T0330241

Cotton and Race across the Atlantic

Rochester Studies in
African History and the Diaspora

Toyin Falola, Series Editor

The Jacob and Frances Sanger Mossiker Chair in the
Humanities and University Distinguished Teaching Professor

University of Texas at Austin

Recent Titles

A complete list of titles in the Rochester Studies in African History and
the Diaspora series may be found on our website, www.urpress.com.

Cotton and Race across the Atlantic

Britain, Africa, and America, 1900–1920

Jonathan E. Robins

UNIVERSITY OF ROCHESTER PRESS

First published 2016

University of Rochester Press
668 Mt. Hope Avenue, Rochester, NY 14620, USA
www.urpress.com
and Boydell & Brewer Limited
PO Box 9, Woodbridge, Suffolk IP12 3DF, UK
www.boydellandbrewer.com

ISBN-13: 978-1-58046-567-0
ISSN: 1092-5228

Library of Congress Cataloging-in-Publication Data

Names: Robins, Jonathan, author.
Title: Cotton and race across the Atlantic : Britain, Africa, and America, 1900–1920 / Jonathan E. Robins.
Other titles: Rochester studies in African history and the diaspora ; v. 73.
Description: Rochester : University of Rochester Press, 2016. | Series: Rochester studies in African history and the diaspora ; v. 73 | Includes bibliographical references and index.
Identifiers: LCCN 2016025372 | ISBN 9781580465670 (hardcover : alk. paper)
Subjects: LCSH: British Cotton Growing Association—History. | Cotton trade—Africa—History. | Cotton trade—England—Lancashire—History. | Cotton trade—United States.
Classification: LCC HD9087.A35 R63 2016 | DDC 338.1751096—dc23 LC record available at https://lccn.loc.gov/2016025372

A catalogue record for this title is available from the British Library.

This publication is printed on acid-free paper.
Printed in the United States of America.

Contents

Illustrations

Preface

While commodity histories are prone to cliché statements about one substance or another "making the modern world," it is an indisputable fact that we live in a world shaped by cotton. There is hardly a corner of our planet that is not somehow connected to the historical and contemporary processes of growing, manufacturing, and consuming cotton. The famous slogan of Cotton Incorporated, the marketing arm of America's Upland cotton growers, reminds us that cotton is "the fabric of our lives."

Cotton is a remarkable fiber, but its ubiquity in textiles and a host of other products is largely due to its low cost. The struggle for low-cost goods has left its mark across the world. In Lancashire, once the dominant center of cotton manufacturing, the brick shells of mills sit empty, awaiting demolition or redevelopment; meanwhile in sites as far-flung as Bangladesh and Haiti, new mills are being erected in pursuit of cheap labor and preferential access to tariff-protected markets in the United States and Europe. The impact of global economic change on cotton agriculture has been less visible, but certainly no less significant. It leaves no urban ruins awaiting transformation into loft apartments, nor does it create sudden (and soon-forgotten) disasters like the 2013 Rana Plaza collapse. We are beginning to take notice of the slow-moving disasters brought by cotton, however, like the desiccation of the Aral Sea. Even my home on Lake Superior, far from the sunny cotton fields of the American South, suffers from the search for cheap cotton: poisonous chemicals like toxaphene have migrated from dusty southern cotton fields to northern lakes, accumulating in the fish we eat.

Cotton agriculture has created human disasters of debt, poverty, and even famine, but it has also brought wealth to farmers around the globe. Today's cotton farmers constitute three distinct classes: one, concentrated in the United States, operates a highly mechanized, capital-intensive industry, protected by an array of federal regulations, subsidies, and tariffs. The second class, spread across the globe from Africa to Asia to Latin America, labors by hand to cultivate and harvest cotton, forced into competition not only with fellow peasant farmers, but also against highly mechanized American farmers. Between the two is a large and still-growing body of laborers in state-run and private-sector mechanized cotton projects in central Asia, Latin America, and increasingly, sub-Saharan Africa.

This book is an effort to understand the divergent paths of development experienced by cotton farmers in the twentieth century. It focuses on Britain's early twentieth-century effort to transform its African and Caribbean colonies into major cotton producers. While other colonial powers embarked on coercive, state-led efforts to create imperial cotton industries, the British Cotton Growing Association attempted to use market forces to transform African and Caribbean colonies into rivals of the American South. British businessmen and government officials assumed that the steady migration of African Americans away from the cotton fields of the American South meant the end of America's monopoly on cotton, opening up a great opportunity for cotton growing in Africa. They believed that black labor was the sine qua non for cheap cotton. Some African Americans celebrated this effort, seeing cotton as an engine for economic growth that would transform Africa and, by extension, the African diaspora. The British project ultimately failed, in part because of the very changes in the American cotton belt that had inspired it. Instead of collapsing, the American cotton industry continued to grow as predominantly white farmers brought government into the business of cotton growing. White farmers and their political allies laid the framework for the protection, and later mechanization, of the American cotton industry in the early twentieth century. When they had a choice, few African farmers chose to compete with the American juggernaut, preferring other cash crops. Instead of abandoning colonial cotton, Britain's manufacturers, like American cotton farmers, turned to the government for help, inaugurating decades of state-led, "scientific" cotton growing in African colonies, a legacy that continues to shape development planning in the postcolonial world.

In writing this book I owe much to the following at the University of Rochester's Department of History. Joseph Inikori provided a rigorous introduction to African and global history, stressing the importance of trade in history as well as the role of state power in shaping institutions and markets. Elias Mandala focused my attention on labor in agriculture, and returning to his books have continued to provide much inspiration. Stanley Engerman and Stewart Weaver provided timely support and invaluable advice. I also owe a debt of thanks to Robert Foster, who introduced me to anthropological perspectives on globalization.

My former colleagues at the Department of History and Geography of Morgan State University, especially Brett Berliner, provided encouragement and a congenial environment for writing major sections of the book between 2010 and 2012. My current colleagues at Michigan Technology University gave further encouragement and helpful comments during the completion of the book. My research was supported by two grants from the Department of History at the University of Rochester, a travel grant from the "Commodities of Empire" project (Open University and the University of London, Institute of the Americas), and additional funding from the Department of Social Sciences at Michigan Technological University. Michigan Technological University also provided funds to support publication of this book, and funds to support the reproduction of images were provided by a grant from the Pasold Research Fund.

Special thanks are due to the organizers and participants of the "Commodities of Empire" workshop series for comments on a paper that formed the basis of chapters 2 and 3. That paper was published by the Commodities of Empire Project (Ferguson Centre for African and Asian Studies, The Open University, and the Institute of the Americas, University College London) as *Commodities of Empire Working Paper 11* (2009), available online at http://www.open.ac.uk/arts/research/ferguson-centre/projects/commodities-of-empire/publications/working-papers.

A revised version was published as "Coercion and Resistance in the Colonial Market: Cotton in Britain's African Empire," in *Global Histories, Imperial Commodities, Local Interactions*, edited by Jonathan Curry-Machado (New York: Palgrave MacMillan, 2013), 100–20. I am also indebted to colleagues for comments received on other portions of the book presented at the 2010 North American Conference of British Studies, the 2012 British Scholar Conference, and the "Cooperation and Imperialism" conference hosted by the University of Bern in 2013. Parts of chapters 1 and 2 were previously published in "Lancashire and the 'Undeveloped Estates': The British Cotton Growing Association Fund-Raising Campaign, 1902–1914," *Journal of British Studies* 54, no. 4 (October 2015): 869–97, and I am grateful to the editor and publisher for permission to reproduce that material here.

Thanks are also due to a long list of librarians and archivists for help in research, and for permission to reproduce archival material. They include: the Special Collections Department of the Cadbury Library of the University of Birmingham, the John Rylands University Library of the University of Manchester, the Oldham Local Studies and Archives and Oldham Council, the Bolton Library and Museum Services and Bolton Council, the Manchester City Archives at Manchester Central Library, the Greater Manchester County Record Office, the National Archives (UK), the London School of Economics Archive, the National Agricultural Library (US), and the University of Georgia Hargrett Library. Special thanks are due to the staff of the Tuskegee University Archives of Tuskegee University for research assistance and for generously accommodating my request to reproduce images from their collections.

Abbreviations

ACC	Association cotonnière coloniale
BCGA	British Cotton Growing Association
BCGC	British Cotton Ginning Company
CO	British Colonial Office
ECGC	Empire Cotton Growing Corporation
FMCSA	Federation of Master Cotton Spinners' Associations
IFMCSA	International Federation of Master Cotton Spinners' Associations (or International Cotton Federation, ICF)
KWK	Kolonial Wirtschaftliches Komitee
NFU	National Farmers' Union
NYCE	New York Cotton Exchange
SCA	Southern Cotton Association
SPS	Sudan Plantations Syndicate
USDA	United States Department of Agriculture

Introduction

John Wesley Hoffman arrived in Lagos on a spring day in 1903 to begin what his employer called "missionary work" among the people of southern Nigeria. Hoffman was not in Africa to win souls for the Lord; his task was to preach the gospel of commercial agriculture and win converts to the cause of cotton growing. Hoffman was regarded by some as "the leading Negro scientist of the world" and had taught at several colleges serving the African American population of the southern United States.[1] He had worked with famous educators like Booker T. Washington at the Tuskegee Institute and could boast of a string of accomplishments in microbiology, human nutrition, and plant breeding.[2] Hoffman was convinced that cotton cultivation—along with a Tuskegee-style education in applied science and disciplined work—was the first step toward the economic development of Africa.

Hoffman was not the first Tuskegee scientist in Africa. Several of his colleagues had been hired by Germany's Colonial Economic Committee (KWK) to start a cotton industry in Togo two years earlier, and they would soon meet with some success in creating a cotton export industry in the small West African colony. Hoffman's employer, the British Cotton Growing Association (BCGA), had bigger plans than the KWK, however. They hired the most distinguished African American scientist they could find and sent him to Nigeria, a recently conquered British colony with vast tracts of fertile land and the largest population in West Africa. (The fact that Hoffman's most important scientific work dealt with dairy microbes did not concern his British patrons.) By educating Nigerians in the latest agricultural knowledge and encouraging them to embrace commodity production for the world market, Hoffman and his backers believed they could rapidly transform Nigeria into one of the world's largest cotton producers. Like Hoffman, many in the African diaspora believed that the economic development of Africa was a critical precondition for the political and economic rejuvenation of black peoples around the Atlantic. Boosters of the cotton-growing movement declared that Hoffman's work "stirred hopes of a future for the race, [and] had awakened dreams hitherto foreign to these Africans, so lately emerged from a darkness as deep as their jungles."[3]

The Europeans responsible for financing African cotton growing observed that cotton grown by African captives and their descendants had made America rich, and they insisted cotton would now make Africa rich. This time, the laborers themselves would reap the profits, though the sponsors of colonial cotton projects were quick to point out that European industries would also benefit from new supplies of raw materials. The colonial cotton movement emerged out of a short-term crisis in the American cotton belt, a moment of uncertainty at the beginning of the twentieth century that promised a fundamental realignment of the world's cotton economy: King Cotton's reign in the American South appeared to be ending, and Africa seemed ready to seize the throne. Cotton proved disappointing as a colonial investment and as a catalyst for economic growth and racial uplift in Africa and diasporic communities in America, however. This book is about that moment of promise, and the starkly different outcomes that ensued for cotton farmers in Africa and America.

British businessmen declared that cotton was "the black man's crop," a fitting industry for Britain's expanding empire in Africa, because they believed black labor was inherently cheap. The inability of Hoffman and other experts to deliver cheap cotton led to a range of coercive interventions in local markets and agricultural systems. Cotton became a tool of colonial power rather than the path to wealth for African farmers. Across the Atlantic, the state also entered the cotton business. After a period of inaction, the federal government came to the aid of cotton farmers—or at least white cotton farmers—to protect America's monopoly on cotton. Research, regulations, and subsidies reshaped the American cotton sector, ultimately displacing African Americans from the industry they and their ancestors had built.

Colonial cotton projects were symptomatic of a broader change in the world of cotton agriculture and manufacturing, a movement away from a bipolar system anchored in the American South and Lancashire and toward a multipolar system with many competing growers of cotton and manufacturers of cotton textiles. We are still living with the legacy of this turn-of-the-century divergence, as a small, heavily subsidized, highly mechanized, and overwhelmingly white cohort of American farmers competes in a nominally free global market with a vast number of poor, small-scale African, Asian, and Latin American cotton producers, many still living with the legacies of colonial cotton.

King Cotton

It was no accident that Hoffman's mission in Nigeria focused on cotton. Cotton had been at the center of economic development in the nineteenth century, and while "King Cotton" had lost some of his influence, cotton remained a vast and profitable industry into the twentieth century.[4] Between 1800 and 1913, raw cotton production grew three times faster than the world's burgeoning population. Cotton consumption increased five times faster than the combined consumption of all other rival fibers, such as wool, flax, and silk.[5] The joint expansion of cotton growing and cotton manufacturing in the nineteenth century made textiles unbelievably cheap. Cotton could be grown by slaves in the American South on specialized plantations, shipped to Great Britain and made into cloth, and shipped again around the world to be sold at a price that could still compete with handspun fabric made from cotton growing in a peasant's garden. Great fortunes were made in cotton, and the industry pulled millions of workers into fields and factories to satisfy the world's hunger for cloth.

Cotton played a leading role in two great narratives of national progress in the nineteenth century. In Britain, the fiber was a key factor in the Industrial Revolution. The sleepy backwater of Lancashire in northwest England was transformed in a few short decades into a smoky, crowded manufacturing region. Cotton textile manufacturing was "the world's first modern industry," using machines, steam power, and proletarian workers to produce goods in a capitalist system.[6] British cloth broke into markets around the globe, and the Union Jack was often not far behind as the British Empire expanded along paths blazed by calico-laden merchants. As other European states industrialized, cotton remained a key industry and an important factor in imperial expansion. Historian Giorgio Riello argued that in earlier periods, no region was able to monopolize cotton agriculture or manufacturing due to the easy diffusion of cotton seeds and simple spinning and weaving machines. Cotton was "the backbone of world trade" long before British entrepreneurs began harnessing water and steam power to drive cotton machinery, but once this new technology took hold, Britain and other European states became machines "that absorbed raw materials and churned out consumer goods in exchange for further raw materials."[7]

On the other side of the Atlantic, cotton growing helped precipitate a war that radically altered the course of government and society in the United States. The American Civil War was about much more than cotton, but cotton was America's most valuable export and the future of cotton—and, by extension, slavery—was the critical factor in American politics leading up to the war. Before and after the war, cotton pushed the American frontier westward. Cotton-crazed planters jealously eyed the lands of the indigenous nations of the American South. When wars swept Native Americans aside, planters replaced them with slaves.[8] Even American expansion outside the cotton belt was linked to the fiber. Pioneers broke ground from the Gulf of Mexico to the Canadian border to feed the cotton belt's slaves, freedmen, and yeoman farmers with wheat and corn.[9]

Cotton survived the abolition of slavery in the United States, and raw cotton production grew phenomenally in the second half of the nineteenth century. Railroads, steamships, and the telegraph practically abolished old constraints on commodity transport, allowing raw cotton and cotton goods to flow around the world with greater ease than ever before.[10] In 1910, a New Orleans merchant could ship one hundred pounds of cotton to the mills at Fall River, Massachusetts, for about 33¢. The same cotton could be shipped forty-five hundred miles across the Atlantic to Manchester for 35¢.[11] The "second Industrial Revolution" of the late nineteenth century corresponded with a steady decline in the price of raw cotton, resulting in a host of new uses for cotton like casing for electrical wires, cords for automobile tires, cellulose for explosives, and "mercerized" cotton that imitated silk. By the start of the twentieth century, the world made by cotton was truly global, connecting the livelihoods of urban workers and rural farmers in nearly every corner of the planet.

If cotton told the story of positive processes in the United States and Great Britain—industrialization, modernization, and globalization—it was at the center of a very different story in Africa. Africans had been growing, spinning, and weaving cotton for centuries, using local plants as well as imported varieties to produce cloth for domestic use and trade. In the early stages of European colonization around the Atlantic, Europeans tapped into the vibrant regional market for cotton cloth in West Africa. Well into the seventeenth century, European merchants transported African textiles—especially those produced in modern-day Nigeria—across the West African coast. Few of these textiles made their way to Europe, but they were important articles of commerce used to buy gold, spices, and captives. West African cloth exports were also an important part of transatlantic trade from the sixteenth century through the eighteenth century, clothing the growing population of enslaved Africans laboring in American plantations and mines.[12] African cloth exports dwindled in the eighteenth century; by the end of the century the main contribution of the continent to the evolving cotton economy came through the forced transfer of African labor to the Americas.[13] Africans continued to grow cotton and produce textiles to meet local and regional demand, but they were increasingly left out of the global system, which combined large-scale cotton agriculture with industrial manufacturing. As Walter Johnson has argued, Africans were not the beneficiaries of the industrialization and economic growth cotton brought to Europeans and Americans; rather they were "transformed into instruments of civilization through free trade in their bodies and the cotton that was extracted from them."[14]

At the turn of the twentieth century, however, Africa's position in the world of cotton changed. Europe's imperial powers looked to Africa for new sources of cotton. The fiber became the focus of dozens of imperial projects. For many Africans, the first practical intrusion into everyday life brought by colonial rule came in the form of a white man armed with bags of cotton seed and promises to buy cotton. European colonizers tried to connect African farmers to the global network of cotton production and consumption, seeing cotton as an important commodity that would feed hungry textile mills at home and also draw Africans down an inexorable path of modernization. As the following chapters will show, African farmers were ambivalent about both prospects, at least under the terms offered by colonial powers. Some embraced cotton growing as a new source of wealth, while others rejected it as a foreign imposition.

Cotton Colonialism

This book argues that the colonial drive for cotton in Africa was a new stage in the evolution of the Atlantic-centered economic system, which had matured in the nineteenth century. "Cotton colonialism" was a response to the breakdown of the division of labor that had characterized the nineteenth-century cotton system. For a century, slaves and then sharecroppers, tenants, and smallholders in the United States provided the mills of Great Britain and continental Europe with cheap cotton. A complex network of economic institutions and financial instruments connected farmers, brokers, manufacturers, and cloth merchants around the world. This network functioned across national borders with a minimum of government intervention or regulation and without any transnational governance or oversight. For the political economists of the late nineteenth century, the cotton industry was a dynamic example of how free trade and unfettered capitalism could create wealth and drive economic growth.

By the early twentieth century, however, the fragility of this ungoverned and unregulated international system was exposed in a series of crises. The first signs of trouble came with a smaller-than-expected American cotton crop in 1902. Brokers in the major cotton exchanges took advantage of poor market conditions and cornered the cotton supply, turning a minor raw material shortage into a "cotton crisis" that paralyzed the cotton textile industry in Europe and America.[15] While politicians on both sides of the Atlantic decried "gambling" in cotton futures and demanded regulation of the cotton exchanges, cotton manufacturers and cotton growers looked for their own solutions to the crisis. Europeans—and especially Britons—looked to their overseas empires for new sources of cotton, hoping to fight the speculators with new colonial supplies.

In Africa, the crisis inspired some of the first attempts at large-scale agricultural development. Colonial cotton programs sought to transform farming communities and environments, seeing cotton exports as the path toward economic growth.[16] Cotton provided colonial planners with an early opportunity to test different models of economic and social change, and Germany, France, Portugal, Belgium, and Italy all launched state-directed programs aimed at turning African peasants into primary commodity producers for the world market. The projects laid the groundwork for a century of colonial and postcolonial economic planning. But British entrepreneurs tried to effect an agricultural transformation through the private sector. They used a "semiphilanthropic" business, the British Cotton Growing Association (BCGA), to create cotton-growing industries across the British Empire, especially in Africa. These imperialist businessmen in Britain found unlikely allies in the African diaspora. For some black thinkers in the Americas, cotton cultivation provided a chance to prove the value of free labor and to affirm the dignity of the "black race."[17] The British model relied on free labor and free market forces, promising a kind of development that was economically—and, the BCGA thought, morally—superior to the coercive, state-centered projects emerging in other European empires. The ultimate failure of Britain's semiphilanthropic model in the first decades of the twentieth century had serious implications for Africans as it encouraged British planners to adopt a much more coercive regime of state-backed "scientific" development after the First World War.

While Britain championed cotton as "the black man's crop" in Africa, American farmers were intent on recasting cotton as a "white man's crop." Reviving the ideas of nineteenth-century populism, white cotton farmers attempted to seize control of a commodity chain that they believed robbed farmers of their rightful profits. Sharecropping, debt peonage, and other coercive elements of the postemancipation cotton economy were part of an "economic system designed for the negro class," but the system had "entangled many whites in its meshes."[18] White and black cotton farmers campaigned for higher cotton prices, hoping to exploit America's monopoly position in the world market. While some African Americans abandoned cotton in favor of emigration to the North or even to Africa, others embraced the historic association between black labor and cotton. Leaders like Hoffman urged black farmers to adopt scientific methods in the hopes that cotton monoculture would lead to economic, and eventually political, advancement. Like their white colleagues, black farmers tried to organize to boost cotton prices but were less successful. White farmers did succeed in bringing the federal government into the business of cotton agriculture and agricultural development. Black farmers in the South were excluded from most of the benefits of government intervention, however. Helped by protective legislation and subsidies, white American farmers had by the 1950s transformed cotton into a crop grown by middle-class farmers on large mechanized farms. Government agencies seized power from private groups like the cotton exchanges, which had long dominated the cotton trade.

Cotton and Global Economic History

This is a book about cotton, but it is not a typical commodity history, focused on the life of a thing across the commodity chain. Cotton is a central element in the story that follows, but it is not a character in its own right. Farmers, businessmen, politicians, and scientists had much more to do with the outcome of Britain's cotton-growing campaign in Africa than the cotton plant itself. As Michael Watts and Peter Little remind us, commodities are not produced in a vacuum: nature sets the stage, so to speak, but the actual processes of production are "always influenced by the larger political and economic environment."[19]

Growing, manufacturing, and selling cotton were dynamic processes connecting people across national borders, and by focusing on the process rather than the state or region we can see how events and decisions made in one place had consequences in many others. It is impossible to understand the origins, and the ultimate failure, of Britain's African cotton-growing adventure without understanding events in the American cotton belt or in Lancashire. For historians, disciplinary boundaries can be just as limiting as national borders, but the history of cotton shows that no single part—agriculture, manufacturing, or consumption—can be understood in isolation. Studies of cotton typically focus on either the agricultural or the industrial sides of the business, artificially dividing a single industry. As historian Sven Beckert observed in an article describing his own attempt to write a global history of cotton, a broader perspective lets the historian bring together "the agricultural, trade, and manufacturing aspects" of an industry "that heretofore have been artificially separated, a flaw that ignores the relations of power between different actors and places in the industry."[20]

By following the economic and political processes associated with cotton, this book moves across geographic and disciplinary boundaries, showing how local events developed out of, but also influenced, global patterns. Commodity-centered approaches have been especially important in the emerging field of global history, which seeks to explain "globalization" as a historical phenomenon. According to A. G. Hopkins, global history is the study of "a process that transforms economic, political, social, and cultural relationships across countries, regions, and continents by spreading them more broadly, making them more intense, and increasing their velocity."[21] Global history has been criticized as a paradigm for African history on grounds that the key process it analyzes—globalization—is identified "by its supposed endpoint," rather than by features of the process itself. Like modernization theory before it, a theory of global history that is preoccupied with explaining the origins of contemporary globalization will invariably measure Africa's past against a Eurocentric yardstick.[22]

For Hopkins, the solution is to push globalization back in history and approach it as a process in motion, rather than a state of being. Hopkins describes global history as the simultaneous study of "local" spaces and "universal" processes, an approach that seeks to understand the local origins of global forces as well as the impact of ostensibly "universal" processes on local spaces.[23] Anthropologist Arjun Appadurai has similarly described globalization as the "flow" of things, people, and ideas across space.[24] Some flows, like bales of cotton, can be counted and analyzed in economic terms. Other flows, such as ideas and ideologies or political power, cannot be measured as easily, but their impact is just as real as that of a physical commodity. Situating Africa's colonial history within this global context requires an understanding of the effects of colonial rule—movements of people, governments, and especially physical commodities in and out of Africa—but also an understanding of the interactions between Africans and Europeans (and, as this book stresses, Americans as well). Colonial history also reminds us that the "flows" of globalization do not move evenly in all directions. Decisions made in a farmyard along the Mississippi were felt along the Niger, but the reverse was not always true.

Throughout the book I have tried to chart a course through the historical evidence that responds to theoretical ideas about globalization, economics, and colonialism without being constrained by them. As the late anthropologist Jack Goody warned, "Africa has been the graveyard of much European based social science" for at least two generations of scholars.[25] While theory can be an important heuristic device, it should not be straitjacket for the researcher. At its core, this book follows a "theoretically eclectic" approach toward African economic history, following the work of Ralph Austen.[26] My analysis relies on two key assumptions from classical economics: that people make decisions about production, exchange, and consumption that serve their own interests, and that markets offer an efficient (if not equitable) way of organizing production and consumption. These claims have been debated by anthropologists and historians for decades, but historians working from the neoclassical tradition have effectively demonstrated that the concept of economic "rationality" is as applicable in Lagos as it is in London. (This issue is addressed in more depth in chapter 2.) The case of the British Cotton Growing Association is compelling because it was, at least ostensibly, a case of colonial development rooted in ideas of economic rationality and market exchange. In subsequent chapters I show how Africans, Britons, and Americans responded to market challenges, sometimes finding that cotton was a good way to earn a living, and more often finding that it was, as Mozambican peasants interviewed by Allen Isaacman said, "the mother of poverty."[27]

The fact that cotton could bring wealth in some places and poverty in others attests to the varied environmental and economic factors at work in different parts of the world, but it also calls attention to the political frameworks that governed (or attempted to govern) economic activity. As Marxian and other structuralist scholars have argued, people often lack the freedom to make the most advantageous decisions for themselves. Marx famously wrote in *The Eighteenth Brumaire of Louis Bonaparte*: "Men make their own history, but they do not make it as they please; they do not make it under self-selected circumstances, but under circumstances existing already, given and transmitted from the past."[28] Constrained by social, political, and economic structures, individuals in this book frequently faced choices that were bad, or that were no choice at all. The importance of political power and even violence in market-making is a key theme of this book. This insight has been absorbed by practitioners of the New Institutional Economics (NIE), who hope to extend neoclassical economic theory by recognizing the importance of social, political, and cultural institutions in shaping economic activity. As Africa's colonial history makes clear, the "perfect competition" assumed in most neoclassical economic models never existed in societies dominated by foreign governments and foreign capital, and the "rules" of capitalist exchange were fluid and unevenly observed in different regions. I draw on work from both Marxian and NIE scholars in this book, seeking a middle ground between the former's preoccupation with class, and the latter's aspirations to mathematical precision.

This integrative approach to economic history has been embraced by historians working in the emerging field of the "history of capitalism." Like the history of globalization, the "history of capitalism" grew out of frustration with the limitations of nationally bounded historical scholarship, which often treated labor, capital, the state, and society in disciplinary isolation. The "history of capitalism" approach is "omnivorous," as one skeptic has described it, crossing disciplinary boundaries to illustrate "systematic connections" and "dynamic changes over extended periods."[29] Like earlier Marxian scholars, proponents of the "history of capitalism" approach argue that capitalism is not "an organic expression of human nature," but rather is an evolving historical phenomenon in need of explanation.[30] This does not require a return to rigid Marxian dogma or to the "substantivist" explanations of economic behavior favored by some anthropologists and historians; one can accept neoclassical claims about universal human economic rationality while emphasizing the importance of environmental, political, cultural, and social structures in shaping and constraining behavior. While scholars continue to debate the nature of the field and the definition of "capitalism" itself, the historians advocating this new approach argue that economic activity cannot be isolated from politics and society, a point that would have been obvious to Marx and other political economists of the nineteenth century.

The "history of capitalism" school is largely a product of historians of the United States, who are beginning to combine their cross-disciplinary approach with the transnational frameworks that scholars working in the related fields of Atlantic history and global history have established in earlier decades. This book continues the process of globalizing American history, by showing how Americans—and especially African Americans—influenced developments around the Atlantic region. The larger aim of the book, however, is to shift the analytical focus in the history of capitalism away from the western corner of the triangular "Atlantic system" toward Africa. African history occupies a prominent place in the fields of Atlantic and global history, but the majority of this work has focused on the period of the transatlantic slave trade, examining the flow of coerced labor out of Africa. Gareth Austin, working from the NIE perspective, has lamented that studies of African economic history occupy a "negligible space in the emerging literature on 'global history'" when studies of the slave trade are excluded.[31] The "history of capitalism" approach offers one way of remedying that problem by giving scholars a way to bridge the disciplinary divides between African economic, social, labor, and political history. The methods and ecumenical theoretical approaches favored by the "history of capitalism" school are well suited to colonial and postcolonial African history, where political and social institutions loom large in historical events, and where the quantitative data demanded by neoclassical scholarship is often woefully inadequate.

Quantities and prices are important for evaluating the significance of economic developments, but for the colonial period economic policies—many of which were unsuccessful—are equally important for understanding the paths that were or were not available to African actors. Policies and politics are necessary if one hopes to avoid the *post hoc ergo propter hoc* fallacy that accompanies some economic history, seeing cause and effect instead of historical contingency. As Frederick Cooper warns, historians seeking to explain patterns of economic change often "[write] history backwards, taking an idealized version of the 'globalized present' and working backwards to show how everything either led up to it ('proto-globalization') or how everything, until the arrival of the global age itself, deviated from it. In neither version does one watch history unfold over time, producing dead ends as well as pathways leading somewhere, creating conditions and contingencies in which actors made decisions, mobilize other people, and took actions that both opened and constrained future possibilities."[32] It is not enough to say, as Patrick Manning does, that colonial cotton campaigns were "poorly designed and had only minimal effect" on African societies.[33] They were not particularly successful in producing cotton for export, but they had far-reaching implications for African farmers. Foreign capital, colonial regulations, and Western scientific concepts were reflected in colonial economic policy, and these forces usually did not work in the best interests of African farmers.

Colonial Cotton

Cash crop production has been an important subject for Africanist historians, linking the older fields of political and economic history to newer areas of inquiry like labor, gender, and the environment. Historians have shown how diverse social, political, and ecological contexts influenced African responses to colonial initiatives, recovering a history where African actors made decisions rather than one in which they were the passive victims of colonial exploitation. In recovering this African past, however, historians have sometimes abstracted the colonial state and colonial business beyond the point of recognition. Complex systems are reduced to what Cooper calls "an abstracted coloniality," which substitutes an adjective—colonial state, colonial economy, colonial culture, and so on—for the tasks of description and analysis.[34] The colonial state is assumed to be a coherent organization with a fixed agenda, while the colonial economy is taken as a real category of analysis, rather than an amalgamation of data reflecting colonial efforts to monitor and control the economic activity of Africans.[35] Some revisionist scholarship has downplayed the importance of colonial states altogether, treating them as "a graft on to pre-colonial African social formations" with little impact on everyday life.[36]

In an influential 1980 article, John Tosh criticized historians for resorting to one-sided studies of African history. In their efforts to refute older interpretations, which celebrated European capitalists for overcoming "the apathy of tradition-bound farmers by introducing them to an attractive range of consumer goods," Marxian scholars conjured up an all-powerful colonial state, wielding coercive power directly or "through its African subordinates, either directly or by means of individual taxation." As Tosh observed, efforts by Africanist historians to find African agency in the midst of expatriate trading firms and colonial bureaucracies often celebrated acts of resistance and entrepreneurial ability at the expense of broader social, political, and environmental contexts.[37]

John Lonsdale and Bruce Berman were among the first African historians to offer a viable alternative to the Marxian idea of the colonial state as an extension of metropolitan capitalism, and their concept of a "semiautonomous" colonial state remains useful despite its inflexible understanding of capitalism in the metropole itself.[38] Historians have increasingly recognized that the colonial state was neither "the crushing leviathan that simply consumed huge peasant surpluses, later digested by metropolitan capital" of Marxist theory, nor an impartial "Great White

Umpire," which simply managed trade between colonial peoples and the rest of the world.[39] As Manning has observed, the colonial state is an amorphous historical object, and ascribing colonial policies to the logic of metropolitan capitalism simply shifts the work of historical analysis from one place to another without explaining the origins and evolution of historical processes. In the case of French Dahomey, Manning doubted whether a group like "the French bourgeoisie" could really be considered the driving force behind the colonial state in West Africa, given their limited involvement with colonial issues. Manning's alternative explanation—that colonial states acted "in response to the interests of individual officers, or in an eclectic reaction to varying pressures from many sources"—is an admission of the inadequacy of theory for describing colonial history but reflects the limitations and contradictions colonial states faced as agents of imperial policy.[40] As with Lonsdale and Berman's idea of a semiautonomous colonial state, Manning's approach allows the historian to follow the actions of individuals—African and European—as they reacted to real economic, social, political, cultural, and environmental forces.

Historians of cotton in colonial Africa were early pioneers in breaking out of the colonial "container" and moving toward a transnational and interdisciplinary approach. Cotton has probably attracted more attention from scholars than any other cash crop in Africa, given its wide geographic distribution and the outsized role it played in many colonial economic schemes. No other commodity generated such interest among colonial powers, and no other proved so systematically frustrating to imperial designs. This work on colonial cotton anticipated the interdisciplinary global turn that much historical scholarship has taken in the last two or three decades. Because the commodity so clearly linked events in African cotton fields to those in European cotton mills, historians of colonial cotton-growing programs were able to follow historical processes from the colony to the metropole. Until important works on "cotton colonialism" began appearing in the 1990s, few historians of Africa had seriously questioned the role of metropolitan industry in colonial policy making. While scholars of European industry were busy downplaying imperial connections, some Africanist historians assumed ties between industry and empire were pervasive and unproblematic.[41]

A series of books published in the 1990s began to challenge the idea that colonial cotton programs were simply appendages of metropolitan capital. The first was Ann Pitcher's study of Portugal's cotton-growing efforts. Reflecting on decades of earlier scholarship, Pitcher identified three inaccurate assumptions scholars had made about Portuguese colonialism in Mozambique during the twentieth century: first, that the Salazar regime's colonial policies were rational and served the interests of metropolitan capital; second, that Portuguese cotton policies directly benefited Portuguese cotton manufacturers; and third, that the interests of Portuguese manufacturers overlapped with the interests of the imperial government. "Many scholars tacitly adopt these assumptions when referring to the relationship between industry and empire; yet, ironically, they chronicle elsewhere in the former colonies a succession of irrational acts, failed and misguided policies, conflicts between the administration and companies over labour, and effective resistance by Africans," Pitcher argued. She called for a broader approach to Africa's colonial history, one that views "the relationship between the Portuguese metropole and the colonies as an interactive process, a two-way exchange (however unequal) of interests and influences rather than a simple top-down imposition of metropolitan initiatives and objectives."[42] Allen Isaacman's 1995 study of African responses to Portuguese cotton colonialism in Mozambique reinforced the idea that cotton colonialism evolved in response to changing metropolitan conditions as well as in response to the decisions of African farmers and laborers.[43]

Another significant contribution was Richard Roberts's 1996 study of French cotton-growing programs in West Africa. Roberts argued that colonial rule created two distinct "worlds of cotton" in French West Africa, emphasizing the survival of a regional cotton economy apart from the worldwide cotton system in which France participated. Roberts sought to reconstruct the West African "world of cotton" to explain its staying power in the face of colonial intrusions, and he saw colonialism as more than an exogenous factor influencing peasant cotton production. He recognized that the lackluster performance of France's colonial schemes concealed real changes—many negative—in the lives of cotton farmers in French colonies. French capitalism and colonial policies interacted with "local social and economic processes to shape the outcome of the interplay between the world economy and the Soudanese market for the cotton harvest," and Roberts found that the failure of French schemes was ultimately due to the strength of local social, economic, and cultural processes rather than changes in metropolitan or global conditions.[44]

Like Pitcher, Roberts recognized that colonial efforts "to develop cotton in the West African colonies must be understood as part of worldwide engagement between globally structured markets, the expansion and periodic crises in capitalist production, and dynamic local processes."[45] Thaddeus Sunseri's study of German cotton-growing programs in Tanganyika went further, digging beneath the assumption that manufacturers were as a matter of course interested in cotton from Germany's empire. German cotton growing, he found, was inspired by efforts to combat the cotton shortages of the early twentieth century, but also to fight growing unrest among cotton textile workers and to show them the tangible benefits of imperialism. The urgency of the cotton crisis in Germany provoked ill-fated attempts at plantation agriculture, as colonial planners desperately worked to relieve discontent at home.[46] "Local" processes in Germany had an impact on events in Africa, but the reverse was also true: the resistance of Tanzanian farmers to colonial policies forced actors in Germany to reevaluate their positions.

Sunseri's work, along with recent contributions by Andrew Zimmerman and Sven Beckert, have brought the history of Germany's African colonies into the same transnational frame as earlier studies of French and Portuguese cotton colonialism. In Beckert's interpretation, cotton was the most important driver of globalization, which he defines as increasing integration among regions. In the ancient world, cotton textiles were a crucial article of trade, but cotton growing and manufacturing easily moved across borders. No single location could dominate the industry for any length of time, given the mobility of cotton seeds and textile technologies. Textiles were usually manufactured in cotton-growing regions. By the seventeenth and eighteenth centuries, however, European capitalists began using military force to disrupt traditional exchange networks. By the nineteenth century, cotton agriculture and manufacturing were disintegrated as European powers began to industrialize and transformed other parts of the world into dependent cotton-growing regions. The capitalist forces represented by the "empire of cotton" turned to colonies to expand supplies of raw materials and keep the price of cotton low. Colonial powers embarked on a mission of "cultivating new lands, persuading farmers to convert more of their existing fields to cotton growing, conducting agricultural experiments to improve yields and quality, and providing state supervision of the selling of the crop."[47] Beckert acknowledges the successful resistance to colonial cotton growing emphasized by Africanist historians, but he concludes that these cases were exceptions that "prove the rule": across the planet, capitalism swept away precolonial political forms, industrialized existing networks of transportation and exchange, and forced European concepts of land ownership and scientific agriculture on cotton farmers.[48] In the United States, Russia, China, Brazil, and many other parts of the world, capitalist firms and national governments were triumphant in their quest to expand cotton agriculture and cotton manufacturing. Beckert's account may appear to marginalize the story of colonial cotton in Africa, but in fact it provides a vital context for understanding the external forces and constraints faced by African farmers and colonial administrators.

One large gap remains in the literature on cotton colonialism, however: the British Empire in Africa. The British Cotton Growing Association was the largest, and by some measures the most successful, colonial cotton project, and this book aims to demonstrate that a global, interdisciplinary approach is vital to understanding the history of cotton in Britain's African colonies. Like the French, German, and Portuguese cases, the experience of cotton colonialism under British rule was shaped by dynamic processes as African and European actors cooperated, fought, and compromised over cotton agriculture. Two-way exchanges between Britain and its African colonies played an important role in this story, but so did exchanges across the Atlantic with the United States, a region usually neglected by African historians studying the colonial period.

The world market is an especially important context for understanding cotton in the British Empire. Because the British Cotton Growing Association was founded on market principles, its efforts to grow cotton in Africa were directly linked to the world market for raw cotton and cotton goods. While French, German, and Portuguese cotton projects were subsidized by the state and were pursued as much for the social engineering they promised as for their economic returns, the British cotton program had to make money if it were to succeed. The BCGA's record in Africa cannot be understood in isolation; connections between Britain and Africa, America and Britain, and even America and Africa are vital in explaining the trajectory cotton-growing programs took in different parts of the British Empire.

The BCGA is an important case in the history of colonial cotton because it was the most successful in actually producing cotton in the years before and after the First World War. While sub-Saharan Africa provided only a tiny fraction of Europe's cotton demand in 1913, nearly three-quarters of it came from British colonies.[49] The francophone states of Africa have taken precedence in recent scholarship, however, reflecting the contemporary geography of cotton in Africa: of the former British colonies in Africa, only Zimbabwe ranked in the top five African cotton producers between 1998 and 2005. Nigeria, where the BGCA had its greatest hopes, ranked ninth and produced less cotton in the same period than either Togo or Benin.[50] As a number of historians and development scholars have shown, colonial history deeply shaped the trajectory of successful cotton producers like Mali. The colonial history of Britain's empire provides an important context for understanding the limits on cotton production in Anglophone Africa and the causes of its decline in the second half of the twentieth century.

The BCGA's history is also important because it is often used as a benchmark for other cotton programs. When Japanese cotton firms launched their Association for the Cultivation of Cotton in Korea in 1904, for example, they explicitly claimed to be "following the example of the British Cotton Growing Association."[51] Historians writing about colonial cotton continued to make these comparisons, arguing that the BCGA was "highly successful" and served as a model for other colonial cotton projects.[52] These comparisons by historians rely on a limited pool of scholarship about the BCGA, however. The historical evolution of cotton policies and cotton agriculture in Britain's African colonies has been widely misunderstood.

Names, dates, and connections between actors are sometimes wrong, or convey the wrong impressions. Pitcher, for example, credits the BCGA with forming the Empire Cotton Growing Corporation, which was in fact formed by the British government to push the BCGA out of key aspects of cotton cultivation.[53] Michael Watts's 1983 study of agriculture and famine in Northern Nigeria badly mischaracterized the BCGA as a "joint state-merchant firm."[54] Watts also mislabeled the group as the British Cotton *Growers* Association, a mistake frequently made by colonial officials and one that generates an impression of the BCGA as a group of expatriate planters.

The first articles and dissertations focused on the BCGA were written while the association still operated in Nigeria and Malawi, and the analyses of their authors were shaped by the political context of the 1960s and 1970s. Historians wanted to know how the BCGA had (or had not) contributed to economic development in the newly independent states of Africa, and most concluded that the BCGA represented a broader policy of imperial exploitation that had enriched Britain at the expense of Africa. Nigerian historian K. Dike Nworah offered the earliest and most balanced analysis, seeing the BCGA as an ineffective attempt by British merchants to redirect colonial development in ways that would benefit the merchants at the expense of Africans, the colonial government, and British industry.[55] Writing a few years later, Marion Johnson and Edmund Egboh both argued that the BCGA was an agent of deindustrialization in Nigeria. Johnson saw "cotton imperialism" as a systematic strategy aimed at transforming cotton-manufacturing Africans into mere exporters of raw fiber, reliant on Lancashire for finished cloth. Egboh claimed that "By growing and exporting raw cotton, and taking European manufactured fabrics in exchange, the [Nigerian] people's traditional cloth industry languished while that of the Europeans thrived."[56] The economic historian Jan Hogendorn took a different approach, seeing the BCGA as an example of imperial hubris, with little long-term impact. In Hogendorn's account, the BCGA served the interests of a powerful "Lancashire lobby," which was foiled by the entrepreneurship of peasants in northern Nigeria, who preferred to grow peanuts over cotton and spent their earnings on local cloth rather than Manchester goods.[57]

While Nworah used records from Lancashire merchants in his article, the other authors all relied on colonial records, rather than the records of the BCGA and the Lancashire cotton firms it represented. The British cotton industry, a central character in these accounts, was seen only through its correspondence with colonial officials. William A. Wardle's 1980 dissertation on the BCGA's activities in Northern Nigeria was the first to make use of the BCGA's own archival records, which were acquired by the University of Birmingham in the late 1970s. Wardle's purpose was explicitly apologetic, aimed at the growing body of neo-Marxian scholarship on

Africa, which blamed colonial business policies for the "underdevelopment" of Africa and the continuing poverty of independent African states. The neo-Marxians of the late 1970s took it for granted that business organizations like the BCGA worked hand-in-hand with colonial governments, and that the colonial state—whether British, Belgian, French, or Portuguese—relied on direct and indirect violence to extract a surplus from African labor. Wardle argued that the BCGA had not in fact used coercion to get its cotton, relying instead on market forces. If African countries were poor when Wardle wrote in 1980, it not because the BCGA had "underdeveloped" them by forcing Africans into cotton production. Wardle's dissertation remains an important, if underutilized, resource despite the limitations imposed by the author's ideological framework. More recent deposits of BCGA records shed new light on the BCGA's activities, however. Along with fresh interpretations of older BCGA materials, these records show that the BCGA undeniably used coercive methods in its pursuit of colonial cotton.

Marxian scholars argued "that force was the midwife of West African commodity production," but the most important studies in this historical school focused on French colonies where coercion was overt and even celebrated by colonial officials. Hopkins, Wardle, and others argued that the British Empire occasionally resorted to violence but generally relied on market principles to extract commodities from the empire. In a survey of economic development in colonial West Africa, Keith Hart concluded that Marxian scholars conflated "the needs of commodity economy" with "those of administration." Hart's position, based largely on his reading of Hopkins and other scholars of British West Africa, was that most colonial coercion was aimed at basic state functions like road-building and tax collection. Taxes rather than home industries occupied the minds of colonial agents who devised forced cultivation schemes. Where commodity exports succeeded, it was because of "West Africans' enthusiasm for new opportunities. The penetration of the market into agriculture did not rest on force."[58]

The BCGA's history offers an opportunity to put the competing claims of Marxists and their opponents to a test. The evidence presented in the following chapters supports Hart's position, with some important caveats. As the BCGA discovered, colonial officials were indeed more concerned with state-building than with Lancashire's fortunes, and they used cotton cultivation as a tool to collect taxes and mobilize labor in many colonies. But the BCGA found willing partners in colonial agricultural departments, who saw cash crop exports as the only viable path toward development for African colonies. Here, the interests of the colonial state overlapped with those of metropolitan capital, and as a result farmers experienced a mixture of market inducements and outright coercion as the BCGA tried to make them into cotton farmers.

Sources

Much of the evidence for this book comes from the records left by the BCGA, Lancashire cotton textile organizations, and the British Colonial Office. The BCGA records are rich in correspondence with colonial officials, but they also offer perspectives from within the British textile industry, the merchant community involved in African trade, and agents at work in Africa. Additional records donated in 1999 by Cargill, the international conglomerate that bought former BCGA facilities in Africa, offer a candid look at the BCGA's day-to-day activities and internal debates over cotton-growing strategies in Africa. These documents include the professional diaries of the BCGA's chairman, J. Arthur Hutton, as well as field journals from W. H. Himbury, the association's main agent in West Africa. (Himbury replaced Hutton as chairman in 1918.) Taken with colonial records, the BCGA archive illustrates the conflicts and compromises that produced colonial policy in the British Empire.

The voices of African farmers who worked under the BCGA's cotton-growing regime are more difficult to find. (The same is true of African American farmers, who feature prominently in chapter 4.) Africanist historians have long wrestled with the problem of sources in the precolonial and early colonial periods, when relatively few Africans recorded their thoughts in writing. Colonial records that purported to capture the sentiments of Africans or that described their actions were products of their time, reflecting the values and assumptions of the men (and they were almost all men) who wrote them. The British writers whose documents provide much of the source material about African responses to cotton growing were not a homogeneous group, however. Some were virulent racists, but others developed nuanced and sympathetic views of African societies. In either case, these records still reflect only one side of the story. To access the perspectives of African peoples, historians have turned to oral tradition and oral history, and the endnotes in following chapters will show my reliance on the work of scholars who collected oral history in previous decades.

In the case of West Africa, and especially southern Nigeria, local newspapers provide another way of accessing the African past from an African point of view. Many of these newspapers were owned, edited, and written by Africans, and while they represent the views of British-educated elites clustered along the coast, they often captured the complex sentiments of Africans living under British colonial rule. These journalists and their informants chafed under colonial regulations and clamored for political rights, but they also celebrated the expansion of trade promised by the BCGA and other groups.

Finally, we can mine colonial records for indirect evidence of the thoughts and actions of people living colonial rule. Historians of the "subaltern school" have been doing this in South Asian history for more than three decades.[59] So long as the biases and limitations of colonial sources are understood and acknowledged, they can be valuable sources for recovering the history of people living under colonial rule. This is not to say that an objective set of facts can be recovered; the "subaltern school" methods call for finding the voice and agency of the colonized within the responses recorded by the colonizers. As Dipesh Chakrabarty argues, "ruling-class documents . . . can be read both for what they say and for their 'silences.'"[60] The ellipses in colonial documents often point to threats of violence, to the remnants of slavery and other forms of social oppression, and to a host of other unpleasant aspects of colonial rule that often went unrecorded in written documents. That said, Britain's African empire generated a wide range of opinion among colonial officials and other writers. Some writers saw Africans as passive objects of colonial policy, but others recognized and even celebrated the ability of Africans to adapt to social, political, economic, and environmental conditions. Some British authors whitewashed colonialism, but others were quite frank about the role of violence and coercion in the process of colonial rule and economic development—either because they thought such violence was reprehensible, or because they thought it was necessary and were not ashamed of it. Writings from journalists, missionaries, colonial agents, and other travelers offer a diversity of viewpoints on what was happening in Britain's African empire. The methodology of the subaltern studies school has not been widely adopted in African history, however. Frederick Cooper warned against the tendency of subaltern studies to flatten the experience of colonial rule into a simple dichotomy of colonizer and colonized, of force and resistance.[61] Recent contributions have shown that it is possible to find African agency by reading colonial records "against the grain," as proponents of the subaltern school argue. Agency could take the form of evasion, collaboration, and even wholehearted cooperation with colonial actors, as well as the resistance so valued by an earlier generation of nationalist historians.[62]

The insights into African responses to cotton growing found in BCGA and Colonial Office records are made richer by personal and professional conflicts within and between the two organizations. Colonial agricultural officials felt that the BCGA's work impinged on the duties of the state, and their sparring with the BCGA produced a trove of documents highlighting the ability of African farmers to resist cotton-growing initiatives as well as their ingenuity and entrepreneurship. Some of these officials shared the BCGA's view that African agriculture was primitive and in need of improvement; they clashed with the BCGA over where, how, and when the colonial state would change African agriculture. Other colonial officials were genuinely sympathetic toward African farmers and took great pleasure in seeing them foil the designs of colonial planners in London and Manchester.

They saw African farmers as rational decision-makers, trying to balance domestic needs and wants with new opportunities and impositions brought by the colonial state. In trying to discredit their rivals, these British officers recorded important information about the preferences and decisions of farmers. Those farmers responded with actions ranging from outright resistance to enthusiastic engagement with the business opportunities offered by cotton.

The Economic Geography of Cotton

This section is a brief survey of the state of cotton growing and cotton textile manufacturing in the early twentieth century. In the period this book examines, the southern United States was the world's largest cotton producer, annually producing more than ten million bales on average (see table I.1). American Upland cotton (*Gossypium hirsutum*) was the most commercially important variety. Upland cotton, with a staple length (the length of fibers in a boll) averaging 0.875–1 inch in length, was a strong, versatile fiber that was widely used in manufacturing low-cost fabrics. Longer fibers are easier to twist together, and thus can be used to make very fine yarns for use in light and strong textiles. If shorter fibers are twisted too finely, the resulting yarn is weak and will not weave well, especially on power looms. India, the closest competitor to the United States, produced a crop one-third the size of the American crop, and most of this cotton was of short-staple varieties suitable for coarser grades of cloth. The average staple length of Indian cotton (generally *G. arboreum*) was under 0.75

Table I.1. Global cotton production (in 500-pound bale equivalents)

	1902–3 Season (August–July)	1912–13 Season
USA	10,758,000 bales	14,129,000 bales
India	3,367,000	4,395,000
Egypt	1,168,000	1,507,000
Russia	342,000	911,000
China	1,200,000 (estimated)	3,931,000
Others	801,000	1,171,000
Total	17,636,000 bales	26,044,000 bales

Source: Scherer, *Cotton as a World Power*, 423.

inches. Egypt was the third largest producer, growing very long stapled cottons to meet a small but growing demand for expensive, high-quality cotton goods. The fibers of Egyptian, Sea Island (both *G. barbadense*), and other exotic long-staple cottons could reach 1.25–2 inches in length, and these cottons commanded sizable premiums over shorter-stapled varieties. Cotton values were based primarily on staple length, although color, strength, and texture were also important characteristics.[63]

Neither Indian nor Egyptian cotton could readily replace American Upland cotton in textile manufacturing. Substituting longer staple cotton for shorter was possible, but doing so greatly increased the cost of the fabric. Cheaper, shorter-stapled cottons could be adapted as well, but their weaker fibers caused frequent yarn breaks unless machines were recalibrated for coarser work. This involved switching to thicker yarns to make an inferior product, or running the machines more slowly to protect the fragile yarn. Smaller quantities of cotton comparable to American varieties were grown in Peru, Brazil, Turkey, Cyprus, Russia, Japan, and China, but much of the produce in these locations was consumed by domestic factories and handicraft producers. Very little cotton grown south of the Sahara in Africa reached the world market at the turn of the twentieth century. The sheer size of the American cotton crop meant that the United States had a de facto monopoly on cotton in the early twentieth century, and the American price dictated all others.

In manufacturing, American firms surpassed their British rivals in cotton consumption by 1900, taking 34 percent of the American cotton crop. Lancashire retained a commanding lead in cotton-spinning spindles, however, boasting more spinning capacity than all of continental Europe combined (see table I.2). Moreover, British spinning firms produced finer yarns than continental or American firms, using less cotton to produce a larger quantity of high-value goods. The significance of cotton to the British economy waned over the course of the nineteenth century, but cotton remained Britain's most important export sector at the turn of the century and the industry provided employment for hundreds of thousands of workers in spinning, weaving, bleaching, dying, printing, shipping, and other ancillary sectors. With respect to market share, Lancashire had little to fear from its rivals. Large as the US manufacturing sector was becoming, American firms exported only $53 million worth of cotton goods in 1906, compared to $78 million from France, or $118 million from Germany. British firms exported a staggering $500 million worth of cotton goods in that year.[64] Britain was singularly reliant on the United States for its raw cotton, however. American imports made up 86 percent of British raw cotton consumption in 1900.[65]

By 1913, Lancashire was home to more than 55 million cotton spindles, more than Germany, France, Russia, India, Austria, Italy, Japan, Spain, and

Table I.2. Cotton manufacturing capacity in 1900

	United States	United Kingdom	Continental Europe	Asia
Spindles (millions)	21.45	45.6	32.64	6.75
Power looms (thousands)	502.1	648.8	790.4	47.1
Cotton consumption (thousand bales)	3,547	3,207	4,691	680 (Japan)

Source: Shepperson, *Cotton Facts* (1901), 2–3; Farnie, "The Role of Merchants as Prime Movers in the Expansion of the Cotton Industry, 1760–1990," 23–25; Jeremy, "Organization and Management in the Global Cotton Industry, 1800–1990s," 215.

Belgium combined.[66] While the glory days of the Industrial Revolution were behind Lancashire, the county still stood at the center of the world's cotton textile industry in the early twentieth century. The British industry was characterized by extreme horizontal and vertical disintegration; 1,977 independent spinning, weaving, and finishing firms were operating in 1910.[67] Except for a few giant firms, like the J. P. Coates sewing-thread company or the Fine Cotton Spinners' and Doublers' Association, Lancashire's productive capacity was in the hands of many small joint-stock companies and family firms. The economic and political center of Lancashire was Manchester, at the southern edge of the county. The city and its suburbs constituted a great "cottonopolis" by the start of the twentieth century. Suburban towns specialized in spinning, while the metropolis itself was home to spinners, weavers, and finishers, sometimes operating under the same roof. In the north of the county, most cotton firms focused on weaving, leaving yarn production to the firms clustered around Manchester. Lancashire mill towns typically specialized in specific products or textile qualities, serving either domestic or export markets. This book draws primarily on evidence from Oldham and Bolton, the largest spinning towns in their respective ends of the textile sector. Oldham firms spun coarse grades of cotton yarn, defined in Lancashire as anything below 40s count yarn (one pound of cotton spun into forty "hanks" of 840 yards each). Oldham relied on American Upland cotton and was heavily oriented toward export markets in India. Bolton stood on the opposite end of the market, spinning Egyptian, Sea Island, and other long-stapled cottons into fine yarn for expensive clothes and home furnishings. Bolton served the high ends of the domestic and foreign markets.[68]

Home to more spindles in 1904 than all of Germany (13,278,705, with another 1,152,000 under construction), Oldham was a stunning example of the growth brought on by the rapid globalization of trade after 1870.[69] Its steam-powered factories churned out huge amounts of cheap yarn, mostly for customers in Asia and Latin America who had previously relied on local textiles. Oldham was home to many competing firms, but it was well organized. Its trade unions were at the forefront of the labor struggle in Britain, and by the 1890s they had achieved remarkable levels of recognition among employers and workers (often called machine "operatives" in Lancashire to distinguish them from mill-owning "spinners" and "weavers"). Many Oldham mills were limited liability companies with overlapping directorships, which facilitated intraindustry cooperation.[70] Mill owners in Oldham launched the Federation of Master Cotton Spinners' Associations (FMCSA) in 1891 to represent employers' interests across the county, uniting existing employers' associations. The FMCSA expanded throughout southern Lancashire, incorporating a majority of spinning firms. In the northern parts of the county, the Cotton Spinners' and Manufacturers' Association (CSMA) developed independently and represented weavers and combined spinning-weaving firms.[71] By the turn of the twentieth century, the employers' and operatives' associations had cooperated on a range of issues and tended to solve labor and trade disputes collectively, instead of turning to the judiciary or legislature.

Bolton's mills were less organized. The town had a higher proportion of family-owned businesses than Oldham, and its trade unions tended to be less militant than Oldham's on account of the higher wages earned in spinning fine counts. Bolton's employers had a history of refusing to cooperate with Oldham's MCSA because they usually enjoyed "buoyant, even expanding, trade with little foreign competition," when "profit margins in the Oldham coarse spinning sector were being seriously squeezed."[72] Taken together, Bolton and Oldham represented a major share of Lancashire's cotton-spinning industry and thus can serve as case studies for the British cotton industry as a whole.

The Cotton Crisis and the Lancashire Cotton Industry

The first chapter examines the "cotton crisis" through the lens of Lancashire, the world's most important cotton textile-producing region. It provides a context for understanding the BCGA's actions and the constraints placed on its activities in Africa. The chapter also clarifies some key facts about the BCGA's origins, correcting early histories that identify the BCGA as an extension of either the Lancashire cotton manufacturers or Liverpool shipping interests.

Despite its commanding position in the world market, in 1902 Lancashire found itself at the mercy of American cotton brokers. These brokers cornered the American cotton market, sending prices to record levels. Factories organized temporary closures to wait out the speculators, but

Lancashire's leaders also began to look for alternative sources of raw cotton, outside the reach of American brokers. The British Cotton Growing Association was born in the midst of this cotton crisis, promising to turn the British Empire, and especially British Africa, into a great rival of the American South. Unlike its European counterparts, the BCGA was a private, for-profit organization rather than a state-run or parastatal entity. The association described itself as semiphilanthropic, believing that it could help Africans become prosperous cotton farmers while also making money for investors and securing the future of Lancashire. It was perhaps the first for-profit nongovernmental development organization, a century before such organizations became common. While it was the most ambitious of the colonial cotton projects before the First World War, the BCGA has been poorly understood by historians, in part because the association's own archival materials were not available and in part because scholars relied on records from the British Colonial Office to reconstruct the association's activities. In the postindependence period, Africanist historians saw the BCGA as a clear example of empire serving the needs of metropolitan business, unaware of the strained relationship between the BCGA and the British government.[73] Other scholars were more apologetic, insisting that "cotton export development was not pursued through coercion of African producers" in an attempt to counter Marxian narratives of imperialist exploitation.[74]

Thanks to recent deposits of records and new research tools that facilitate full-text search of published materials from around the world, the BCGA's internal organization, government relations, and policy activities can now be better examined. The picture that emerges in the second chapter is of a divided and often ineffective organization, pulled in different directions by business interests, politicians, colonial administrators, scientists, as well as by the Africans the BCGA hoped to turn into cotton farmers. This history of the BCGA offers a new perspective on the long-running debate over the place of imperialism in British society. Economic historians have more or less abandoned the idea that manufacturers were the driving force behind British imperialism, and recent accounts have emphasized how marginal the empire was to all but a small group of privileged elites. As P. J. Cain and A. G. Hopkins demonstrated in their comprehensive study of British imperialism, manufacturers were outsiders in London, excluded from the high politics of empire. Industry "rarely got its way, whereas the City's needs were very much to the fore." "The wealth of most manufacturing capitalists remained limited and their interests local," the pair concluded.[75] While economic historians were busy demonstrating how little empire mattered to most Britons, however, cultural historians began to argue that empire lay at the very center of British society. Scholars following the "cultural turn" took a further "imperial turn" and have produced an enormous body of literature that tries to show how imperialism penetrated every aspect of British life.[76]

Cotton workers and their employers certainly "thought imperially," as contemporary proponents of empire-building urged, but they did so pragmatically. Imperial markets were necessary for Lancashire's survival, and imperial sources of raw materials attracted a great deal of interest among labor and capital. The evidence in this book shows that there were clear limits to imperial enthusiasm, however, and many in Lancashire refused to trade in their historic commitment to free trade and laissez-faire for statist imperialism even when it stood to benefit the cotton industry. A rift emerged between pro- and antiempire cotton camps, and the failure of the BCGA to transcend this debate shows the limited extent to which imperial ideologies guided political and business thinking in Lancashire. It was one thing to enjoy the idea of an empire; it was a very different matter to financially or politically support activities within that empire. Lancashire's cotton industry did not strongly support the campaign for empire cotton, and as a result the BCGA and its successor organizations developed policies that were far from what Lancashire firms had in mind when they founded the association in 1902.

Cotton, Imperialism, and Economic Development in Africa

The second and third chapters look at the BCGA's actual work in Africa, and the response of Africans to the cotton campaign. The chapters compare the BCGA to contemporary German and French cotton-growing programs. While the BCGA did not succeed in transforming Britain's empire into a major source of cotton, its activities brought hundreds of thousands of colonial subjects into contact with the world market. The semiphilanthropic BCGA tried to combine scientific research and "missionary" work among prospective farmers with profit-seeking activity, operating from the contradictory premise that markets were the best way to develop cotton-growing industries, but that Africans needed extraeconomic pressures and incentives to respond to those markets rationally. Prevailing ideas about race shaped agricultural policies as Europeans debated whether or not Africans were "economic men." Their answers to the question shaped the institutions and incentives they developed to encourage cotton growing in the colonies. The BCGA's strategies generally failed, and Africans only willingly grew cotton for export markets when relative prices made it an attractive endeavor.

Chapters 2 and 3 use records from the BCGA, the British Colonial Office, African newspapers, and Lancashire's cotton organizations to show that British cotton-growing policies did not respond to specific demands from

Lancashire, but rather developed out of the interests of the BCGA's leadership. The association was not managed by manufacturers but rather by a clique of prominent Manchester and Liverpool merchants with their own interests. Taken together, the chapters provide a new perspective on how British business and colonial government approached cotton growing, and how Africans reacted to these policies. In keeping with its philanthropic aims and with Lancashire's historic commitment to laissez-faire and free trade, the BCGA sought to control labor by indirect and often innocuous-sounding methods. The market was at the center of BCGA cotton-growing efforts, but the BCGA was tied to a world market for cotton that had little to do with local conditions in Britain's African colonies. When African farmers found that prices favored cotton, they grew it, but more often than not the world price for cotton was far lower than the price necessary to tempt African cultivators. The BCGA and colonial state responded to this behavior with regulation and scientific agricultural regimes, ultimately using coercive control over cotton markets, cotton cultivation, and cotton seed to reshape African farmers into producers of American cotton.

American scientists helped transfer American varieties of cotton to British colonies, but they also transferred American agricultural theories and work regimes. Most, like Hoffman, succumbed to disease and left Africa before their work could reach fruition. African American scientists helped *Gossypium hirsutum* take root in Africa, but their work subjected far more Africans to colonial oppression than it raised to prosperity. The most successful British cotton project, the Gezira irrigated cotton scheme in Sudan, was perhaps the most significant American contribution to colonial cotton growing. There, an American adventurer launched a project that effectively replicated the oppressive conditions of Southern sharecropping in Africa, a model the BCGA embraced as its other projects failed. Rather than functioning as a tool for pan-African progress, the "black man's crop" ushered in a new era of oppression in twentieth-century Africa.

Hardly any African colony was spared from the rush for cotton. These cotton programs are important not just for their immediate impact on Africans and Africa, but because their legacy shaped the course of colonial and postcolonial development. The lessons learned (or more often, learned incorrectly) had a lasting influence on agricultural policy, and the abject failure of private initiative and private capital to make markets work for cotton in Africa led states to sideline both as tools of development.

Making Cotton a "White Man's Crop"

The fourth chapter travels back across the Atlantic and explores the reactions of American farmers to the cotton crisis. For Southern cotton growers, the politics of the cotton crisis were global as well as intensely local. Rising cotton prices during the cotton corners raised farmers' hopes; the subsequent collapse of prices stirred the embers of populist politics back into a raging fire. While Europeans proclaimed that cotton was a "black man's crop," white Southerners argued that cotton was in fact a white man's crop and that the time had come for cotton to reach a price sufficient to sustain white farmers. Two groups—the Southern Cotton Association and the National Farmers' Union—emerged and promised to radically change the way farmers grew and sold their crops, diversifying Southern agriculture while eliminating the "speculator" and connecting the farmer to the Lancashire spinner who bought his crop. In this forgotten episode of Southern history, white cotton farmers organized and ultimately succeeded in changing the discourse of cotton in the United States.

White farmers saw the BCGA as a sign of desperation on the part of Lancashire, rather than a threat to America's cotton monopoly. They mocked African agriculturalists as hopelessly primitive, but also pleaded with European cotton buyers to not "drag the Southern cotton planter to the Indian level" by insisting on cheap cotton. Their reactions to colonial cotton projects, though unsuccessful in raising the price of cotton, resulted in a raft of state and federal legislation aimed at helping landowning (and thus predominantly white) cotton farmers. The cotton populists started a chain of events that would leave cotton securely in the domain of the middle-class white farmer for the rest of the twentieth century.

Many black Americans and pan-African thinkers living in the shadow of this racialized "cotton populism" saw Africa as their best hope for economic and social advancement. Booker T. Washington had famously urged African Americans to "cast down their buckets" and work within the racist society of the South, but white populists ensured that black farmers were excluded from cooperative organizations and from the growing array of state and federal services aimed at improving the lot of cotton farmers. Seeing no future in Southern cotton, African American newspapers triumphantly advertised the achievements of scientists like Hoffman and introduced readers to "civilized" Africa. African Americans encountered stories about Lagos entrepreneur Richard Blaize and the Alake Gbadebo I of Abeokuta, both of whom owned BCGA shares and promoted cotton growing in Nigeria. The efforts of white farmers to make cotton a "white man's crop" drove some black Americans to support Britain's quest for the "black man's crop" in Africa.

The fourth chapter reconstructs an important episode in American agricultural history, but it also puts the history of "cotton populism" in a global context. Historians have come to see the American South as a "peripheral" region, to use the language of world-systems theorists, supplying raw materials to the North and to the world economy.[77] For many

Southerners, constructing a "New South" meant reasserting Southern economic and political strength within the United States as well as on the world stage. By 1910, the South was not only the world's largest raw cotton producer but also the third largest cotton manufacturer after Great Britain and the Northern states. White Southern farmers campaigning for economic reform during the cotton crisis were not trying to restore the lost glory of the plantation past, but rather to ensure their place in a new economic order.[78]

Conclusions

The final chapter looks at the effect of the First World War on farmers in Africa and America and on manufacturers in Britain. The war brought on a new crisis, one that magnified the failings of the existing system. American farmers were burdened with the largest crop in history when war broke out, and they demanded and won groundbreaking federal agricultural legislation to protect their livelihoods. The war exposed the BCGA's failings, as the organization proved unable to secure a large and reliable supply of cotton from Britain's colonies. After the armistice its private development model was scrapped in favor of a state-managed system. European manufacturers became more closely linked to cotton-growing projects in the colonies as a matter of politics, but these relationships had little impact on industrial production.

The 1920s were a turning point in British colonial agricultural policy. In most accounts, the transition toward a more scientific kind of development is attributed to a sudden decision to get serious about development, as government officials abandoned old policies that had "evolved out of day-to-day needs of the different colonies."[79] This view misses the reason for that transition, which was disappointment with the old liberal imperialist model of development that the BCGA characterized. British administrators did not embrace scientific methods because of their changing educational backgrounds or because of new knowledge about agriculture; they did so because they were disgusted with two decades of amateurish experiments and halfhearted investment by the BCGA and Lancashire. When the colonial state got serious about cotton, it used cotton as a state-building project rather than a tool for economic development. This process was marked by increasing regulation and coercion aimed at African cultivators.

By the 1930s, the world of cotton was characterized by state intervention rather than unfettered capitalism. On both sides of the Atlantic, government assumed development tasks that had previously been left to private enterprise. In the United States, white farmers continued their work of making cotton a "white man's crop," using subsidies and other government interventions to create large and—by the late 1940s, mechanized—farms that made a cotton a viable crop for middle-class cultivators. In Africa, colonial states used science, regulation, and coercion to push cotton cultivation on unenthusiastic cultivators. British planners used the tools of control devised by the BCGA but jettisoned its commitment to the market. A few colonies did become significant exporters of raw cotton but empire cotton proved insufficient to save Lancashire from collapse. Until independence, colonial powers continually tried to change African environments and African agriculturalists, believing that science and state power could solve what was really an economic problem. The problem with African cotton was not African soil, African pests, or African farmers. As a farmer from the Gold Coast told a British official, cotton simply "does not pay to grow."

1

The Cotton Crisis

Lancashire, the American South, and the Turn to "Empire Cotton"

To understand the origins of the British Cotton Growing Association and its impact on Africa, we must follow the commodity chain of cotton to its centers at the beginning of the twentieth century: the southern United States and Lancashire. These sites were respectively the largest exporter of raw fiber and the largest exporter of finished fabric, and events in these places shaped the movement of the cotton industry across the world. The transatlantic relationship between American agriculture and European industry was made possible by the labor of African captives and their descendants in America, but as workers they had little ability to influence prices and other developments.

The turn of the twentieth century was an uncertain time for American cotton farmers, black and white, as well as for their trading partners in American and European textile mills. American farmers still dominated the world's cotton supply, but cotton prices were at their lowest point since the Civil War. Manufacturers were recovering from the depression that followed the "Panic of 1893," and Britain's cotton mill owners were concerned about growing competition from rival European and Asian exporters. When cotton prices began to move upward in 1900, few took notice: most manufacturers were lamenting a new decline in textile demand, caused by horrific droughts and famines in places as distant as China and Brazil.[1] The value of British textile exports to a key market like Brazil fell 40 percent between 1899 and 1901; exports to China and India fell only about 5 percent in value, but the quantity of goods sold fell by nearly three times that amount, as Asian consumers paid more for less cloth.[2]

By 1901, attention shifted from demand to supply as prices for raw cotton shot up dramatically. Manufacturers slashed prices to prop up flagging sales, but they were caught between stagnant demand and rising raw material costs.[3] The cost of raw cotton was becoming an increasingly important part of the final price of textiles, and raw cotton prices were out of the control of European manufacturers. In Lancashire, all eyes were on the "margin," the trade term for the difference between the cost of one pound of raw cotton and the sale price of the yarn spun from it. This was not the profit margin, but rather the gross earnings from which manufacturers had to cover labor and capital charges, with any leftover money returning to investors as profit. While cotton prices might swing erratically, spinners' margins tended to be stable. Fierce competition among spinning firms ensured that yarn prices closely followed the price of raw cotton (see fig. 1.1). By 1902 the margin fell to 2d. per pound in Britain, a low not seen since the Great Depression of the 1870s.[4]

By 1903, textile manufacturers had identified "speculators" working the world's cotton exchanges as the main culprits behind rising cotton prices. Investors rallied around Daniel J. Sully, Theodore Price, and other famous American cotton brokers who battled for ever-higher prices.[5] American farmers enthusiastically followed the speculative bubble, hoping that it signaled the end of a decade-long decline in raw cotton prices. As table 1.1 illustrates, prices for American cotton moved upward across the first decade of the twentieth century. Cotton mill owners organized local efforts to mitigate the effects of high cotton prices, but they realized that there were only two ways to put cotton out of the reach of speculators in the long run. The first, regulating the cotton exchanges, was politically impossible in Britain and the United States, where the most important cotton exchanges operated. In Lancashire, cotton men were among the staunchest defenders of laissez-faire capitalism and free trade, and the idea of government intervention in commodity markets was anathema to them. The second option was to grow more cotton, flooding the world's markets with fiber and shifting the sites of production away from the American South. As long as the world relied on the South for its raw cotton, operators in the New York and New Orleans exchanges who handled American cotton would be able to corner the crop and manipulate its price. Cotton grown outside America would still flow through the Liverpool Cotton Exchange and other important commodity exchanges in continental Europe, but it would be insulated from the vagaries of the American cotton crop and the predations of American speculators.

While French and German cotton spinners turned to the state to launch new cotton industries in overseas colonies, British spinners formed a private organization to pursue the same goals. The British Cotton Growing Association, founded in 1902, was designed to invest in colonial cotton agriculture on Lancashire's behalf, creating new industries in British Africa to rival the American South. Instead, the BCGA project foundered, caught between competing political factions and competing visions of imperial

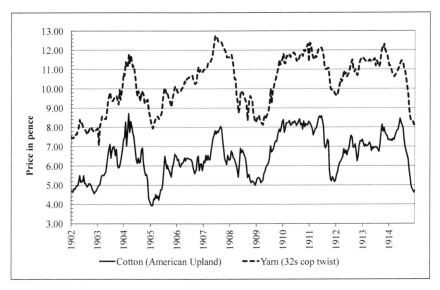

Figure 1.1. Spot prices of "good middling" American Upland cotton in Liverpool and standard yarn (32s twist on cop) in Manchester, 1902–14. *Cotton Factory Times* (January 1902–January 1915).

development. On one side stood "Tariff Reformers" and other imperialists who wanted the state to assist capitalists in developing the colonies. On the other side were free-trading Liberals who found the idea of state-supported colonial development fiscally unsound and morally dangerous. A small group of Manchester and Liverpool merchants took the reins of the association and tried to steer a course away from political controversy, but their efforts produced a plan for colonial cotton that favored merchants rather than Lancashire spinners. In the decade leading up to the First World War, British capitalists made only desultory investments in the BCGA and other colonial cotton projects. They wanted more cotton from Britain's empire, but they did not want to pay for it. Surprisingly, Lancashire's workers supported the BCGA more uniformly than their employers, seeing the association's work as an investment in Lancashire's long-term security. As the final chapter shows, the commitment of workers to "empire cotton" helped transform the BCGA after the First World War, leading to an entirely different kind of development than what the BCGA's founders had envisioned.

An "Unnatural Proceeding": Speculation and the Cotton Futures Market

After reaching a post–Civil War high of more than eleven million bales in 1898, growth in the American cotton crop stalled. Total production

Table 1.1. American cotton production, exports, and prices, 1896–1914

Year	American crop (in 500-pound bale equivalents)	Bales exported	Liverpool price (average per pound in pence)
1896	8,515,640 bales	6,124,026 bales	4.22
1898	11,435,368	7,626,525	3.28
1900	10,123,027	6,806,572	5.16
1902	10,630,945	6,913,506	5.46
1903	9,851,129	6,233,682	6.94
1904	13,438,012	9,057,397	4.91
1905	10,575,017	6,975,494	5.95
1906	13,273,809	8,825,236	6.38
1907	11,107,179	7,779,508	6.19
1908	13,241,799	8,889,724	5.5
1909	10,004,949	6,491,843	7.86
1910	11,608,616	8,025,991	7.84
1911	15,692,701	10,681,332	6.09
1912	13,703,421	9,199,093	6.76
1913	14,156,486	9,256,028	7.26
1914	16,134,930	8,931,253	

Source: Scherer, *Cotton as a World Power*, 419; Todd, *World's Cotton Crops*, 100.

actually dropped in the first years of the twentieth century, and it was this shortfall that was the immediate cause of rising cotton prices. Europeans and Americans quickly blamed speculators for turning a minor cotton shortage into an artificial crisis, however. In a market where demand exceeded supply, speculators could "corner" the cotton crop by purchasing large amounts of cotton or cotton futures contracts, later offering them for sale at inflated prices. If buyers were unable to find alternative sources of cotton, they would have to pay the speculator's high prices, and brokers and manufacturers with stocks of cotton often raised prices alongside speculators to take advantage of a bull market. The British and American press identified futures traders in the New York and New Orleans cotton exchanges as the leading figures in the "bull campaign" for higher prices.[6]

Speculation was not a new feature of the cotton industry. Complaints from merchants and spinners about speculative corners in cotton date to at least 1825, when Britons blamed false crop information and clever manipulation by American brokers for wild swings in cotton prices.[7] Before the Civil War, the American cotton crop was shipped and marketed by specialized "factors," merchants who supplied farmers with credit and bought their cotton, selling it on to brokers in seaports and eventually to European and New England cotton mills. It was hard for factors or brokers to corner the market, given the slow speed of information in the pretelegraph era. Rumors might help a broker corner a local market for a short period of time, but no individual could possibly know how much cotton had been grown, how much was desired, and who owned it.

After the American Civil War, cotton futures markets emerged alongside new forms of marketing and communication to replace the old cotton factor system.[8] Commodity futures were initially tools that allowed buyers and sellers to protect themselves from unexpected market fluctuations by agreeing on a price for a given commodity before the commodity was available for sale. Spinners and weavers had to sign contracts for yarn and cloth delivery over long periods, and they needed to know that they could get the cotton they needed at a certain price. Futures helped manufacturers hedge their purchases, protecting them from the fluctuations of the market. Futures markets also disseminated price information to farmers, merchants, and manufacturers around the world; after telegraph cables were laid across the world's ocean, futures quotations were "flashed over the world." An American broker claimed, "they are known in Shanghai a short time after they are known here in New York."[9]

Major cotton exchanges emerged in New Orleans, New York, Liverpool, Bremen, and Le Havre, and the exchanges in New York and Liverpool developed especially large futures markets alongside their spot markets (where bales of cotton were physically sold). In New York, spot sales were a tiny fraction of the exchange's business by 1900, and its huge transaction volume in cotton futures led contemporaries to declare that "The New York price rules."[10] The New York Cotton Exchange (NYCE) stopped issuing data on futures transactions in 1898, but in that season more than twenty-nine million bales were traded on paper for a crop that only amounted to eleven million bales.[11]

The global cotton industry of the early twentieth century articulated a regional, unmechanized, and seasonal agricultural sector with a highly industrialized, year-round manufacturing industry selling to customers around the world. To keep the commodity chain moving, buyers and sellers needed reliable information.[12] Individuals who did not deal in futures still used them as a price reference and as an indication of which direction the market for cotton was moving. In this environment, information was a powerful weapon in the hands of competing brokers. Major cotton dealers ran their own statistical bureaus, usually keeping their information secret. On the New York and New Orleans exchanges, however, a number of highly visible brokers used their data and crop predictions to influence petty speculators and casual investors, whose purchases and sales could make or break cotton prices. "Cotton guessers" and "cotton prophets" battled over crop predictions as they sold pamphlets and books to investors, merchants, and manufacturers.[13] These high-profile brokers also aimed their predictions at farmers, hoping to influence the amount of cotton farmers grew, as well as when farmers took their cotton to market. A federal investigation into cotton brokers reported that although "undoubtedly in some instances misinformation is deliberately given out," many brokers did "publish the actual material which they obtain."[14]

The US government began distributing cotton crop data in the late nineteenth century, but its figures were, at best, imprecise. The US Census Bureau gave the most accurate reports, releasing reports obtained from cotton gins as the harvest arrived. The Census Bureau also issued retrospective reports after the crop had been marketed, giving farmers and brokers a good sense of historic trends in the cotton supply. Predictions were the business of the US Department of Agriculture (USDA), which tracked acreage, weather, and other factors to estimate each year's anticipated cotton crop. Secretary of Agriculture James Wilson boasted that his department's 1900–1 estimate was "commented upon throughout the entire cotton world as a marvel of statistical forecasting," but there was little to brag about in most years.[15] USDA agents used a confusing and unscientific measure called "crop condition" as an important measure of crop expectations, and the result was often far off the mark.[16] Alfred Shepperson, a New York cotton broker and one of several prominent "cotton prophets," accused "the present presiding genius of the [USDA] statistical division" of taking "a great deal of trouble to reach a thoroughly inaccurate result."[17] Shepperson and other amateur statisticians sold annual handbooks for cotton traders and had a clear financial incentive to criticize government statistics, but the numbers were usually on their side (see table 1.2). In 1901–2, for example, the USDA predicted a crop of

Table 1.2. American cotton crops, 1897–1901

	USDA estimate	Actual crop
1897	9,100,000 bales	11,216,000 bales
1898	10,300,000	11,256,000
1899	8,900,000	9,422,000
1900	10,100,000	10,500,000
1901	9,674,000	10,700,000

Source: Shepperson, *Cotton Facts* (1901), iii.

9,674,000 bales; Shepperson predicted 10,531,000. The final Census report found 10,700,000 bales.

American farmers typically hated commodity futures. Charles Barrett, the first president of the National Farmers Educational & Cooperative Union (now the National Farmers' Union), fulminated against commodity speculation as a sin and an economic crime: "Irrespective of the welfare of the producer, gambling in farm products, like other species of gambling, is contrary to sound public policy, and for that reason it is the duty of the government, in so far as possible, to suppress it. This is axiomatic."[18] Critics considered futures sales fictive because the delivery clause in the futures contract was almost never exercised. Instead, buyers and sellers exchanged money to cover the difference between the price of the futures contract and the spot price of cotton, even if both parties had no intention of ever buying an actual bale of cotton.[19] This practice made futures attractive as a hedge, as merchants and manufacturers did not need to take delivery of a specific order of cotton and store it, but could take the proceeds (or losses) from the futures sale and use it to buy cotton on the spot market when needed.

By the late nineteenth century, American farmers often blamed their problems on commodity exchanges and Wall Street; they "saw their enemies not in small, inefficient operations or in overproduction, but in the money lenders, the supply merchants, and the cotton buyers, who were tied to the country's large financial, transportation, and industrial corporations."[20] This fear and hatred of wealthy men who "gambled" with the lives of farmers did not stop farmers from using cotton futures themselves. Many used futures prices as a guide for planting; an NYCE member testified that farmers consulted futures prices "not only daily, but hourly; every fifteen minutes, if he can get them, and now he is complaining because he can not get them every minute."[21] Farmers also used futures to gamble in rural "bucket shops," illicit venues that let farmers place sporting bets on commodity prices.[22]

Futures were supposed to stabilize prices across the season and from year to year, but farmers argued that they had a depressing effect on prices. Rural buying agents closely followed New York and New Orleans markets, only bidding for farmers' cotton within a narrow range "on" or "off" the futures price for a given grade of cotton.[23] Even a momentary swing in futures prices could drive farm gate prices up or down. If prices were down during harvest time, farmers still had to sell. The "rush to market" happened each autumn in the American South, as farmers were forced to sell their cotton quickly to pay debts and crop liens. "If he could hold his cotton for even 60 days," a Southern politician argued, "he would receive a higher price."[24]

While farmers felt that futures drove cotton prices down, cotton spinners held that futures actually inflated prices for raw materials because so many transactions in the cotton exchanges were between brokers rather than between producers and consumers of cotton. An American manufacturer complained that cloth buyers wanted to pay prices consonant with futures prices, regardless of the fact that "the quotation here [NYCE] of 11 cents for January cotton does not represent the actual value of cotton, or the value of cotton we can buy for two or three months; yet they keep on insisting on 11 cents as the value of cotton when in the South we are paying 12 cents."[25] Unlike farmers, manufacturers actively participated in futures markets, using them to hedge on long-term contracts. They differentiated between legitimate hedging and outright gambling, identifying the latter with individuals in the cotton exchanges "who have no direct connection with the cotton trade."[26] Lancashire was peculiarly vulnerable to the abuse of futures markets. While American and European manufacturers often stockpiled cotton in mill warehouses to ensure a consistent raw material supply for long production runs, British manufacturers specialized in shorter runs and took advantage of the large Liverpool Cotton Exchange to avoid the charges inherent in storing cotton.[27] British spinners bought spot cotton to meet their yarn contracts, and used futures to hedge when accepting contracts several months in advance of production. This practice left Lancashire vulnerable to short-term disruptions in the markets for spot cotton and cotton futures.

Daniel J. Sully and the "Dawn of the Cotton Century"

As the cotton crop began to arrive in September for the 1902–3 season, rumors swirled about the direction prices would take. Henry G. Hester, the bullish secretary of the New Orleans Cotton Exchange, predicted a short crop. In Liverpool, the city's most respected cotton statistician, Thomas Ellison, estimated global demand for the upcoming year at 10.8 million US bales, requiring a crop several hundred thousand bales larger than Hester's prediction.[28] As the final USDA crop condition reports were released in the autumn of 1902, their pessimistic contents sent cotton futures prices surging upward. The *Commercial & Financial Chronicle* warned that "too much dependence is usually placed upon these monthly condition figures because they are Government reports" and urged caution.[29]

In the New Orleans Cotton Exchange, a broker named William Brown was gathering money, cotton, and allies for a cotton corner, which he hoped would fix cotton prices at a level high enough to guarantee prosperity for Southern cotton farmers.[30] While Brown quietly bought large amounts of futures contracts, a brash Rhode Island trader named Daniel J. Sully entered the market. Biographical details are scanty, but Sully claimed to have begun studying the historical price movement of cotton while working at a cotton brokerage in the late 1890s. He was struck by the fact that spinners in 1898 paid 5¢ per pound for cotton, and for "the same cotton that Lancashire had fought to get in 1864 at $1.90 a pound. It was the same cotton for which lives were risked in running blockades in the Civil War." As he saw it, "There appeared to be something the matter."[31] Observing that demand for cotton was expected to rise worldwide with growing populations, Sully argued that various supply-side factors would invariably lead to higher prices.[32]

In late 1902 Sully started to buy futures for May and July deliveries, joining Brown's bull campaign. Sully bought whenever futures contracts or spot cotton came on the market.[33] He bet heavily on a short crop and succeeded in cornering the market. Spot prices jumped almost 50 percent, up to 7d. per pound in Liverpool. When Sully liquidated his contracts and reaped the profits of his corner in the spring of 1903, the New Orleans brokers reentered the market. They formed a pool to protect the gains of Sully's campaign and refused to sell cotton or settle futures deals until their July contracts matured, forcing a massive difference (a "break") between New York and New Orleans prices. The New Orleans pool took advantage of the disparity and invaded New York's market, buying up cotton, as they saw it, "as a matter of self preservation."[34] By mid-summer, the largest partner in the New Orleans pool, the firm of Vincent & Hayne, held 61 percent of New York contracts and 48 percent of New Orleans. Financed by Southern banks and "foreign correspondents," the pool bought a record-setting 130,000 bales in one day—at a price of $4 million—to protect their corner.[35] Cotton landed in Europe had to be repatriated to New York to settle contracts.[36] Newspapers proclaimed that "Anybody who wants to buy cotton has to see [William] Brown, and he is selling it now to mills all over the world." Brown maintained, "legitimate demand and the strong statistical position have put prices where they are. If this were not the case I wouldn't be bulling cotton at present prices."[37]

Sully reentered the market as the 1903–4 crop began to arrive in September, betting on another short crop. Sully and other brokers published circulars urging Southern planters to hold their cotton as long as they could to defend the corner Sully and his allies were assembling.[38] Unlike the 1902–3 period of speculation, which occurred after the crop had been sold to merchants and brokers, farmers arriving in Southern towns with wagons of cotton in the autumn of 1903 found themselves selling cotton at high prices. Ignoring Sully's call to hold back cotton, farmers sold enough cotton to depress prices slightly between October and November.[39] Sully was well received in the South as a prophet of prosperity. He was, in the words of one editorial, "a man to whom the people of the South very naturally feel profoundly grateful" for "putting the price of this season's cotton up to what he believed to be its real value."[40] Sully eagerly sought this public attention. In newspaper interviews and a major article published in the *North American Review*, he explained why the price of cotton should and would inevitably rise even higher. He began with the large crops of 1897–99 and the low prices that resulted. Cheaper raw materials allowed manufacturers to sell cheaper cloth, encouraging manufacturers to expand. In Lancashire alone, 3.4 million spindles were added between 1898 and 1904.[41]

Sully explained that cheaper cotton "created new outlets and new factors in consumption." Mercerized cotton competed with silk, and heavy cotton goods with wool. Armies needed the fiber for gun-cotton, uniforms, and tents. Products like automobile tires, which had not existed a decade earlier, offered huge new markets for cotton fibers outside the traditional realm of textiles. Sully concluded that cotton's low price during the 1890s "caused the staple to be used for things never before dreamed of."[42] He found it unlikely that manufacturers using cotton to make the new products of the second Industrial Revolution would abandon the fiber when prices rose. Sully declared in a later article, "The dawn of the cotton century is here."[43] He was right that cotton had entered a new phase in the industrial world, appearing in a seemingly infinite array of new products as chemists and manufacturers transformed the fiber.

Optimists predicted that new cotton-growing regions in Texas, Oklahoma, Arizona, and California would meet the demand, but Sully argued that four factors limited the growth of the cotton supply. First was the boll weevil, which was making a slow but steady advance northward from Texas. Contemporaries were concerned about the pest, but Sully accurately gauged the devastation it would eventually wreak in the cotton belt. Sully next pointed to the rise of Southern cooperative movements; the nascent Southern Cotton Growers' Protective Association, for example, asked cotton farmers to hold back cotton, plant more corn, and raise hogs. Its founders called on farmers to "Help break the shackles which have bound the Southern farmer to Wall street and Liverpool gamblers, and become freemen, priceing [*sic*] your own money product at a fair and just value. The opportunity is at hand, and 9 cent cotton is in sight if united concert of action is secured."[44] Combined with soil exhaustion—the third factor—Sully believed that calls for diversification among Southern farmers would lead to the slowing or even a reversal of the growth of acreage devoted to cotton in the South. In fact, acreage continued to increase at an average annual rate of 3 percent between 1890 and 1913, though cotton yields dropped precipitously from 240 pounds per acre in 1898 to a low of 170 pounds in 1903, recovering to 207 pounds in the 1904–5 season. Rainfall and other weather conditions were partly to blame, but the data (based on admittedly poor USDA "crop condition" reports) suggest that cotton farmers simply cut back on labor (weeding and careful harvesting), fertilizer, and other inputs in response to low prices, instead of switching their fields to corn or other crops.

Sully's final factor involved a theory of "seed degeneration," allegedly caused by the South's notoriously poor handling of cotton and the rise of the cottonseed oil industry. Unginned seed cotton was left in sacks outdoors, exposed to freezing temperatures, which Sully believed damaged the seeds.[45] The best lint-producing seeds were also the highest yielding in the oil mill, encouraging ginners to crush the good seeds and return the worst for replanting. The result was "a sterilized seed, which . . . has manifested itself in a less hardy and vigorous plant, bearing a shorter staple of less tensile strength, generally showing 10 to 15 per cent. less in producing power than obtained before the days of the oil mill."[46] Theodore Price, Sully's avowed enemy at the NYCE, was won over by the seed theory. Price concluded that a shrinking pool of seasonal African American labor in the South would further limit the size of the American crop, and by August 1904 he had joined the bull campaign.[47]

Sully's arguments had an appeal in their own right, but his charismatic influence was important. Unlike the faceless Wall Street "gambler," Sully was often favorably described in the press. The bullish circulars Sully sent around the South urging farmers to withhold crops were nothing new, but his celebrity grew as Southern newspapers heaped adulation on him for driving up the price of cotton. A widely circulated sketch depicted Sully as a serene master of the trading floor, as rival brokers smashed each other with chairs during a trading frenzy.[48] Sully's office was deluged with flowers on birthday, sent by grateful Southerners.[49] He personally broke the post–Civil War record for cotton prices in January 1904, when he marched to the NYCE floor to pay 16¢ per pound for a one-thousand bale order.[50] Sully paid the unprecedented sum of $68,000 for a seat on the New York Cotton Exchange, allowing him to trade on the exchange in his own name.[51] Believing that the forward inertia of his bull movement was about to receive a boost from the looming Russo-Japanese war, Sully continued to promise farmers higher prices. "When the first gun is fired in case of war cotton will advance 2 cents a pound," he told his followers.[52] He warned cotton spinners, "there isn't a cotton plant in the South that hasn't been picked of every ounce of its product."[53]

Sully insisted that he was not a gambler, declaring "that no price is speculative at which a commodity can be actually sold."[54] Behind the scenes, however, Sully worked hard to defend his market position. Knowing that the consumers of cotton textiles would ultimately decide the price of cotton through their buying habits, Sully launched what he called an "educational campaign."[55] With a fund of $275,000, Sully and some allies in the American manufacturing sector tried to influence "the American press and the American people to accept the high prices."[56] As a later editorial put it, manufacturers selling cheap cotton goods in the 1890s had "taught the consuming public to believe that the abnormal was the normal."[57] Sully believed that most buyers would ultimately pay "a level of cotton goods prices consonant with the price of cotton." While a number of newspaper articles used Sully's "talking points" almost verbatim, the campaign was not well received.[58] A retrospective editorial from the following year charged that "education" about the true value of cotton was of little interest for consumers: "the real intention on that occasion was to help along a speculative bull movement."[59]

British and American manufacturers knew that passing price increases on to consumers would simply decrease demand, and their short-term response to higher cotton prices was to cut production and reduce working hours (see below). As figure 1.1 shows, yarn prices followed raw cotton prices closely. No one wanted to be caught holding large inventories of yarn spun from expensive cotton if the price of cotton fell, and so throughout the 1902 and 1903 seasons, manufacturers bought on "a rigid hand-to-mouth basis."[60] In Lowell, Massachusetts, mills were reported to be selling their stocks of cotton back to the spot markets during the Sully corner, making money on cotton that was too valuable to spin while their machines sat idle and their workers went unpaid.[61]

Sully triumphantly sold off some of his cotton in February 1904 and planned a vacation. Rumors spread that Sully had dumped a million bales of cotton, and nervous sellers sent prices down by sixty points before Sully reappeared and refuted allegations that he was bailing out of the corner. According to the *New York Times*, a "bear faction" in the NYCE was behind the rumor, having warned Sully "that if he did not desist he would find no mercy."[62] The outbreak of war between Russia and Japan on February 4 further weakened prices, as merchants with business in Asia cut back on textile orders, contrary to Sully's prediction. Sully reentered the market the next day, prompting the panicked business columnist of Dallas's *Morning News* to announce in a headline, "SULLY TO THE RESCUE."[63] Newspapers carried exhilarating reports of Sully's cool handling of the mob on the NYCE floor, with headlines describing the "Generalship of 'Cotton King' in Moments of Excitement."[64] Sully's corner recovered, and the *New York Times* even reported a rumor that Standard Oil was forming a $50 million pool to back Sully.[65]

Sully should have quit while he was ahead, when his profit stood at nearly $8 million. Whether Sully really cared about Southern cotton farmers or was too proud to end his winning streak, he held on for too long as rivals attacked his corner in February and March. His primary financial backer in New York forced him to liquidate cotton contracts, but Sully decided to fight on alone and bought new contracts.[66] Allying with New Orleans brokers, Sully declared war on short-sellers who had snatched up contracts for spring and summer deliveries earlier in February when Sully's panicked disciples sold their futures contracts. Promising that he would force the short-sellers to buy cotton from him at 20¢ per pound to meet their summer contract deadlines, Sully kept his office open twenty-four hours a day, providing free in-house meals and lodging for his clerks.[67]

The collapse of Sully's corner on March 16, 1904, took many by surprise. The previous day, papers reported that spinners had "considerably extended their demands for American cotton," and rumors circulated that Sully was forming a new pool.[68] Futures prices slumped as trading opened on March 16, until the NYCE suddenly announced suddenly that Sully's firm had been suspended from trading. The announcement "caused a panic on the Cotton Exchange, smashed the wheat market, and depressed stocks." On the exchange floor, "A wild shout went up, and there was a rough-and-tumble fight to execute orders."[69]

Sully's opponents had found a liquidity problem in his operation and forced him to settle contracts early, knowing that he could not get cash fast enough to settle contracts under NYCE rules. Rival brokers banded together to prevent Sully's reinstatement, "even if this opposition should result to in a loss to them by reducing the chances of securing full payment for his debts."[70] They also blocked the attempts of a New Orleans broker to buy an NYCE seat, leading the *Manufacturers' Record* to charge the Exchange with waging "war upon the cotton growers!" "None but cotton bears need apply," the paper groused.[71] From a high of 9d. per pound in Liverpool, cotton prices fell down to 7d. and then 6d. over the spring and summer.

Supporters of Sully argued that there had not been a corner at all, and that the bulls delivered every bale contracted for. The *Manufacturers' Record* made a martyr of Sully in the South, decrying the victory of industrial capitalism over the farmer:

> The 'bear' element in this country and in Europe is powerful and untiringly active in its effort to force the price of cotton down. This element never sleeps. . . . Against this speculation to force prices down, to the impoverishment of millions of cotton-growers, the newspapers of the world have uttered no protest, but when Sully and his associates take the lead to make the world pay to the South a fairer price for cotton, to the enrichment of millions of growers who have been almost ruined by five and six-cent cotton, then the 'bear' element bring into play their vast machinery of capital and influence to break them, and thus break prices.[72]

New York's *Commercial & Financial Chronicle* compared the Sully corner to the 1898 Leiter wheat corner, blaming failure on novice leadership. "But this a secondary cause," they added. "The real and invariable reason for failure in experiments of this sort lies in the nature of supply and demand, which regulates all markets."[73] The Times (London) agreed that basic economic laws remained unshaken, and they reminded critics that prices would have risen even without Sully. "It must not be forgotten that there was a real basis for some advance in prices," wrote an editor, "and higher prices were inevitable without any effort on the part of Mr. Sully for any one else."[74]

Southern cotton farmers disagreed. In their view, the Sully corner showed that "the price of cotton was not the remote, inevitable grinding of the law of Supply and Demand, as they had always supposed, but a mere man-made affair."[75] The *Chronicle* observed that the corner succeeded "partly because the total supply was actually very limited, but chiefly because producers of cotton were themselves participating in the campaign for higher prices, and therefore holding back their product."[76] It was indisputable that Sully's short-lived corner enriched the cotton belt. The world paid $516,764,000 for the South's cotton in the 1903–4 season, $100 million more than the previous season. Bank deposits in the South increased 100 percent between 1900 and 1905, compared to a 50 percent increase nationally, while Southern land values rose at triple the rate of the 1890s. All over the South, newspapers reported paid-off farm mortgages. One Southern banker proudly stated that "the dependence upon crop liens and mortgages to make the coming crop will be confined almost entirely to the negroes and the less thrifty class of white farmers."[77] Even the anti-Sully *Chronicle* concluded with satisfaction: "Probably never have producers of cotton in the South secured such a profitable return for their labor."[78]

Unfortunately for cotton farmers and the world's consumers of cotton, the Sully corner sent cotton prices on a roller-coaster ride that lasted until the opening salvos of the First World War. The New York *Chronicle* had warned farmers during the early stages of the corner that windfall prices would "work a lasting injury." "For the time being, the producer looks upon it as a great boom . . . [but] the planter is led by the abnormal value to largely add to his acreage in cotton . . . the result the following season must presumably be a phenomenal crop with outcome to the producer of a minimum price for his staple."[79] The *Chronicle*'s editors were right. Inspired by the high prices of 1903–4, farmers produced a bumper crop for the 1904–5 season. Speculators rushed into manufacturing, especially in Lancashire, hoping to capitalize on plentiful cotton and pent-up demand for textiles. Manufacturing capacity and cotton agriculture could not find equilibrium.

In the 1909–10 season, bad weather damaged the crop and allowed a pool led by William Brown and other New Orleans brokers to launch a new corner. The conspirators agreed to hold seventy-five thousand bales each until November 1910, although the deal fell apart in June.[80] Prices skyrocketed, mills shut down, and spinners complained of the worst trade in memory. This time, the US government took action and indicted the pool members for "combination in restraint of trade," "conspiracy in restraint of

trade," "monopoly of trade," and having "power to fix prices," all in viola-
tion of the Sherman Anti-Trust Act. The pool managed to deliver on all its
contracts, totaling some 337,000 bales, yet its members were still charged.[81]
In a case that reached the US Supreme Court, the brokers finally agreed to
plead *nolo contendere* and paid $5,000 in fines, the maximum allowed under
the Sherman Anti-Trust Act.[82] The prosecution struck many Southerners
as unfair, and few enjoyed the irony that the weapons populists had helped
to create in their war against "bear cliques" in the 1880s and 1890s worked
just as well against bullish speculators pushing for higher prices.[83]

Cotton Corners and Cotton Spinners

From the spinner's perspective, the American brokers had used their
market position to manipulate prices in a way that had no bearing on the
actual supply of cotton or the demand for textiles. "What merchant or
manufacturer can make provision against such an unnatural proceeding?"
they complained.[84] While factories around the world were affected by the
Sully corner and subsequent shocks in cotton prices, Lancashire bore the
brunt of the "cotton crisis." As we have seen, Lancashire firms did not keep
large stockpiles of raw cotton and were exposed to rapid shifts in the price
of cotton. Lancashire also depended on price-sensitive customers in competitive, open markets in countries like India and China. India alone took
one-third of Lancashire's textiles in 1900, some two billion linear yards
of cloth.[85] Continental and American spinners did most of their trade in
domestic markets, protected by high tariff walls. Their customers had little
choice but to absorb any increase in the cost of raw cotton that manufacturers passed along. In Lancashire's export markets in Asia, Africa, and
Latin America, customers could buy cheaper grades of cloth from rival
manufacturers, turn to homespun fabrics, or simply do without. The low-
cost fabrics Lancashire firms sold in these markets were primarily made
from American cotton, which offered strong fibers at a low price, unlike
cheap but short-stapled Indian cotton or expensive long-stapled cottons
from Egypt. To sell cotton to the world, Lancashire had to buy cotton from
America (see table 1.3).

Lancashire's cotton mill owners and cotton workers pursued three strategies in their fight for cheaper cotton and stable prices. First, manufacturers and workers demanded the "international suppression of gambling
transactions in cotton," insisting, as socialist MP Keir Hardie put it, that
"it was a scandal that speculators should be able to gamble on the Stock
Exchange not only in scrip, stock, and shares, but also in the lives and
comfort of thousands of their fellow subjects."[86] Irish MP and labor advocate William Field proposed the prohibition or taxation of cotton futures

Table 1.3. European takings of American cotton

	Britain	Continent
1901–2	2,708,000 bales	3,696,000 bales
1902–3	2,603,000	3,946,000
1903–4	2,361,000	3,595,000
1904–5	3,620,000	5,148,000
1908–9	2,988,000	4,663,000
1909–10	2,606,000	3,748,000
1910–11	3,194,000	4,098,000

Source: Shepperson Publishing, *Cotton Facts* (1912), 37.

many times between 1904 and 1912. He was outraged that a "body of men operating between England and America should be allowed to shut out from employment thousands of persons, and bring disaster upon the cotton operatives of this country."[87] The *Times* of London agreed that it was "hard to convince a Lancashire artisan that it should in any way depend on Mr. Sully whether he is to be in employment next week," but the editors warned that futures markets were "an exceedingly complicated mechanism which cannot be roughly handled without sacrificing the benefits received from it by industry in normal times."[88] Nothing ultimately came of these calls for regulation in Britain, but they reflected a feeling in Lancashire that "gambling" rather than real supply issues were to blame for the cotton crisis.

The second response was a boycott of American cotton, which in Lancashire took the form of a work-sharing strategy called "short time." By reducing working hours, short time reduced cotton consumption and, at least in theory, would force down cotton prices as demand for raw cotton fell. Short time had originally been organized by powerful trade unions like the six-thousand-strong Oldham Operative Spinners' Union. Workers preferred to cut hours for all rather than see some factories operating as usual while others closed completely.[89] Employers eventually came to agree with workers that, as economist Sydney J. Chapman put it, "Low wages for the many are certainly better than no wages for the few."[90]

When the first rumors of a cotton corner reached Lancashire in the spring of 1902, Lancashire's de facto leader, Sir Charles Macara, launched a short-time campaign.[91] Macara was president of the Federation of Master Cotton Spinners' Associations (FMCSA), a trade group representing Lancashire spinning firms. Macara famously negotiated the Brooklands Agreement, which ended a vicious 1892 strike and established a wage-adjustment mechanism for spinning mill workers. The Brooklands Agreement established Macara's reputation as a leader of industry, capable of balancing the needs of workers and capitalists.[92] His role as self-appointed spokesman for Lancashire was not always appreciated (Andrew Bonar-Law sarcastically called him "the incarnation of the cotton trade"), but his success in leading the FMCSA made him a powerful public figure.[93]

Two institutions encouraged participation in short time among mill owners. Mill managers met at the Manchester Royal Exchange to buy and sell cotton, yarn, and cloth, and their personal interactions created a social network that facilitated cooperation among businesses that were otherwise fierce competitors.[94] The Liverpool Cotton Exchange was perhaps the most crucial institutional element, as it relieved manufacturers of the burden of carrying large stocks of raw cotton. Spinners bought spot cotton at Liverpool to fill orders as needed; mills with substantial capital locked up in raw cotton would have had little incentive to participate in short time.[95]

By May 1902, 90 percent of Oldham's fourteen thousand operatives were on short time. Nearly all Oldham firms (93 percent) participated.[96] The FMCSA had no way of enforcing short time beyond censure and public shaming, but the sharp increase in the price of raw cotton encouraged mills to cooperate. When spinning profits improved slightly in early April 1902, Macara took it as evidence of short time's efficacy and pressed for more of it. Through the Cotton Employers' Parliamentary Association, a loose lobbying group representing Lancashire's capitalists in Westminster, Macara appealed to spinners in Bolton and other towns that were less dependent on American cotton. Macara warned that "there was no hope unless combination could be secured." Bolton's spinning mills joined the movement during the height of the Sully corner, but in 1902 its representatives insisted "that five and a half out of seven million spindles would have nothing to do with short time," demonstrating the uneven impact of the crisis and the heterogeneous composition of Lancashire's textile sector.[97]

As the Sully corner gained momentum, Macara became convinced that "gambling" was solely to blame for the rising price of cotton. The FMCSA issued new plans for short time, using fines collected from FMCSA firms that declined to participate to compensate firms whose machinery stood idle. The *Times* praised the plan as "on the right lines," crediting Macara with recognizing that "the only way to deal with speculators who force up the price of an article is to refuse to buy it from them."[98] Cotton spinning firms that had previously avoided cooperative action joined the FMCSA in large numbers, uniting behind Macara's war against Sully.[99]

Many employers continued short-time work when the first FMCSA-sanctioned term expired in February 1903. Eight more months were approved for the winter and spring of 1903–4 to fight Sully's corner, with some firms voluntarily reducing hours for the rest of 1904.[100] When Sully's corner finally fell in March, Macara was quick to credit short time with the feat. The FMCSA report for the year concluded: "There can be little doubt that [Sully's failure] was very largely brought about by the loyalty of the trade to the short-time movement."[101] Oldham's operative spinners' union agreed, but noted that "it has been done at an immense pecuniary sacrifice by [mill owners] and their workpeople."[102] Short time haunted Lancashire's workers and capitalists for years after Sully's corner collapsed. The "Panic of 1907" sparked a fresh wave of cutbacks in late 1907, and by May 1908 a number of firms were reported to have shut down completely. Manufacturers eagerly locked out workers across Lancashire in response to a strike in late 1908. FMCSA votes for short time failed in 1909 and 1911, garnering support from only about 80 percent of firms instead of the 90 percent needed. Hundreds of firms nonetheless implemented short time. Conditions were so bad in 1909 due to unstable cotton prices that Macara believed "as far as England is concerned the mills might as well be stopped as running."[103]

Short time proved to be a costly weapon for Lancashire. During the Sully corner, Macara estimated that employers lost at least £40,000 a week, while workers in all branches of the cotton trade lost £110,000 in weekly wages. Oldham firms ran at a loss and paid dividends only by tapping cash reserves. The 1909–10 corner had a similar effect. In Bolton, which was insulated from many problems by virtue of its specialization in Egyptian cotton, firms nonetheless ran at losses worth an average of 10.26 percent of share capital in 1910.[104] The cost to organized labor was particularly significant. Short time cut working hours from about fifty-five to forty hours per week, nearly equivalent to a 30 percent pay cut. A well-off spinner might normally earn 45–60s. per week, depending on the type of yarn being spun, while his helpers (sometimes his own children) could earn 10–20s. each.[105] Most of that income was consumed in everyday expenses, which for a family of four might average £2 10s. (50s.) per week.[106] Short-time wages could easily spell the difference between a comfortable working-class existence and an inability to meet subsistence needs. Workers in the spinning industry endured at least forty months of FMCSA-sanctioned short time between 1902 and 1913, and those unfortunate enough to be employed by firms that voluntarily restricted output further suffered much more. Beyond the two hundred thousand spinning operatives affected, more than three hundred thousand weavers and many thousands of bleachers, printers, and workers in other trades suffered the downstream effects of short time.[107]

Trade unions paid out enormous sums to support their members during the crisis. When the first rounds of short time hit in 1902, rank-and-file members of the Minders and Twiners Union forced their leaders to draw on union funds to make up lost wages. Other workers followed suit, and by the end of January 1903, Oldham's operative spinners had paid £15,000 out of their funds.[108] For the decade between 1901 and 1910, Oldham's Operative Spinners' Union paid out more than £100,000 in lost wage benefits. Across Lancashire, trade union payments for short time and other related out-of-work benefits for spinning operatives exceed £320,000 by 1909. This was a huge amount, considering that the resources of all cotton-spinning trade unions combined were reported at only £400,514 in 1904.[109] Thomas Ashton, secretary of the Oldham union, warned his colleagues in 1902 that "members have driven a nail in their own coffin, by demanding and obtaining payment from the funds of the association for short-time working, as per the new rule. No trade union in the country can stand the strain put on funds."[110] He was right; the drain on organized labor's resources limited the ability of unions to fight with employers over wages and working conditions.

Macara asserted that operatives "would choose rather a continuance of their privations and suffering than a return to full time under conditions so ruinous to the trade,"[111] and labor leaders indeed chose to suffer the lesser of Macara's two evils, but in several corners the stirrings of labor's revolt against the paternalistic "millocracy" and the Liberal Party were beginning.[112] Bolton's relatively prosperous spinners' union warned the employers: "It is too much to expect that the working classes will continue to submit to a policy of starvation, in order to checkmate a body of wealthy gamblers. We venture to think that if the position was reversed, and the working classes were the aggressors, some effectual action would soon be taken by the Authorities to put an end to a system which produces such bad results."[113] Ironically, the Brooklands Agreement—which protected workers from arbitrary cuts to their pay—also prevented workers from claiming large wage increases during periods of recovery.[114] Manufacturers reaped windfall profits as cotton prices fell in 1905–6, but labor was entitled to only a 5 percent pay increase. In April 1906, Bolton's workers won their 5 percent increase in a year that saw profits jump 17 percent for employers. When unions finally pushed back in 1910, the "near-famine price of American cotton" caused by the 1909–10 cotton corner checked their bargaining power.[115] While there is no documentation showing that employers intentionally used short time to beat back labor demands, employers were quick to lock out workers and contest strikes when cotton prices were high.[116]

When the Brooklands Agreement finally collapsed in 1913, it was due to a growing "bad spinning" problem, as well as Macara's refusal to budge from the principle that capital be allowed a 5 percent profit—no matter what the trading conditions—in any negotiations to raise the operatives' rates. "Bad spinning" described abnormal yarn breakage during spinning, usually caused by the substitution of shorter and weaker cotton for a given grade. Broken yarn forced mill operatives to stop their machines and mend the yarn, lowering output and decreasing the operative's piece-rate earnings.

Employers saved money by using cheaper cotton, but forced operatives to work harder mending yarn.[117] As more expensive American cotton reduced margins, manufacturers had a strong incentive to substitute cheaper inputs to hold down unit costs. Sully's corner thus contributed to the end of two decades of industrial peace in Lancashire, pitting labor and capital against each other in a struggle neither would ultimately win.

The Cotton-Growing Movement

Short time was an important response to high cotton prices, but it was a negative strategy, a way to mitigate damage in the hope that time would set the market right. The third response Lancashire pursued was to grow more cotton in regions outside the reach of American speculators. It was this movement that would have the greatest impact, as Lancashire turned to Africa as a replacement for the American South. The first stirrings of a cotton-growing movement came in Oldham. At a meeting of the Oldham Chamber of Commerce in late 1901, the town's business leaders recalled the efforts of an earlier Lancashire cotton-growing group, the Cotton Supply Association (CSA). The CSA had been founded in 1857 in anticipation of the American Civil War, and its membership swelled when the war began and the "cotton famine" ensued in 1861. The CSA identified plantation sites, distributed information and equipment to would-be planters, and lobbied governments to provide services and subsidies.[118]

In India, the colonial government refused CSA's requests to spend money on roads, ginneries, and agricultural experts. Indian cotton did reach Lancashire in increasing quantities during the cotton famine, but most of the fiber was too short for the typical yarns spun in Lancashire, and the available supply did not come close to replacing the American crop. Although the CSA tried to improve the quality and size of the Indian cotton crop, its plans were "geared to the needs and interests of English industry, not to the interests of India," and they ultimately had little impact on the Indian cotton industry.[119]

The CSA's involvement in West Africa was equally unsuccessful. A Manchester merchant named Thomas Clegg financed a Church Mission Society plantation program in Nigeria, combining his Christian zeal with his own need for cotton.[120] Nigerian farmers exported several thousand bales of cotton to Britain during the war, but the CMS program and other cotton-growing efforts in the Gambia and Gold Coast succumbed to poor weather, land and labor problems, and high production costs. Even given the outrageous prices paid for American cotton during the war, African cotton proved expensive. The return of cheaper American cotton in the 1870s doomed any hopes for future development, and the CSA dissolved in 1872.

If the Oldham Chamber of Commerce's minutes are accurate, nobody could quite recall why the CSA had failed in its mission to transform the British Empire into a major supplier of Lancashire's cotton. Still, the Oldham manufacturers resolved that Lancashire should once again work "to increase the 'Growth of Cotton' particularly within the Empire."[121] Cotton growing appeared on the agenda of Oldham's Master Cotton Spinners' Association several times during the rest of 1901 and early 1902, but manufacturers devoted most of the organization's energy to enforcing short time.[122]

Manchester's business community soon got wind of Oldham's cotton-growing meetings, and public meetings were held across Lancashire in early 1902. At a joint meeting of the Oldham and Manchester Chambers in April, leaders of the textile industry decided to incorporate the British Cotton Growing Association (BCGA). The new association's mission was: "[to] Dispatch expert expeditions to report on the best methods of procedure; Acquire land on which to make experiments and establish plantations; Distribute seed amongst the natives, and to encourage them by advice and assistance to grow cotton on their own land, and to engage experts for this purpose, if necessary; [and to] Establish stations to buy and sell cotton."[123] According to its founders, the BCGA was to be a semiphilanthropic organization, with a nominal capital of £50,000. Manchester and Oldham leaders wanted to use subscriptions to pay for scientific and "missionary" work in the empire, viewing this as a philanthropic service to the empire. Once the cotton-buying arm of the operation became profitable, subscriptions would become dividend-paying shares. Many were hopeful that the British Empire would soon be feeding Lancashire's mills. "We want to compete with American [cotton] in the market," said John Newton, president of the Oldham Chamber and first chairman of the new BCGA.[124] A *Punch* cartoonist captured the mood in Lancashire with an illustration of John Bull issuing orders for cotton growing in Africa, Egypt, and India, while a sullen Southern planter looks on (see fig. 1.2).[125]

Lancashire was not alone in looking to its empire for alternative sources of cotton. German manufacturers launched the Colonial Economic Committee (KWK) in 1896 to promote raw material exports from Germany's empire, and a branch within the KWK focused extensively on cotton agriculture after the American cotton corners began in 1902. German manufacturers feared that shortages in the American cotton supply would cripple their growing textile industry and also lead to social unrest. Unlike Lancashire's stoic trade unions, German unions were unwilling to accept short time and factory shutdowns when cotton prices rose. German manufacturers argued that colonial cotton would secure the domestic textile industry, concluding that "a prosperous cotton industry was essential to combatting working-class upheaval."[126] France's Colonial Cotton Association (ACC)

TOUCHED ON THE RAW—MATERIAL.

JONATHAN. "HELLO! STARTIN' OUT TO GROW COTTON, IS HE? GUESS I MUST HAVE 'CORNERED' HIM ONCE TOO OFTEN!"

Figure 1.2. Cartoon of John Bull. Raven-Hill, "Touched on the Raw Material," 201.

had similar aims, though the regional textile syndicates that created the group in early 1903 seemed more focused on the strategic and economic benefits of colonial cotton, rather than domestic labor issues.[127] While the ACC, BCGA, and KWK were all independent organizations representing manufacturing interests, the BCGA stood out from its counterparts by emphasizing the role of private industry in developing colonial cotton industries. The French and German groups believed governments needed to help home industries exploit colonial resources, but Lancashire's manufacturers initially did not seek anything more than the cooperation of colonial officials in implementing the BCGA's ideas.

The British government and the colonial administrations did not have much to offer the BCGA in any case. Colonial governors had a hard enough time raising capital to pay for basic services like railroads or sanitation, and did not have the political latitude or the money to fund cotton growing.[128] While "the services of [the Royal Botanical Gardens at] Kew were at the disposal of both the self-governing and the Crown Colonies on a vast range of agricultural and botanical matters," Kew's experts had little to share with regard to cotton.[129] A Colonial Office (CO) official told the BCGA in 1902 that "there is no one at Kew with practical knowledge of growing cotton," urging the association to find its own experts. Only five CO officials out of forty-three had any specialized education in science in 1903. Nearly a decade after the BCGA's founding its chairman could still complain that "There is no single official at the Colonial Office or in the Government who is imbued with any idea of the necessity of Tropical Agriculture or Tropical Medicine," although by then scientific expertise in colonial agriculture was rapidly expanding.[130]

Competing Interests: J. Arthur Hutton and Sir Alfred Jones

Manchester came to the cotton-growing movement from two different directions. Like Liverpool, its trading rival, Manchester was home to a merchant community with business interests around the world. Manchester was also a textile-manufacturing center in its own right, however, and its mill owners shared the interest of Oldham's spinners in solving the cotton supply problem. Two men who would lead Lancashire's campaign for imperial cotton—Sir Charles Macara and James Arthur Hutton—represented each of Manchester's perspectives on the cotton trade. Macara was initially offered the BCGA presidency but accepted a vice-presidential role, preferring to focus his energy on organizing FMCSA support for the new association. The merchant J. Arthur Hutton was initially nominated by the Manchester Chamber of Commerce to serve as BCGA vice-chairman, and he quickly rose to chairman. Hutton and his colleagues in the West Africa section of the Manchester Chamber of Commerce ultimately determined the course of the BCGA by directing Oldham and the other manufacturing towns toward West Africa.

Hutton's interest in Africa had several dimensions. His family had a business history in West Africa dating to the late eighteenth century. There are few details of the Hutton family's early dealings in Africa, but several Hutton men served with the Company of Merchants Trading to Africa on the Gold Coast in the eighteenth and nineteenth centuries. The Huttons traded imported manufactures for gold and slaves on behalf of the company, and on their own account. A 1784 invoice from the ship *Venus* in the Hutton family's papers links William Barnard Hutton, founder of the family firm, to the London merchant house of Camden and Calvert (later, Camden, Calvert, and King, a major slaving firm).[131] The 1784 voyage of the *Venus* took it from Cape Coast Castle, where 320 slaves embarked, to Charlestown, South Carolina. Only 280 captives survived the journey.[132]

The family business weathered abolition and the arrival of "legitimate trade," and records from 1811 show an active trade on the West African coast.[133] The family developed a specialty in palm oil and supplied European forts and other merchants with trade goods. A Hutton served as British consul to Asante and published a travel narrative in 1821, and references to the family appear throughout British administrative records relating to the Gold Coast.[134] The Huttons moved eastward to Whydah as early as 1838, and the firm used "strong-arm tactics" to force out rivals in Nigeria in 1850. They were apparently a small concern in the palm oil trade with only thirteen shipments (amounting to 2,905 casks of palm oil) recorded between 1830 and 1855.[135] The firm also manufactured cotton cloth, putting out yarn to hand-weavers and exporting the finished products to Africa. While no data are available on the extent of this business, the firm continued its putting-out operations until the 1880s, when competition from power looms drove the last hand-weavers out of work.[136]

The Hutton family also had links to African cotton growing, although this piece of family history seems to have been lost on J. A. Hutton. The family firm responded to the CSA's call for more cotton in the 1860s, and Anthony Calvert Hutton partnered with the newly formed Manchester Cotton Co. in 1861 to launch a cotton plantation at Winneba on the Gold Coast. A. C. Hutton's 350-acre cotton plantation was an illustrative failure: it relied on two English farm workers as managers and agricultural experts, neither of whom knew anything about cotton. Imported inputs in the form of two bulls and workers from Cape Palmas were substituted for scarce local labor. Some £600 worth of machinery was lost in a shipwreck, leaving the plantation without a cotton gin. By 1862 the plantation experiment was over, and A. C. Hutton returned to trading.[137]

While Oldham and Manchester formed committees and founded the BCGA, Liverpool beat them to the actual work of growing cotton. Sir Alfred Jones, owner of the Elder-Dempster steamship line, had been trying to get entrepreneurs in Africa to cultivate the crop for years. Jones had no direct connections with Lancashire's cotton interests, seeing cotton only as a useful return cargo for his freighters.[138] Jones's initial response to the creation of the BCGA was to simply take it over. The shipping tycoon went to Oldham's business leaders directly and convinced them to join forces. Oldham's Chamber of Commerce curtly informed Hutton in April 1902 that Liverpool would be joining the movement under Jones's leadership, and that Jones was going to be the association's new president.[139]

Jones explained to Hutton that he had been sending cotton seed and tools and encouraging cotton production in West Africa for several years: "It is a pity that Manchester and Liverpool don't confer together a little oftener. You will see how fully we have gone into the subject, and I was delighted to see you suggest Cotton growing in Africa the other day, although it is two years after we have started it."[140] Instead of fighting Jones, who was unloved among the Manchester merchants trading in West Africa for his monopolistic practices and his wholehearted support of Joseph Chamberlain's plans for government intervention in colonial economies, Hutton accepted Jones's arrival with resignation.[141] Jones brought publicity, connections with cottonseed suppliers in America, a fleet of steamships, and a network of merchants in West Africa to Lancashire's cotton-growing crusade. He used his patronage of the journalist E. D. Morel (soon to be famous for his reporting on the Belgian Congo) to raise the profile of cotton in the press. As Morel prepared to launch his new paper, the *West African Mail*, Jones told him, "I hope you will push the Cotton growing movement. I am confident that you will be able to increase the radius of public interest in West African affairs. Every living Englishman ought to take an interest in West Africa. It is a great country, with a great future."[142] Jones also brought his personal fortune into the cotton-growing venture, pledging £10,000 toward the BCGA's initial capital of £50,000, later contributing another £15,000.[143]

While Jones was an outspoken admirer of Germany's KWK and its state-subsidized cotton-growing program, he wisely kept quiet about in meetings with free-trading Lancashire merchants and manufacturers. Instead he urged the rapid commercialization of cotton growing in British Africa, rather than the cautious semiphilanthropic approach endorsed by the BCGA's founders in Oldham and Manchester. In the midst of the 1902 Sully corner, Jones insisted that "America was not proceeding on philanthropic lines at present."[144] Hutton agreed, saying it was "no use going to Governments and asking them to stop speculation." The cotton industry's salvation "lies mainly in her own hands," he said.[145] At a BCGA meeting in late 1903, J. A. Hutton argued that the crisis was an opportunity for the BCGA:

> as business men, we ought not to sit idle and cry out for help like children to the Government to come and help us to put a stop to the proceedings of the speculator. It is for us, as business men, to find the remedy for ourselves. . . . Here are these speculators, who want to have the cotton. I say, let them have the cotton, and let us grow as much we can everywhere, and push it on to them. The only way to deal with speculators is to smother them in cotton. (Hear, hear, and laughter).[146]

In his speech, Hutton laid out a plan of work for the BCGA, moving beyond the tentative ideas circulated in 1902. He urged the association to focus on recruiting cotton experts to train colonial subjects in cotton cultivation, and to establish ginneries and cotton buying stations to create demand for cotton in the empire. If ginneries offered to buy cotton at good prices, Hutton was sure farmers in the colonies would start growing it. Ginning profits would fund further expansion of the colonial industry, in addition to paying dividends to the BCGA's financial backers.

The merger of manufacturing and merchant interests in Lancashire was not a smooth process. Emboldened by Jones's support, Hutton proposed "to confine our attention absolutely to West Africa and to the possibility of successful extension of cotton cultivation in our colonies there."[147] Oldham businessman John Newton, who had not yet yielded the BCGA chairmanship to Hutton, pointed to recent news from Germany's experiments with cotton in Togo and argued that "there was no commercial value in it," given the high cost of production and transportation.[148] Newton "referred to the efforts of the Oldham Chamber with regard to other parts of the world than West Africa and especially in Egypt," vetoing Hutton's call for an exclusively African focus. Newton was taken aback when he heard that E. D. Morel's *West African Mail* was, according to its masthead, "the official organ of the British Cotton Growing Association." Hutton and Jones both encouraged Morel to publish articles about the BCGA, and either one might have given Morel the "official organ" designation with an eye toward steering the imperial cotton movement toward West Africa.[149] Newton and other manufacturers were not amused that a small newspaper serving the West African merchant community was claiming to be the mouthpiece of what was supposed to be an empire-wide movement. Newton retaliated by withholding BCGA reports from Morel and by publishing material on cotton growing in India, Egypt, and other parts of the empire.[150]

Newton soon resigned from the BCGA, however, giving Hutton and his friends in the Manchester merchant community a chance to seize control of the cotton-growing movement. Records for this early period in the association's history are scant, but it appears that the Executive Council's decision to open a permanent office in Manchester gave vice-chairman Hutton control over official correspondence and planning. By 1904, Hutton was effectively running the BCGA, and he succeeded Newton as chairman in short order.

Outside of Oldham, the most vocal critic of the BCGA and its new focus on Africa was John Holt, a Liverpool merchant and bitter rival of Jones in the West African shipping business. Holt was a true believer in the colonial "civilizing mission," and believed that commerce was its best tool.[151] He attended early BCGA meetings in Manchester in 1902, but told his friend Morel,

> I cannot claim to take any great interest in a scheme which seeks with £50,000 to increase the world's supply of cotton and is to embrace the world in its area of experiments. I cannot enthuse on spending my money or time in order to cheapen the price of cotton for the world—the idea is beyond me and my cramped ideas. It is as much as I can do to think of growing cotton in Africa, not to make it cheap in Europe, but to give the native another outlet for his energies and provide a new field for the use of British Capital. Cheapening will not help that operation. Dearness would be more likely to give the desired result. The professed aims of mere philanthropists would justify the employment of £5,000,000, rather than of £50,000.

Holt was also suspicious of Jones's role in the scheme. He rhetorically asked, "Would not Jones himself put £100,000 in it to give his steamers freight if he thought there was a margin even to pay expenses—not to speak of profit? Don't be deluded."[152]

Selling Empire Cotton in Lancashire

Holt and the BCGA's new leaders agreed on one point: cotton growing was not the government's business. The BCGA needed private investment to begin its work in the colonies, but Lancashire's capitalists proved to be unenthusiastic investors in African cotton. The first BCGA appeal assumed that the inherent business potential of cotton growing would attract investment, but by October 1903, only £31,000 had been subscribed, and less than £2,500 of that sum came from individuals or groups not directly connected to the cotton trade. Lancashire trade unions and cooperative societies contributed the most (£9,541), with Oldham's spinners and Manchester's spinners and merchants taking second and third place (£8,635 and £5,241 respectively).[153] Disappointed, Hutton tried a new tack, emphasizing the damaging effects of Sully's corner on Britain's economic health. Hutton argued that only new supplies of cotton—preferably in British hands— would check American speculators: "Let Lancashire only realise that it is no use going to Governments and asking them to stop speculation. Let her learn a lesson and realise to-day, if she has not done so already, that her salvation lies mainly in her own hands, and then, and not till then, we may be able to look on Mr. Sully and all his gang as benefactors in disguise."[154] For audiences outside Lancashire, Hutton emphasized the far-reaching impact of disruptions in Lancashire's business. Textile workers operating on short time had to "economise in clothes . . . [and] restrict their purchases of food, and the brewers are also suffering because the people cannot afford to drink so much beer." Hutton went to list effects on farmers, bootmakers, and other trades who relied on patronage from factory workers.[155] In the *West African Mail*, Morel followed a similar line, expanding his analysis to Britain's African Empire. Empire cotton offered: "For England: Safety for the most important of our industries. Self-protection against a peril which might become a National Disaster. For Lancashire: Cessation of dependence upon America. . . . For West Africa: The Creation of a new Native Industry. Increase in Native Purchasing Power, and consequent advance in the Development of the Colonies."[156] This new approach, which cast cotton growing as a national and imperial economic imperative, was more successful than the first appeal. Local committees spontaneously formed in at least ten large and small Lancashire towns, representing both spinning and weaving centers. Coverage in the Times (London) was restrained but uniformly positive. BCGA officials reported that papers in smaller towns "helped with good articles."[157]

The BCGA's semiphilanthropic status was an important part of the association's new fund-raising campaign. BCGA spokesmen argued that cotton growing would help colonial subjects and the empire as a whole through "the provision of profitable employment for the natives, freights for the railway, cargo for the steamers, and raw material for the most important industry of this country, bringing prosperity to a vast number of the subjects of the king, whether in England or in Africa, whether white or black."[158] The BCGA hinted at a concept of imperial cooperation across geographic and racial boundaries, though it never systematically developed the idea that white workers in Lancashire were partners in a global cotton industry with black workers in Africa (or America, for that matter). The BCGA's use of imagery was limited, but illustrations used by the association and press outlets tended to stress the benefits of imperial cotton for Britain, rather than for imperial subjects. An unpublished 1904 illustration by *Punch* illustrator Bernard Partridge depicts imperial subjects laying cotton bales at the feet of Britannia (see fig. 1.3), accurately capturing the tone of BCGA propaganda in Britain.

The association made its claims to philanthropic status by stressing the differences between its own plans and those found in other industries and empires. As the Duke of Marlborough argued, the BCGA's plans to distribute free cotton seed would give Africans "healthy as well as remunerative

Figure 1.3. Bernard Partridge, unpublished illustration (ca. 1904), printed on a BCGA banquet menu, BCGA 10/4/3. Courtesy of the Cadbury Research Library: Special Collections, University of Birmingham.

employment," whereas most expatriate-owned plantations ruthlessly exploited African laborers.[159] G. D. Hazzledine, who served as Sir Frederick Lugard's secretary during the conquest of Northern Nigeria, boasted that cotton growing would be "the easiest way of earning money they [Nigerians] have known. Then the Yankee may keep all his cotton, and gamble and fool with his crop to his heart's content, to the injury of his own industries instead of the industry of Lancashire."[160]

While the BCGA carefully maintained a matter-of-fact tone in its official propaganda, the association's friends in colonial governments and the press enthusiastically used empire cotton growing to promote their own political agendas. Hazzledine linked the BCGA to his own jingoistic vision of imperialism, arguing that cotton growing would allow Britain to achieve its true purpose in Nigeria:

> to change the darkest spot in darkest Africa back again into a land flowing with milk and honey. . . . Is it to be thought that the British public will grudge the money for a work like this? France is doing her share . . . Germany, in the Cameroons and Adamawa, has more than she wants. Are we, muling and puking, to follow the finger of the Little Englander, invest all our moneys in electric railways, schools, and scientific experiments, and leave the real work of the world to be done by nations who *can* breed men like those who made Great Britain the leader in civilization?[161]

On the opposite side of the political spectrum, E. D. Morel argued that the BCGA was a model for Liberal imperialism, offering a way to develop the empire without costly and coercive government interventions. Business, rather than government, would lead the development of Africa according to the laws of supply and demand, delivering benefits for the metropole as well as the colony. According to Morel, the BCGA's investments in Africa would bring wealth to African farmers and stability to Lancashire's cotton industry.[162]

Morel and Hazzledine's positions do not strike the contemporary reader as philanthropic, but the context in which they made these claims is significant. European empires were rocked by labor scandals in the early twentieth century, and the BCGA's supporters contrasted the association's model with contemporary episodes like the "Chinese slavery" scandal in South Africa.[163] The most important comparison was with the Congo Free State. In 1904, articles publicizing the BCGA's work and new royal charter appeared alongside news of a campaign against King Leopold's genocidal rule in Congo. The Congo scandal put BCGA president Sir Alfred Jones in an awkward position, as he remained a staunch defender of Leopold's regime. E. D. Morel, who had worked as a clerk for Jones before starting his own newspaper, helped lead the British campaign against Leopold as well as Jones, who refused to suspend his shipping business in Congo. Morel's *West African Mail*, which declared on its masthead that it was the "official organ of the BCGA," published stories celebrating the BCGA next to articles fiercely condemning the "Leopoldian system" in Congo.

For Morel, the BCGA—despite Jones's involvement—offered an alternative to exploitative capitalist development in Africa.[164] Through a combination of "philanthropic" work like distributing free cotton seeds, and commercial activity like buying cotton at ginneries, the BCGA promised to draw millions of African workers into cotton production through market forces alone, free of all hint of coercion. As the editors of the African-owned *Lagos Weekly Record* put it, "the true object and policy of British rule in West Africa" was to facilitate this kind of private investment in the colonies and to promote unfettered trade, not to unjustly exploit the labor and resources of the colonies.[165] Morel held that the most vital aspects of imperial development were not government-backed railroads or land concessions to plantation companies, but rather "the maintenance of the right of the native to trade, not with the Englishman only, but with all men: the right of the native to sell his labour and the fruits of his hand, which his labour can alone gather and reap. We hesitate, but too frequently alas! To use the word TRADE, lest we be accused of interested motives; lest humanitarianism be described as utilitarianism."[166] BCGA supporters like Morel made a powerful case for the association's approach to cotton, especially when contrasted with the coercive measures used in German and French cotton-growing projects. By combining claims about national and imperial economic benefits with the rhetoric of philanthropy, the BCGA hoped to convince individuals across Britain to join the campaign for empire cotton as investors and as philanthropists.

Public interest in the BCGA waned as Sully's corner collapsed in March 1904, however. Instead of scaling back, the BCGA's leaders boldly expanded their plans for cotton growing in the British Empire. Political allies warned that "those interested in the greater production of cotton that when their pockets were full, that was the time to increase their subscription." "Hay must be made when the sun still shone," declared David J. Shackleton, a mill worker turned Labour MP.[167] Some of the association's prominent backers convinced the British government to award the BCGA a royal charter to enhance the association's flagging appeal. King Edward mentioned the BCGA favorably in his 1904 speech before Parliament, and the government "recorded its approval by the grant of a Royal Charter."[168] The royal charter marked a substantial reorganization of the association. To finance Hutton's vision of a network of imperial ginneries and cotton-buying stations, the association raised its capital goal tenfold, to £500,000. Under the charter's terms, the BCGA agreed to postpone dividend payments to shareholders for at least seven years in exchange for government recognition of the association's semiphilanthropic status. Hutton claimed that the royal charter elevated the association "above all ordinary commercial ventures," giving it a special role in the development of the colonies.[169]

To rekindle interest outside Lancashire, the BCGA council decided to hold a public exhibition where information, photographs, and artifacts from cotton-growing experiments could be displayed. The first "Empire Cotton Exhibition" attracted more than eighteen thousand visitors to the exhibition rooms of the Imperial Institute in London.[170] The BCGA displayed a copy of the royal charter, maps, a telegram from the King, samples of cotton, and examples of African looms and clothing, while a professional canvasser worked the crowds. The exhibition later went on tour, though a reviewer from the *Times* was sure that it would "make only a vague impression on the man in the street." He held out some hope that it might "touch the woman in the street in a way she can understand" by connecting the idea of empire cotton to "those charming or useful articles with which the shops are decked at the present moment in bewildering profusion."[171] Railway stations allowed the BCGA to post advertisements for free, and banks accepted subscriptions for BCGA shares at local branches.[172]

Despite all this, the BCGA failed to become a popular movement. By the end of 1905, only about £40,000 of the £188,098 subscribed had come from individuals and companies outside Lancashire and not directly connected to the cotton industry. Discouraged by the initial failure to raise all the BCGA's capital at once, Hutton submitted his resignation in February

1905. Only "representations that it might injure the Association" convinced him to stay.[173] Lancashire MPs then introduced a resolution in Parliament expressing appreciation for the BCGA, "to let it be seen that the movement was not dead, and that they did not mean to let it die."[174] The association hired three canvassers to solicit contributions, but they raised only £3,408 in four months and took a 6 percent commission.[175] Two of the canvassers reported that "it was useless to continue further canvassing outside the trade, until there had been a much larger response from Spinners and Manufacturers." They noted that "several mills with which members of the [BCGA] Council are connected have not subscribed the full amount."[176]

In response, Hutton came up with a new scheme that targeted Lancashire alone, hoping to compel the cotton industry to commit money for its own defense. In cooperation with Macara and trade union leaders, the BCGA instituted an annual levy on manufacturers of 10s. per thousand spindles and 3d. per loom, as well as a day's wage from every cotton worker. Ambitious as this plan was, Hutton calculated that it would bring in only £210,000, and required unions and firms that had already subscribed to pay again.[177] Historians have assumed that the cotton textile sector was behind the BCGA's work in Africa, but Hutton's struggle to wring even £210,000 from Lancashire showed how apathetic many manufacturers were to the idea of imperial cotton growing.[178] Surprisingly, mill operatives supported the BCGA much more than their employers. The BCGA used appeals to both imperial patriotism and labor's pragmatic sense of self-preservation to build support for colonial development.

Macara thought that Lancashire would meet its commitment to the new BCGA plan and he told FMCSA members that he hoped to have raised the full BCGA capital of £500,000 in time for the second meeting of the International Cotton Federation in Manchester in June 1905. "Lancashire will be able to take the proud position of having set a worthy example to the rest of the world," he said.[179] Yet BCGA finances languished as good trade replaced short time in 1905. Firms did not respond to levy notices, and Hutton issued an "Urgent Appeal to Spinners, Manufacturers, and Operatives" in September 1905, saying "if Lancashire chooses to defeat America's monopoly and manipulation, she can do so, but at present her spinners and manufacturers are content to stand by in apathy."[180]

Oldham's MCSA launched a door-to-door canvass of local firms to convince firms to pay the levy, but Bolton's mill owners rejected the idea. The local MCSA instead wrote letters to uncooperative firms, hoping to stave off embarrassing in-person solicitations from the BCGA.[181] During the door-to-door campaign in Oldham, the BCGA ran into outright hostility. The Willow Bank mill directors said they were "in sympathy with the general movement," but "have fully decided not to increase our support until we see some attempt upon the part of the Cotton-Spinning Authorities to deal with the undue expansion of mill-building."[182] A less tactful firm told the MCSA, "We are not in favour of receiving a deputation, nor scarcely in favour of 'The British Cotton Growing Association' in face of the continuous and reckless Mill Building that is continually going on by persons that are in the trade one day, and out another."[183] The BCGA's mission was effectively being undermined by the expansion in mill capacity, which would increase pressure on the cotton supply. In Oldham alone, FMCSA member firms added 1,138,900 spindles in the second half of 1904, and another 1,886,938 in 1905.[184] FMCSA leaders failed to take these complaints seriously, and weakly suggested to the BCGA that "if new mills would undertake to subscribe for the number of shares recommended . . . it would remove a serious obstacle to the work of getting further support to the movement."[185]

Other firms observed a free rider problem, promising to give more only when all firms had subscribed.[186] In the small spinning town of Stalybridge, all but one of the important firms had subscribed to the first BCGA appeal, but they refused "to increase their amounts until Messrs. Wilkinson [the laggard firm] subscribe."[187] Excuses of "extravagance" at BCGA headquarters were offered by a number of other firms that refused to subscribe. High salaries and wasteful spending allegedly "deterred the firms . . . from subscribing although they supported the objects of the BCGA."[188] The directors of the Townley Mills raised these issues as well as more basic questions: "Has a balance sheet been issued? Is there any guarantee that whatever cotton is raised by the B.C.G.A. it will be first offered to subscribers?"[189] (The association issued only general overviews of its finances in annual reports. Regular auditing of expenditures in the colonies did not begin until 1908.)[190]

The FMCSA fund-raising drive in Oldham was supposed to prove that Lancashire stood behind the cotton-growing movement, and it was successful in increasing Oldham's stake in the BCGA (see table 1.4). Smaller towns like Rochdale and Stockport did not receive such intense lobbying, and in any case had raised funds proportionate to their size. In districts less closely associated with cotton, like Lancaster or Glasgow, the increase in contributions was insignificant, indicating that the initial BCGA appeal had reached nearly all those it would attract outside Lancashire.

When the BCGA tried to raise funds from Lancashire spinning mills again in 1910, they found that firms representing more than 60 percent of Oldham's productive capacity ignored the appeal.[191] Macara blamed the BCGA for the fund-raising failure. An FMCSA report in early 1910 suggested that India had been neglected as a site for cotton growing, and that too much money had been spent (and spent unwisely) in West Africa. The committee approved continued support for the BCGA, but demanded that two FMCSA members sit on the merchant-dominated BCGA Executive Council.[192]

Table 1.4. Change in mill owners' BCGA subscriptions

	1904	1906
Oldham	£11,603	£29,138
Bolton	5,662	12,335
Rochdale	3,992	5,603
Stockport	2,661	4,058
Preston	3,096	11,008
Lancaster	707	807
Scotland	2,086	2,393
Total subscriptions	188,098*	248,116

Source: Reports, BCGA 2/2.
Note: *Figure for early 1905.

The BCGA's inability to secure significant amounts of cotton from Africa certainly did not help the fund-raising effort. All cotton landed in Liverpool by the BCGA was sold, but it was not until 1908 that the BCGA could report "a considerable increase in the demand for West African cotton."[193] The BCGA did not even bother sending its own agent to the cotton exchanges to sell African cotton until late 1909, leaving the commercial end of their work in the hands of major cotton brokers (and BCGA Executive Council members) like A. A. Paton and C. M. Wolstenholme.[194] Most firms found the kinds of cotton being offered by the BCGA unsuitable. Native short-staple cotton from Africa was not priced competitively with Indian short staple, and the more valuable long-staple cottons were too long for Oldham and too rough in texture for much of Bolton's fine-spinning. Firms found that African cotton "was not suitable for their purposes," and tried to buy it at bargain prices.[195]

In contrast to Lancashire's capitalists, cotton textile workers contributed a great deal of money to the BCGA. Organized labor's leaders saw the BCGA as a hedge against short time and future unemployment in the cotton industry. While the BCGA assumed that workers—especially relatively well-paid mule spinners—would "see their way to take their share of the responsibility and pecuniary risk involved," organized labor had no place in the early organization.[196] By June 1902, the BCGA council invited representatives from spinning and weaving trade unions to join the association.[197] The following year, a special appeal for contributions was issued to the operatives.[198] By August 1904, unions and other groups of employees in Lancashire firms had subscribed more than £3,200. Another £4,500 came from more than forty cooperative societies, which counted many workers among their members.[199] When Hutton introduced the "day's wage" scheme as part of the 1904–5 fund-raising campaign, the BCGA and labor leaders were confident the rank-and-file would participate, sending a powerful message to mill owners and the rest of the country.[200] Initially, the day's wage collections were a great success. Oldham's trade unions held a football match as a BCGA fund-raiser, and dozens of local committees were formed to distribute cotton-growing propaganda and to pool money to buy additional BCGA shares.[201] The promise of dividends from BCGA operations was important to union officials managing investment portfolios, as well as to the upper ranks of workers who personally invested in shares. Bolton's Cardroom union explicitly told its members that their contributions bought two hundred share certificates, expanding their union's portfolio.[202]

Workers made it clear to the BCGA "that universal support from the Labour bodies in the Textile Districts could be relied upon if the Employers generally responded to the Levy."[203] The failure of many firms to subscribe embarrassed leaders like Macara and Hutton, and it gave workers little incentive to continue supporting the BCGA. The *Cotton Factory Times* chided employers for their lackluster response to the BCGA's appeals, saying, "It is really time they decided to pay up."[204] When pressed in 1906 to pay the second installment of the day's wage collection, the chairman of Oldham's cardroom union said he "was not in favour of Cardroom workers paying a day's wages, especially seeing that the employers had not given the movement the support which they ought to have done."[205] Bolton's spinners lambasted employers for not contributing enough, proudly saying workers had "done your duty and set an example to more wealthy people."[206] In Oldham, collections for the second installment of the day's wage collections in 1906 were a "dismal failure."[207] Union leaders blamed employer apathy, and elected to pay the next installment out of reserve funds.

The BCGA's lead fund-raiser, Henry McNiel, blamed problems on "Socialistic opinions amongst the Operatives." Workers told McNiel "the Employers are making such large profits that *they* ought to find all the money wanted." Workers admitted that since the end of the Sully corner "Operatives are doing better than they were some time ago, but argue that they are not getting anything like an equitable share of the present exceptional profits which they allege are being made by the Employers." Some workers argued "neither Employer nor Operative ought to be called on to contribute, but that the work of Cotton growing in the Colonies should be done entirely by the Government."[208]

Cardroom unions, representing the lowest-paid operations (which included female ring spinners and workers in other parts of the cotton mill), led working-class opposition to continued BCGA fund-raising.[209]

The cotton corners had caused long periods of "depressed trade, bringing with it short-time working and reduced pay packets," weakening the hand of organized labor.[210] Lancashire unions lost several important fights in the first decade of the twentieth century, and workers began to see cotton mill owners as free-riders, ready to benefit from empire cotton but unwilling to pay for it. When the day's wage scheme was relaunched in 1910, one district of the Oldham Cardroom workers' union sent back the account books issued to monitor compliance, and leaders in other mills refused to take collections at all.[211] Oldham's cardroom union secretary told their membership that it was "to Lancashire's disgrace the [BCGA] has to beg" for money from employers and workers.[212] During the last BCGA drive in 1914, Oldham cardroom representative W. H. Carr refused all further contributions, despite pressure from the mule spinners' unions. He "considered that if the Employers thought that the work of the Association was so desirable and necessary, they ought to have no difficulty in finding the requisite money, and he did not see why the operatives should be asked to subscribe at all."[213]

Still, labor took a long view of empire cotton, blaming lackluster support from capitalists for the BCGA's slow results: "Financial support from certain quarters has hardly been as liberal as might have been expected," said one union report. "With the means at its disposal the Association has no opportunity of patiently prosecuting its work."[214] Labor representatives clearly understood what the BCGA was trying to accomplish by erecting cotton gins in Africa and carrying out "missionary work," and they took a long-term view of colonial cotton agriculture. While labor records shed little light on working-class views of Africans, union minutes and labor newspapers discussed Africans as rational economic actors, who had to be convinced that growing cotton for Lancashire was a worthwhile task. The Oldham Cardroom Union reminded its rank and file that "The work of interesting native farmers in different parts of Africa to grow cotton require time, money, and patience. One failure to obtain good result must not be allowed to daunt them." The union added, "If the efforts now being put forth by the Cotton Growing Association are allowed to lapse for want of funds, it will be the everlasting disgrace of the reputed keen, capable, far-seeing business men of Lancashire."[215] Instead of recognizing the failure of capitalists to hold up their end of the bargain, Hutton attacked workers for not giving the money their leaders had promised. He threatened to shut down the BCGA in one meeting with employers and labor leaders, citing his "great disappointment that the Appeal to the Operatives had not received the response which had been hoped for."[216]

Foreign observers were surprised that workers contributed anything at all. The Boston-based *Textile World Record* suggested that the subscriptions coerced, coming "only when the appeal for aid has been made to a working population of whom many are working on short time, facing hunger and deprivation because of a shortage in the cotton supply."[217] Hutton's counterpart in Germany, Moritz Schanz, complained that German workers would not "follow the example of their broad-minded English colleagues, who, in spite of privations caused them through the short-time movement, contribute to the B.C.G.A. 1s. 3d. per head." He admitted that "efforts to induce the German operatives to a similar step have failed."[218] Lancashire's working class did commit substantial sums of money to the BCGA. The first Day's Wage appeal raised £24,000 from workers, nearly 27 percent short of Hutton's estimates, but still far better than the 39 percent shortcoming among FMCSA member firms. The second (1910) appeal raised another £21,500, falling 35 percent short of labor's goal.[219] All told, Lancashire's working class raised at least £45,500 for the BCGA.

Colonial Investment and Imperial Politics

One group was conspicuously absent from BCGA shareholder rolls: the "gentlemanly capitalists" who historians P. J. Cain and A. G. Hopkins suggest were the main drivers of imperial economic policy. Only a handful of wealthy, politically influential imperial enthusiasts like Sir Alfred Jones bought in BCGA shares, and while the BCGA enjoyed the patronage of important men like the Duke of Marlborough, the aristocracy was generally uninterested in financing empire cotton. Social elites were precisely the segment of British society from which "the most strident Empire support could have been expected,"[220] but as investors, this class preferred specific kinds of imperial investments, such as government bonds and railroad debentures. BCGA shareholder records show only a few gentleman shareholders. Many of these were Lancashire gentry, representing local sentiment rather than a nationwide imperial ethos.[221] The BCGA was not the only colonial cotton-growing operation trying to raise capital in Britain. As chapter 2 explains, private firms tried to launch cotton plantations in Africa to take advantage of the "empire cotton" movement, but most were unsuccessful. When a Lancashire cotton firm finally made a serious investment in cotton agriculture, it was not in the British Empire, however. In 1911, the Fine Cotton Spinners' and Doublers' Association paid nearly £1 million for a cotton plantation—in Mississippi.[222]

National politics did not help the BCGA win over skeptical investors. The association had the misfortune of launching just as Joseph Chamberlain launched his controversial "Tariff Reform" campaign for protectionism and imperial development.[223] Chamberlain envisioned a customs union spanning the entire British Empire, allowing imperial manufacturers and raw material suppliers to trade without facing foreign competition.

Chamberlain also hoped to use state funds to promote new agricultural, mining, and manufacturing enterprises across the empire. He was friendly to the BCGA during his tenure as secretary of state for the colonies, but Chamberlain, Jones, and other Tariff Reformers knew that linking cotton growing to Tariff Reform would poison the BCGA in Lancashire.[224] BCGA president Sir Alfred Jones was an enthusiastic supporter of Tariff Reform, however, and saw colonial cotton as an important part of Chamberlain's plan. He chided E. D. Morel for publishing anti-Chamberlain rhetoric in 1902, arguing that Chamberlain had "put his shoulder to the wheel" and was "doing everything he can to help the [cotton] trade."[225] In public, however, Jones was careful not to link the BCGA to Tariff Reform.

Hutton, a free-trading Liberal Unionist, argued that empire cotton stood apart from the Tariff Reform debate: "on the common ground of cotton supply all parties have joined hands—Free-Traders, Freefooders, Tariff-Reformers, Fair Traders, Protectionists, Little Piggers, Whole Hoggers."[226] As a pamphleteer put it in 1911, cotton growing was "without doubt of immediate and overwhelming importance to Lancashire, and so long as it is accomplished it matters little or nothing if what is called fiscal orthodoxy is or is not outraged in the effort."[227] George Harwood, a Liberal MP and Free Trader representing Bolton, expressed this feeling early in the BCGA's fund-raising campaign when he insisted that Lancashire was not "pursuing a selfish policy." Borrowing a line straight from Chamberlain, he said, "All they wanted was that the Government should regard the Empire as an estate to be developed in the interest of the whole Empire." (The statement provoked "much hilarity on the opposite side of the House [of Commons].")[228]

The central political issue for the BCGA was public financing for railroads in the empire. Without cheap transportation, cotton could never be profitably exported from Africa, but private investors were unlikely to build railways into agricultural areas. Egged on by Frederick Lugard, the governor of Northern Nigeria, the association declared that "Northern Nigeria was the only country which offered any possibility of producing cotton suitable for Lancashire in large quantities." They warned that without a railroad "it would be hardly worth while the Association carrying on its work, for what could be obtained from other parts of the Empire would only be small in quantity, and therefore absolutely insufficient to keep Lancashire Mills running."[229] The Nigerian railroad put some Lancashire men, like Hutton, in an uncomfortable position: as free-trading, laissez-faire liberals, they had fought against earlier colonial railway projects, such as an 1898 proposal for a state-financed railway to gold fields in Ashanti.[230] As a Conservative MP reminded his Free Trade colleagues, they were "asking for a bounty and departing from the pure milk of the Cobdenite theory" when they voted for colonial railroads.[231]

A Tariff Reformer argued in 1907 that a bill for a railroad into cotton-growing areas of Nigeria "was practically a policy of subsidy and bounty, and he cordially supported it. . . . It was a good Tariff Reform Bill." Winston Churchill, a BCGA supporter and a Liberal at the time, retorted that "he had never heard a line of argument which was more capable of producing the opposite results to that which the hon. member desired."[232]

Despite the BCGA's efforts to remain aloof from politics, both sides invoked empire cotton as a campaign tool in the 1906 and 1910 elections. Two Conservative candidates in Oldham ran under the slogan, "Vote for Hilton and Stott and Support and help British Cotton growing."[233] Liberals won the January 1906 election, and while the party remained committed to free trade, its leaders saw government-backed development as necessary "to avoid making continual calls on the British tax payer" for the maintenance of African colonies.[234] The government was still wary of spending taxpayer money on "white elephants" like the outrageously overbudget British East African railroad that had embarrassed the previous administration.[235]

Winston Churchill, the new undersecretary of state for the colonies, assured Lancashire's MPs that the new Colonial Office was "warmly interested in the work of the British Cotton Growing Association."[236] Churchill moved from Oldham, which he represented from 1900 to 1906, to a safer Manchester district for his election as undersecretary. He made cotton growing the centerpiece of his colonial policy outside the white dominions. "A well-considered and thrifty policy of railway development," he argued, "would do more for the Lancashire cotton industry than will ever be gained by Mr. Chamberlain's food taxes or Mr. Balfour's tariff wars."[237] Building on the BCGA's "philanthropic" status, Churchill, Morel, and other BCGA supporters argued that state-backed railways would contribute to a humane form of development in the empire, with benefits for colonial subjects as well as metropolitan investors and workers.[238]

Historians have assumed that the BCGA's success in building the Northern Nigeria railroad demonstrated Lancashire's influence in imperial policy making.[239] Governor Lugard had convinced the association that a light-gauge railway from the cotton districts to the Niger River was the most economical choice. A rail connection all the way to Lagos, the main Nigerian port, threatened Lugard's dream of maintaining Northern Nigeria as a separate colony from the south. Chamberlain thought the rail-to-river route was a poor investment, and he backed a more expensive standard-gauge railway connected to the existing Lagos railway. Lord Elgin, the new colonial secretary in 1906, was emphatic that Lagos be the terminus and that a "battle of the gauges" be avoided by using the standard three-foot six-inch gauge already in use in Southern Nigeria.[240] The BCGA pleaded that Lugard's light and fast railway was Lancashire's only hope, insisting that "No other Colony is capable of producing millions of bales."[241] The government agreed with the BCGA that Nigeria merited a railroad, but they initially refused to build it on the BCGA's terms.

For years, Lancashire MPs and BCGA deputations harried the Colonial Office about the Nigerian railway. The BCGA finally bypassed the CO by bringing a huge deputation of Lancashire's leading men to lobby the prime minister in 1906.[242] Faced with a serious challenged from the Tariff Reform campaign, Britain's Liberal government approved *both* lines. This allowed the government to seize the mantle of imperial leadership the Tariff Reformers claimed for themselves, and the bill passed in part because of support from Conservatives and Tariff Reformers in Parliament. Elgin was unhappy but concluded that the light gauge line to Baro on the Niger River was a temporary expedient that would (and did) fall into disuse when the direct line to Lagos was finished.[243]

Tariff Reformers celebrated the Nigerian railway as "an extremely elementary form of protection to subsidise cotton-growing, which cheapened cotton from Manchester."[244] Arguments like this fell hard among supporters of the BCGA. George Bowles, an embattled Conservative MP and a committed Free Trader, turned against the BCGA and the railway in 1907.[245] Churchill tried to change the terms of the debate, defending the railway as an example of a Liberal, free-market version of imperialism. "This miserable Little Englander Government came into power, and we are building a great railway 450 miles long through the heart of the cotton districts of Africa," he boasted, adding that "It has cost less than half of the Uganda Railway, which Mr. Balfour and his friends constructed."[246] Churchill pointed to his support for the BCGA during his tenure in the Colonial Office during a 1908 by-election, and Sir Alfred Jones reluctantly endorsed him instead of the Tariff Reform candidate.[247]

The Nigerian railway was the BCGA's greatest political victory, but it was a one-off event. As later events illustrate, the BCGA had little influence on government in Britain. Churchill took a prestigious post at the Board of Trade in April 1908 and promptly lost interest in empire cotton; his replacement was skeptical of the BCGA and began to restrict some of the special access to colonial officials the association had enjoyed. When the BCGA's access to political power waned, Sir Alfred Jones prepared to turn the BCGA into a minor cotton-buying operation, "a specialist, but subsidiary, part of his business empire."[248] As Jones's rival John Holt observed, "he finds he has not got the hold of the present C.O. leaders that he had when Marlborough and Churchill reigned there." "It is a great pity but with Jones in charge of Liverpool and Hutton leading Manchester it is all cotton growing and steamships instead of the wider interests of the community and the promotion of the moral and material welfare of the natives of Africa," Holt complained. "[They] are interested adventurers and are too apt to overlook other more important matters in their eager pursuit of their own special hobbies."[249] Jones's sudden death in December 1909 gave the association a chance to start a new relationship with the CO, however, and it gave Hutton (who had threatened to resign in November 1909) a second wind.[250]

The BCGA chose Lord Derby, a staunch Conservative and a free trader, to replace Jones as BCGA president. The council hoped Derby's prestige would help disassociate cotton growing from domestic politics. Derby told the public, "we have never had one word of politics in any of the [BCGA] meetings I have had anything to do with, and I take good care we don't," quipping that the "Free Trade lamb has lain down with the Tariff Reform lion, and neither, I think, is the slightest bit the worse."[251] Hutton was further encouraged when the Oldham mill owner and BCGA vice-president Alfred Emmott was elevated to the peerage and made the colonial under-secretary in November 1910.[252] Unfortunately, the new secretary for the colonies, Lord Harcourt, was not impressed by the BCGA's semiphilan-thropic aims and government support for the association dwindled.[253] Harcourt told African colonies to avoid a cotton exhibition planned for 1915, which the BCGA hoped would reinvigorate public interest in the cotton-growing movement. Only Uganda's government prepared an exhibit, and only after insisting that rubber and other crops be exhibited alongside cotton. Hutton was so disgusted that the BCGA withdrew, refusing to spend any more money on propaganda.[254]

Conclusion

The association ultimately got the railroads it wanted, and it made sure that Lancashire—often marginalized in imperial politics by more powerful financial interests—was heard in imperial policy making. Still, Hutton and other BCGA leaders envied the support German and French cotton-growing programs had received from their governments. From Lancashire's perspective, Britain's government had spent a pittance on a project that was supposed to make African colonies wealthy and financially self-sufficient, while also protecting Britain's biggest export industry from the depredations of American speculators. But a lack of government aid was only one of BCGA's problems; more important was a lack of capital. The BCGA might have gotten off to a strong start with or without government help if it had enough capital to invest in cotton growing. Instead, the association struggled for more than ten years to raise £500,000.

By the end of 1914, the BCGA had delivered almost three hundred thousand bales from Africa and the West Indies to Lancashire. More than ninety thousand bales came from West Africa, where the bulk of BCGA experimental work was directed. The rate of increase was impressive, from thirteen hundred bales in 1903 to thirty-three thousand in 1909, but the quantity was a drop in the ocean as far as Lancashire's spinners were concerned.[255] BCGA supporters hoped that the association's "philanthropic" model would attract investors, but few in Lancashire were interested in the empire in any serious way. E. D. Morel was the most vocal proponent of the idea of a partnership on equitable terms between the "black races" of Africa and the "white races" of Europe, but his ideas did not translate into financial commitments to empire cotton. When Lancashire's workers talked about cotton growing, they were focused on their own jobs, rather than the welfare of African farmers. Likewise, Lancashire's capitalists were apathetic about the idea of building partnerships with African cotton farmers either as a philanthropic or a business venture. All told, Lancashire's workers and employers subscribed £278,500 to the BCGA, while railroads, collieries, banks, insurance firms, and brewers offered a further £21,745. Less than £10,000 came from London and the rest of Great Britain. Merchants and investors in Manchester and Liverpool contributed the rest of the nearly £500,000 that was raised by the start of the First World War.

Historians have argued that British colonial policy was beholden to a "Lancashire lobby," but this chapter shows that Lancashire's influence on government was modest, and that Lancashire itself was not fully committed to imperial cotton growing.[256] Industry and government did not react to the crisis in the American cotton market in a coordinated fashion, and Lancashire was not uniformly convinced that the BCGA offered a solution to volatility in the American cotton market. The Baltimore-based *Manufacturers' Record* was no friend of the BCGA, publishing many diatribes against colonial cotton schemes, but its editor was right to observe that "The most significant fact about the [BCGA] appeal is the necessity for making it. If the growing of cotton within the British dominions to satisfy the needs of Lancashire was a practical business proposition, the long-headed, alert and aggressive capitalists would have subscribed to it over and over again."[257] There was little tangible to invest in under the association's semiphilanthropic model, aside from a few ginneries. Most of the BCGA's capital was locked up financing cotton crops, and until 1916, the association's merchant activities consistently lost money. Ultimately, British capital liked to invest in railways and mines, not merchants and farmers.[258]

2

"The Black Man's Crop"

The British Cotton Growing Association and Africa

> Whether planted in West Africa or in any other part of the world, cotton of any variety other than Sea Island must necessarily be a black man's crop. The return per acre is not sufficient to adequately remunerate white men.
>
> —William Howarth, Lancashire cotton
> spinner and BCGA member

All of the imperial powers of Europe were affected by instability in the American cotton supply and looked for ways to end America's monopoly on long-staple cotton. British, French, German, Belgian, Italian, Dutch, Portuguese, Russian, and Japanese cotton manufacturers hoped that their nations' colonies could replace America as a source of long-staple cotton. While cotton could be grown in Asia and the Americas, Africa attracted the most attention from imperial powers. This chapter explains why Africa appealed to cotton manufacturers and colonial development planners, and why the British Cotton Growing Association invested so heavily in the continent at the expense of India and other parts of the British Empire. The chapter then examines the BCGA's plans for cotton growing, comparing its strategies to those of its French and German counterparts. While all of the colonial cotton programs exchanged ideas about cotton growing, the BCGA was uniquely burdened by its semiphilanthropic orientation and private-sector status, and its struggles to raise capital in Britain limited its ability to implement projects in Africa.

Three themes connect this chapter and the next. First, the chapters show a clear disconnect between metropolitan interests and colonial decision-making. While Lancashire and the British government claimed to be in full support of "empire cotton," the BCGA received little investment. As a class, British capitalists were apathetic toward the entire cotton-growing enterprise.[1] A few private cotton companies were floated during and after the Sully corner, but only one (the Sudan Plantations Syndicate) operated for more than a few years. On the other hand, Lancashire had little influence on the BCGA's plans. British cotton manufacturers and workers were shut out of the BCGA executive committee and made no effort to dictate what kind of cotton the BCGA should pursue, or where and how it should be cultivated. Instead, one man's preoccupation with finding a British-controlled replacement for American long-staple cotton drove most of the BCGA's decisions. Until his resignation as chairman in 1918, J. Arthur Hutton designed BCGA programs around the premise that the American cotton supply would become increasingly expensive and would eventually be consumed entirely by American manufacturers. Hutton believed that the survival of Lancashire depended on the transplantation of American long-staple cotton to the British Empire, and he believed that only Africa could meet Britain's needs. Many failed policies emerged from this mistaken assumption.[2]

The second theme concerns the variety of ways in which Africans responded to the BCGA. As Allen Isaacman has argued, Africans were not "passive recipients of a colonial mandate."[3] Some farmers eagerly embraced cotton; others resisted colonial impositions directly or "used the market against the state" by cheating merchants, jumping colonial borders to access better paying markets, and otherwise subverting cotton-growing regimes.[4] Further, some African entrepreneurs were able—at least for a time—to redirect BCGA programs to serve local handicraft textile industries. Context was critical: where the BCGA made cotton a competitive crop, cotton flourished. Where the BCGA could not—or would not—make cotton lucrative, African farmers chose other outlets for their labor. J. A. Hutton and other BCGA leaders saw resistance and redirection as market failures, rather than rational responses to economic conditions.

Finally, the two chapters outline the long-term consequences of the BCGA's successes and failures. To fix perceived "market failures," Hutton gradually steered the BCGA away from the private sector and toward the state, imposing monopsonistic and monopolistic conditions, fixed prices, and expert supervision on African farmers. These policies made fictions of Britain's supposedly free markets in colonial produce and limited the economic freedom of Africans. Apathy from Lancashire capitalists and incompetence on the part of the BCGA gradually engendered hostility toward cotton agriculture in government circles. Colonial officials abandoned cotton with alacrity wherever more promising industries turned up. By 1918, the BCGA's semiphilanthropic model was thoroughly discredited, clearing the way for new development ideologies that marginalized private enterprise and free markets in favor of state-sponsored agricultural science and the expert management of rural labor.

Race and Place

The director of the German Colonial Economic Committee's (KWK) cotton department, Moritz Schanz, addressed the annual meeting of the International Cotton Federation in 1910 and declared, "We consider the following to be the *fundamental conditions for a remunerative cultivation of cotton*: Suitable climate and soil, large extension of suitable tracts, sufficient supply of cheap native labour, and finally, reliable and cheap means of transport" (emphasis in the original).[5] The southern United States had all of these things, thanks to the twin legacies of slavery and capitalist development in the cotton belt. What Schanz and other Europeans feared was the disappearance of that "cheap native labor" in the South that made cheap cotton, cheap cloth, and the global system of mass textile consumption feasible. European manufacturers believed their African colonies already had three out of Schanz's four requirements; the missing factor, transportation, was seen as merely a matter of time and political will, given the potential of African land, labor, and climate.

Schanz was right about the criteria for the cheap production of labor-intensive commodities. Unfortunately for the colonial powers, he and his colleagues were quite wrong in assuming that these conditions could be easily met in Africa. Transportation was neither easy nor cheap, and while there was plenty of arable land in Africa, little of it was anything like the Mississippi delta.[6] There was little extant scientific work on African environments, and Schanz and his colleagues in Britain and France based their own plans on reports from travelers and administrators who knew little or nothing about cotton. Many European travelers in West and Central Africa described large fields of cotton growing apparently without care and harvested haphazardly to meet domestic needs. Heinrich Barth's 1857 account was typical:

> Having heard that the wealth of the inhabitants of Dikowa [Dikwa, northeast Nigeria] consisted of cotton, I expected to find extensive, well-kept cotton plantations; but although the article was cultivated to a great extent, I was astonished at the neglected appearance which it exhibited, the cotton-fields being almost buried beneath the thicket, and overgrown, not only with rank grass but even with trees and bushes, so that scarcely any space was left for the plants to spread out; nevertheless, their luxuriant growth bore ample testimony to the rich nature of the soil, and gave an idea of the wealth that lies buried in these regions. I have already observed on another occasion that the natives of Negroland take very little care of their cotton-plantations; and there is no doubt that, if sufficient care was bestowed, quite a different quality might be produced.[7]

On the other end of the continent, David Livingstone reported "cotton growing luxuriantly all around the market-places from seeds dropped accidentally." Livingstone believed the plants he saw were derived from American seeds, "so influenced by climate as to be perennial."[8]

Secondhand information further inflated cotton's prospects. Thomas Clegg, a promoter of the Civil War–era Cotton Supply Association, reported in 1858:

> Abbeokuta [*sic*] is but just on the border at one corner, I may say, of the great cotton field of Western Africa, extending from Abbeokuta to the Niger and away into the interior . . . the Rev. Mr. Clark had seen at Ilja near Ilorin in the Yoruba country fifteen or sixteen packages of clean cotton offered for sale weighing seventy five to eighty pounds each, and had been assured by the natives that on market days (every fourth) from one to two thousand such bags were offered for sale and this for their own country manufacture.[9]

Stories like this demonstrated that Africans could grow cotton on African soils on a large scale. Yet these accounts emphasized the "neglected" nature of the crop, and promoters of cotton-growing schemes intimated that production could be rapidly scaled up if Western agricultural methods were applied. With tropical agricultural science in its infancy, however, naive assumptions about the innate fecundity of African soils rather than empirical research guided the early cotton-growing projects.[10]

Cotton is an adaptable plant and will grow in a range of soils, but the conditions under which it will produce a commercially viable quantity of lint are more particular. There are regions in Africa well suited to commercial cotton growing, but even these are hindered by the inescapable fact that tropical latitudes receive fewer hours of sunlight in the summer than the subtropics. Cotton lint production is strongly correlated with sunlight exposure, and the extra hours of summer light enjoyed in the American South (along with Egypt, the Mediterranean, and central Asia) results in higher yields than tropical environments can offer. As geographer Philip W. Porter put it, "Never was so much misplaced effort devoted to an enterprise as the production of cotton in sub-Saharan colonial Africa. The photosynthetic difference and cotton's wide production in large, better-suited areas doomed from the start the metropolitan dream of developing a competitive cotton industry in tropical Africa."[11]

Africa might have lacked ideal soils and sunlight, but the continent definitely had an African population, which was for imperial powers synonymous with "cheap native labor." As Isaacman has argued, "Race became a powerful organizing principle and rhetorical device to legitimate forced cotton cultivation" across Africa.[12] Race allowed colonial planners to break with economic orthodoxy because African farmers were viewed first and foremost as Africans, rather than as economic actors participating in local, regional, and global markets. As Hutton told a wartime committee on cotton in 1917, cotton was "a crop for the small man. It is the black man's crop."[13] What made it a crop for the "small man" was Hutton's assumption that cotton had to be cheap, and that black labor was inherently cheap. When Australians asked the BCGA for help launching a cotton industry in Queensland, Hutton strongly discouraged them from investing cotton. "Owing to the prohibition of coloured labour being imported," Hutton argued that white farmers could not and would not grow cotton at a competitive price. Other colonial experts shared Hutton's belief that black labor—and especially African labor—was cheap. Schanz explicitly listed "a strong coloured population, easily accustomed to agricultural work at low wages" as Togo's most crucial asset for the German cotton growing project.[14] While the KWK and BCGA did experiment with plantations, Schanz and Hutton agreed that peasant production was the way forward; many colonial planners found through experience that "owing to their low fixed costs and flexible use of family labor, [peasants] could consistently undersell state-managed or private-sector plantations."[15]

What separated cotton from other commodities was the explicitly racial dimension of cotton production. Cotton's history in the United States had given Europeans, Americans, and Africans a shared stock of racial discourse that shaped the development of colonial cotton growing in Africa. Europeans readily accepted prevailing American stereotypes about the supposed relationship between Africans and cotton.[16] White Southerners insisted that "the white man cannot stand the continuous exposure hour by hour in the position that is necessary to pick cotton." Various contrivances for mechanically picking cotton were doomed to fail, they argued, because the best cotton picker was "invented in Africa some thousands of years ago, which found its place in our fields; they could not improve on it."[17] Some members of the African diaspora endorsed this association between black skin and white cotton bolls. Frederick Douglass, the great African American political campaigner, agreed with white Americans that cotton was destined to remain a crop cultivated by black workers. He claimed that cotton farming in hot climates was "uninviting and harshly repulsive to the white man," whereas "the Negro walks, labors, or sleeps in the sunlight unharmed."[18]

Journalist E. D. Morel put a positive spin on the association of Africans with cotton, arguing that "What the West African Negro has done in a land of exile as a slave, or hired servant, he can accomplish in his own land, as a free man, and landowner in his own right." For Morel, the transfer of cotton to Africa was part of "the irrevocable march of events which mould the ultimate destinies of peoples."[19] The editors of the *Lagos Weekly Record*, an African-owned paper with proto-nationalist leanings, argued that while the BCGA was working "to supply the wants of Europe," it was also establishing "a safe-guard against oppression and wrong in Africa and upon the African" by creating a great new industry for African farmers.[20] Cotton appeared to offer a way for African farmers to participate in the world economy on fair terms without the coercion required for plantations and wage labor. As Sir Alfred Jones declared at a 1903 BCGA meeting, "Africans had made America and he believed that the people who would make Lancashire would be the Africans again."[21]

Europeans tended to ignore the fact that white farmers cultivated about 60 percent of the American South's cotton land, and that many could not afford to hire black labor.[22] At the same time that Europeans were promoting cotton in Africa, Americans were encouraging the immigration of Italians and other European laborers to the South, believing that they could replace black Americans in cotton fields. In Sir Charles Macara's opinion, Italians "were infinitely superior to the negroes, who are hopeless as regards getting to be possessors of the soil themselves."[23] Still, the link between cotton and race proved hard to break.

Turn-of-the-century racial theories often differentiated between the "black" and the "brown" races, but they shed no light on why the BCGA favored Africa over India or Egypt, both of which produced appreciable quantities of cotton and had, from the European point of view, "black" populations. European manufacturers might have pursued cotton growing in peripheral regions in Latin America or Asia, where European capitalists had a long history of extracting vital commodities.[24] Latin America failed to interest European cotton manufacturers, despite the modest success of cotton agriculture in places like Peru and Brazil. The Argentine government published a pamphlet encouraging settlers and investors to start cotton plantations in 1904, hoping to take advantage of the interest generated by the Sully corner.[25] An anonymous pamphlet published in Manchester in February 1904 urged investment "in the fertile northern states" of Brazil.[26] Nothing came of these efforts. Brazil was only taken seriously as a cotton producer by Lancashire in the 1920s, when the boll weevil infestation in Mississippi annihilated a variety of cotton that typical Brazilian cotton could replace.[27]

Colonial powers did pursue cotton growing in Asia. The Russian Empire had wanted to transform central Asia into a cotton-producing region for nearly a century, with leaders predicting that the subjugated peoples of the region "would be our Negroes" and supply Russian mills with raw materials.[28] The Dutch implemented a program along the lines of the German KWK in Indonesia.[29] Japan expanded cotton production in occupied Korea and China. In British-ruled India, cotton had been an important industry for millennia and it was the world's second-largest producer of raw cotton. Instead of investing heavily in India, the BCGA ignored it. This was largely J. Arthur Hutton's doing, although business opinion in Lancashire stood behind him. Lancashire men bitterly remembered the poor grades of Indian cotton that merchants rushed to market during the US

Civil War. The president of the Cotton Supply Association set the tone for the next half century when he said in 1862, "I do not hold India to you for imitation. You have nothing whatever to learn from India, except how to mismanage your business, and produce the worst quality of cotton that is grown on the face of the earth."[30] Indians had once grown the best cotton in the world, but low prices and inattention to seed selection contributed to a process of adverse selection that resulted in a shorter and weaker fiber. A British traveler observed in 1863, "the cotton is always sold in advance, and there is no market whatever for quality, only for quantity."[31] Much of the cotton Lancashire received was uneven, dirty, and too short to replace American Upland cotton. Even the quantity was insufficient to meet British needs. The *Economist* complained that "The primitive prerequisites of common political economy . . . are not satisfied. You have a good-demanding Englishman, but, in plain English, not a good-supplying Indian."[32] The passage of four decades did nothing to erase these negative memories in Lancashire. The "spinners' prayer" of the 1860s cotton famine was a favorite joke in Lancashire whenever the topic of Indian cotton came up: "O Lord, send us more cotton, but, O Lord, not Surat."[33] New research by Sandip Hazareesingh has stressed the importance of environmental factors in foiling British efforts to increase the cultivation of cotton varieties desired in Lancashire, suggesting that British critics may have exaggerated the extent to which Indian business practices affect cotton supplies.[34]

Hutton believed that Indian business institutions posed an insurmountable obstacle to expanded and improved cotton growing. He reported, "local buyers will not pay a higher price for the improved varieties of cotton, and complaints to this effect have been received in all parts of India."[35] Adverse selection worked against cotton quality by encouraging farmers to pursue quantity over quality. A long line of Indian middlemen separated the farmer from the exporter, making it difficult to pass along price incentives for higher-quality cotton. Agricultural reform would require the overhaul of tenancy, finance, and contract law, to say nothing of the agricultural extension services that would be required to raise the quality of the cotton seed supply. Cotton, therefore, was the Indian government's problem as far as the BCGA was concerned. Lancashire may have had more base motives for ignoring India as well: there was little profit to be had in a place where the association would have to compete with local and expatriate firms for raw cotton. Strong demand for ginned fiber from handicraft spinners and weavers and the growing Bombay textile-manufacturing industry threatened to make cotton too expensive for Lancashire. At a minimum, competition would eat into ginning profits, which the BCGA hoped to use to pay dividends to shareholders in Britain. The secretary of the International Cotton Federation, Arno Schmidt, alleged that "some Manchester people" really opposed Indian cotton because "an extension of the spinning industry in that country would inevitably follow, and that industrial competition would thus be made keener."[36]

Whatever the reason, the BCGA dedicated very few resources to India despite repeated requests for assistance from missionaries, businessmen, and administrators in India. Over and over, Hutton told government officials and public audiences that "The bulk of the cotton produced in India is absolutely useless for Lancashire's needs."[37] A BCGA India subcommittee met infrequently, and only once discussed setting up cotton buying centers with the Indian government. When Sir Charles Macara went behind Hutton's back and tried to arrange new cotton-growing programs in India on behalf of the International Cotton Federation, BCGA leaders bitterly resisted and convinced the imperial government to abandon the plan.[38]

With India out of the question, the BCGA focused on Africa, where Britain controlled colonies with large black populations, in regions with a proven ability to grow cotton. Beyond determining the site of production, racial ideologies also had an impact on how Europeans shaped cotton-growing strategies. The politics of race determined where the BCGA worked, how its capital and services would be administered, and how free workers would be to control their land and labor. Race ultimately became an excuse to put organizations like the BCGA between producers and the market.

Utter failures by plantation companies in British and German colonies settled the fundamental question of plantation versus peasant production early in the cotton crisis (see below). Except for a few "white man's colonies," colonial planners saw peasant agriculture as the way forward. But the peasant mode of production was an amorphous thing, as was the very definition of "peasant." I have generally used "farmer" in this book to describe African and American cultivators alike, to emphasize similarities in the economic conditions experienced by each group. Both groups engaged in subsistence production as well as production for the world market, both worked under a variety of land tenure arrangements, and both used varying combinations of household and hired labor. While there were many sociocultural and environmental differences in their experiences, the most salient differences related to their respective levels of integration with the world market, and their relationship to the state. The former were colonial subjects, many newly connected to global commodity markets, and they became subjects of state action. The latter had long been enmeshed in the global cotton industry, but were able to actively use the structures of government to improve their position.

The word "farmer" carried different meanings in different contexts. British writers usually preferred "farmer" to peasant in the period under study, obscuring diverse African land tenure arrangements with an image of African yeomen. German colonialists explicitly identified cotton as a "people's agriculture," implying a similar sense of free, landowning farmers.[39] But in German (as in French and British) colonies, participation in the market economy as a "free farmer" was mandatory. Varying levels of coercion and different incentives were used to push and pull farmers into cotton production for export markets. Across Africa, colonial officials took it for granted that indirect pressure like taxation was necessary to transform subsistence producers into market-oriented farmers, and indirect pressure to participate in the colonial economy often gave way to more direct coercion.

Thomas Bassett has described three models of agricultural development that operated in European empires. In the "rational peasant development discourse," farmers "were treated as knowledgeable and rational economic agents who would increase cotton supplies if purchase prices were sufficiently attractive and if they were allowed to grow cotton following customary methods." States merely enforced the rules of the market. To liberal apologists for Britain's empire and to some later historians, this model best characterized the colonial experience in British Africa. Opposite this approach was the "compulsory development discourse," in which peasants were seen "as unwilling to produce cotton for export markets unless forced to do so by the colonial state. This generally racist view represented Africans as apathetic and lazy by nature." Here, the state's "primary role was surveillance," policing farmers to ensure that they grew cotton and did so in the ways colonial officials demanded. Finally, there was a "paternalistic development discourse" that "combined elements of these first two."[40] The BCGA was officially committed to the "rational peasant" model, but it moved very quickly toward the paternalistic model as its early efforts failed to produce large amounts of cotton.

Historian Andrew Zimmerman argues that colonial powers in Africa resolved the paradox of coercion in a free market by appealing to "the pathological nature of the 'Negro,' whose freedom demanded supervision and coercion."[41] This racial ideology identified Africans, as well as African Americans, as a group that could not be expected to respond "rationally" to economic incentives. Social science theory added respectability to the centuries-old stereotype of "lazy" Africans, who supposedly enjoyed easy access to food by virtue of living in a tropical paradise, and therefore would not work hard.[42] Whether biology or social conditions were supposedly responsible for perceived differences in the races—and most of the British imperialists considered here emphasized the latter—the black man was often not viewed as *homo economicus* by white observers in Europe or America. It was the task of the missionary, the merchant, and the civilizing state to remedy this. The BCGA's leaders saw themselves as agents of this civilizing mission: they hoped to "try, as far as possible, to get inside the black's mind," not to understand the actual needs and desires of Africans, but rather "so that we can most readily lead him on the line of his natural development."[43] The BCGA chose cotton production as the most desirable activity for Africans and took action to ensure that it happened.

Of course, not all white Europeans and Americans were swept up in racist rhetoric. Early in the cotton-growing campaign, one American cotton expert remarked, "The natives of Africa . . . are not especially interested in the matter of an abundant supply of cotton at a low price for the cotton spinners of Europe. . . . They will not grow cotton from sympathy for European spinners, nor can they expect to derive any fun or amusement from a crop requiring careful attention the greater part of the year."[44] The author of this editorial concluded that only a good price would tempt Africans into cotton growing. This assertion turned out to be true in Britain's colonial cotton experiment. When prices were right, farmers indeed grew cotton for export markets. When market incentives alone failed to entice Africans into cotton production, however, colonial planners fell back on what Richard Roberts called a "tool kit" of coercive strategies, tweaking levels of force, market freedom, and agricultural regulation to produce the desired outcome.[45]

Colonial Cotton and Imperial Government

The interplay of imperial and industrial politics was important in shaping colonial cotton policies. France's cotton-growing program, the ACC, represented the interests of French spinners and weavers and functioned as a not-for-profit corporation. Under French law, the ACC had to remain a nonprofit group to get government subsidies, and French manufacturers traded potential profits for immediate assistance getting the cotton-growing industry started in French West Africa. French colonial administrators took the lead in formulating cotton policy; the ACC lobbied for or against particular choices but generally played a subsidiary role, managing the buying and ginning of cotton that French colonial officers convinced or compelled farmers to grow. While tactics varied widely from region to region, French officials often openly used corvée labor to grow cotton, as well as employing in-kind taxes and labor taxes to extract cotton from producers.[46] In effect, the ACC entrusted cotton cultivation to colonial administrators, who used the tools of state power to force farmers to grow cotton.

Germany's KWK also had a semiofficial status, representing private industry but working closely with government. The KWK became a colonial department for all intents and purposes, and its policies reflected the "compulsory development discourse," which assumed a need for state action in the colonial economy. In Togo, the KWK initially conscripted men to work on its plantations and bought cotton at inflated prices from local women, who already grew the crop for domestic handicrafts. Cotton exports grew quickly in Togo, but the amounts were insignificant for German industry. Efforts to impose a more thorough system of cotton cultivation in the larger East African colony of Tanganyika were disastrous. Men were forced to "leave their household farms and work for virtually no compensation to grow cotton for the state or German planters," and new agricultural regulations designed to increase cotton production "severely encumbered rural food production."[47] Animosity against the program contributed to the Maji-Maji uprising of 1905, in which the colonial regime killed more than two hundred thousand people. The KWK responded to the Tanganyika disaster by discouraging new plantations, reverting to a passive style of peasant management that relied on African initiative, albeit under the supervision of colonial inspectors and with the threat of tax collection forcing farmers to produce for the market.

In Britain, the political environment limited the role government would play in colonial cotton growing. Conservative and Liberal governments of the early twentieth century were both wary about spending large sums in the Empire, particularly in Africa. The penny-pinching "Gladstonian garrison" in the Treasury ensured that raising funds for even basic infrastructure in the colonies was a torturous ordeal.[48] As we have seen in the last chapter, British politicians tried but failed to elevate cotton growing above "Little Englander" sentiment and the controversy over Tariff Reform. Colonial administrations could ask officials in the colonies to carry out cotton propaganda work at little cost, but they were in no position to build cotton gins or purchase and distribute cotton seeds. Beyond the construction of a few key railroads, the actual work of development was left to the BCGA's administration, especially its Executive Council, which was run by experienced merchants like Sir Alfred Jones and Hutton rather than cotton manufacturers.

Historian K. Dike Nworah argued that the Lancashire merchants were split into two camps, the humanitarian-minded "Liverpool Sect" and the social-Darwinian "Radical Imperialists."[49] The "radical imperialists" thought that economic progress was held back by an unwarranted faith in the economic rationality of black peoples. Armchair imperialists like Benjamin Kidd, having concluded that "the tropics *must* be developed" (emphasis in the original), were convinced that "such a development can only take place under the influence of the white man."[50] Opposing these imperialists was a circle of humanitarian writers and their friends in and around Liverpool such as Mary Kingsley and E. D. Morel. They argued that Africans were rational agents who needed only a "vent" for their labor. This discourse was a significant departure from earlier humanitarian expressions rooted in Christian missions and the abolitionist movement. The abolitionists often viewed Africans as fallen or backward peoples who needed "civilizing." Kingsley and Morel argued that all Africans needed from colonial rule was access to markets, capital investment, and good governance. If Africans wanted to become Englishmen, it was their own business, so far as the "Liverpool Sect" was concerned.

Kingsley died before the BCGA was founded, but Morel quickly attached the BCGA to his Liberal humanitarian agenda. As the cotton-growing campaign got underway in Britain in 1902, Morel told readers, "If the native can see a profit in the business, he will take it up. That is morally certain."[51] The Liverpool humanitarians and their business allies argued that Africans could greatly increase agricultural exports if proper incentives (i.e., higher prices) were provided.[52] Hutton and some of the Manchester and Liverpool merchants on the BCGA Executive Council shared this view, concluding that they would get the most cotton with the least investment by setting up cotton-buying agencies and building ginneries, rather than actively cultivating cotton. By creating demand for cotton, the BCGA hoped to lure African producers into commodity production, and it claimed it could do so without resorting to coercion and the violence accompanying the making of labor and commodity markets seen in other parts of the Africa. An illustration of the BCGA's "Churchill Ginnery" in Lagos (see fig. 2.1) emphasized the transformative power of technology, depicting the ginnery alongside a train loaded with neatly packed cotton bales.[53] The BCGA imagined that ginneries and railroads would break through labor bottlenecks in Africa, allowing cotton to flourish as an export commodity.

Although he was likely the originator of the BCGA's demand-side, ginnery-centered policy, Hutton was ambivalent about the rational peasant model. Maintaining a near-religious faith in the power of markets to create supply in response to demand, he nonetheless doubted the ability of Africans to respond to the "invisible hand" without a strong push from business and government. When Africans did not follow the roles prescribed for them by humanitarian theorists, Hutton and his colleagues drifted toward the "radical imperialist" side of the political spectrum. A pointed letter from Hutton to Morel over the question of land expropriation in Nigeria illustrates this ambivalence. Hutton wrote, "We want the land for the good of the native, and it would really be idiotic if we were to allow native prejudices to stand in the way of all progress. If you will think the matter over, you will see that our plantation is in exactly the same position as the railway, and I don't think anyone . . . would argue that native prejudices should be allowed to stand in the way and prevent the construction of the railway."[54] Cotton was too important to be left to native entrepreneurship and decision-making; the BCGA therefore had to stand between farmers and the market to overcome the backwardness and conservatism of African farmers. The BCGA's contradictory adherence to a classical economic model and a racist view of African farmers produced ineffective and, over

THE CHURCHILL GINNERY
LAFENWA, LAGOS

Figure 2.1. Illustration of the BCGA's flagship Churchill Ginnery in Lagos, ca. 1907, BCGA 2/2/7. Courtesy of the Cadbury Research Library: Special Collections, University of Birmingham.

time, coercive policies. BCGA and colonial leaders readily made political and moral compromises when reality failed to meet their expectations.

Initially, the British Colonial Office (CO) encouraged the BCGA to promote cotton in Africa. From Joseph Chamberlain's perspective as secretary of state for the colonies, the BCGA offered to perform a useful service that government lacked the personnel and money to provide. Chamberlain told colonial governors to request scientific experts, cotton seed, and gins from the BCGA, hoping to get cotton programs moving with minimal government involvement.[55] One governor, Sir Frederick Lugard, actively courted BCGA assistance. Lugard thought cotton was the key to the economic development of his new governorship in Northern Nigeria and he arranged for the covert distribution in Lancashire of cotton samples and speculative statistics promoting Nigerian agriculture. E. D. Morel hid Lugard's role in publicizing Nigeria's potential for cotton growing, crediting reports in his newspaper describing Northern Nigeria as a "cotton growing paradise" to impartial business travelers.[56] Lugard and his subordinates fed the BCGA frequent press releases on the existing Nigerian cotton sector, estimating in 1904 that farmers produced tens of thousands of bales annually for the local textile industry. Eager to develop the new territory, the BCGA pushed for a railroad to Northern Nigeria despite finding early cotton samples from the region "disappointing."[57]

If Hutton was encouraged by the warm reception offered by Chamberlain's CO, he was emboldened by the replacement of Chamberlain with Alfred Lyttelton in 1903. Chamberlain resigned to pursue his Tariff Reform campaign full-time, and his successor at the CO was described by the press as "a comparatively unknown man" chosen for his experience in South Africa and his zealous support of Tariff Reform. Lyttelton was reputed to be "not as forceful as Chamberlain."[58] The BCGA requested and received privileged access to the new administration. Meetings with high-level officials were held monthly, and the association was given unprecedented access to colonial officials as they returned to Britain on leave. The CO also agreed to provide funds to help pay the salaries of cotton experts in West Africa. The Imperial Institute, the CO's quasi-private scientific arm, diverted resources to cotton research at the urging of its director, Wyndham Dunstan. Dunstan prepared a report to the Board of Trade in 1904 outlining what he thought was the vast potential of the British Empire for cotton production. The report noted the retarding effects of poor transportation, unregulated marketing, and unscientific agricultural practices.[59] Drawing on this report and the association's own published reports, the BCGA requested increasingly unorthodox concessions from the CO to remove these obstacles.

The CO gave the association land for experimental plantations in Sierra Leone and Southern Nigeria, overruling the objections of officers on the scene who pointed out scarcities of both labor and land. (BCGA and CO policies toward land expropriation and plantation agriculture are addressed below.) The CO granted ginning monopolies to the BCGA in several colonies, on grounds that competition might disrupt the BCGA's efforts to monitor cotton quality and to deliver consistent prices to farmers. The BCGA went so far as to demand "that the export of cotton seed from Lagos should be prohibited, and that the Association should be given control over all seed, with a view to their distributing it for sowing purposes." Lyttelton's administration rejected this last demand outright, recognizing that BCGA control over the seed supply meant de facto control of the entire cotton sector.[60] The CO did approve a ban on cottonseed exports in Lagos, however. The BCGA planned on crushing the seed and using it as fertilizer, giving farmers a useful agricultural input while also depriving them of the ability to replant local cotton varieties. This was part of a broader BCGA strategy to eradicate African varieties of cotton (see chapter 3). With its limited capital the BCGA was unable to install a crushing facility and as a result piles of seed accumulated around BCGA gins. The BCGA begged the CO to lift the export ban in 1905, and the CO obliged.[61] Hutton continued to push for control of seed in other areas, and succeeded in gaining control over the cottonseed supply in much of Nigeria and in Nyasaland.

When a new Liberal government took control in Britain in 1906, it challenged Chamberlain's legacy at the Colonial Office, but did not upset the CO's close relationship with the BCGA. Winston Churchill, who became undersecretary for the colonies, took a keen interest in cotton and personally chaired monthly meetings with the BCGA. Churchill had an independent idea of how colonial development should work, however. He urged the BCGA to divert its resources away from Nigeria as well as from white settlers in Rhodesia and Nyasaland. Churchill favored Uganda, which offered the most promising field for peasant-driven export agriculture and which already had access to a railway. The BCGA demurred, maintaining that West Africa (where Hutton and other merchants associated with the BCGA had commercial interests) should remain the association's focus.[62] Churchill and Hutton soon clashed over railway policy. Hutton complained that freight rates on existing lines were too high, suggesting that "the Governments looked perhaps too much for immediate returns on their railways." Churchill responded that he "failed to grasp what the commercial community really wished in that matter, as at the time it was urging that railway should be made, it contended that they could and should be made as commercial enterprises, which entailed of course that they should be made to pay not only their working expenses but a return on the capital invested. It now seemed that the Association considered the railways might be run at a loss if industries, infant or otherwise, could be fostered and encouraged thereby." Churchill "did not deem it desirable that the railways should be run at a loss" and insisted that cotton pay its own way.[63]

Whenever critics like Churchill objected to subsidies, monopolies, or other special treatment for the BCGA, the association's leaders appealed to their semiphilanthropic status and Lancashire's dangerous reliance on American cotton. Hutton insisted that he had no interest in stifling competition from rival ginners, claiming that through BCGA ginning monopolies "all the bad type of seed might be eliminated from the country." According to Hutton, government grants and subsidies were warranted because so much of the association's work was "such as should be performed by an Agricultural Department of an Administration."[64] Hutton and other BCGA promoters argued that its provision of these "philanthropic" services to African farmers entitled the association to special privileges, even if they went against the laissez-faire, free trade doctrines the BCGA ostensibly represented.

Models of Development

Cotton prices were at the center of the BCGA's cotton campaign in Africa. Having argued the Africans would respond to price incentives and grow cotton, the BCGA had to figure out whether it could pay Africans enough to lure farmers into cotton production while still making a profit on cotton sold in Liverpool. Outside the BCGA, many colonial officials believed that Africans were unresponsive to prices, producing only enough cash crops to buy luxuries while enjoying the security of subsistence food production. British agricultural scientist Samuel Simpson claimed that Africans were "not enthusiastic cotton growers" because "Their food plants, maize and cassava, grow luxuriantly, and they see no reason to exert themselves by growing cotton. Besides, their wants are few and very easily satisfied."[65] From the perspective of colonial governments and private businesses, the chief problem of colonial development (outside the mining sector and settler colonies) was the construction of appropriate institutions and incentives to shift Africans away from subsistence farming and into the production of cotton, cocoa, palm oil, and other cash crops.

Historical interpretations of development in the first decades of colonial rule in Africa frequently invoked the "vent for surplus" theory to explain the boom in commodity exports observed between 1900 and 1930. Drawing on economist Hla Myint's research on economic development in the Third World after 1945, historian A. G. Hopkins applied the vent for surplus model to West African development on the basis of three observations: that there was a boom in commodity exports that occurred without a major increase in population; that it was apparently achieved without diverting land and labor from traditional agriculture and industry; and that it was accomplished without "any major improvements in agricultural technique."[66] Hopkins's aim was to demonstrate the economic rationality of Africans and to refute the "substantivist" school of historical analysis, which rejected the narrow focus in economic history on profit-maximizing activity in favor of more holistic explanations of behavior rooted in culture and the natural environment. More recent scholarship has largely supported Hopkins's findings, though the turn by some scholars toward the "New Institutional Economics" has incorporated many of the cultural forms and social relationships that the substantivists found so vital in explaining historical behavior in African communities.[67]

Marxian critics flatly rejected one key element of the Smith-Myint model used by Hopkins: the idea that increased commodity exports reflected a costless reallocation of "idle" resources. Drawing on the anthropological approach of Claude Meillassoux and other scholars, Marxian historians argued that export booms in fact reflected profound social changes. Social reproduction, gendered labor divisions, and access to land, food, and other resources were all transformed by colonial rule and the arrival of foreign capital.[68] Outside the Marxian camp, historians have further criticized Hopkins and other supporters of the "vent for surplus" theory for extending a few exceptional cases like the Ghanaian cocoa industry and

Northern Nigerian peanut production to the entire African continent, overlooking wide disparities in environments, crops, and labor systems.[69] Even these two cases, where farmers allegedly traded leisure time for cash crop production, have come under scrutiny in recent studies. Gareth Austin's detailed study of the cocoa industry in Asante shows that "that extra-subsistence output was much larger in the pre-cocoa era than can comfortably be reconciled with any meaningful notion of such a reserve [of leisure time]."[70] Most Africans were already enmeshed in local markets for foodstuffs and other produce alongside subsistence production, and adopting cash crops meant "either a difficult reordering of priorities or an intensification of effort far beyond accustomed levels."[71] Producing new cash crops or intensifying production of existing ones was never a costless process, these scholars argue.

J. A. Hutton, the BCGA chairman, understood the importance of providing a "vent" to stimulate a new industry like cotton. He was less convinced of the existence of a labor surplus in Britain's African colonies. He rejected outright any notion that Africans were idle. Speaking about Nigeria, Hutton said, "The West African is a born trader and agriculturalist. It is constantly stated that he will not work; but this is absolutely untrue."[72] Hutton realized that even without competition from other export commodities, cotton had to be competitive with foodstuffs, craft industries, and other outlets for labor. The BCGA's model did not rely on a sudden reallocation of "surplus" labor, but rather on rational decision-making among farmers who would grow cotton for export instead of committing labor to other cash crops, food crops, or handicraft textile manufacturing. The BCGA focused on Nigeria precisely because farmers there already grew cotton for domestic consumption. The association aimed to make cotton profitable for farmers by increasing yields through improved seed and new farming techniques, while also pulling cotton away from domestic industries through the construction of export-oriented ginneries and railroads. The assumption was that the handicraft textile industry would wither in the face of manufactured imports, freeing up cotton as well as labor to serve Lancashire's needs. French and German colonial planners had similar expectations, although as we shall see, African textile industries proved resilient in the face of competition from manufactured goods.[73]

Because African farmers were distant from world markets, marketing and transportation costs ate away at the prices merchants could offer for cotton. By providing these services at a "philanthropic" rate, the BCGA was supposed to make cotton competitive with other economic activities in British colonies. The BCGA did erect "pioneer" ginneries in the Nigerian hinterland, like the modest "Hutton Ginnery," equipped with saw gins in a metal building and a single baling press (see fig. 2.2). These ginneries did create a "vent" for local cotton farmers. Unfortunately, Hutton severely

Figure 2.2. View of the Hutton Ginnery at Aro, Nigeria, ca. 1904, BCGA 7/3/1. Courtesy of the Cadbury Research Library: Special Collections, University of Birmingham.

underestimated the price at which African farmers could be convinced to grow cotton. France's ACC and Germany's KWK drew on state funds to subsidize African producers of cotton, taking a short-term loss in the hopes of a long-term payoff. Because the BCGA was privately funded (and struggled to raise capital in Britain) it could not sell its cotton at a loss. Its activities in Africa were thus constrained by prices in the global market. Hutton ultimately failed to appreciate how little that price had to do with relative prices in colonial hinterlands.

When cotton failed to arrive in appreciable quantities even after the provision of railroads and ginneries, Hutton moved beyond the problem he could not fix—world prices—and instead searched for social or cultural constraints on cotton growing. BCGA and colonial officials understood at a basic level that farmers were responding rationally to prices when farmers chose not to grow cotton, but Europeans frequently fell back on racist assumptions to explain away this behavior. One BCGA agent at work among would-be cotton growers in rural Nigeria complained, "the desire for wealth has not so far appealed to them." Another official complained that the African farmer's plans "seldom reach beyond his immediate wants," making it difficult to convince them to plant new cash crops.[74] Out of this contradictory view of human nature, which held that humans responded rationally to price incentives, but that Africans were irrational for ignoring the prices offered by the BCGA, came a contradictory and ineffective set of policies. The BCGA took the market as the proper mechanism of development, but insisted that the market alone was not sufficient to convince Africans to grow cotton. In short, the BCGA—largely in the person of J. A. Hutton—came to believe that only extramarket forces could make the market work in Africa.

Fixed Prices

The BCGA's fixed-price policy was its original sin against the doctrines of laissez-faire and classical economic theory. The policy itself was not wrong-headed; a simple price guarantee gave BCGA experts something tangible to offer farmers when they introduced the crop. Colonial officials generally agreed with the principle of fixed prices, believing that African cultivators could not follow rapid price movements in global markets. They shared the BCGA's view "that that it was imperative to avoid setting [prices] too high in case the price should come down later."[75] Believing that the high prices of the cotton corners would last, the BCGA planned to pocket the difference between the wildly fluctuating prices paid in Liverpool and the fixed price offered to African producers. The profits would fund BCGA operations and build a reserve fund to allow the maintenance of the fixed price in later years when world prices might fall. (State-run marketing boards used the same arguments to justify their monopolization of export crops in subsequent decades.) As it turned out, prices crashed in the summer of 1904, forcing the BCGA to reexamine its price targets immediately. Under the BCGA, fixed prices proved highly variable.

Racial prejudices about the economic rationality of Africans also lurked beneath the idea of a temporary price floor for cotton. In their reports, BCGA experts intimated that African farmers were incapable of long-term planning and were focused only on immediate returns. J. W. Hoffman insisted that "the price of cotton must not undergo any fluctuations, as the people are not in a condition to meet such changes. They will become discouraged at once." Like other BCGA experts, Hoffman was exasperated that many African farmers doubted the promise of fixed prices. He complained that they were "under the impression that the greater quantity of cotton produced the lower will be the price paid for it."[76] Clearly these Nigerian farmers understood the relationship between supply, demand, and prices. The BCGA, however, took this as a sign of peasant conservatism or economic irrationality and wondered why its fixed-price promise failed to attract more cotton.

Even before the BCGA was forced to lower its prices, the decision to depart from economic orthodoxy opened up a range of additional anti-market policies that hurt producers. The measures were justified by the need to maintain the fixed price policy. Most important was the BCGA's demand for monopoly cotton buying and ginning privileges in Africa.

Hutton and other BCGA officials argued that a monopoly on cotton buying and ginning was required to minimize losses under the fixed-price policy, and to prevent commercial rivals from raising producer prices through competitive buying. As Hutton later put it, monopoly was needed to avert the "danger of the industry being fostered on an artificial basis," portraying the association's own artificial prices as a mechanism for saving farmers from disappointment when world prices invariably fell.[77]

By only partially abandoning free-market principles, the BCGA opened the door to practices that worked against the interests of producers. The association claimed in its propaganda that all the cotton grown in the empire would be purchased, but it refused to pay more than the fixed price for cotton in local markets. Farmers and colonial officials were often put in awkward situations, having responded to Lancashire's appeals for cotton only to find that the BCGA refused to buy it at a price farmers deemed worthwhile. In southern Nigeria, farmers who had raised cotton eagerly in 1902–3 in response to BCGA propaganda balked at the prices set by the BCGA office in Manchester. J. R. Prince, the local BCGA expert, begged for a modest increase in the fixed price. The BCGA council flatly denied the request on grounds that "false hopes for the future would be raised." Hoffman was scolded in September 1903 for paying 1.5d. per pound, a price that the BCGA insisted "cannot be maintained." In Gambia, the BCGA was appalled to hear that the governor was buying seed cotton at 2d. per pound, a price that would have brought the association a penny per pound loss at current Liverpool prices. CO officials in Nyasaland, having taken the BCGA at its word that all cotton that could be grown would be bought, were criticized by the BCGA for "buying cotton in places where there were no transport facilities, which would mean a heavy loss."[78]

Farmers in southern Nigeria produced the most cotton for the BCGA in its first years of operations, but their enthusiasm was not appreciated in Manchester. Hutton asked the CO for permission to abandon the fixed-price policy in the south in 1906. Nigerian farmers who had invested in cotton agriculture on the basis on fixed prices soon found themselves competing directly with the American South in the Liverpool market. As chapter 3 will show, Nigerian farmers who tried redirect cotton from the export market toward more lucrative local textile manufacturers were charged outrageous fees for the use of BCGA gins. The BCGA claimed that cotton had taken off in the region by 1906 and that market forces should prevail, and it even offered to give up subsidized rail freight privileges in exchange for the CO's consent to early termination of the fixed-price agreements.[79]

The BCGA's lack of ideological commitment to maintaining competitive prices for cotton was fully exposed during the First World War, when the association fought efforts to raise prices up to 9d. for seed cotton despite record cotton prices on the world market. A BCGA council member "pointed out that the natives were formerly well satisfied with 6 cents per lb.," in effect arguing that global market prices should have no correlation to the remuneration of labor in Africa.[80]

Colonial officials grew frustrated with this contradictory approach to markets. As they saw it, the BCGA demanded special privileges but refused to take special responsibilities. Gov. Hesketh Bell excoriated the association for prematurely retreating from the Benue River area in Nigeria, complaining that "the results of 4 years' work by the Political Staff have been for nil."[81] Farmers there had begun to grow cotton, but the BCGA refused to buy on grounds that it was too expensive to purchase and transport. In the Gold Coast, the CO compelled the BCGA to continue working long after it was proven that cocoa, gold, and other products would be that country's future exports. Hutton was told that the ginnery at Labolabo "should be kept open for the benefit of those natives who are already committed to the cultivation of cotton." Governor Thorburn warned, "if operations cease in the Northern Territories the natives will regard such cessation as a breach of faith."[82]

BCGA leaders accused colonial officials of sabotaging its efforts to set cotton prices, "either by trying to fix the price [themselves] or suggesting to the natives that they should not sell their cotton, but hold for better prices."[83] In Lancashire, BCGA members complained that colonial officials did not understand the market for cotton and were in no position to offer guidance on prices. H. R. Wallis, chief secretary of Uganda, fought back, arguing that he could not "properly advise growers to accept a price which is obviously inadequate." Wallis stated that the BCGA's own demands that administrators act as cotton experts led farmers to "not unnaturally apply to them to solve their perplexities in connection with fluctuating prices."[84]

Besides not really being fixed, the fixed-price policy had other limitations. First and foremost, farmers were under no obligation to sell the cotton they raised with the BCGA's free seed. BCGA manager W. H. Himbury was forced to double (to one penny) the price paid for seed cotton in southern Nigeria after chiefs refused to sell their cotton or plant any more in response to a drop in the BCGA's fixed price.[85] Because many colonial farmers were not fully committed to cash crop production, they could easily hold their cotton and wait for better prices. Governor Lugard observed in 1919, "The native of Nigeria is extremely shrewd in his estimate of what pays best to cultivate, and . . . will prefer to take his cotton back again, even after he has brought it to the buying station, rather than accept an unremunerative price."[86]

Farmers also exploited fixed-price policies by ignoring the arbitrary political barriers created by colonial powers, shopping their cotton to merchants in neighboring colonies who offered higher prices or better subsidies. Portuguese Mozambique was a convenient alternative for farmers in

British Nyasaland, and Gold Coast growers could sell their cotton to German buyers in Togo. When the German railroad from the interior to Lomé opened at the start of the 1909–10 cotton season, cotton exports from Gold Coast ports dropped from 505 bales to ninety-eight, demonstrating the extent to which this strategy was practiced.[87] Entrepreneurial Africans also took advantage of uneven policies within colonial borders. In Nigeria, the Alafin of Oyo exploited special price incentives the BCGA offered in his district and gathered cotton from far and wide, dumping it on the association for a windfall profit. Himbury told the Alafin that the BCGA "only promised to buy cotton actually grown at Oyo at a certain price" and put a stop to the practice, but only after buying the Alafin's stocks.[88]

Another unanticipated outcome of fixed prices was the elimination of incentives for quality. The BCGA imagined fixed prices as a floor, but they also functioned as a ceiling for producers of high-quality cotton that might fetch high prices in Liverpool. Farmers knew that they would get the same price regardless of the condition of their cotton, and they tended to hastily pick the crop or even adulterate it with water or debris to increase its weight. As happened in India a century earlier, a cycle of adverse selection threatened to wreck the industry through tit-for-tat drops in price and quality.[89] In Southern Nigeria, Governor Egerton warned the BCGA about this, citing the positive influence competitive pricing was having on the cocoa industry in the Gold Coast. The "present rule of one price for any quality retards and even discourages any attempts by the growers to improve the product," he argued.[90] Instead of acknowledging the economic rationality of Africans and opening up cotton pricing to competition, the BCGA responded to the quality and quantity problem with draconian legislation, working with colonial agricultural experts to control how cotton was grown, processed, and sold.

One of the reasons the fixed prices offered by the BCGA and other colonial cotton programs failed to entice Africans into widespread cotton cultivation was the lack of integration between local markets for raw cotton and the global market that European manufacturers competed in. Across Africa, French, German, and British cotton buyers battled with local spinners and weavers whose economic world remained unconnected to the global prices that regulated European buyers. As Governor Bell observed regarding Northern Nigeria, "The whole future of the export trade depends . . . upon the question whether the natives will find it profitable to grow cotton on a large scale at the price which the B.C.G.A. or other cotton dealers can afford to pay them."[91]

Farmers needed easy access to rivers or railroads to get cotton to export markets at a competitive price, limiting cotton production for export to areas adjacent to transport. Bell believed a man would carry sixty pounds of cotton a distance of fifty miles, "but beyond that distance the price that he would receive for his cotton would not pay him for his trouble."[92] The BCGA worked hard to get railroads built and to erect ginneries in potential cotton-growing regions, but the integration of African producers with the world market through railroads and waterways often worked against cotton. Africans who did gain access to distant markets were not limited to cotton growing and pursued many new opportunities. The growth of tin mining and other industries in Nigeria and the expansion of urban centers created markets for food, and a frustrated BCGA field agent reported that "Within a belt of about 30 miles of the river, I believe, it is more profitable to grow food-stuffs."[93] During his 1910 tour of Nigeria, E. D. Morel found that an acre of yams could bring £8 to £10 per year, while an acre of cotton would net only £3 to £4 at the penny per pound being offered by the BCGA at the time.[94] Another study found that the average Northern Nigerian could earn 16d. per day growing millet, while cotton paid only 12d.[95] Cocoa cultivation yielded an order of magnitude more money than cotton, although it could be pursued only in a limited region. Peanuts could often grow on the same land as cotton and paid 100 percent more than cotton per acre, requiring less labor to boot.[96]

When the BCGA finally began buying cotton on a wide scale in Northern Nigeria as the railroad reached northward from the Niger River, the BCGA set its fixed price at half a penny, ignoring high prices caused by the 1909 cotton corner in America. To the BCGA's dismay, local spinners in Kano paid as much as 12s. per kororo (a sixty-pound bag) of seed cotton, or 2.4d. per pound. Governor Bell reported that "if a ginnery were opened at Zaria tomorrow, it would remain absolutely idle. There is no surplus cotton in the country." Had the BCGA operated its gins on a strictly commercial basis, the machines would undoubtedly had been very busy processing fiber for the highest bidders—Nigerian spinners and weavers. Instead, the BCGA refused to sell machine-ginned cotton back to African farmers and merchants. Because the Liverpool price constrained BCGA buying prices, the only way to increase cotton exports was to glut the local market with cotton, growing far more cotton than local handicraft spinners could handle. The BCGA sought to do this by "inducing the peasants to extend their cultivations." While the BCGA hoped distributing free seed would achieve this end, colonial officials helped out by impressing "our desires in this direction" on the ruling emirs in Northern Nigeria.[97]

Despite his earlier support for the BCGA, Lugard ultimately abandoned cotton as the key crop for Nigeria, finding that it could not thrive "except as a secondary crop planted with yams" in equatorial regions. In drier climates the local price had to exceed 1.5d. per pound to be competitive with peanuts. Indeed, Lugard had learned by 1919 that "the Hausa peasant is fully alike to the advantages of a leguminous crop for his fields, while cotton involves much more work, and greater risks from weather, parasites,

&c."[98] Only the relative bulk of peanuts in shipping and the possibility of intercropping worked in favor of cotton. As the BCGA discovered, most CO staff shared E. D. Morel's free-market view that the African farmer "cannot be expected to devote his attention to raising one particular raw material which a certain home industry may desire, if he can make larger profits in another direction."[99]

Only in southern Nigeria did the BCGA come close to matching the cost of American cotton, although Hutton was convinced that the region would never be an important supplier in the long run. Railroads, rivers, and roads connected these Nigerian farmers to the port at Lagos, and the population was dense enough to support intensive cash-crop production. The BCGA in fact earned sizable profits in southern Nigeria, making £1,098, £4,918, and £10,228 annually on its ginning and buying operations between 1905 and 1907.[100] Hutton compiled a table of costs for his southern Nigerian ginneries in his journal, showing a range of prices paid to Nigerian farmers as well as the revenue generated by BCGA ginneries and European merchant and shipping firms (see table 2.1). Ginning costs were the single largest charge on the BCGA's African cotton, significantly higher than transportation. The prices the BCGA paid to Nigerian farmers amounted to nearly three-quarters of the final value of the cotton in Liverpool, but the BCGA managed to capture a substantial portion of the total value in its ginneries. While a typical American farmer might pay $2.50 to gin and package a bale's worth of cotton, the BCGA paid itself at least three times more for ginning services on cotton it sold in Liverpool.[101] This was hardly a philanthropic service, and when Nigerian entrepreneurs tried to use the BCGA's gins to process cotton for local purposes, they were charged even higher rates. In 1907, the BCGA demanded a full penny per pound to gin seed cotton for local businessmen and expatriate merchants outside the BCGA's network of cotton buyers. This was three times higher than the charge the BCGA collected on cotton ginned for its own account, and it added 3d. to the price of each pound of ginned cotton.[102]

Hutton was secretive about the actual costs of ginning in Africa, and he resisted pressure from the CO to publish figures that would, as the CO put it, "encourage merchants to establish [rival] ginneries." This was a troubling position, given that the BCGA was supposed to be encouraging the growth of a cotton industry in Africa. At the CO, Undersecretary Churchill told the BCGA he was wary "to take any steps that might be suggestive of monopoly," although he acknowledged the difference "between allowing and encouraging others to establish ginneries." Hutton argued that the need to maintain control of the seed supply justified the BCGA's monopoly (de facto or de jure, depending on the colony), but the profitability of ginning was a crucial factor in the BCGA's intractability on the issue.[103] After all, the long-term goal of the BCGA was to pay dividends to shareholders,

Table 2.1. BCGA estimates for ginning costs in Southern Nigeria, ca. 1907

	Ibadan	Oshogbo	Ilorin	Lokoja	Ojuda?*
Farm gate price for 3.75 pounds of seed cotton with 1/8d. merchant commission	3.75d.	3.75d.	3.28d.	4.22d.	3.28d.
Ginning and baling	.75	.85	.95	1.00	1.10
Bags	.04	.04	.04	.04	.04
Freight to ginnery	.10	.10	.10	.10	.10/.14
Freight to port	.23	.28	.30	.18	.18
Subtotal in Africa	4.87	5.02	4.57	5.54	4.84
Shipping to Liverpool	.25	.25	.25	.25	.25
Liverpool charges	.13	.13	.13	.13	.13
Total cost per pound ginned cotton	5.25d.	5.40d.	5.05d.	5.92d.	5.22d.

Source: BCGA 7/2/3 (* *illegible*).
Note: The average Liverpool price for American middling cotton in 1907 was 6.55d. per pound. Hutton's calculations assume 3.75 pounds of seed cotton yielding 1 pound of ginned cotton.

and cotton ginning and associated cotton-buying activity were the only profit-making aspects of the BCGA's work.

The BCGA's public shareholder reports aggregated expenditures and profits, concealing the real rate of return on ginning. Ginning profits were supposed to subsidize the BCGA's research and propaganda work under the terms of the association's charter, but Hutton came up with a scheme in 1907 to bypass the charter and raise more capital. He sold the BCGA's ginneries to a dummy corporation, the British Cotton Ginning Company (BCGC), which leased the facilities back to the BCGA at prices that earned a fixed 7 percent return for BCGC investors. The investors were, of course, businessmen like Hutton, Sir Alfred Jones, and other Lancashire cotton merchants, who felt that "they were undertaking further burdens to make up for the capital which ought to have been subscribed by others interested in the Cotton Trade."[104]

Officials at the CO were not amused; they felt that the dividend payments to BCGC investors were "in effect, a diversion of the profits on the existing ginneries, and of profits which may be made on the ginneries which may be erected in the near future, from the purposes to which . . . they should have been devoted."[105] In the end, the CO let the BCGC arrangement proceed, and in exchange for a quick infusion of £100,000 from investors, the BCGA gave up its ginning income for a decade.[106] The BCGC effectively set ginning costs until the expiration of the arrangement in 1916, charging high fees instead of providing services to expand African markets at a "philanthropic" rate. These fees generated profits but also discouraged African entrepreneurs from integrating the BCGA's mechanical ginning process with domestic textile production. In any case, the BCGC/ BCGA preferred to own the cotton it ginned, ensuring that the ginned product would find its way to Liverpool rather than Kano or other African textile centers.

Unexpected Outcomes

Africans did not stand idly by while the BCGA tried to convince its shareholders and the Colonial Office that it could balance philanthropy and profit. Across the continent, farmers took advantage of the relative disintegration of local and global markets to exploit colonial subsidies and to redirect colonial agricultural policy for the benefit of local industries. Local weavers were willing to pay far more than the BCGA, KWK, or ACC for cotton because indigenously produced cloth remained a popular and highly valued commodity. Beckert argued that in Togo "such price discrepancies show that a market in cotton never developed," but in fact the difference between local and global prices simply illustrated the strength of African markets and the relatively high costs of international trade.[107] Colonial agents tried to buy African-grown cotton, and cotton farmers could choose between selling it to domestic producers, or exporting it and buying imported textiles. The best choice for farmers usually favored local textile producers.

Far from sounding "the death knell of indigenous handicraft industries," colonial cotton growing actually gave local textile producers a brief stimulus.[108] New long-staple cottons introduced by colonial powers were easier to hand-spin, and in French colonies their introduction "led to new opportunities for economic growth and new ways for women [hand-spinners] to enhance their autonomy and their income."[109] The ACC's pioneer ginnery at Segu sold cotton to the highest bidder, and as a result the ginnery could send only samples back to France after its first year at work. Local spinners paid an unbelievable two francs per kilogram for the machine-ginned cotton.[110] There, the advent of machine ginning broke through a major bottleneck in local textile production.

In British West Africa, the expansion of transportation infrastructure and the widespread distribution of cotton seed aided domestic textile industries by increasing the local supply of cotton, thereby lowering local prices. Handicraft producers could buy cotton from farmers just as easily as BCGA agents, regardless of where the seeds came from. C. A. Birstwistle, the commercial intelligence officer for Southern Nigeria, explained this fact to a disappointed BCGA audience in 1907. The Nigerian cloth industry was thriving because of expanded cotton growing, he said. "Although their methods are primitive, it is really a wonderful industry."[111]

The BGCA's hard-won railroad across the Niger River to Kano also brought unexpected outcomes. The first trains were packed with peanuts, produced by free farmers and slave-owning landlords eager to cash in on the high prices being offered by European merchants. In the following years, the peanut industry exploded as farmers reduced "the amount of land under other foodstuffs and cotton" and introduced "minor, though highly effective changes in technique" like shorter fallowing and greater fertilization and intercropping.[112] Ironically, Hutton may have encouraged the emergence of the Nigerian groundnut industry. His initial plans for peasant agriculture called for crop rotations of cotton and maize, but field agents told him maize was an "Exhausting crop—not to be encouraged without deep ploughing." Hutton recorded his solution to the problem in a short note in his 1907 diary: "Push ground nuts."[113]

The windfall brought by peanut exports was not spent on imported Manchester fabrics as the BCGA and colonial officials expected, but on goods like Kano's famed handmade cloth (some of it spun and woven from BCGA-sponsored cotton).[114] Director of Agriculture P. H. Lamb reported that Kano's spinners faced such high demand that they were importing cotton from other parts of Nigeria, and did so in quantities that noticeably reduced exports to England. He observed, "the prices paid locally bear no relation to those of the Liverpool Exchange and happen to be on such a basis that to compete for purposes of export is often a most unprofitable undertaking."[115] Lamb savored the irony of the situation. He rather unconvincingly expressed sympathy for the BCGA, stating, "It is a regrettable thing, from Lancashire's point of view (and therefore perhaps from the Imperial standpoint) that the native weaving industry retains its popularity." He could not resist pointing out, however, that "the home-spun" was a superior product, "preferred, largely I understand on account of its greater durability."[116] In the midst of the First World War, which further detached local producers from global markets, Lamb reported that Nigerian spinners and weavers enjoyed "brisk demand." Surprisingly, he reported that the "the popularity of Kano cloth is spreading not only to Europeans but to natives of Lagos and other large towns."[117] By the 1930s, an estimated fifty thousand people still worked in northern Nigeria in the cloth-dying industry alone, processing up to fifty million square yards of locally made cloth.[118]

By late 1915, the metropolitan government recognized the strength of local markets for cotton and withdrew its support for the BCGA in Nigeria, declaring that "the work of the Association there has mainly consisted in an attempt to provide an export market in competition with local markets. . . . That attempt, in Mr. Bonar Law's opinion, must be deemed to have failed."[119] After the war, Lord Milner vetoed the idea of erecting cotton factories in Nigeria "with a view to destroying the local hand weaving industry." "It may very well be that, in time, machine made cloth will gradually oust the native hand made article," he observed, but he added that "this would, I consider, be regrettable, and the Government, at any rate, should do nothing to hasten the change and to throw the native weavers out of employment. It should rather endeavour to make the change, if it is inevitable, as gradual as possible." Milner suggested that resilient local weavers would not simply roll over in the face of modern industry. "On the contrary, it is probable that they would then turn their attention to competing with Lancashire itself in the Nigerian and other similar markets."[120]

In mid-1916, the BCGA exported 10,500 bales of cotton from northern Nigeria, surprising some who were ready to abandon the entire region to peanuts. According to a BCGA report, the "purchasing power of the native has stimulated the trade in imported cotton goods." Because "cotton land is not the best for ground-nuts, and vice-versa," the crops were able to coexist once peanut prices fell below a half penny per pound.[121] The BCGA did benefit as Lancashire cloth gradually displaced handmade goods, but the association did not dump Lancashire cloth in Nigeria or other markets as part of an active strategy to capture raw cotton, as some scholars have claimed.[122] Manchester cloth, like the blue-and-white cotton textile fragment J. W. Hoffman kept as a souvenir of his time in Nigeria (see fig. 2.3), complemented indigenously produced cloth, rather than driving the latter to extinction to free up cotton for Lancashire. After the First World War, British imports were often cheaper than local goods and were offered on credit to farmers, obliging them to sell cotton back to BCGA merchants. The steady increase in cotton exports from northern Nigeria seen in the 1920s and 1930s was the product of the growing commercialization of African societies and the entrenchment of export-oriented merchants, ginners, and transport networks, rather than the annihilation of local textile industries through BCGA policies.

The Plantation Model

Given the BCGA's strong support for the peasant mode of production, it is surprising that the association also attempted to launch a full-fledged plantation program alongside its initial "missionary" work with farmers. There has been considerable confusion over these abortive plantations. Most scholars accept the BCGA's own explanation that its plantations were

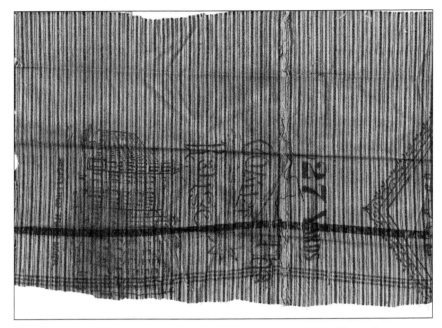

Figure 2.3. Fragment of a typical trade cloth sold in West Africa. From the collection of J. W. Hoffman, Tuskegee University Archives. Reproduced by permission from the Tuskegee University Archives, Tuskegee University.

purely experimental, precursors to later colonial agricultural research stations. The Colonial Office was not convinced, suspecting ulterior motives. A telling sign was the frequent misidentification of the BCGA as the Cotton *Growers'* Association, implying that it actually represented would-be white planters.[123]

The plantation model had its backers, and at the turn of the twentieth century, leaders of the German and Portuguese cotton-growing campaigns in southeast Africa "initially assumed that cotton had to be a 'white man's crop,'" in the sense that "plantations worked by Africans under the immediate supervision of Europeans would yield the highest returns."[124] A German company, the Deutsche Togo Gesellschaft, obtained concessions for a large cotton plantation in Togo in 1897. The DTG relied on the state to deliver contract labor, but it faced opposition from administrators and local merchants who feared that low plantation wages would stifle the import trade in manufactured goods. The KWK eventually sided against the company, favoring the peasant model over plantations.[125] Plantations did little better in Tanzania, where Africans fiercely resisted labor conscription by German cotton companies.

In British colonies, the plantation model was adopted for different reasons in different places. White settlers in the east African colonies like

Rhodesia were encouraged by the state and the BCGA to set up plantations for political reasons. These were to be "white man's colonies," and state economic policy was designed to encourage white settlement. No yeoman farmer could afford the costs of striking out alone, and settlers wealthy enough to emigrate had no interest in working the land without hired labor. Plantation agriculture was the only way to attract settlers, and with them the capital and tax base needed to further develop the colonies. The colonies of West Africa were barred to settlers, however, first by default and later by government policy. The climate took a heavy toll on Europeans stationed in the region, making settlement an unattractive prospect in the nineteenth century. By the time effective antimalarial drugs arrived in the late nineteenth century, British administrators had decided that the land was too heavily populated to alienate large tracts for expatriate planters.[126]

Nonetheless, the BCGA sought and obtained plantation rights in West Africa. The reasons were twofold: first, plantations could show investors in Lancashire immediate returns and demonstrate that cotton could be grown commercially in Africa. Populations in West Africa were large enough to make wage labor a plausible option, at least near the coast, and if the plantations succeeded they could be scaled up and replicated to offer the American South real competition. The second reason, and the one that the BCGA offered to the public and the government, was that plantations were necessary for noncommercial reasons. Seed farms had to be established to breed new varieties and to free the BCGA from the expense of buying seed in America. Hutton also argued that the plantations would serve an important educational function, as they had done for the Germans in Togo. Wage laborers would be trained as indigenous cotton experts during their service on the plantation, and having been convinced of the profitability of cotton, were supposed to return home as agricultural missionaries for cotton growing.

Officially, Lancashire's employers and workers backed the idea of peasant production, finding it ideologically preferable to capitalist plantations and their association with slavery and other labor abuses. But the representatives of labor and capital on the BCGA council cared little about how cotton was actually obtained. The "labour question" first came up in BCGA meetings in 1903 when R. B. Blaize (a Nigerian businessmen and BCGA shareholder) urged the association to create plantations around Lagos. BCGA members expressed concern with the idea of wage labor plantations, but referred the issue to the merchant-dominated Executive Council and never discussed the issue again.[127] BCGA propaganda in Lancashire was emphatically in favor of peasant production, but the association's financial support of white planters and its own plantation experiments show that BCGA planners were not wholeheartedly committed to peasant agency as a means of developing African cotton industries.

The best clue about the BCGA's intentions comes from a tour diary kept by W. H. Himbury, the BCGA's field manager in West Africa. He noted in 1904 that "Manchester's idea is to start a very large plantation and grow cotton with hired labour. Personally I do not agree with this policy, I believe in a small plantation as an object lesson, and to raise seed for distribution; but to try and grow cotton on the plantation principle in Africa is, in my mind all wrong, and the venture will not be a success. Anyhow, Manchester is in a hurry to get a lot of cotton, hence this new attempt."[128] Himbury was skeptical but nonetheless helped set up the BCGA's plantations and worked to find and train local farmers as cotton experts. Morel later claimed that "many of the Association's advisers contended that systematic agriculture was totally beyond the intelligence and power of the tropical African native," and that from this "tap-root of error," the plantation schemes were launched.[129]

Hutton had a great deal of difficulty explaining to audiences in Europe why, "notwithstanding the fact that the [BCGA] Council is firmly of opinion that the native will work better when farming on his own account than when working as a hireling," the BCGA attempted plantation agriculture in Africa at all.[130] When speaking on the supposed advantages of peasant agriculture over plantations, Hutton told audiences that he did not "like to dogmatise on a doubtful point."[131] In the Gambia, he noted, farmers continued growing groundnuts instead of switching to cotton, while in the Gold Coast farmers found cocoa far more profitable.[132] Lancashire needed cotton, not cocoa, and plantations seemed to be the fastest way to grow the fiber in Africa.

Hutton insisted in public that BCGA plantations were strictly "experimental," designed to educate natives "in the best methods of cultivation, and for this purpose nothing could be better than a plantation under white supervision." These stations were to be "more or less self-supporting," but Hutton effortlessly circled from the idea of philanthropic, educational research stations to a conventional model for a capitalist plantation: "At the same time, every endeavour is being made to make these plantations a commercial success, and should the efforts be successful there will be a large additional opening for European capital, and more rapid developments may be possible; otherwise it will take a considerable time longer before West Africa is able to produce a million bales annually."[133] The CO saw what Hutton meant, and its officials noted a continued need for "our keeping the idea of profit-making quite subservient to that of the encouragement of cotton growing by the natives."[134]

With the help of a few allies in the CO and the Imperial Institute (especially Wyndham Dunstan, the institute's director) the association pushed past opposition from officials stationed in the colonies and established commercial-sized plantations in Sierra Leone and Nigeria. In Southern

Nigeria, where the two largest plantations were launched near Ibadan and on the Sobo Plains, colonial officials complained that obtaining land was "impossible," and that "their policy is to discourage any such development."[135] The resident at Ibadan warned that purchasing land for a plantation would "possibly necessitate the use of force and certainly the loss of the goodwill and peace of the Yoruba nation."[136] The local officers were overruled, and the BCGA even convinced the CO to hand over an existing experimental coffee and rubber plantation near Onitsha to "put the whole plantation under cotton."[137]

Unhappy officials in the CO reported that the BCGA was creating "plantations worked by paid native labourers under European supervision intended to produce considerable quantities of cotton." Noting that the Sierra Leone plantation was expected to grow to ten thousand acres, they warned the metropolitan government that the plantations were of "a size much larger than that of the small experimental stations originally proposed." Oldham manufacturer J. C. Atkins responded to these criticisms by insisting that smaller model farms would be "ruinously expensive."[138] Arguing that a larger plantation brought economies of scale with regard to white managers, Atkins showed that salaries for white managers on a thousand-acre farm would add 2d. to every pound of cotton, compared to a half penny on a ten-thousand-acre estate. It was sound fiscal policy, he argued, that experimental plantations be self-supporting.

Another argument in favor of the plantations came from Northern Nigeria's governor, Frederick Lugard. Lugard was supported by one of the BCGA's plantation experts, Shelby Neely, a white farmer from Mississippi.[139] Lugard believed cotton would give the new Northern Nigeria colony a valuable export staple, and Neely suggested that the ruling emirs would shift their plantations and sharecropping systems to cotton monoculture in imitation of BCGA plantations. Neely thought this would have a profound modernizing effect on the region, as the emirs would embrace mechanized farming on a massive scale to compensate for the declining pool of slave labor brought about by the colonial conquest and subsequent antislavery proclamations. Neely observed that the British administration did not encourage slaves to desert, but warned, "it is inevitable that large numbers should have done so."[140] The solution was to save labor with machinery and plant valuable cotton for export, allowing the landowning classes to offer competitive wages to former slaves while still earning profits. Plantation cotton would thus pave the way toward African capitalism.[141]

Neely never got a chance to test his theory in Northern Nigeria. BCGA headquarters chose the Sobo Plains in southeastern Nigeria as the first plantation site, and in 1904 they dispatched Neely to oversee the project and recruit wage labor. Although the Sobo site did not push many farmers off their land, the act of expropriation set an alarming precedent for humanitarian activists. Critics feared the beginnings of a new kind of slavery as the BCGA and other corporations gained land concessions and reduced free farmers to wage laborers, as happened in the French and Belgian Congo. BCGA officials vigorously countered accusations of wrongdoing, declaring that "it is not the intention of the Association to develop cotton growing by a system of large plantations." Alfred Emmott argued that "As soon as slavery was abolished in the United States cotton ceased to be grown in large plantations even there," insisting that the Sobo Plains plantation was strictly experimental.[142] E. D. Morel reluctantly defended the plantations-as-experiments excuse in his newspaper, the *West African Mail*, though he warned "that a certain school outside the Association thinks differently" about the need for large plantations in Africa. He added, "as far as the Sobo experiment is concerned, I think it is only right to say that that experiment is viewed with very little enthusiasm by many competent men on the spot."[143]

The Imperial Institute backed the Sobo experiment, however, and its survey agent was convinced that the region had "large areas of sandy loam apparently suited to cotton," calling the site "sufficiently favourable to justify [an] experiment of 1,000 acres."[144] When Neely arrived, he found the estate failing on its first crop. He tersely reported to Hutton, "Sobo plains [are] unsatisfactory."[145] The BCGA nonetheless continued with the project, egged on by Dunstan at the Imperial Institute and encouraged by Sir Alfred Jones's promise to extract a railroad to the site from the colonial government.[146] Hutton dutifully spent the association's money at the Sobo plantation, but privately remarked that the "Sobo plains await development but [we will] probably abandon."[147] By 1905, the BCGA had squandered £2,891 on the Sobo plantation—nearly twice the BCGA budget for all of Sierra Leone.[148] The site was abandoned early in 1905, along with an abortive plantation at Moyambo in Sierra Leone.[149] Hutton's experts told him that location was the only problem, and the BCGA committee responsible concluded, "Find more [in] N[orthern] Nigeria . . . land no trouble."[150]

Moor Plantation (named after Sir Ralph Moor, former high commissioner for Southern Nigeria and later an employee of Jones) was a more spectacular failure. The BCGA "was of opinion that it was most desirable that a large plantation should be started in Lagos as soon as possible principally with a view to pushing on the cultivation of cotton on a large scale, and towards the education of the natives in the best modern methods." They repeated the argument that "even if it did not pay [it] would be more or less self-supporting, whereas small model farms and traveling educational experts would be most expensive."[151] After the Egba nation refused to turn over land for the plantation near Abeokuta, north of Lagos, the BCGA settled on Ibadan, about forty miles northeast of Abeokuta.[152] The proposed plantation site spanned five thousand acres and was leased for thirty years at 3d. an acre, with what K. D. Nworah described as the "sullen, silent but greedy acquiescence of the Bale [of Ibadan]."[153]

Hutton dispatched eighty tons of cottonseed and an array of plows, tractors, and planting machines to the site. If it was a research station, it was on an audacious scale. It was also suspiciously well equipped for the commercial production of American Upland cotton: several thousand pounds of miscellaneous seed were allotted for experimental purposes, but fifty tons of Black Rattler and another twenty tons of Richmond (both American long-staple varieties) made up the bulk of the initial seed shipment.[154] Prof. J. W. Hoffman was reassigned from his model farm at Oyo to oversee the Ibadan plantation.

The project generated controversy before it even broke ground. The land was inconveniently occupied by several hundred people, and their eviction sparked protests in the West African press. A complaint made it all the way to Parliament.[155] Several harsh articles appeared in the European press, and Hutton sent Himbury to personally examine the project in 1905. Himbury was appalled by what he found. Hoffman turned out to be "a nuisance" and "a bit of a waster." The BCGA's plantation manager had embezzled funds and spent his time building a racecourse and a polo ground.[156] In a tense meeting with Captain Elgee (the local resident), the Bale, and two hundred angry farmers, Himbury heard that the BCGA was "taking the land and turning them off their farms. They also complain about our growing corn, and building a race course."[157] Himbury told Hutton, "unless we give them some concession, cotton growing here is going to be a failure, and we shall be pretty badly boycotted and our money will be wasted." Elgee sided with the farmers, and the Bale himself was browbeaten by his subjects and forced to support a revision of the land deal.

Unable to find workers, the BCGA gave in and invited the farmers to return. The compromise agreement allowed the BCGA to retain its lease on the land, and the farmers were not charged rent on the condition that they "plant cotton—not all cotton of course, but as much as we think they should plant."[158] One thousand acres were retained for research. Experiments were dutifully conducted at Moor Plantation for several years after the failure of the initial scheme, but the whole enterprise was turned over to the state in 1910 "in a very neglected condition."[159]

Moor Plantation had been an embarrassing failure, and the BCGA did what it could to whitewash the affair. In 1921, Himbury (who replaced Hutton as BCGA chairman in 1918) completely ignored the problems of labor and land rights in a retrospective article, disingenuously suggesting that the debacle might "possibly be due to the fact that the land was only a few miles from the town, and was in consequence exhausted."[160] The BCGA continued to dabble in plantation agriculture despite these costly failures. In 1911, Sir Percy Girouard tried to find "some Lancashire capitalists, to take an interest in the development of cotton growing in the Juba Valley" in East Africa. Some members of the BCGA council dourly noted that even in the United States it was more profitable to grow maize than cotton, but the merchant members nonetheless decided to float a company, with the BCGA providing some of the initial capital.[161] Despite its official commitment to peasant agriculture, the BCGA actively supported plantation agriculture beyond the failed West African plantations. In early 1904, for instance, the BCGA advanced £1,000 to Mr. Walker, a planter with twelve hundred acres in Nyasaland. On the basis of a short interview in London, the BCGA agreed to help him expand his holdings by another five thousand to ten thousand acres. Walker convinced the association that "there is a good supply of cheap labour," and he was sure he could get cotton to Liverpool for a mere half penny per pound in transport costs.[162] Walker suggested that many of his friends were interested in cotton growing, and would readily take BCGA advances at 6 or 7 percent interest. The entry costs to cotton cultivation were not prohibitive: in Nyasaland, the director of agriculture believed white planters could bring cotton to market for £3 8s.10d. per acre, meaning a price of about 3.6d. per pound of ginned cotton landed in Liverpool. It would be sufficient to set up an estate with £2,000.[163]

British entrepreneurs floated at least ten cotton plantation corporations during the prewar period.[164] The enthusiasm for cotton revealed in their prospectuses was matched only by the ignorance they displayed about cotton growing and land and labor conditions in Africa. Two companies founded to work in West Africa in 1902 never broke ground and were dissolved by 1906. One, the West African Cotton Growing Company Ltd., was founded by Athanasius Buckle, chief clerk in Sierra Leone. He was backed by two mill owners in Burnley, a cloth finisher, and three Manchester merchants. The firm raised only £617 and soon dissolved.[165]

The more ambitious New Cotton Fields Ltd. was founded by several London-based gentlemen and associated itself with the BCGA in its prospectus, implying that generous tax and transport subsidies could be expected for pioneer cotton growers. The firm assured investors that "Native labour is easily obtainable at low rates." Imitating the KWK and BCGA, the firm tried to hire Tuskegee graduates to manage its as-yet imaginary land concessions in West Africa. Henry Francis Downing, an African American jack-of-all trades who had fought in the American Civil War, worked for the Liberian government, and been a major proponent of the pan-Africanist movement, was charged with leading a preliminary expedition. Downing promised "to supply at lowest possible rates, Trained Coloured Labour from the American Cotton Fields," adding that "if expedient," entire black families could be resettled in Africa.[166] Downing wrote to Booker T. Washington in 1902 asking for Tuskegee-trained experts, although he admitted to Washington that "the methods the Company may adopt . . . have not been fully formulated." Washington was not amused by the emigration scheme and declined to help Downing with recruitment. Downing soon quit the company. Two merchants in Africa signed on as directors, but the company managed to raise only £235 before it was dissolved.[167]

Two syndicates were formed to grow cotton in the Caribbean, where the BCGA maintained a small cotton-growing program. The Jamaica Cotton Co. was founded in late 1904 by a group of Lancashire spinners. They paid £6,000 for a three-thousand-acre estate in Jamaica and operated until 1909. Another company bought an estate on Demerara for cotton; it failed in a year.[168] A third British company paid £22,000 for a cotton estate in Chiapas, Mexico.[169]

Proposals aimed at East Africa drew the most commercial interest, although they were as unsuccessful as the West African ventures. The East African Cotton, Rubber, and Fibre Co. tried to get Hutton's support for a three-thousand-acre plantation north of Mombassa, apparently not realizing that cotton and rubber were not especially complementary crops.[170] The Rhodesia Cotton Syndicate Ltd. was launched in late 1903 with the backing of a number of merchants, stockbrokers, and gentlemen. Sir Alfred Jones and two cotton brokers on the BCGA council served as directors. The company tried to purchase thirty thousand acres in Rhodesia for cotton and tobacco, but had difficulty securing the land and the firm was reorganized in March 1906.[171] A new company, the East African Cotton Syndicate, was launched the following year as a private corporation; it leased five hundred acres on the Tana River and took options for thirty thousand more acres. By 1910 the firm had issued £15,023 in shares, but its revenue failed to cover costs. In 1909, £3,800 in operating expenses and capital expenditures yielded only £991 4s. 5d. worth of cotton, while in 1910 the plantation made £1,170 11s. against costs of £4,496 19s. 8d., two-thirds of which went for new buildings, machines, and improvements on the estate. The expenses overwhelmed the syndicate's resources, and it was liquidated in 1911.

The last two firms were latecomers, both founded in 1911. Both went to East Africa as well, seeing the best prospects for plantation agriculture there. Nyasa Cotton Estates Ltd. was launched by a planter and several gentlemen but failed to raise enough capital.[172] The East African (Jubaland) Cotton Growers' Association, launched by a merchant and an engineer, bought an estate but does not appear to have had any notable results.[173]

Plantation companies that overcame the first hurdles of raising money and obtaining land quickly discovered that where wage labor was available, it was not cheap. As Erik Green has argued, would-be planters faced a "Nieboer problem," first described by H. J. Nieboer in his 1900 book, *Slavery as an Industrial System*. Because most African societies had access to large reserves of land, there was "no wage which it would be profitable both for a prospective employer to pay and for a prospective worker to accept, as opposed to working for himself or herself."[174] As a form of organizing land and labor, plantations did not offer any clear productivity gains over peasant agriculture. Only labor-saving technologies or population growth could alter this formula. For Nieboer, this phenomenon provided an economic explanation for slavery as a form of labor control.[175] For colonial entrepreneurs, the availability of land meant that the potential pool of wage workers was simultaneously a pool of independent peasant producers who could grow the same crops as plantations on a smaller scale. Workers who had the opportunity to match or beat plantation wages by growing cash crops on their own land invariably chose to be their own bosses.

Planters across Africa found wage labor surprisingly expensive. In northern Nigeria, where the BCGA had its greatest hopes, a touring scientist remarked that "apart from the cost of white supervision," the 9d. per day local workers demanded would "be practically prohibitive" to plantation agriculture.[176] In Nyasaland, planters of cotton and tobacco were unable to find wage workers at all without resorting to coercive tactics.[177] BCGA workers at the Abeokuta ginnery even went on strike in July 1904 because of the manager's demands that they "work six hours on end and pay nothing for overtime." "They refuse to do this, and wisely," Himbury wryly remarked, noting the local seller's market for labor.[178]

Himbury argued that the plantation drive failed because of the success of Britain's civilizing mission. "Natives of British territory have grown in our image as liberty-loving subjects, and many are not prepared to undergo the comparative discipline of life on a plantation for a shilling a day," he argued.[179] The soap magnate William Lever reached the same conclusion following his own failure to gain land concessions in Nigeria. Lever told E. D. Morel that he was moving operations to Congo, where "The Natives, in all probability, will not have been spoiled and contaminated."[180] Arguments like this concealed the economic nature of the labor problem with cultural and racial rhetoric.

For its part, the Colonial Office tried to steer the BCGA away from supporting new cotton plantations. In 1906, Churchill harshly criticized BCGA plans to create new plantations in East Africa, suggesting that their resources would be better spent supporting peasant agriculture in Uganda.[181] Officials eventually discouraged the BCGA from backing established white planters as well, leading to a near-total disengagement from plantation cotton in Africa. Several officials approached the BCGA with suggestions for new plantations, however. Sir Percy Girouard, then governor of British East Africa, told the BCGA that unoccupied land near the Juba River could be developed; with regard to labor he assured the BCGA that "We have the Indian population, and more particularly we have our native population, whom we would sooner provide for than import indentured labour."[182] The fast gains promised by plantations continued to tempt British officials and investors for decades to come, though most schemes were utter failures.

Race and Finance

One of the most transformative elements of BCGA policy was its financing of crops and machinery, giving farmers the capital needed to dramatically increase yields per acre and per unit of labor. New technologies like tractors would let farmers break through the "Nieboer problem" by improving productivity. Unfortunately for Africans, this aid was strictly regulated by a conflation of race and class. To the BCGA, white farmers were "planters," landowners or leaseholders worthy of loans and subsidies. Black farmers were regarded as peasants and received only free cottonseed and the dubious gifts of expert advice and supervision.

While the BCGA's initial statement of purpose made no mention of support for white planters in the colonies, the association was soon deluged with correspondence from aspiring and established planters eager for information about cotton and financial aid.[183] BCGA leaders never expressed a clear policy toward private cotton growers, and the association used financial aid for different functions in different colonies. In Africa, the BCGA lent money to white planters because they were seen as a quick route toward a large-scale British cotton-growing industry. Armed with capital, expertise, and cheap African labor, these planters boasted that they would challenge the American South within a few years.

Sir Alfred Jones was responsible for BCGA loans to West Indies planters; rejuvenating moribund colonial economies was one of his hobbies and he saw cotton as a crop that could replace the region's ailing sugar plantations.[184] Supporting white planters there was a patriotic gesture, and Jones was not at all concerned that the region was best suited to growing extralong staple cotton varieties, rather than the typical American Upland types the BCGA was founded to provide. The BCGA gave £400 to West Indies planters in 1902–3, but only £47 14s. 8d. was advanced for cotton planting and harvesting, with BCGA reports explicitly stating that the sum was to be repaid upon sale of the cotton. By the next season, however, the association advanced more than £5,600 for crops and machinery. A certain Mrs. Howe of Monteserrat received the first loan of £150, and other planters received smaller loans and advances.[185] Mrs. Howe got special treatment for several years, and the BCGA West Indies committee gave her regular advice, encouraging her "to use only the very best seed, and be more careful in the preparation of her cotton."[186] By 1905, the BCGA was annually lending more to white planters in southern Africa and the Caribbean (£13,757) than it was spending on seed, transport, experts, and propaganda for black farmers in all of Britain's African colonies (£9,975).[187] Mrs. Howe and other white plantation owners were quite successful in raising Sea Island and other exotic varieties of cotton, and they developed close relationships with Lancashire's fine-spinning firms. Across the Caribbean, colonial officials and local business leaders praised the BCGA for its support of cotton growing. The industry grew quickly, with exports rising from 9,676 to 186,510 bales between 1902 and 1907.[188] BCGA officials also encouraged the consumption of other Caribbean products like cassava and arrowroot (for sizing) and citric acid (for bleaching) in Lancashire's textile industries.[189] The BCGA funded at least one mill for processing cotton seed into oil and cattle feed, despite numerous financial troubles with the oil firm, further diversifying and enriching the regional economy.[190]

Meanwhile, the commissioner of Agriculture for the West Indies, Francis Watts, reported that black peasants in the Virgin Islands—"not a capitalist amongst them"—produced more than fifty thousand pounds of cotton lint annually by 1911. They did so "managed by the Government," without a penny of BCGA money.[191] The association completely ignored black smallholders like these in the Caribbean, despite their proven ability to grow good-quality cotton. Beyond denying these farmers financing, the BCGA made sure that only white planters could have their cotton classed as "superfine," though black farmers on the same islands were producing "first class ordinary cottons." Cotton growing was ultimately an effective way for white and black farmers to break out of sugar monoculture,[192] but white planters were given a clear advantage by the BCGA's unequal financing policies. The association's support of white planters merely prolonged the decline of the plantation system in the Caribbean, and in the long run, the real key to cotton's success across the region was the existence of a strong market for valuable long-staple cotton rather than the expert guidance of the BCGA or its money.

Hutton allocated ever-smaller amounts of money to research across the British Empire as advances to planters consumed greater proportions of the BCGA budget. The BCGA dedicated a paltry £686 to research in 1912, with the unlikely prospect of Natal taking the lion's share.[193] The association advanced £44,128 to white planters in the Caribbean and Africa for crops and equipment in the same year.[194] The BCGA did earn £13,722 in commissions on cotton it sold for white planters between 1908 and 1914, but this income was entirely negated by the failure of many planters to repay BCGA advances.[195]

The BCGA flatly rejected the idea of financing black farmers in Africa in the same way it advanced cash to white planters. H. H. Lardner, who described himself as an "educated native" of Sierra Leone who was in full support of "the great Cotton Growing Movement in Lancashire," pointed out the need for rural credit early in the BCGA campaign. In a February 1904 speech, he argued that subsidies or cash advances were critical to the success of peasant cotton farming, along with an introductory period of fixed prices: "Unless this announcement is publicly made it is feared that confidence will never be so far restored in the natives as to induce them to grow cotton."[196] Lardner knew that while peasant farmers did not need money to buy or rent land, they still required money to buy tools, seed, and food, and to pay wages during harvest time when the demand for labor on a family-sized farm outstripped a typical family's labor supply. The BCGA ignored Lardner's proposal. Hutton stated that African peasants could "get on perfectly well without any advance whatsoever," in contrast to the desperate conditions of American sharecroppers or Indian *ryots*, who survived on merchant capital lent at usurious rates.[197] BCGA officials argued that Africans were inherently entrepreneurial, and that entry costs to cotton growing were low enough that no credit facilities were needed. One told the West African Lands Commission in 1913 that "my experience of the African is that he will take on risks that people in civilised countries will not."[198] A key asset of many African farmers—their ability to respond rapidly to market opportunities—became an excuse to deny them access to capital.

The Colonial Office raised the question of an Agricultural Bank for West Africa with the BCGA in 1906, pointing out the success of experimental "micro-lending" schemes in Jamaica. The BCGA rejected the idea on grounds that in Africa, "The native could give no individual security as he did not own the land, and there were objections to a tribal security."[199] The CO's land policy in West Africa, which discouraged land alienation and encouraged traditional communal property rights, saved Africans from expropriation, plantations, and a new landlord class but left individuals without capital in land. French colonial authorities took a different approach, and by 1910 had launched a network of rural credit societies in French West Africa. These agencies provided funds but also agricultural advice, allowing French administrators to "improve" cotton-cultivation techniques while also offering much-needed credit to farmers.[200]

With the minor exception of the Caribbean and its Sea Island crop, the BCGA's plantation strategy was a failure. Rejecting his own early support for planters, McCall, Nyasaland's director of agriculture, said that "if the [BCGA] had spent the same money as they have spent on advances to planters in erecting ginneries and aiding the native cultivation . . . a much larger cotton Industry would be established in the country."[201] By 1912 the BCGA realized this fact and began to disengage from its commitments to white planters in Africa.[202] By 1918 it had lost £90,826 (more than 20 percent of the association's capital) on bad loans and failed investments across Africa and the West Indies. Only £3,479 was lost in the West Indies, compared to £24,700 in Nyasaland and Rhodesia, £12,902 in East Africa and Uganda, and £42,000 in West Africa, most of which was spent on the BCGA's own failed plantations in Nigeria and Sierra Leone.[203]

Labor and the Politics of Empire

Besides financially supporting white planters, the BCGA withheld its support for peasant production in some settler colonies. The BCGA promised that it "had no intention . . . to encourage Native cultivation in that part of Rhodesia, suitable for plantations carried on by Europeans."[204] In Uganda, the BCGA tried to discourage peasant cotton agriculture, arguing that the region was ill suited to the crop. In fact, the BCGA was in conflict with the local department of agriculture from an early date over several key issues. Hutton had dispatched cottonseed to missionaries in 1902–3 but took little interest in the region for several years, and by the time the BCGA focused its attention on Uganda, cotton was already well established as a peasant industry.[205] A number of merchants erected ginneries and established buying networks, and the colonial department of agriculture refused to grant the BCGA the monopoly ginning privileges it had obtained in West Africa. As a result, Uganda failed to appeal to the BCGA as a commercial ginning proposition, and the proliferation of private ginneries prevented the absolute control of the seed supply that Hutton believed was crucial to the spread of American long-staple cotton. When questioned by Churchill about his lack of interest in Uganda, Hutton weakly protested that "owing to want of capital, the Association were not able to take an active part in Uganda in the earlier stages on the same lines as in West Africa."[206]

In settler colonies, the BCGA supported plantation agriculture instead of standing up for more efficient peasant producers. When planters protested arrangements for the export of labor from southeast Africa to the South African mining sector, the BCGA firmly backed the planters. J. E. B. Seely, who had replaced Churchill as undersecretary of state for the colonies in 1908, had little sympathy for the BCGA or the white planters, however. The enormous mining sector in South Africa took precedence over cotton growing, and Seely replied that "It was . . . thought better to control an emigration which could not be prohibited, so as to ensure that the natives who did go, went under the most favourable conditions."[207] The interests of the mine owners were paramount to the CO in southern Africa, and the failure of schemes to import Chinese indentured labor or hire contract workers from the Portuguese colonies made it imperative to secure alternate sources of labor.[208]

The BCGA lobbied against the transfer of labor to the mining sector for several years and found a champion in Nyasaland's former governor,

William Manning. Manning warned the BCGA that "Nyasaland could never be properly developed as agriculture cannot afford the high wages that are paid in the mines." Men returned from South Africa flush with money, "and instead of saving it they utilise the money to pay the taxes of their friends with the result that in some villages they simply stay in their huts and do not work." Manning believed that keeping workers in Nyasaland was critical to the development of the colony, and he was willing to encourage limited peasant agriculture at the expense of white planters to achieve that end. He said, "The idea that Nyasaland should become a country where the native only should be the producer would not hold, neither would the idea that all cotton should be produced on European plantations."[209] His ideal model of colonial development combined plantation and peasant production: plantations would draw the young, dispossessed, or desperate, while peasant cotton growing would keep everyone else anchored in the villages.

McCall, the director of agriculture for Nyasaland, promised to not "encourage native cotton cultivation in close proximity to European estates," although he did intimate that the plantations were doomed to fail in the long run.[210] The same policy was enacted in Rhodesia, where the BCGA maintained that it "had no intention at the present time to encourage Native cultivation in that part of Rhodesia, suitable for plantations carried on by Europeans."[211] McCall believed that the BCGA's advances to planters in southern Africa were well spent: "men with a little capital had been liberally assisted by the Association that now they were independent planters, and very useful members of the community out there."[212] McCall wanted "a limited number of the right class of men," and even offered to let the BCGA interview would-be planters in England.[213]

Peasant production was therefore pursued as an adjunct to, and eventually a replacement for, white-owned plantations. Producer agency was crucial in all stages of the evolution of these British policies. Plantations were favored initially because of fears that farmers with choices would not choose to grow cotton. But as the BCGA discovered, even white planters abandoned cotton rapidly. In Nyasaland, for instance, planters switched the bulk of their acreage to tea or tobacco. "It has not occurred with the natives," Hutton complained, "but it has with the white planters." By supporting cotton through ginneries and free seed, the BCGA ensured that cotton remained accessible to peasants in need of a cash crop to meet tax demands. By 1914, Hutton was convinced that cotton was "essentially a crop for the small man. It is the black man's crop."[214] A dependent peasantry, controlled by colonial officials, indigenous elites, and expert advisers, and restricted by monopsony was perceived as necessary for cost-effective cotton production.

Most historians have overlooked the BGCA's serious interest in plantation agriculture. Historian K. Dike Nworah suspected that the BCGA intended to develop commercial cotton plantations in West Africa, but he lacked access to BCGA records. W. A. Wardle's study was the first to use the association's archival materials, but he defended the experimental excuse for plantations, characterizing the BCGA as a genuinely philanthropic organization representing a model of development that, Wardle argued, should have been used more widely.[215] The evidence is clear, however, that BCGA leaders had every intention of commercially growing cotton on plantations.

Conclusion

J. A. Hutton wanted a replacement for the American South, and he was convinced that only Africa fit the bill. Hutton believed that plantations could get the industry started rapidly, giving Lancashire meaningful quantities of cotton while the slower process of creating a cotton-growing peasantry began. But plantations were failures across Africa, and those white planters in southern Africa who survived did so by switching to tobacco, coffee, or tea. Peasant cultivators were equally disappointing, however. It was not for lack of enthusiasm; in many regions peasants did grow cotton, either at the urging of colonial officials or on their own initiative, lured by the prices offered by BCGA merchants. But those prices—dictated by Liverpool and New York—were disconnected from local African economies, and the BCGA simply could not compete with domestic textile industries or rival export commodities in many places. The fast growth of cotton exports from West African and Caribbean colonies (see table 2.2) was not nearly fast enough to replace or even compete with American cotton in the world market.

Hutton blamed a lack of infrastructure, peasant conservatism, and even sabotage by colonial officials for the failure of cotton to blossom as a large-scale peasant industry. But he refused to confront the price problem directly. In the Gold Coast, for instance, Hutton (backed by Wyndham Dunstan at the Imperial Institute and Gerald C. Dudgeon, the agricultural inspector for West Africa), explained failure by claiming that the experimental region was simply unsuited to cotton.[216] As the local director of agriculture reported, however, the Labolabo site was in the very heart of the local cotton-growing zone. "During my tours through the Colony I have tried to get the natives to take an interest in cotton-growing, but have, so far, been unsuccessful," he said. From his perspective, the problem was simple: "The natives state that it does not pay to grow."[217]

Table 2.2. Approximate estimates of cotton grown more or less directly under the auspices of the BCGA (figures given in 400-pound bales)

	1903	1904	1905	1906	1907	1908	1909	Total
Gambia	50	100	300	0	0	0	0	450
Sierra Leone	50	100	200	150	100	0	0	600
Gold Coast	50	150	200	200	250	200	300	1,350
Lagos	500	2,000	3,200	6,000	9,500	5,500	12,000	38,700
Southern Nigeria	50	100	150	150	250	200	300	1,200
Northern Nigeria	50	100	500	1,000	1,500	500	1,000	4,650
West Africa (subtotal)	750	2,550	4,550	7,500	11,600	6,400	13,600	46,950
Uganda	0	150	300	500	2,000	5,000	7,000	14,950
British East Africa	50	100	150	200	200	300	300	1,300
Nyasaland	100	550	1,500	2,200	2,300	1,500	2,500	10,650
Rhodesia	0	50	50	100	200	300	500	1,200
East Africa (subtotal)	150	850	2,000	3,000	4,700	7,100	10,300	28,100
West Indies	1,000	2,000	4,000	5,500	6,500	7,000	6,000	32,000
Scind [India]	0	0	500	1,000	1,800	2,000	2,500	7,800
Sundries	0	100	150	200	300	500	600	1,850
Total	1,900	5,500	11,200	17,200	24,900	23,000	33,000	116,700
Approximate Value	£29,000	75,000	150,000	260,000	390,000	360,000	480,000	£1,744,000

Source: BCGA 2/2/9.

3

"The Scientific Redemption of Africa"

Coercion and Regulation in Colonial Agriculture

All the colonial powers discovered that African farmers usually did not choose cotton when offered a choice of cash crops. Development planners, like those at the BCGA, found that producers abandoned cotton in favor of less labor-intensive or more lucrative crops whenever they gained access to world markets hungry for tropical commodities. Colonial rulers then had three options: they could give up on cotton, they could compel Africans to grow cotton, or they could try to make cotton competitive with other crops. The BCGA officially focused on the latter strategy, but British and other European colonial officials used all three options at different times and places. Local contexts, rather than overarching metropolitan visions, ultimately determined where and how cotton export industries developed in Africa. As Anne Phillips argued, "colonial policies necessarily developed in response to a complexity of local constraints."[1]

Outright coercion has been the best-studied aspect of "cotton colonialism" in Africa, but overt force was used sporadically and reflected the failure of the colonial state to exercise authority through less costly mechanisms. Colonial powers learned early on that forced cultivation was inefficient and expensive. Reflecting on the German experience in Togo, KWK director Moritz Schanz admitted that "there are no means in existence to force them to a cultivation of any certain product, although the Government authorities may express the wish and use some influence in getting the natives to grow that product which is most *necessarily required by the mother country*" (emphasis in the original).[2] Sven Beckert and Andrew Zimmerman have both demonstrated how German policy toward cotton drifted between the poles of freedom and compulsion. Despite their belief in theories of scientific racism, German officials were unable to justify the use of forced labor for cotton growing.[3] Compulsion was inefficient, expensive, and engendered outright resistance to colonial regimes. As a result, German as well as British and French planners used force alongside more subtle policies of propaganda, taxation, regulation, and surveillance to push Africans into cotton growing and to ensure cotton was cultivated in the manner Europeans wanted. As Europeans realized that the prices they could offer for cotton were not attractive to African farmers, they focused on making African cotton competitive by increasing yields and improving quality. These efforts invariably required more labor and were rarely well received by farmers. As Allen Isaacman and Richard Roberts observed, "Persuasion often gave way to coercion" in such situations.[4]

This chapter surveys the BCGA's approach to cotton agriculture. First, it shows how the BCGA used outright coercion to force Africans to grow cotton. The reality of coercion is abundantly clear in the historical record, but historians have downplayed its significance in Britain's empire or even claimed that it never occurred.[5] The BCGA and the Colonial Office used their own agents as well as local partners to manage African labor and to ensure that cotton was grown in preference to other crops. Violence, taxes, and collaborating local elites were all employed to create new cotton industries. Africans responded to this coercion in a range of ways: some fought colonial impositions, some cooperated, and others found ways of creatively cheating, sabotaging, or otherwise frustrating colonial demands for cotton. African elites were enthusiastic partners of the BCGA at times, but also pursued their own interests and clashed with the BCGA. In some cases, the BCGA and CO responded to resistance by intensifying coercion, but in other instances they admitted defeat and abandoned cotton growing.

The second theme the chapter identifies is scientific agriculture, which was intended to make cotton competitive with other crops but which also served as a form of indirect coercion imposed on African farmers. Under the guise of "improving" African agricultural practices, BCGA and CO agents compelled Africans who chose to grow cotton to do so in tightly prescribed ways. Farmers were discouraged from using indigenous agricultural techniques as well as indigenous varieties of cotton in the mistaken belief that American long-staple cotton and American cotton monoculture could be easily transferred to Africa. Many African farmers found that cotton cultivation increased their labor commitments to agriculture without additional earnings, and subjected them to a high level of surveillance from the colonial state.

The ability of Africans to resist direct and indirect coercion produced two unrelated results in the BCGA's cotton project. First, it encouraged a dissident faction within the Colonial Office to fight the BCGA, ultimately putting scientific agriculture in the hands of government officials rather than BCGA experts. Resistance from CO officials contributed to a collapse of government support for the BCGA in Britain and the eventual recasting of the association as a specialist cotton-ginning service corporation after the First World War. African resistance also turned the BCGA's attention to an alternative model of agricultural development for Africa, one that bridged the gap between peasant and plantation cultivation and that brought some of the exploitative tools of the American sharecropping system to Africa. In the pioneering Gezira scheme in Sudan, the BCGA found that a marriage of private capital and state power could produce large amounts of high-quality cotton. Massive irrigated schemes like Gezira appeared in French and Portuguese colonies as well as in British India, bringing capital and technology to bear on the problems of efficient cotton cultivation. Tenants on the Gezira scheme were nominally free farmers, but their rights to the land depended on their submission to the scientific oversight and regulation of the project's managers. Throughout the remainder of Britain's rule in Africa—and well into the postcolonial period—the Gezira model competed with the peasant model for the attention of policy makers.

Direct Coercion in the British Empire

Instead of intensifying its investment in infrastructure or encouraging Africans to take up remunerative niche products, as the West Indian planters had done with Sea Island cotton, the BCGA responded to poor results in Africa by turning to direct and indirect coercion. Although it was rarely discussed in frank terms, forced cultivation was on the minds of BCGA and colonial officials from the start of the twentieth century. The forms of compulsion available to the BCGA were more limited than the methods available in the French, German, Belgian, or Portuguese colonies, however. As the American journalist Herbert Adam Gibbons observed, Germany's initial success with cotton "was largely due to the greater power over the native given to Europeans by the Germans than by the British." By contrast, "In British West African colonies, a European is fined who strikes a native. In the German colonies, one can flog a native up to twenty-five lashes." Gibbons concluded that violence "helps greatly in making the native work; But the method is incompatible with Anglo-Saxon ideas of the way things should be done."[6] W. H. Himbury concurred, warning that physical coercion was tempting for the foreign overseer but that "one must guard against excesses creeping in."[7] Still, the BCGA could draw on an arsenal of subtle forms of coercion, with and without the aid of colonial states, to push and pull African farmers into cotton cultivation.

One of the first things the BCGA proposed—before it had even sent any agents to Africa—was the collection of cotton in lieu of money for the "hut taxes" that colonial administrations began to impose in the late 1890s and early 1900s. Hut taxes promoted crop production when they were enforced because farmers had to produce for the market to earn money to pay taxes. The 1898 "Hut Tax War" in Sierra Leone was a clear demonstration that British administrators were willing to use violence to enforce taxpaying, thereby encouraging production for the market. Ironically, J. A. Hutton and other Lancashire merchants had ferociously attacked Chamberlain for waging the "Hut Tax War," calling it an abuse of power and a hindrance to economic development.[8] Hutton changed his tune when he joined the BCGA and began trying to stimulate cotton production in Africa. The possibility of collecting taxes in kind would ensure that farmers grew cotton instead of other marketable crops. The BCGA's interest in this strategy reveals early contradictions in the group's free-market approach.

The Colonial Office opposed cotton taxes on practical as well as ideological grounds. Besides the ethical quandaries such a policy posed (could such taxation lead to corvée labor or forced plantation labor?), cotton taxes would have required government officials to enter the cotton business, learning how to buy, grade, store, and market a bulky commodity in which the state had no intrinsic interest. Not deterred, Hutton discreetly asked Governor Lugard if he could compel farmers to pay taxes with cotton in Northern Nigeria in late 1904, hoping to achieve some quick results to combat waning public interest in colonial cotton. Lugard replied that "the paying of taxes in cotton was long ago sanctioned," but he complained, "I cannot *force* them to pay in cotton if cash is tendered" (emphasis in the original).[9]

Colonial states did use taxation to stimulate cotton production in some areas; Nyasaland's government doubled its poll tax but offered 50 percent discounts to those holding certificates showing that they had worked on a white-owned plantation growing cotton, tobacco, or coffee.[10] In Uganda, the performance reviews of chiefs were tied to cotton production in their districts, and farmers who grew "2 good sizeable cotton shambas [gardens]" were relieved of corvée labor, in which villagers gave labor in lieu of cash to meet tax obligations.[11] Taxation had its limits, however. As frustrated planters in Nyasaland found, workers would quit as soon as they earned tax certificates. Across the continent, taxation was an important "push factor," but it "was never a sufficient one" for creating large pools of wage laborers or commodity producers.[12]

In her study of British colonial tax policy, Leigh Gardner found many reasons "to doubt that taxation was a very effective means of compelling Africans into the labour market." When groups like the Kamba and Maasai in East Africa refused to pay taxes, colonial officials "would grant exemptions or agree to collect arrears the next year." Even when taxes could be collected, "exemptions and tax evasion also served to limit the coercive effects of the direct tax." Tax evasion strategies included "borrowing tax receipts from other taxpayers, leaving the place of employment just before the collector arrived so that the taxpayer would be difficult to trace, moving across territorial borders, and bribing tax counters to have their names omitted from the count."[13]

British colonial governments ultimately saw taxation as a means to financial solvency, rather than a tool to help metropolitan industries. In Uganda, the government encouraged peasants to grow cotton, but "in areas where alternative employment options existed, the government decided not to press the peasants to grow cotton."[14] Cocoa prevailed in the Gold Coast and parts of southern Nigeria, and peanuts beat out cotton in northern Nigeria and the Gambia. Cotton lost in the marketplace because it simply did not pay enough, and British colonial governments were all too happy to take the larger revenue brought by other commodities. The BCGA was unable to "capture" the colonial state, and the interests of government were not synonymous with the interests of Lancashire. As an early study of colonial development in Uganda put it, "the people were not taxed in order that they might be made to grow cotton; rather, they were urged to grow cotton in order that they might be able to pay taxes."[15]

Colonial rulers did work to some extent on Lancashire's behalf, however, and it is clear that some British officials ordered their subjects to grow cotton in preference to other crops. Journalist E. D. Morel received a letter alleging that "The people [in Nigeria] dare not object to grow it because the Government tells them to do it. The village chiefs in their turn tell them that the Government has ordered this to be done, and out of fear these men go on planting cotton and receive no compensation in any way commensurate with the work done."[16] A Ugandan official proudly told Hutton in 1912 that "For some years the Government have pointed out that it is the Duty of every good Citizen to cultivate Cotton and the increase is almost entirely due to Government influence."[17] These cases were the exception to the rule, but as Jan Hogendorn found, the perception of official coercion was quite common even when direct orders were not issued.[18] Nigerian director of agriculture P. H. Lamb was in fact concerned that government distribution of cotton seed had "a moral effect by creating an impression that 'Government expects' cotton to be grown for export in preference to other crops." Lamb feared that colonial subjects might lose out on more profitable crops and thereby deprive the colonial government of additional revenue.[19]

Local Elites and the BCGA

The colonial state undoubtedly had a privileged position from which to influence the behavior of producers, but the BCGA and other cotton programs also used indigenous elites to extend cotton cultivation. Five decades ago, Ronald Robinson argued that European imperial expansion could only be understood as a product of European and non-European interactions. "Without the voluntary or enforced cooperation of their [non-European] governing elites, economic resources could not be transferred, strategic interests protected or xenophobic reaction and traditional resistance to change contained."[20] Few scholars today would disagree. The editors of a recent volume on colonial intermediaries felt no need to qualify their claim that "there could be no colonization without some forms of collaboration or implicit acceptance of colonialism."[21] As Elias Mandala has argued, the successful production of export commodities in colonies often "depended on [the state's] capacity to deploy the indigenous elites."[22]

Robinson's model "had the merit of locating much of imperial government in Africa and Asia in pre-imperial structures," but it implied a dichotomy of collaboration and resistance that does not give "detailed answers to puzzles about the strength and weakness of imperial rule or about the political gains or losses for the protagonists."[23] In postcolonial scholarship, collaboration has been too frequently "contrasted with resistance and condemned as its antithesis," ignoring the often blurry boundaries between resistance and cooperation.[24] For Marxian scholars writing in the postcolonial period, the role of local elites in the colonial economy posed a special problem. If elites were collaborators who facilitated the workings of capitalism in traditional societies, why had capitalism failed to supplant other "modes of production" such as peasant agriculture? To one group of historians, the answer lay in the "articulation" of different modes of production within an imperial and even global economic system. Elites served as intermediaries between peasant production and colonial capitalism, connecting two very different socioeconomic worlds.[25] According to this theoretical interpretation, capitalist industries outside Africa captured an extraordinary surplus from peasant cash crop producers because prices for those crops failed to cover the costs of social reproduction (producing foodstuffs, raising children, and other domestic activities). Village elites helped maintain existing structures of land tenure and labor to ensure that peasants remained more or less self-sufficient, while also extracting surplus labor in the form of cash crops for sale on the world market.

As Michael Watts and other critics argued, the debate over modes of production and articulation in the 1970s and 1980s devolved into "an abstract and sterile taxonomy," concerned with theoretical precision rather than descriptions of reality.[26] Still, the idea of articulation captured an essential theme in the early history of cash crop production: that colonial states did not—and could not—simply sweep away African economic systems and replace them with capitalist models, such as plantations staffed with wage laborers. Even when colonial legislation abolished indigenous forms of labor control like slavery, colonial governments and private firms continued to rely on local elites to recruit and discipline workers for projects.[27]

Colonial administrators lacked the terminology of postcolonial historians, but they were well aware of the advantages of articulating indigenous socioeconomic systems with capitalist industries in their home countries. The French colonial administrator Emile Baillaud recognized that preserving local institutions of power would reduce the need for colonial oversight. While he hoped that Africans would be "encouraged [to engage in cash crop production] by seeing the fine crops of the whites" on model farms, he also advocated "task-work, or contracts made with the more intelligent heads of houses, and . . . farms on the metayer system."[28] The methods Baillaud listed were all ways of using local elites to recruit and control labor without resorting to violent coercion or paying wages competitive enough to lure laborers away from other opportunities. In Northern Nigeria, the colonial government ordered local administrators to organize cotton growing through local elites. Officials were told to "impress on the Emir, local chiefs, and people, that if they grow this cotton they will find a ready sale to the European traders." Recognizing the importance of the local handicraft textile industry, the author of this memorandum encouraged officers to show local leaders that the BCGA's cotton varieties "will also be much better for their own local manufacturers."[29] During his tenure as governor of Northern Nigeria, Hesketh Bell "strongly impressed upon the Emir [of Zaria] our desires" regarding cotton and found that local elites were eager to earn money from new export industries.[30]

In his study of plantations in the Kano region of Nigeria, Mohammed Bashir Salau demonstrated that slave plantations were an important feature of the northern Nigerian economy and continued to operate well into the colonial period.[31] While Lugard and other CO officials claimed to be ending slavery, they quietly encouraged slave owners to shift production toward cash crops like cotton. Even when Nigerian slaves gained their freedom, limited access to land forced them into sharecropping arrangements with their former masters. Vagrancy laws imposed by the British restricted the ability of runaways to settle and earn a living in towns or wastelands.[32]

In regions of Africa that lacked an existing infrastructure of slave plantations, the BCGA and Colonial Office still managed to find ways of harnessing local labor systems to the cash-crop economy. The African Lakes Corporation, a merchant firm allied to the BCGA, tapped into age-cohort power relations in Nyasaland to secure cotton. BCGA agents had initially "sent Capitaos into the district, asking the boys to bring their crop to them" and met with little success. The "boys" growing cotton may well have been working for higher-status men rather than cultivating cotton as peasant farmers, and they would not have been free to dispose of the produce as they saw fit. The corporation, which had more experience trading in the region, "called in the various chiefs, and arranged with them that they would see that their boys brought it [cotton] to Mandala which, as results show, proved effectual."[33] By identifying local leaders who were willing to cooperate with colonial agents, colonial powers could mobilize large numbers of workers for cash-crop production without investing in the manpower and administrative apparatus a plantation system would require.

Some of the closest cooperation between the BCGA and African elites occurred in southern Nigeria and Uganda. In Nigeria, the BCGA recruited the Alake of Abeokuta, Gbadebo I, at an agricultural show in Lagos in 1903.[34] He became a fervent supporter of cotton; by 1904 he had spoken to more than two thousand farmers and had overseen the distribution of over twenty tons of cotton seed. "The Alake delights to make personal visits to inspect the cotton fields," Gov. MacGregor wrote, adding that the Alake offered "prizes for the best fields" and had cotton cultivation advice printed in the Egba government gazette.[35] Local farmers praised "their King the Alake, who had not thought it derogatory to his high and exalted position to visit their farms and encourage them to take up cotton growing."[36]

W. H. Himbury, the BCGA field agent in West Africa, described a 1905 meeting with Gbadebo and J. W. Hoffman: "The Egbas are glad they planted cotton and have promised to plant more this season. . . . The Alake opens some champagne and agrees to subscribe for 100 shares in the Association as he seems very pleased with the work we are doing."[37] Gbadebo was not alone in purchasing BCGA shares; Lagos businessman R. B. Blaize bought 250 shares, and other notables in the Lagos and Southern Nigeria colonies bought a total of 175 shares.[38] Hoffman also enjoyed a good relationship with the Alafin of Oyo. The professor claimed that the Alafin offered to adopt him as a son, in addition to granting him land for cotton experiments.[39]

In Abeokuta, the Alake took his role as cotton promoter seriously, adding a regulatory role to his early propaganda work. By 1905, the cotton-growing industry was well established, and farmers had begun to find ways of inflating their incomes at the expense of the BCGA and other European cotton buyers. Farmers added dirt, leaves, rocks, and water to cotton to increase its sale weight. The Alake's government responded with a law making "the adulteration of Cotton a punishable offence."[40] To appease farmers who had to meet new quality standards, Gbadebo promised to limit the high fees charged by porters who carried cotton to market. Gbadebo's work in Abeokuta fit with the narrative of development the BCGA and its allies were promoting in Britain, which emphasized the partnership of philanthropic capitalists with progressive African leaders. According to the editors of the African-owned *Lagos Weekly Record*, the free-market, export-oriented cash-crop economy this cooperation produced was "the true object and policy of British rule in West Africa and the policy which alone can give efficiency and stability to such rule in these parts.[41]

In the summer of 1904 the Alake visited Britain, a trip that coincided with the BCGA's first major publicity campaign.[42] Gbadebo met King Edward VII and a number of Colonial Office and BCGA officials. In Lancashire, he told cotton manufacturers that he understood "what the cotton trade is to the people of this country," promising that "My people can grow cotton and I have already encouraged them to do so. When I go back I shall encourage them still more."[43] He took every opportunity to play the role of an improving monarch in Britain: he split granite at a quarry, examined motors, went to sea on a trawler, and tried to use (with little success) a horse-drawn plow at an agricultural fair. He told the British press, "Until I came here I had never seen a plough. We have none in my country. I have bought six, and my people will be taught to use them."[44] The Alake caused a sensation in Britain. Some papers praised him as "one of the most enlightened and progressive rulers on the West Coast of Africa" while others made racist jokes.[45] An excited student in Aberdeen tore the Alake's robe, and in Oldham, women working in a spinning mill swarmed him to examine his clothes.[46] James Joyce viciously satirized the Alake's visit (or more precisely, the coverage of it in the *Times*) in a skit in *Ulysses*.[47]

> A delegation of the chief cotton magnates of Manchester was presented yesterday to His Majesty the Alaki of Abeakuta by Gold Stick in Waiting, Lord Walkup of Walkup on Eggs, to tender to His Majesty the heartfelt thanks of British traders for the facilities afforded them in his dominions . . . after which he visited the chief factory of Cottonopolis and signed his mark in the visitors' book, subsequently executing a charming old Abeakutic wardance, in the course of which he swallowed several knives and forks, amid hilarious applause from the girl hands.

Joyce's literary reaction tells us more about British racial stereotypes than it does about Gbadebo, but in any case the Alake's impact on Britain was fleeting. His visit did not result in trade deals, new British investment, or improvements in the uncertain political status of Abeokuta within the colony of Southern Nigeria. One paper complained that Britons "spent money and wasted valuable time and energy . . . to whoop enthusiastically for a colored brother whom they supposed to be the prince of one of his majesty's dominions over the seas, but who turns out to be of much less importance than the average head waiter."[48] After the British tour, Hoffman tried to bring Gbadebo to America for the 1904 Louisiana Purchase Exposition in St Louis, but nothing came of the plan. Hoffman left few records about this plan, but it was probably his intention to show off Gbadebo in America as a representative of African civilization and industry.[49]

The real significance of Gbadebo's career as a cotton promoter lay in southern Nigeria. His government was intent on modernizing Egbaland, "clearly trying to create the transportation and marketing infrastructure that would enhance production and trade."[50] This plan included cotton but was not defined by it. The Egba were well aware that British development aid, such as the BCGA's free cottonseeds came with strings attached. When Governor Egerton offered the Alake's administration £2,000 annually for road construction to facilitate the export of cotton and other crops, he also demanded British oversight of the Egba judicial system. The Alake's government refused. One local notable said, "For the last six or seven years the Alake has busied himself with [nothing] more than ROADS! ROADS! ROADS! and MARKETS! . . . If we are to give away Abeokuta let us give it up in a straight way and not in any enticing ways."[51]

Gbadebo eagerly took the BCGA's free cottonseed, but he also promoted palm oil, coffee, cocoa, and kola as alternative industries.[52] His government warned the BCGA that it had "distinctly agreed that 1d. per lb. is to be paid for all cotton offered," and that failing to meet this fixed price commitment would "be grave breach of faith which will not be lightly forgiven or forgotten."[53] The BCGA abandoned fixed prices in southern Nigeria anyway, arguing that the industry no longer needed artificial support. When the BCGA clashed with Egba farmers over ginning policy, the Alake defended his people's interests. Local farmers wanted to use BCGA gins without selling their cotton to the BCGA, so that they could sell the fiber locally or hold it until export prices rose. The farmers complained, "When the steam ginning machine was to be brought out, they fully understood and were assured that it would be for their benefit, and that if they liked they could have their cotton ginned, at a fixed rate before placing same in the market thus solving for them the labour difficulty. But since the establishment of the ginning machine the Egba farmers had been completely shut out and no application from them could be entertained."[54] A community leader added that he had "several hundred pounds weight of cotton already picked . . . but owing to the fluctuating condition of the prices offered, he had decided not to sell." The BCGA manager scoffed at these complaints, alleging that the Egba had brought only two hundred pounds for ginning. The Alake and Hoffman both defended the farmers, saying that that the true figure was "not less than about 30,000 lbs. of seed cotton."[55] In the end the farmers won access to the gins without having to sell their cotton to the BCGA, though the association charged dearly for the service. The BCGA charged a full penny to gin one pound of seed cotton, which amounted to nearly as much as the cotton was worth in Liverpool.[56]

When the BCGA asked for land to establish an experimental plantation, Gbadebo turned them down. Abeokuta would have been an ideal location with easy access to a railroad, but citizens protested that they had "no public land to spare" and the BCGA instead turned to Ibadan.[57] Gbadebo further angered the BCGA when he began enforcing transit tolls on goods, including raw cotton and the manufactured goods British merchants imported to buy cotton.[58] Hutton warned that "the cause of cotton growing has suffered very severely" because of the tolls.[59] Eliminating import tolls would have made British manufactures cheaper in Abeokuta's shops and allowed the BCGA to buy cotton more cheaply on barter terms. The Alake ultimately backed down on transit tolls but retained the import tolls; he celebrated the decision by distributing free cottonseed.[60] Governor Mac-Gregor surprisingly stood by Gbadebo on the tolls question, writing that "Tolls are as necessary at Abeokuta as municipal rates in any town in the United Kingdom." He noted that they were a time-honored institution.[61] Gbadebo saw import tolls as a vital means of raising revenue and regulating trade, duties that he was unwilling to cede to the colonial government in Lagos. He explained that "he could not promise to support anything that would mean to the people selling away the country."[62]

Ultimately the BCGA turned its back on Abeokuta and the rest of southern Nigeria. The BCGA got exactly what it asked for in the region: a class of farmers willing to invest in cash-crop production for exports, so long as prices were competitive. Gbadebo's enthusiasm for cotton had been an asset to the BCGA early in the cotton campaign, but the association found that the Alake and Egba farmers would not turn the country into a BCGA plantation. Mechanical ginneries, which were key to the BGCA's strategy, were used to stifle the cotton market instead of stimulating it. The BCGA dropped price guarantees in southern Nigeria after 1906 and focused its investment further north.[63]

In other parts of Africa, the BCGA found more pliable leaders. The most useful were in Buganda, where the ruling elite became enthusiastic supporters of the cotton industry. Britain had reached a compromise with ruling elites in Buganda in 1900, recognizing them as a landed aristocracy with considerable authority over their subjects.[64] The ruling Kabaka, Daudi Cwa, was a child when Buganda formally came under British rule; real power lay in the hands of the regent and prime minister, Apollo Kaggwa.[65] Kaggwa had no qualms about forcing his subjects to grow cotton, and the industry rapidly expanded as a result. Chiefs ordered villagers to grow cotton on communal plots, rewarding laborers with beer and food.[66] As chief Samwiri Mukasa put it in his short autobiography, "It was not enough introducing cotton; I urged people to grow it."[67] Gov. Hesketh Bell noted approvingly that "the bare orders of the chiefs were expected to suffice to ensure effective obedience" to new cotton-growing ordinances.[68]

When Daudi Cwa came of age in 1913, the BCGA worked to win his favor. The association spent £150 hosting the Kabaka's entourage during a 1913 visit to Manchester, and BCGA minutes state that it "was money well spent."[69] During the visit, Hutton addressed Daudi Cwa as a pupil rather than a visiting monarch: he needed "to see what we have to show him and to learn all that he can in order to help him and to enable him to carry on the government of his people in the future." "We look to Uganda to supply us with still larger quantities [of cotton]," Hutton said, quickly adding "that we do not wish that there should be any compulsion; every part of the British Empire is a free country, and all we want is that the inhabitants of Uganda should grow the crops which pay them the best." Hutton concluded his speech by urging the Kabaka to remember that "the prosperity of Uganda means also the prosperity of Lancashire."[70] Daudi Cwa replied, "Now that we understand how much cotton is needed here, we shall try more than ever to increase the quantity that leaves Uganda for Manchester every year." As a souvenir of his visit, Daudi Cwa received a working model of a cotton gin.[71]

The Kabaka's government promoted cotton well into the 1930s on royal estates as well as among the peasantry. An early student of Uganda's history concluded in 1951 that "there can be no doubt" that coercion was employed by local elites in the service of cotton agriculture. "In the abstract, so to speak, most Ganda agree that cotton-growing started under compulsion—often adding that this was one of the best things that the British have ever done for them. On the other hand, there are many individuals who assert that they personally began to grow cotton, in the years before 1914, of their own will and motion."[72] These remarks should not be seen as contradictory. It was possible for compulsory cotton growing to be profitable for local farmers, and the incredible success of cotton in Uganda perhaps made it easier for officials and outside observers to acknowledge the coercive role of colonial and indigenous governments in the process of economic development.

Across Africa, local elites cooperated with colonial authorities in a wide range of economic and political matters. An earlier generation of Marxian historians painted these elites as collaborators and "compradors," serving the interests of European capital by marshalling labor and natural resources in colonized and postcolonial states.[73] Some colonial elites undoubtedly profited from colonial rule and were loyal to the colonial state. Many others tried to balance the political realities of colonial overrule with the demands of local economic and social life, however. As Mandala warns, we should not hold the crude view that such elites were either "the selfish collaborators of Marxist theology" or "the foolhardy rebels of nationalist propaganda." These elites were "human beings who made compromises."[74] Sometimes these compromises worked in the interests of the BCGA and cotton cultivation, but in other cases they proved inimical to cotton growing.

Resistance to Overt Coercion

Farmers across Britain's African colonies did not passively accept the new burdens of cotton cultivation, whether imposed by colonial officers or local elites. Some examples of resistance were overtly political, defying the claims the BCGA and the British Empire made on land and labor. Most of the evidence from the cotton-growing campaign suggests more mundane resistance, however: farmers were unhappy with the kind of work cotton growing involved or the prices the commodity fetched. Like unhappy workers throughout history, they found ways to manipulate economic systems "to their minimum disadvantage."[75]

As James C. Scott argued, the difference between politicized resistance and mere theft, vandalism, or idling is a difference of intention, and it is a difficult thing to discern: "The English poacher in the eighteenth century *may* have been resisting gentry's claim to property in wild game, but he was just as surely interested in rabbit stew. The slaves in the antebellum US South who secretly butchered their master's hog may have been asserting their right to a decent subsistence, but they were just as surely indulging their fondness for roast pork." Scott asked, "Which of these inextricably fused motives are we to take as paramount?"[76] He is right to reject a dichotomous view that privileges "*Real* resistance" over "token, incidental, or epiphenomenal activities." African farmers may have disliked British rule *and* wanted to make more money; their choices were constrained by colonial policies but also forced changes in those policies.

As the BCGA discovered, African farmers had a wide array of resistance strategies at their disposal. In Northern Nigeria, where many people were still bound by slave status at the onset of colonial rule, some individuals simply walked away from cotton farms. While Governor Lugard had no intentions of serving as Northern Nigeria's emancipator, his official proclamations against slavery inspired many slaves to rebel. One British official reported, "There is now practically nothing to prevent slaves asserting their freedom by the simple process of walking away from their masters and earning wages on the railroad or elsewhere."[77] In southern Africa, where slave status was less common, colonial officials and white planters nonetheless complained of frequent "desertion" among workers. Often forcibly recruited, these workers fled after receiving tax certificates or when higher wages in the mining sector beckoned. One South African farmer quipped that "cheap labour is expensive when three-quarters run away."[78]

In Uganda, farmers slipped away at night with cotton and sold it directly to private merchants, avoiding the fees imposed by local chiefs, as well as colonial or BCGA quality inspections.[79] The arbitrary borders erected by colonial states provided another way for cotton growers to exploit colonial cotton projects. In the Gold Coast, for example, the local BCGA agent complained that farmers had taken free cottonseed but were selling their cotton in Togo, where Germany's KWK was happy to buy and gin the fiber. The better-subsidized KWK offered higher prices.[80] BCGA and colonial officials filed similar complaints in Nyasaland, where Portugal's colony in Mozambique offered farmers an alternative market.[81]

African farmers also increased their income by adulterating cotton, a time-honored practice in India and America. Because cotton was sold by weight, a farmer could make more money through fast and careless harvesting. This left stems, leaves, dirt, and other trash mixed with the cotton lint, in addition to saving labor. Malicious farmers could intentionally adulterate their cotton with trash, or add small rocks. Water was the easiest way to increase cotton weights; cotton can absorb an appreciable amount of water before it feels wet to the touch. These strategies were especially effective in Africa because of the BCGA's fixed-price policy, which did not allow buyers to discriminate against low-quality cotton. In southern Nigeria, officials complained that farmers were using all of these dirty tricks to boost their incomes.[82] This behavior infuriated the BCGA, but British officials did not usually see this kind of fraud as a political issue. As one officer in northern Nigeria put it, the tax evasion, cheating, desertion, and sabotage he faced was "a great game" and colonial subjects "were expert players at it."[83]

Africans openly challenged colonial authority when the costs of compliance outweighed the possible dangers of rebellion. In Uganda, Governor Bell was shocked to find fields full of cotton rotting in neat, tidy rows. Local farmers had feared British officers enough to plant the cotton, but as soon as the watchful eyes of the empire withdrew, farmers stopped cooperating. Local chiefs, who were supposed to supervise the care and harvesting of the cotton, were unable to convince their subjects to continue working. Bell explained with some sympathy that "The idea of having now to carry their crops on their heads all the way to ginnery at Kampala, ninety miles off, was . . . much more than they were prepared to do, even to please the chiefs or the government."[84] In 1912, peasants in some regions of Uganda went so far as to burn their fields instead of wasting labor harvesting what they deemed to be a poorly paying crop.[85] Such acts were uncommon, but they illustrate how flimsy the mechanisms of coercion could be in Britain's African empire.

Experts, Cotton, and Race

The ability of farmers to defy colonial authorities as well as indigenous elites convinced the BCGA's leaders that surveillance, regulation, and education would be required to extract large quantities of high-quality cotton from African producers. Initially the BCGA saw agricultural experts as "missionaries," encouraging farmers to adopt cotton and teaching them improved cultivation techniques. When prices were right, this strategy worked. Elsewhere, the prices the BCGA offered for cotton were not sufficient to convince farmers to risk their land and labor on new cotton varieties and new farming techniques, or to subject themselves to new agricultural regulations. In these cases, as John MacKenzie has argued, "the success of the expert was dependent on the effectiveness of the colonial state."[86]

A state-backed, technocratic agricultural regime would not mature until the 1920s and 1930s in Britain's African empire,[87] but its origins lay in the cotton campaign of 1902–14. No other agricultural commodity excited such attention and frustrated so many metropolitan visions. BCGA chairman J. A. Hutton came to believe that noneconomic coercion and scientific management were essential to the success of cotton production by free farmers, a contradictory position that emerged out of his frustration with the rational reactions of farmers to low cotton prices. Two aspects of this "rule of experts"[88] stand out: the deployment of technical expertise to reshape African work processes, and the use of a cotton monopsony for coercive and regulatory purposes.

Expert supervision was intended to fight the resistance of African farmers to cotton-growing regimes, but cotton experts also battled the cotton plant itself. Left to its own devices, cotton is a promiscuous pollinator. Commercially valuable cotton landraces were bred over millennia to emphasize long, strong, and white fibers, but wild cottons feature an exuberant variety of fiber lengths and colors. If wild cotton is allowed to flower near a planted cotton field, cross-pollination might produce hybrid varieties with short or colored fibers, lowering the value of the crop. Only careful pollination or generations of felicitous natural selection could produce plants that thrived in local environments and also produced economically viable amounts of fiber. Thus to grow American cotton in Africa, the BCGA had to do more than simply convince Africans to grow cotton: it had to prevent its imported seeds from hybridizing with local cottons, to keep American cotton from losing the color, texture, and staple length that made it so desirable. The agronomy of cotton justified interventions in local economies and agricultural systems that went far beyond the regulation of farmers who willingly participated in BCGA projects.

The BCGA's approach to agricultural expertise was informed by contemporary ideas about race. Germany's KWK had set a remarkable precedent by turning to Booker T. Washington's Tuskegee Institute for help in 1899–1900, believing that his philosophy of "accommodation and self-help" for black Americans could be transplanted to Africa to produce a politically docile and economically productive peasantry.[89] Hutton admired the German experiment, stating in 1902 that "The experts and farmers, most if not all of whom were American Negroes enjoyed excellent health and got on well with the natives."[90] African Americans also promoted the idea that they were the ideal agents of economic change in Africa. One prominent educator argued that colonial experts should be "full-blooded or black negroes, not the brighter mixed bloods. They should be black people, like the natives, so as to make the natives feel that these were men of their own race. This would give the natives confidence in themselves."[91]

Yet when the BCGA began hiring experts for British colonies, the association's leadership was reluctant to hire black scientists for the most prestigious posts. A. A. Paton, a cotton merchant on the BCGA council, used his agents in America to recruit experts in 1902 and they strongly discouraged the selection of black men. One said, "Everybody I have spoken to on the subject has been against the idea of a nigger. They say he would not be any earthly good and that he would be unable to make any other nigger work, also he wouldn't work himself." Another commented that "a coloured man would not have the executive ability requisite and that a white man from the Miss[issippi] Bottoms inured to malaria, etc., would be the best."[92] German officials, too, expressed concern about the "executive ability" of African Americans, stating that "Negro-planters might find some difficulties . . . in finding the necessary authority toward the native population, and in having at the same time the necessary respect towards the German government official."[93] For the Moyamba plantation in Sierra Leone, the BCGA sent John Neely, a white planter from Mississippi, accompanied by "three negro farmers" who served as subordinate cotton experts.[94] John Neely's brother, Shelby Neely, was selected to oversee an expedition to the Sobo Plains in Nigeria. Edward Fisher, a white planter from Tennessee, was dispatched to the Gold Coast; Fisher left the Gold Coast in 1907 and went on to direct cotton programs in Congo for the Belgians. Experienced black farmers were hired for lower-ranking jobs on BCGA plantations and agricultural stations, but they initially were under the supervision of white experts.[95]

The Colonial Office was not convinced of any need for white supremacy in agricultural science. When the British cotton campaign got underway in 1903, the high commissioner of Southern Nigeria, Sir Ralph Moor, insisted that he get a Tuskegee scientist of his own for cotton work. At the CO's insistence, a black professor of agriculture named J. R. Prince was sent to Southern Nigeria, his salary and expenses paid by the BCGA.[96] The BCGA eventually warmed to the idea of hiring black experts and hired J. W. Hoffman (see fig. 3.1) later in 1903. Economy was one compelling reason to cross the "colour bar": Moor pointed out that a black expert commanded a salary of only £300. The white inspector for agriculture, Gerald Dudgeon, had a salary of £700 plus expenses. When Governor McGregor complained that two experts had been sent to Nigeria instead of the one he had requested, the BCGA replied that "the joint salaries of Hoffman and Barnes only equal the cost of one white expert."[97]

The BCGA and Colonial Office hoped that black cotton experts like Hoffman would get a better reception in Africa than white experts. The only known photograph of Hoffman in Africa shows him seated in front of a tent, surrounded by a group of Egba farmers (see fig. 3.2). Hoffman's

Figure 3.1. Portrait of Prof. John Wesley Hoffman, BCGA 2/2/1. Courtesy of the Cadbury Research Library: Special Collections, University of Birmingham.

Figure 3.2. Prof. John Wesley Hoffman (*center, seated*) addressing Egba farmers, BCGA 2/2/2. Courtesy of the Cadbury Research Library: Special Collections, University of Birmingham.

attire and equipment mark his status as a colonial official, but there is no evidence suggesting that he intentionally distanced himself from his African audiences. The professor seems to have been well liked by the Nigerians he worked with. Hoffman promoted his work in the Lagos press as well as in African American publications. A letter from farmers in Pine Bluff, Arkansas, captured the sentiment of some African Americans who read about Hoffman's exploits: "From what we read between the lines we are convinced that the work in which you are engaged will in the end solve the mysterious & vexing problem concerning our race."[98] Still, Hoffman and his colleagues in Africa preached the same message they had offered in the United States: that black people should focus on hard work instead of politics. Hoffman wrote in 1909: "Back to the soil must be the cry of every African, and the Government ought to do everything to introduce the teaching of Agriculture in Africa." His colleague warned, "the Anglo-Saxon race will just waste time and increase trouble by making the negroes a race of educated clerks." Cash-crop production, on the other hand, would lead to "a true and natural evolution to a higher state of civilization and culture."[99]

Black or white, the BCGA got little out of its American cotton experts. Most resigned, were struck with malaria and sent home, or died within one or two years of arriving in West Africa. W. H. Himbury brought Hoffman with him to help in negotiations with Nigerian elites, but he was unimpressed with Hoffman's expertise in cotton.[100] When Hoffman fell ill in 1905, he was not replaced. (The professor had secretly accepted a position at Prairie View College in Texas during his summer leave in 1904. He returned to Nigeria for a second tour but resigned on grounds of health.)[101] When urged to hire more experts by the CO, Hutton complained, "Our experience of Americans has been utterly hopeless, and as far as we can judge it will be absolutely necessary to send out young men to be trained as experts in either Egypt or elsewhere."[102] The CO ultimately agreed, and when new supervisors were required for Togo following the British invasion in 1914, the officers on the scene requested a colonial agricultural officer in preference to a BCGA man or even former employees of the German Tuskegee scheme.[103]

The main contribution of the American experts was their propagation of American-style agricultural extension work in Africa. Black educators like Booker T. Washington and George Washington Carver had long been advocating for agricultural and industrial education as a solution to poverty in the American South. Scientists, including Hoffman, hosted "farmers' institutes" across the South, teaching black and white farmers about new crops, tools, and techniques. Farmers typically "distrusted government demonstration farms because they were operated by salaried farm managers whose financial security was not contingent on the success or failure of the crops."[104] The new demonstration method, usually credited to Seaman A. Knapp, involved getting farmers to try out new techniques and technologies on a portion of their own land, with a guarantee to make up any shortfall in income if the sample plot failed. The method was wildly successful, and was used by universities, state governments, and the US Department of Agriculture in conjunction with farmers' institutes to disseminate new agricultural techniques.[105] The BCGA surely knew of the USDA's demonstration work: Hutton subscribed to the USDA's technical series on cotton and had a good collection of USDA publications from the late nineteenth and early twentieth centuries.[106] Hoffman helped transplant these American methods to southern Nigeria, where he delivered lectures and set up model farms to let local farmers test new cottonseeds and new tools. "The people can never be trained by one visiting their farms and showing them," Hoffman wrote. "They must first see for themselves how crops are produced under modern methods."[107]

Racial ideas permeated these experts' views of agriculture. Europeans and Americans often caricatured Africans as ignorant of agricultural science, barely "scratching" the earth with hoes and reaping a bountiful harvest thanks to the supposed fecundity of African soils.[108] Klas Rönnbäck traced the stereotype of the "lazy African" back several centuries, showing the durability of the idea in European writing about Africa. Practically from the first contacts between Europeans and Africans, Europeans complained about "bestial sloth" among Africans, especially men, who were "unwilling to exert themselves to sow more than will barely support them through the year." Rönnbäck argues that the "lazy African" was a "hegemonic" idea, so pervasive that even writers who observed industrious activity firsthand were reluctant to challenge the broader stereotype of laziness.[109] As we have seen, some Britons, like Hutton, rejected the "lazy African" thesis. The stereotype was widespread among BCGA staff and in the Colonial Office, however. To take one example, the Guggisbergs (who would eventually be governor and first lady of the Gold Coast) argued that foreign experts would quickly discover the "simple devices by which the natives, far too lazy to attempt such a feat themselves, can improve both the quality and quantity of their crops."[110] The trope of peasant laziness (or alternately, peasant conservatism) was widespread: in one of the BCGA's first field reports, its expert in the Gambia complained that the natives "were very slow in adopting new methods," words to be repeated by foreign experts for decades to come.[111]

The task of the expert, then, was to make African labor work harder and more scientifically. Touring instructors gave lessons and distributed leaflets in local languages, explaining how cotton should be grown. New techniques like deep hoeing of fields, ridging between rows of crops, heavy thinning of plants, and total uprooting of plants at the end of the season were emphasized, all tasks that greatly increased labor inputs.[112] These steps increased yields and reduced losses to pests and disease, but they were alien to most regions of Africa, where mixed cropping and bush fallow practices kept weeds and pests under control and maintained soil fertility. Agricultural experts did use some positive incentives to convince farmers to adopt new farming practices, and they pointed out that farmers would earn higher incomes if they adopted strategies designed to increase crop yields. The BCGA offered £20 for the best cotton grown under the BCGA's conditions in southern Nigeria early in the cotton campaign. To win, farmers had to sell all their cotton to the BCGA, follow a specified farming regimen, and cultivate at least seven acres.[113] As with the fixed price policy, however, the BCGA dropped most prizes and bounties for cotton as the price of American cotton fell.

An enormous disincentive for would-be cotton farmers was the BCGA's requirement that its imported cottonseeds be cultivated as annuals in a monoculture, disrupting traditional work patterns and complementary ecologies. Monocropping was lifted straight from the southern United States, where the practice increased cotton yields by eliminating competition for sunlight and soil nutrients from other plants. In a report from 1904 Hoffman observed that farmers near Alabata in Nigeria had gotten a yield with American cotton that "was twice as much as their own native cotton," and he was "very sure if they had only planted the cotton alone the

yield would have been nearly three times the yield of the native cotton."
He blamed food intercropping for the lower yields, concluding that "if we
had a model farm they would be able to see the cotton grown under modern methods."[114]

For all of the colonial cotton programs, monocropping was a critical
step toward the improvement of agriculture through new methods, seeds,
machines, and chemicals. One French official remarked that clearing
new land for cotton would be "of little value . . . if the methods were to
remain the same and the yields inferior."[115] The BCGA also believed that
monocropping reduced the risk from diseases and insects, as other crops
could harbor pests.[116] Single-crop fields were easier for colonial officials
to monitor, to ensure that the right kinds of cotton were being grown in
the specified way. French planners imposed monocropping and row-field
layouts for the same reasons, following the latest scientific cotton-growing
standards while also making it "easier for district guards to delimit cotton
fields and to supervise their cultivation."[117]

Monocropping in the South relied on animal-drawn equipment to efficiently prepare large tracts of land, however, and Southern farmers with
access to regional and national markets in foodstuffs did not have to produce subsistence crops as a life-or-death matter. In tsetse-infested regions
of Africa, only human labor was feasible and producers had little access
to imported food. Intercropping cotton and food made sense as a survival
strategy, and growing cotton alone could mean starvation if the crop failed,
or even if cotton prices fell too low.[118] Drawing on evidence from Malawi,
Wapulumuka O. Mulwafu noted five distinct benefits that peasant cultivators obtained from intercropping: first was food security from planting a
variety of crops, followed by "enhanced soil fertility, though few peasants
could explain exactly how this farming technique helped to accomplish
this." Leguminous plants in the crop mixture helped restore nitrogen to
the soil. Third, "inter-cropping helped to maximize labour use since peasants could plant different crops on one piece of land that had already
been cleared." The fourth benefit was protection from soil erosion and the
preservation of moisture, due to extensive leaf cover in a cultivated plot.
Finally, intercropping "reduced the growth of weeds and, in the process,
reduced the amount of labor required."[119]

The broad diversity of crop mixes and agriculture techniques seen in
Africa reflected the "accumulated wisdom of peoples living on their own
land for generations," knowledge that prioritized survival over cash crop
production.[120] The BCGA paid little attention to the balance of subsistence and market production that characterized much African farming,
and it should come as no surprise that a crop like groundnuts, which could
be marketed but also eaten in an emergency, were preferred over cotton
in many places. By the 1930s, colonial agricultural officials wrote about

intercropping cotton and maize as if it were an agricultural innovation, rather than a return to sound local practice.[121]

Ridging soil was a particularly onerous task imposed by colonial agricultural experts, and it had no immediate payback in terms of labor productivity. Colonial experts imposed ridge-building across slopes as a conservation measure to check erosion in the 1930s. Mandala argued that the way ridges were often constructed—under threat of punishment from village chiefs—was intended to "make peasants revere and respect the authority of their traditional rulers" as much as it was intended to protect farmland. The policies bred resentment among farmers, and CO staff admitted that the benefits brought by ridging had only been won "by fear and not willing co-operation."[122] In Lesotho, Kate Showers demonstrated that soil ridges constructed on the orders of colonial experts in fact "induced the growth of gullies in fields and pastures," worsening erosion in the marginal lands the Basotho had been pushed into by white settlers.[123]

The BCGA and CO rarely examined the sociocultural context of labor in Africa, just as they imposed cotton cultivation without a sound understanding of local ecologies. The BCGA assumed that the unit of labor was the "native farmer," and that the (male) farmer would mobilize household labor as needed. This was based in part on a lack of understanding of African societies, and in part on a simplistic understanding of cotton production in the American South. On American cotton farms, the household under patriarchal authority was indeed the key unit of production, but the farming family usually relied on a pool of wage labor during harvest time. This labor was traditionally supplied by landless, underemployed African Americans. In the United States, harvest labor operated through wage relations, but in many African societies reciprocal labor exchanges served the same function, maximizing efficiency during key steps of the agricultural process. In addition, gendered divisions of labor in African societies meant that male or female labor might be unavailable for cotton cultivation. These labor systems were not inherently incompatible with individual cash-crop production, but they often relied on reciprocal exchanges of labor, food, and other goods outside of the cash economy. A farmer who used family or community labor to harvest cotton would receive cash from the BCGA, and this was difficult to redistribute among contributors to the labor process. According to conventional economic theory, a money economy for commodities leads to a money economy for wages, but in many parts of Africa commodity prices were too low and wages too high for wage labor to take off as a dominant labor system.[124] The BCGA effectively isolated the "native farmer" from society, assuming that familial or market mechanisms would take care of labor and subsistence inputs.

In addition to the threat to subsistence posed by cotton monoculture, monocultures of cotton also led to rapid degradation of soils, in Africa even more so than in America.[125] American farmers regularly had to abandon "sour land" even when using crop rotations (usually maize and tobacco, both as nutrient-hungry as cotton), and the BCGA tried to convince African farmers to adopt this short-sighted model on thin, nutrient-poor soils. American farmers' organizations and the US Department of Agriculture had already learned the dangers of monoculture by 1900, and they encouraged cotton producers to diversify their crops. Booker T. Washington warned Germany's KWK against making "the same mistake that has been made in the South among our people, that is, teach them to raise nothing but cotton."[126] Whether in Africa or America, the only way to sustain such cultivation was to bring more land under the plow or hoe, or to add fertilizers to replace nutrients.

Surveillance, Regulation, and Control in a Colonial Free Market

The association's "pioneer" work—establishing ginneries, distributing seed, buying cotton in remote areas, and offering fixed prices—was part of a trade-off with colonial officials. In exchange for offering agricultural services on a "philanthropic" basis, the BCGA received special privileges from colonial governments. Colonial rules restricted competition in cotton buying and ginning and allowed the BCGA to control what cotton could be grown, where seed would be distributed, and how cotton would be raised.

After initially failing to convince the CO that "the Association should be given control over all seed" in its first major policy request, the BCGA settled for a monopoly on ginning.[127] The BCGA recognized from the beginning that cotton agriculture could be controlled at the ginnery level. Ginners could reject cotton that they thought was mishandled or of an undesirable variety, shaping the actions of cotton farmers. Centralized machine ginning allowed the BCGA to collect all cottonseed from an area, preventing farmers from replanting their own cotton. In effect, the BCGA's ginnery strategy allowed the association to manage the production of cotton in British colonies without controlling the land, labor, and other economic resources of Africans.

Effective enforcement required a monopsony, however, to prevent producers from selling "substandard" cotton to less scrupulous buyers who might return the seed to farmers. The BCGA argued that "undue competition in cotton buying" was "responsible for a good deal of inferior cotton being shipped to Liverpool," suggesting that only the BCGA, with its semi-philanthropic status, could serve as an effective guardian of quality.[128] In its propaganda in Lancashire, the BCGA tried to ease concerns over this apparent abandonment of free trade principles, saying that "All authorities are agreed *that the most vital factor* in successful cotton growing is the provision of the best selected seed" (emphasis in the original), and that "this control can only be effectively obtained by retaining the ginning in the hands of the Association."[129] In effect, Africans were free to grow cotton, as long as they grew it from BCGA seed and sold it to BCGA ginneries.

The BCGA's desire to control the supply of cottonseed in Africa also meant that the association suppressed the diffusion of the hand-cranked roller gin (based on the Indian *churka*), a simple technology that could have greatly facilitated the adoption of cotton as a cash crop. Cottonseeds make up anywhere from 60 to 80 percent of the weight of raw cotton bolls, and removing the seeds locally would have saved African farmers a great deal of labor by reducing the weight of cotton packages. Farmers and porters could have carried more ginned cotton over longer distances, expanding the number of potential participants in the export-oriented cash-crop economy. Roller gins also would have helped local textile producers get access to cotton, however, and they were ineffective at ginning the American Upland cotton the BCGA had hoped to grow in Africa.

The Nigerian government requested hand-cranked gins early in the BCGA's cotton campaign, but the BCGA refused to send more than a few samples. Instead it deployed steam-powered ginneries, which required farmers to travel long distances to a central ginning location.[130] The ginneries concentrated cottonseed in the hands of the association, allowing it to determine which varieties farmers would replant after each harvest. Unginned cotton must be kept very dry to prevent the seed from germinating and ruining the fiber, and this fact probably forced some African farmers to sell cotton quickly instead of waiting for better prices. As the dispute over access to gins in Abekouta illustrated, African farmers knew that ginned cotton gave them power in the marketplace, allowing them to sell to local spinners or wait for better prices. Roller gins in private hands would have given local textile manufacturers ready access to ginned cotton because BCGA gins exported all the cotton the association purchased. Thus roller gins would have diverted cotton away from export markets while reducing demand for Lancashire cloth.

In Uganda and Nyasaland, Indian and African entrepreneurs who had erected hand-cranked roller gins in remote locations were shut down by expensive government licensing requirements at the urging of the BCGA. Hutton warned that if local ginners were allowed to continue operating, East African cotton would "soon acquire as bad a reputation as East Indian cotton—viz., sown anyhow, grown anyhow, ginned anyhow."[131] The BCGA feared that these gins would allow peasants to collect and replant their own seeds, rather than the imported varieties Lancashire desired. Writing fifty years later, Cyril Ehrlich defended the BCGA's position by arguing that roller gins produced poor-quality fiber, though he admitted that roller gins also "put peasant growers in the position of being able to provide their own seed for sowing purposes without any supervision."[132] By suppressing small-scale roller gins, the BCGA also limited the ability of African entrepreneurs to accumulate capital. The BCGA and its affiliated companies owned all of the steam-powered saw ginneries in Uganda and many other colonies, and the ginneries used European merchant firms to purchase cotton in rural areas. For crops like cocoa, new processing techniques and simple equipment allowed African farmers and merchants to add value to the raw material.[133] As the rich historical literature on cocoa farmers illustrates, African farmers used their new wealth as capitalists, hiring wage labor and purchasing or renting land to expand production.[134] Under the BCGA regime, there was no path toward indigenous cotton capitalism, save perhaps for plantation owners in former slave economies like northern Nigeria.

Nearly all of the seeds the BCGA imported to Africa were American Upland varieties, the kind Lancashire most needed. Hutton, who was responsible for ordering seeds, adopted a scattergun approach, trying many varieties in the hopes that one would be successful (see table 3.1). Despite finding commercially attractive native cotton varieties in West Africa, the BCGA decided to eradicate local varieties. When they found good native cottons, experts like Hoffman were initially instructed to "buy as much as you can" and "gin it and save the seed for planting," but the BCGA quickly changed its position as Hutton took control of the association's day-to-day operations.[135] In Lagos, the BCGA asked the CO to ban cottonseed exports as part of a broader effort to control the stock of available seed. If merchants bought native seeds with the intention of exporting them to foreign oil firms, they could also sell seeds back to African farmers and allow them to perpetuate their preferred landraces. The BCGA did eventually erect an oil mill to crush seeds in Nigeria, but before the equipment was installed, the BCGA found that farmers were helping themselves to the ginnery stockpiles to replant cotton.[136] The BCGA hastily asked the CO to repeal the export ban to rapidly clear out these seed stocks, which could not be used for fertilizer or cattle feed without being processed by a crushing mill, and Governor Egerton obliged.

By 1908, the BCGA instructed its agents to take "particular pains to eliminate all undesirable varieties . . . and to issue only pure sound seed to the natives."[137] Pamphlets in English and local languages gave literate farmers and agricultural officials clear instructions:

34. What kind of cotton should be grown?
A: The best kind to grow in Uganda is American.
35. Should the native cotton be grown?
A: No; it is best to root up all plants of the native kind, because the cotton is a very bad kind, and the plants growing on from year to year breed insects and disease.[138]

Table 3.1. J. A. Hutton's cottonseed orders, 1905 (*G. hirsutum* unless otherwise indicated)

	Gold Coast	Sierra Leone	Lagos	S. Nigeria	N. Nigeria	Buganda (?)
Black Rattler (tons)	1 T	2 T	5 T	5 T	20 T	9 T
Rumella(?) Big Boll (bags)	2 bags	2 bags	2 bags	2 bags	2 bags	8 bags
Jones Improved	2	2	2	2	2	9
Culpepper Big Boll	2	2	2	2	2	8
Sunflower Long Staple	2	2	2	2	2	9
Allen's Improved	1	1	1	1	-	-
Hawkins' Extra Prolific	2	2	2	2	2	4
Smooth Peruvian	2 T	2 T	2 T	2 T	2 T	8 T
Joannovitch (Egyptian)	2	2	2	2	2	8
Abassi (Egyptian)	2	2	2	2	2	8

Source: J. A. Hutton daybook 2, BCGA 7/2/2.
Note: Illegible entries indicated by "?"

Favoring one landrace over another was not a trivial issue. American cottons introduced by the BCGA were not suited to African environments, and the bolls they produced demanded additional labor at harvest to keep the lint clean of debris. The burs of the Black Rattler variety had the unfortunate habit of "lacerating the hands of pickers," but Hutton nonetheless sent eighty tons of it to West Africa in 1905.[139] In French colonies, the ACC also provided American seeds to grow cotton that was, in the words of a colonial Agricultural Service report, "adapted to a type of [spinning] machine and giving yields that are most advantageous to buyers [in Europe]." Colonial planners never asked "whether the high performing plant was one that brought the biggest economic return to the grower."[140]

Indeed, if Nigerian farmers were given a fair choice, some might have chosen the native Ishan variety. A *G. barbadense* cotton that was probably transplanted to Africa from the Caribbean in earlier centuries, Ishan cotton produced long fibers that were competitive with Egyptian cotton on the world market.[141] A study conducted at Moor Plantation in 1915 showed that this localized cotton was competitive with several American varieties, in terms of yield as well as market price (see table 3.2). As an extra-long staple cotton, it also would have appealed to local hand-spinners, who could more easily produce fine, strong yarns with it than with shorter-stapled cotton. By contrast, the BCGA favored heavy-yielding American Upland varieties with shorter, less valuable fiber. These cottons consistently failed to thrive in different conditions across Africa. After many years of failure, the BCGA and Nigerian agricultural department got lucky in the early 1920s with Allen's Improved, an American long-staple variety that did well in northern Nigeria. According to O. T. Faulkner, Nigeria's director of agriculture between the world wars, Allen cotton "proved able to adapt itself to the climatic conditions, and has now completely replaced the indigenous cotton in all the main cotton-growing areas." Faulkner championed Allen cotton because of its value in export markets, but he nonetheless pondered "Whether or not an even better type of cotton might in time have been evolved by scientific selection from the indigenous cotton."[142]

The BCGA and CO also struggled with farmers over perennial cotton. In many parts of West Africa cotton was traditionally grown as a perennial, yielding the most lint in the second or third year with deterioration in successive years. By the fourth or fifth year, fiber yields declined and the cotton was uprooted and the field planted with other crops.[143] As A. G. Boyle, the acting governor of Southern Nigeria, put it in 1912: "A native naturally prefers a crop which [is] of a more or less permanent nature and personally were I a planter I should be inclined to agree with him."[144] By insisting on growing American cotton as annual, the BCGA greatly increased labor requirements for African farmers. Ironically, the BCGA did search for perennial "tree cotton" in Australia, where labor costs seemed prohibitive for American-style cotton cultivation and harvesting. The Caravonica cotton variety was tested unsuccessfully as a perennial crop, and Australians concluded that they would never be competitive cotton producers without a source of cheap labor to imitate the American monocultural, annual model for cotton.[145]

To ensure that Africans grew the right cotton plants in the right way, the BCGA turned to the colonial state regulation. In an early example, BCGA managers in Lagos sought punishments for farmers who arrived at ginneries with cotton that failed to meet the association's standards, instead of offering a price differential to encourage higher quality produce.[146] A decade later in Sudan, Hutton asked colonial officials to supervise and discipline farmers during cotton picking, because farmers were sensibly harvesting the crop as fast as they could to take advantage of fixed prices. If farmers "were compelled to gather their cotton in the proper manner and if there were careful selection of seed," he argued, "we might produce a really satisfactory type of cotton most useful to Lancashire."[147]

In Nyasaland, the BCGA worked closely with the agriculture department and Samuel Simpson, the director of agriculture, to produce the 1910 Cotton Ordinance. Simpson was one of a handful of scientifically trained officials at work in British Africa before 1914. A graduate of Edinburgh

Table 3.2. Cotton yields at Moor Plantation, Nigeria, ca. 1915

Variety	Lint/acre	Value/pound	Value/acre
Georgia*	125.8 lbs	5.58 pence	£2-18-6
Upland*	119	5.53	2-14-10
Ishan [localized *G. barbadense*]	112.2	5.81	2-14-4
Hawkins Extra Prolific*	116.8	5.49	2-13-5
Allen's Long Staple*	88.2	6.56	2-8-3
Truitts Big Boll*	102.3	5.51	2-7-0
Griffin Long Staple*	91.7	6.04	2-6-2
Nyasaland Upland [localized *G. hirsutum*]	91.3	5.96	2-5-4
Jones' Improved*	95.2	5.52	2-3-10
Mebane*	92.4	5.68	2-3-9
Meko [localized *G. peruvianum*]	91.4	5.38	2-1-0
Nyasaland Upland [localized to Nigeria]	38.4	6.16	0-19-9

Source: BCGA 6/1/4.
Note: * = American Upland varieties, *G. hirsutum*

University, Simpson won a posting to the agricultural department in Egypt, where he researched cotton. The CO dragooned him into service as a cotton expert at the BCGA's request, pulling him from the prestige and comforts of a university laboratory in Cairo to work in Nyasaland. He complained, "This practically ruined my career, but it has not been allowed to spoil my life which I have tried to make useful."[148] The scientist tried to make the best of his situation by rigorously applying scientific methods to the problem of colonial economic growth. Simpson thought little of the BCGA's early work, and he condemned the association's policy of giving seed and loans to white planters who "have no experience of agricultural work whatever, and would absolutely starve in most countries."[149]

The cotton ordinance did not specify how cotton was to be grown, or how much farmers were to plant, but it deeply affected the lives of farmers by prescribing new tasks and by restricting the market for cotton and cottonseed. Farmers had to grow something to earn tax money, and cotton was the only commodity the BCGA would buy. Under the ordinance, all cotton plants were to be uprooted and burned after the harvest to prevent disease, adding a new step to labor routines and eliminating the perennial cotton option. Government agents destroyed the plants of farmers who failed to comply, and charged them for the cost of clearing the field. All seed sales to farmers required the agricultural department's approval, and non-BCGA cotton buyers faced strict licensing rules. All native-grown cotton was to be ginned within the Protectorate, cutting peasants off from outlets in Mozambique and denying them access to their own seed stock, as BCGA ginneries kept all seed for crushing or redistribution. Violators of any of the seventeen rules could be fined up to £5 or imprisoned for a month.[150] Such rules were intended to improve the quality and quantity of cotton, but they did so by dramatically increasing the surveillance of producers and by intensifying farmers' labor inputs without additional remuneration. Similar laws were passed in Nigeria when the BCGA finally settled on the Allen's Improved variety of *G. hirsutum* as the most likely to succeed. Certain sectors were zoned as "American cotton areas" and farmers were heavily fined for growing other varieties.[151]

Ugandan peasants were successful—with the aid of the local Department of Agriculture—in resisting BCGA efforts to wipe out the Uganda long-staple varietal. Uganda cotton (a localized variant of *G. barbadense*) found a ready market in Lancashire and even commanded a premium over the cotton varieties the BCGA distributed. Hutton complained that local officials were encouraging farmers to plant the more valuable cotton instead of American varieties, and he used a momentary fluctuation in the price of Ugandan cotton to assert that "whatever local evidence there may be as to the quality of Uganda cotton having been improved . . . it is not supported by what is after all the final test, namely, the price a spinner will pay for the cotton."[152] The Ugandan government's cotton expert, P. H. Lamb, retorted that Hutton had a distorted view of market conditions, looking only at the comparison of Uganda cotton to American. In fact, Uganda cotton competed with Egyptian cotton, and the low price for Uganda cotton Hutton had used as evidence of the fiber's deficiencies was due to a fall in the price of Egyptian long-staple cotton, rather than any fault in the Ugandan product.[153] Lamb was a partisan of specialization in the finer grades of long-staple cotton, having concluded after a 1908 tour of the American South that competition with American Upland producers was futile.[154]

The CO promoted Samuel Simpson from Nyasaland to a new post as Uganda's first official director of agriculture in 1911; Lamb moved to a post in Nigeria. By the time Simpson arrived in Uganda, he was, according to one account, "a man of radical outlook," with a "strong antipathy to capitalistic enterprise."[155] Simpson used his newfound authority to harshly criticize the BCGA for all manner of sins, beginning with the decision to send seeds for Black Rattler and other American cotton varieties to Uganda. Simpson taunted Hutton (who viewed Germany as a model for cotton growing) with the fact that "Uganda cotton is having very satisfactory sales in Hamburg and Havre, and the German East Africa Government has given us an order for 60 tons of [Uganda] seed for German East Africa."[156] Simpson charged that Hutton had maliciously dispatched saw gins to Uganda, intending to destroy the better-paying local cotton varieties and replace them American Upland cotton. The saw gin had been invented to remove the fibers of *G. hirsutum* from the seed, and it did so by violently pulling and cutting the lint.[157] The roller gin was perfectly adequate for cleaning long-staple cotton like the *G. barbadense* being grown in Uganda, but saw gins mangled these cottons and reduced the value of the lint. Every single BCGA ginnery in Uganda was outfitted with saws designed for American Upland cotton instead of rollers.[158] Simpson complained, "the work of this Department is being nullified to a great extent" by the BCGA's choice of machinery.[159] Ultimately Simpson's defense of Ugandan cotton was vindicated by the market, and firms in Lancashire praised Ugandan cotton as "rather better than Texas."[160] Private ginning firms in competition with the BCGA chose roller gins to protect the long staple, and by 1918 rollers outnumbered saws by four to one.[161]

White plantation owners were also pressured by the BCGA to plant specific varieties of cotton, although they were not held back by the monopsonistic conditions imposed on black farmers in Africa. During a conference with planters from the West Indies, Hutton warned the growers that "some of you have been aiming a little bit too high. Longer and longer staple you have been aiming at. That is a mistake; there you are going into a limited market."[162] White planters chose to grow long-stapled Sea Island cotton because, besides being native to the area, the variety fetched extremely high prices in Lancashire, where it was used for the finest yarns. When asked to provide a prize of £15 for the best Sea Island cotton by the Jamaica Agricultural Society, Hutton curtly told them "to recommend experiments with American Upland or Egyptian cotton" instead.[163]

In the long run, the BCGA was wrong about the kinds of cotton that would find a market and pay the grower. Sea Island and other "superfine" varieties succeeded admirably in the West Indies, and Ugandan cotton flourished (exports increased from fifty-four bales in 1904–5 to 321,348 bales in 1936).[164] Hutton lamented that Sudanese farmers were having so much success with Sakellarides (Sakel) cotton, a variety that Hutton thought "very few spinners can use," making it "unsaleable even at a low price" despite being "a heavy cropping variety, early maturing and very fine and strong."[165] In short, despite its many virtues, it was not American Upland cotton. Sakel was in fact very successful commercially; even Hutton was forced to admit by 1917 that there was "a large and growing demand for [long-staple] cotton, which is solely limited by the supply."[166]

The BCGA was also wrong about the viability of African cottons. Imported American seeds, when they successfully germinated, often did not produce good crops. P. H. Lamb "regretted that the old acclimatised variety had been destroyed [in Nigeria] through measures to extinguish the mixed seed in 1908,"[167] and another agricultural official agreed that there was "no doubt that cultivation using native varieties was the way forward." BCGA efforts "to introduce exotic American and Egyptian cottons on large-scale plantations had ... been a failure."[168] Governor Egerton reminded the BCGA in 1907, "The American product is the result of over 100 years careful selection and cultivation. Was it originally better than the West African plant? Is it not more than probable that greater success will result in careful propagation of this plant rather than by the introduction of an exotic of doubtful superiority?"[169] According to Governor Macgregor, J. W. Hoffman did succeed in "developing a new type of cotton suitable to the climate as to yield and line, by crossing an American variety of cotton with a hardy native type" during his time in Nigeria. No other evidence appears to corroborate this claim, however, and it was not until much later that colonial breeding programs succeeded in creating an American-type cotton suited to African conditions.[170]

The BCGA's experts gradually realized that, like African cotton plants, many African agricultural practices also had merit, though the foreign experts were still burdened by the agricultural paradigm of the American South. Hoffman's experience working with Nigerian farmers led him to challenge a few conventional stereotypes. He praised the Yoruba as "keen farmers, enthusiastic over the idea of cotton-growing and agricultural work generally, very intelligent, and anxious to get all the latest views on farming."[171] Near Ekiti he was impressed by cotton plants "as carefully tilled with native hoes as the American Negro would cultivate his cotton with the best American plough." Yet he was convinced that the American model of cotton monoculture with mule-drawn plows was the only way forward for African cotton. "The people will have to be trained in the way of cultivating cotton by itself," he insisted, noting that "At present you will find growing together cotton, yams, corn, and beans."[172]

After Hoffman, the most influential figure in the early push for cotton education was Gerald C. Dudgeon, who served as inspector of agriculture for West Africa. A former planter from India, Dudgeon was appointed to the CO at the BCGA's behest.[173] While experts in London like Wyndham Dunstan of the Imperial Institute took an optimistic view of African farming, calling it "primitive yet effective," Dudgeon's "man on the spot" observations were far more critical. He condemned African farming practices like shifting cultivation and soil mounding as wasteful and primitive, and thought Africans spent insufficient time weeding, used insufficient fertilizer, and carelessly collected seeds for replanting.[174] Early in his career Samuel Simpson also decried African farming practices as "exceedingly primitive." "The seed distributed should be of the best and grown under

European supervision," Simpson argued, lest the seed be "badly mixed" with local varieties.[175] Back in Manchester, Hutton frequently complained of inefficient practices and blamed a conservative mindset that sought to maximize production while minimizing labor. This was a completely rational response, and Hutton understood why farmers chose certain agricultural methods, but he nonetheless lamented that "The native is too much inclined to go in for quantity irrespective of quality."[176] Many colonial agricultural experts agreed that African farming practices were inefficient and also "ruinous to the environment in the sense that they encouraged deforestation and soil erosion."[177]

Such negative views of African agriculture were not universal, however. As a 1932 report from Nyasaland put it, some colonial officers understood that "Natives have a great knowledge of agriculture and are clever at choosing soils."[178] A number of colonial officials, like Sir C. A. King-Harman (governor of Sierra Leone), told the BCGA that cotton experts were quite unnecessary; Africans clearly knew how to grow cotton and had been doing so for centuries. "It did not appear to me that the natives required any special instruction in the matter," he said.[179] It was capital, not expertise, that King-Harman believed Sierra Leone lacked, and he expressed disappointment that the BCGA failed to follow through on early promises of bounties and free seeds, tools, and freight.

Hoffman did not stay in Africa long enough to see the limitations of the American model, but other experts eventually came to appreciate the benefits of indigenous farming practices like mixed cropping. Even Dudgeon admitted that African farms boasted higher cotton yields than the BCGA's model estates. After being transferred from Nyasaland to Uganda, Samuel Simpson too became a partisan of "traditional" agriculture, although he continued to believe in the close management of farming by colonial experts. As will be seen below, these views eventually prevailed in the Colonial Office. By 1913, the author of the *Historical Geography of the British Empire* could confidently state: "In mere agricultural methods it is doubtful if a people, who for many years have raised rich crops from soils, in some places by no means promising, without apparent sign of exhaustion, can learn much from European agriculture."[180]

Inappropriate Technology

The African farmer and the cotton plant were not the only things the BCGA hoped to revolutionize in Africa. Hutton knew that increasing cotton yields was the only way cotton could become viable as anything more than a marginal peasant crop in British colonies, and he looked for technical solutions to the environmental, economic, and social problems of

African cotton. Records of activities in Africa were not well kept and the BCGA did not even audit its accounts until 1908, but the existing documentation reveals much about how Hutton approached cotton cultivation at a practical level. A gross of hoes were sensibly sent to Sierra Leone along with seeds for cowpeas, rye grass, and clover (for experiments in crop rotation) early in the association's work, but Hutton sent exceptional amounts of sophisticated equipment to his favorite sites. The BCGA council sanctioned only basic implements for Moor Plantation in Nigeria, but Hutton sent out modern plows, tractors, and planting machines, fully expecting that the results would justify the expense.[181]

BCGA records reveal that Hutton also sent agricultural machines to many white planters in Africa.[182] He hoped to raise funds for the association by retailing cotton machinery to the plantation sector, but the plan was vetoed by the BCGA council on grounds that it would not encourage the spread of cotton growing.[183] Still, Hutton sent heavy plows to Port Herald to jump-start Nyasaland's cotton plantation industry, seeing possibilities in economies of scale.[184] McCall tried to stop this transfer of "inappropriate technology" in Nyasaland, warning Hutton that German experiments with gasoline-powered plows had not been successful. After suggesting steam plows, an exasperated Hutton asked, "You don't know of any motor ploughs which are of any use whatever?" McCall flatly told him that fuel would be too expensive, and that the plows were inappropriate for the soils where cotton grew best. Furthermore, the kinds of plows Hutton sent to Nyasaland were suited only for plantation agriculture, doing nothing for the peasants that McCall was beginning to believe were the real future of the region's agricultural production. Despite McCall's protests, Hutton shipped a "Conqueror" disc plow anyway.[185]

Hutton also looked for chemical solutions to pests like the leaf stainer and pink bollworm, which took a toll on Egypt's cotton crop and threatened the new African cotton industries. He brought up Paris Green, an arsenic-based pesticide, several times in early BCGA meetings. Hutton repeatedly tried to get Paris Green distributed in West Africa, and it was not until his visit to Egypt and Sudan in 1911–12 (where he tried to convince an Egyptian manager to start using the stuff) that Hutton learned of its lethality to cattle and humans.[186]

The end goal of the BCGA's program of education, modernization, and regulation was to transform free peasant farmers into commodity producers for the world market. Each component of the BCGA program had a rather benign objective: improving the yield and quality of cotton, which would increase farmer incomes (as well as the supply of cotton available in Britain). Yet these individual pieces often had negative side effects. African farmers were forced to choose between food crops and monocropped cotton, threatening their food security. African entrepreneurs were shut out of a lively market for mechanical ginning by blanket bans on hand-powered ginning machinery. Hardy local landraces were replaced with exotic imports, forcing farmers to gamble each season against the soil, weather, and pests. In turning African farmers into cotton exporters, the BCGA overturned centuries of indigenous agricultural knowledge. The same was true of agricultural development schemes across the continent: "Before monocrop specialization for export became normal, West Africans used to employ a highly differentiated set of production strategies. . . . All of these considerations constitute the accumulated wisdom of peoples living on their own land for generations. They are liable to be lost from sight when development programs are formulated for large, generalized areas."[187] In its expert research, its plantation experiments, and its regulatory work the BCGA ignored local knowledge and abstracted the wide variation in natural and social conditions found across Britain's African colonies, following the reductionist logic of the "black man's crop."

The Gezira Model

Frustrated by the inability of peasant producers to rapidly scale up production along the lines envisioned by the BCGA and by the abject failure of early plantations, Hutton looked for an alternative model for cotton growing in Africa. He found it in Sudan, where an American capitalist and several African American farmers had launched a bold experiment on the banks of the Nile.[188] With the blessings of the colonial government, the Americans and their British successors leased land from local owners, built irrigation and transportation networks, and hired Sudanese families first as wage workers and then as tenant farmers. A privately owned company (later called the Sudan Plantations Syndicate) managed the scheme and provided inputs and services—seed, fertilizers, agricultural education, mechanical plowing, and water—and also marketed all the cotton. This irrigated cotton experiment on the Gezira plain was an early example in Africa of a global phenomenon, dubbed "high modernism" by James C. Scott. Across the world, states embarked on massive projects that used science to produce "a simpler and more manageable reality" in spaces marked by complex social and environmental interactions.[189] In Gezira, the SPS, BCGA, and colonial state brought together mechanical cultivation, irrigation, seed selection, and chemical inputs with close supervision of Sudanese labor to overcome the difficulties faced in other BCGA cotton projects. Although the model was advertised as a harmonious balance between capital, labor, and the state, it in effect transformed free farmers into sharecroppers, entrapped by the global cotton economy and laden with new dependencies for farm inputs and credit.

Leigh Hunt, a brash and well-connected American capitalist, visited Sudan in 1902 as part of a vacation to Cairo.[190] Unknown to the BCGA, Hunt devised a plan to replicate Egypt's irrigated cotton farms along the banks of the Nile River in Sudan. Moreover, he wanted to resettle African Americans there as cotton growers, to produce fiber, and to teach the Sudanese how to become capitalist farmers. Hunt believed he could "help at least a million negroes to happy productive homes," solving the race problem in the South while also making money off of high cotton prices. He told his friend Gen. J. S. Clarkson, "Once the South realizes that there is a safe and sure way for them to lose the black men who do all their work, I am inclined to think they will conclude that the black man is not such a dangerous fellow after all." Hunt saw "little hope for the negro through the channel of party politics, nor can he be aided by charity. It must be done if done successfully along business lines." Reflecting on his plan for Sudan, he said, "I think I have laid those lines."[191] Emigration to Africa was an old theme in American race politics (see chapter 4), but Hunt thought his scheme would succeed where so many others had failed. On June 15, 1903, Hunt and Clarkson dined with President Theodore Roosevelt and explained Hunt's cotton "repatriation" project. According to Hunt, Roosevelt called his plan "a revelation and a timely one in a day of great need," adding that it "would help mightily in solving the sad and serious problem of the negro and his oppressed condition in the south." Hunt insisted that his plan "was not only a humanitarian project, but also a great business and money-making enterprise."[192]

The *Seattle Times* prematurely reported some details of Hunt's plan in September 1903, saying that Hunt "and Booker T. Washington, recognized as the leader of the negro race in America, have joined hands in a colonization undertaking which promises to go a long way towards solving the negro question in this country." The paper falsely stated that there were "thousands of Negro families in the South [who] would gladly embrace the chance of going to the Sudan and making new homes," and that President Roosevelt "promised his help in every way possible."[193] Clarkson did in fact introduce Hunt to Booker T. Washington, but the latter was not amused with Hunt's proposed solution the American race problem. "I am not in favor of wholesale colonization of the Negro people to Africa, or anywhere else," he told Hunt. Yet Washington had already sent Tuskegee graduates to Togo with the KWK, and several of his colleagues and former students were being courted by the BCGA at the time Hunt's proposal arrived. Despite misgivings about Hunt, the educator agreed to find a few volunteers for a pilot scheme. "The opportunities which you suggest the Sudan offers are opportunities which, it seems to me, large numbers of our Negro people should take advantage of," Washington remarked, treating the project as one of humanitarian colonization rather than the "repatriation" of the African diaspora.[194] Three Tuskegee students were chosen, and after some haggling over wages, the trio left for Sudan in 1904. Washington told them that he would "watch your work here, with a deep interest and anxiety," warning them that "a great many persons going to a warm climate, go to ruin from a moral standpoint." Having staked his school's reputation on the venture, he warned that failure would "not only [carry] you down, but us as well."[195]

To gain the approval of the British administration in Sudan, Hunt emphasized his support from high-profile backers like Washington and Roosevelt. He promised that African Americans would "assimilate with the natives . . . without causing friction, whereas Turks, Spaniards, Italians, or any people who might be expected to live comfortably in the Sudan, would make serfs of the natives." After initially telling Lord Cromer, the consul general in Egypt, that he wanted to give black Americans what they "do not now possess—a country to which they might safely migrate," he backtracked and downplayed the idea of mass emigration.[196] Hunt told Cromer he was not "ambitious to remove negroes from the United States, nor any portion of them, but I do believe that enough of them can be transplanted to serve our purpose of teaching the Sudanese how to raise cotton."[197]

Hunt had a reputation as a reckless self-promoter, and many were skeptical about the sincerity of his emigration plan. Yet he was taken seriously in some the most important financial circles of the day. Mining magnate Lionell Philips and millionaire investors Julius Werhner and Alfred Beit worked closely with Hunt and agreed to invest £600,000 in a plantation company, pending the results of an £80,000, five-year experiment.[198] Hunt boasted to Philips, "Leaders of thought may be arrayed against me and all the avenues of capital closed. I will defy these influences and win out, starting a steady Negro migration that will live longer and outlast the German, Scandinavian or Irish emigration to the United States."[199] Although Hunt toned down his rhetoric by 1905, he still insisted—quite incorrectly—that "the ancestors of many of our negroes came from the Nile region," and that since Sudan was "not a white man's country," African Americans were the perfect agents of Western-led economic development.[200]

British authorities awarded Hunt a concession for 10,000 feddans at Zeidab, along the Nile in northern Sudan, with an option for another 20,000 feddans. The first year at Zeidab was a total failure. Not a single cotton plant survived, but the three Tuskegee experts learned from the experience and had more success in following years. Encouraged by their positive reports on the potential of the site, Hunt asked Washington to send out two additional Tuskegee students. Over the next year, the five African Americans built a short railroad line and an eighty-foot smokestack for the pumping station boiler, and raised good crops of cotton with local laborers once the irrigation system was worked out.[201] Malaria took a toll on the group—including Hunt—and three of the Tuskegee men returned to the United States in 1907. One died in Sudan later the same year; the fate of the last man, John Jerry Powell, is unknown.

Back in Cairo, Hunt sold his stake in the Sudan Experimental Plantations Syndicate to Donald Peterson MacGillivray, a Scottish investor with a banking business in Egypt. MacGillivray struck the word "experimental" from the company name and ruthlessly purged inefficiencies to get the firm's ledgers into the black. Where Hunt relied on wage labor drawn from farmers and herdsmen displaced by his concession, MacGillivray instituted a sharecropping system. Hunt had paid generous wages and did not penalize workers for the failure of the early crops, believing that the cost-effective production of high-quality cotton was a technical problem rather than a question of labor. MacGillivray's new sharecropping system essentially sold water to tenants, who were responsible for the success or failure of their cotton. He expelled laborers-turned-tenants who failed to meet production quotas. "MacGillivray had no patience with tenants who either failed to or did not care to learn the tenets of capitalism," wrote Hunt's biographer. "After two or three warnings, he ousted tenants he considered indolent or irresponsible." In contrast to Hunt's model of warm paternalism, the new management's "main charge was to provide water, which it did with impressive efficiency." By 1910, the syndicate made £8,934 in profits from Zeidab and began work on the larger Tayiba estate at the top of the Gezira plain, this time in cooperation with the colonial government.[202] By 1912, the Sudan Plantations Syndicate returned its first dividends to shareholders at a handsome rate of 12.5 percent, and the SPS and colonial government looked to expand across the Gezira plain with a gravity-fed irrigation system rather than the pumps used at Zeidab and Tayiba.

BCGA chairman J. Arthur Hutton watched the Zeidab experiment closely and corresponded with Werhner and Beit. When MacGillivray took over the company, the BCGA used some of its capital to buy ten thousand SPS shares, giving the BCGA chairman a seat on the syndicate's board of directors. Hutton and other BCGA officials also invested their personal fortunes in the venture. Irrigated cotton appeared to have a bright future in Sudan, but the full-fledged Gezira project still needed two things that private capital could not provide. First, the colonial administration in Sudan had to secure rights to land across the Gezira plain. After that, the metropolitan government had to approve financing for irrigation works. Since the British government was unlikely to hand control of the waters of the Nile River to a private business, the irrigation scheme demanded government participation. To win these two objectives the BCGA launched its biggest campaign since the 1902–4 cotton corners.

Sir William Mather, a Lancashire industrialist and occasional MP, spearheaded the effort with public lectures in 1910. Mather emphasized the BCGA's core messages: Lancashire was still dangerously dependent on America for its raw materials; countless Britons depended directly or indirectly on the fortunes of Lancashire; and Britain had a collection of underdeveloped colonies in need of new industries. Mather also hit on a theme close to the hearts of Britons when he connected cotton growing with Britain's 1898 reconquest of Sudan. The celebrated martyrdom of General Gordon at the hands of the Mahdi's army in 1885 would be made worthwhile, Mather suggested, if the British government would fund irrigation and "afford the natives opportunities to work out their own salvation by utilizing the natural resources of their country." Mather acknowledged that Sudan was jointly ruled by Britain and Egypt, but he argued that the "greater responsibility and higher duty devolves upon Great Britain." Citing Hunt's success at Zeidab, Mather claimed "The effect [of laboring in cotton fields] on the natives has been to develop self-respect, and to inspire them with the ambition to become tenants of the 30-acre plots."[203] Mather ignored the question of government investment in colonial economies (let alone state aid for the benefit of one firm!) and the Tariff Reform controversy. He urged audiences to "bring your influence to bear, through the BCGA, upon the British Government, to induce it to move without delay, and to do its part in the development of the Sudan." The campaign was successful in pulling Lancashire's MPs and other politicians back onto the BCGA bandwagon, and Mather was elected an honorary vice-presidency of the BCGA in 1913.[204]

The Gezira scheme had impressed Hutton enough to warrant this last-ditch campaign in Britain, one that exhausted much of the association's waning political capital.[205] Hutton decided to personally inspect the Tayiba site in 1911. He was immensely satisfied:

> I can hardly describe what I have found here. . . . We have seen to-day some of the best cultivated cotton fields in the world, and with cotton bursting open which will delight the Lancashire spinner; and all this has been done in spite of immense difficulties in little less than a year. . . . I cannot dwell too much on the fact that many of the tenants have never grown cotton before in their lives, and yet I have never seen cleaner or better cultivation anywhere, and what is more important, the quality of the cotton is really excellent.[206]

The new model was a radical shift away from the BCGA's previous model, which relied on African farmers to bring cotton to BCGA ginneries. The Tayiba model placed farmers under close British supervision, ensuring that they planted and harvested cotton in prescribed ways. As an early photograph of the project shows, farmers at Tayiba were required to store cotton in front of their homes in bags that kept cotton free from dirt, but which also made it easy for British supervisors to inspect the cotton (see fig. 3.3). Hutton still clung to the philanthropic ideals of the original

Figure 3.3. Photograph of cotton tenant's farm at Tayiba, ca. 1912. Schmidt, *Cotton Growing in the Anglo-Egyptian Sudan*, 34.

BCGA mission, however, assuring Lancashire and government officials that tenants would get "a fair reward" for their work growing cotton. SPS control saved peasants "from the clutches of low class money lenders or unscrupulous buyers," while ensuring that "the land is not ruined by reckless methods of cultivation." "Capital," Hutton noted, should of course "have a fair reward," given the services investors were providing to Sudanese farmers.[207]

While the Gezira scheme moved past bureaucrats in London, Hutton ran into unexpected opposition from civil servants in Khartoum. During his tour, he found "There are two schools here, one for securing commercial co-operation and the others who believe in the Government doing nearly everything, which means practically keeping all commercial men out of the country."[208] Hutton met with the consul general in Egypt, Lord Kitchener, but failed to convince him that capitalist rather than state management was the best way forward. Businessmen complained that Kitchener "has ideas of developing the country purely for the Sudanese peasant—this is a general hobby at present," and there were fears that private capital would be shut out. As a correspondent told Hutton in 1913, there was "no country where a purely peasant proprietary makes a success of things and the only way to make the Sudanese grow cotton is to supervise him as is done at Zeidab and Taieba [*sic*]. And only private enterprise with financial resources can supervise successfully."[209]

Kitchener wanted to move quickly, with or without the SPS, and he told Hutton to pursue government funding for irrigation without an explicit agreement between the Sudan government and the SPS. Hutton complained, "I tried to impress upon [Kitchener] that it was absolutely essential to secure the co-operation of big commercial people; but he seems have a down on people like Werhner, Beit because they are Jews."[210] Hutton told the BCGA, "our instructions now are to get £1,000,000 out of Lloyd George [then Chancellor of the Exchequer]" to pay for irrigation works. Anti-Semitism aside, the Foreign Office staff who managed Sudan were rather hostile to capitalist investment, believing that sudden economic change would upset their system of "indirect rule."[211] For several decades, they restricted economic activity in the hopes of preserving traditional elites as political allies.

Other British officials had their own reasons for supporting the Gezira scheme. Sir Reginald Wingate, who succeeded Kitchener as governor-general of Sudan in 1899, was eager to "free" Sudan from Egyptian control and came to see Gezira as the fastest way of severing Sudan's fiscal ties to Cairo. Kitchener had replaced Lord Cromer as consul general in Egypt, but he was unwilling to publically support a scheme that would undoubtedly provoke Egyptian nationalists. Many Egyptians wanted to retain control of Sudan as a colony, and they feared irrigation works that might allow an independent Sudan to control the Nile's waters. Kitchener and Wingate were also unable to secure financing for the Gezira irrigation works through the usual colonial channels because of Sudan's awkward status as an Anglo-Egyptian condominium (hence Foreign Office rather than Colonial Office oversight in Sudan).[212] Parliament had to approve a special funding bill, and the BCGA struggled between 1911 and 1912 to get this bill passed.[213] By 1913 Kitchener finally stepped in, and claimed most of the credit for the passage of the Gezira loan guarantee.[214]

The Gezira episode revealed how far Hutton—and, by extension, the BCGA—had moved from his laissez-faire roots. The SPS had a government-backed monopoly on cotton sales from Gezira, and relied on government force to secure land for the project. When Hutton heard about resistance among some Sudanese landowners to the project, he remarked, "It is a great pity when the Government conquered the country that they did not declare all land Government property by right of conquest; it certainly would have saved complications in dealing with the irrigation of the Gezira."[215] Ten years of disappointment with African cotton growing had transformed Hutton from a man who condemned colonial wars and landgrabs as grave injustices to a man who wholeheartedly supported imperial conquest. State power transformed free farmers into tenants at Zeidab, Tayiba, and then across the Gezira plain, much to Hutton's satisfaction. Gezira was a model farm in which Africans had no choice but to play the role of apprentice farmers, using the seeds and techniques prescribed by British experts. A correspondent of Hutton enthusiastically commented on the possibilities for social engineering, arguing that "several Taiebas should now be started to train up a race of cultivators. The Arab [*sic*] is by nature avaricious and when he sees there is money in it and has [been forced] to working himself without slaves he will make a good worker."[216] Historian Victoria Bernal has argued Gezira was ultimately about power as much as it was about cotton: "The colonial order imposed by the schemes was about disciplining a rural population to accept not only the rigors of irrigated cotton production, but also British authority."[217] As the scheme matured, Gezira featured schools, hospitals, and other services alongside commercial agricultural, creating a model society of dependent commodity producers.

The First World War delayed construction of the irrigation works, but the colonial administration embraced the project with unusual energy after the war. They boasted that the state's partnership with the SPS avoided "the danger of rapacious 'land-lordism,'" and that the benefits of the tenancy system soothed landowners' "sense of grievance at the compulsory renting of their land."[218] Once in operation, the Syndicate distributed 40 percent of profits to tenants and returned another 35 (later 40) percent to the state for infrastructure costs. Gezira was praised in the West an example of enlightened colonial development; one visitor beamed that the scheme kept natives "on the land without any suspicion of exploitation."[219]

In Gezira, market forces had been supplanted by monopoly capital, government power, and scientific management. The SPS monopolized the entire cotton crop on grounds "that the population at Gezira was too sparse and too inexperienced in dealing with the international market" to manage production and export operations themselves.[220] Hutton argued that the SPS "would have a lien on the crop through making advances to the tenants," chaining labor to the land through crop liens and loans.[221] Farmers were utterly dependent on the syndicate for agricultural inputs, and they had no choice but to follow the syndicate's rules. As had been the case in northern Nigeria, many workers on the new cotton farms were slaves or former slaves, bound by custom, debt, and social ties to local elites and limited by colonial vagrancy ordinances and land controls.[222]

British writing on "empire cotton" took on a new tone after Gezira, embracing the coercive and explicitly racist models that Germany had pioneered. An anonymous account of the early years of Gezira is revealing: instead of the using prewar rhetoric of "economic men" and proper incentives, the author described the Sudanese as "wasters" and "hardened sinners," complaining about the "inveterate idleness" of tenants. "Some of them seem to forget entirely that the more they pick the bigger their profits will be, and have to be driven daily to bring in more [cotton]." The racial dynamic of the American plantation system was reborn, complete with white overseers on horseback shouting abuse at black workers. A more generous account from the following year still portrayed the Sudanese as "a most exasperating race of people from whom to extract work!"[223]

Figure 3.4. Bernard Linott, "A Sudan Cotton Field," Empire Marketing Board poster, 1927–33. Reproduced by permission from the National Archives of the United Kingdom.

French essayist Odette Keun, who also wrote about the Tennessee Valley Authority and development projects in the Soviet Union, repeated British propaganda about Gezira almost verbatim in her 1930 book on Sudan. "Not even a Bolshevik could say that by taking over Sudan in 1898 England made an enviable haul," Keun wrote, trying to establish that Sudan was a wasteland without civilization or history. For Keun, Gezira was "the latest thing in European exploitation, and it is the best." Instead of seizing land for European plantations, the SPS had given the Sudanese "seed, water, technical supervision, and yet left him his own master." Coercion was "indispensable; it ensures the complete cultivation and the good husbandry of the irrigated area, for, abandoned to himself, the native would certainly never have succeeded."[224] Imperial propagandists celebrated the Gezira scheme for decades, holding it up as a success for cotton growing and planned colonial development in the midst of many failures. A 1933 poster commissioned by the Empire Marketing Board depicted African men harvesting cotton in a scene reminiscent of postcard photos of the American South; only the clothing and structures in the background suggest that the scene had been transposed to a new continent (see fig. 3.4).[225]

The Gezira project even inspired an American adventure novel, in which a witty black manservant named "Old Reliable" and his white friend ramble through Sudan and visit a fictional Gezira plantation.

"Old Reliable" confirmed racial stereotypes while also highlighting the disciplined nature of agriculture in Gezira. He explained that African Americans would never work on Gezira because planting, chopping, and picking cotton were constant tasks under the SPS: "Dis work comes too stiddy an' reg'lar. Back home . . . a nigger breaks up his lan' den he rests a while." "Old Reliable" endorsed the idea that colonial authorities had to impose order on Africa, quipping that African Americans immigrants would "be runnin' naked in de woods," as the natives supposedly did before the Gezira project opened.[226]

The Tuskegee experts who crossed the Atlantic with Leigh Hunt hoped to use science and technology to revolutionize agriculture in Sudan. But instead of replacing the old American cotton system with a new, enlightened model in Africa, the Gezira project reproduced the structures of racial hierarchy, agrarian poverty, and dependency that plagued the South. Hutton saw this as a great success, and hoped to create new projects like Gezira across Africa. In his testimony before the wartime Empire Cotton Committee, he disavowed wage-labor plantations, citing his own experience of failure. Sharecropping put "the cultivator so much at the mercy of the land-owner," but Hutton believed that the Gezira system offered an ideal solution. Labor, capital, and government would work harmoniously to produce cotton in a scientific and economical manner.[227]

During the boom years of the 1920s, irrigated cotton in Sudan did succeed. The introduction of cash quickly monetized the local barter economy. Consumption of luxuries like coffee, tea, and sugar increased, and increases in meat consumption and the use of better building materials marked a general improvement in standards of living among those fortunate enough to get a tenancy in the scheme.[228] Tenants often fell into a debt trap, however, and the intensive irrigation of the region created a breeding ground for crop pests and human diseases.[229]

The End of "Semiphilanthropic" Development in Africa

A layman surveying cotton exports from British Africa in the 1920s would have noticed several bright spots. Ugandan farmers, who had not exported a single bale of cotton in 1903, exported nearly 200,000 bales annually by 1925. Sudanese exports grew prodigiously after irrigation at Gezira began, rising to more than 160,000 bales by the late 1920s. While Nigeria was not the new American South the BCGA claimed it would be, farmers there sent more than 50,000 bales abroad in 1926.[230] One might be tempted to conclude that despite early setbacks, the BCGA's private-sector development model was successful in bringing a new staple industry to Britain's African colonies.

Such a claim fails on two points. First, the BCGA did not meet its goal of providing Lancashire with a significant supply of American cotton from the empire. British Africa never became a replacement for the American South. In 1927, for instance, British Africa and the West Indies combined met just over 6 percent of Britain's cotton needs, and two-thirds of that came from Sudan. Most of that cotton was also extra-long staple *G. barbadense* rather than *G. hirsutum*. Some scholars have put a positive spin on these figures, arguing that the fine-spinning sector in Lancashire benefited from "special stimuli" like the Gezira project, which "must have lowered the price of fine cotton, at least a little."[231] This would have been little consolation to the Oldham spinners who had founded the BCGA. While finespinning and extra-long staple cotton were crucial to the tenacious survival of Lancashire's cotton industry through the mid-twentieth century, the fact remains that the BCGA failed to provide Lancashire with the American cotton that most of its factories relied on. The American-spinning sector was just as vulnerable to wild swings in the price of American cotton in the 1920s as it had been during the Sully corner two decades earlier.

The second point is that the two biggest cotton-growing successes in British Africa, Sudan and Uganda, had little to do with the BCGA directly. In Sudan, the BCGA was merely a shareholder and a promoter in a larger capitalist and government enterprise. The Tuskegee experts hired by Leigh Hunt proved the viability of irrigated cotton cultivation in the region, and the SPS provided the management and capital to expand operations into the Gezira plain. BCGA lobbying was an important, but not sufficient, factor in the government's decision to sign the loan guarantee for irrigating the Gezira project. In Uganda, the BCGA worked against the local cotton industry. Hutton sent very little money to the colony to support research, and the gins the BCGA erected were not suitable for the long-staple cotton being grown by peasant farmers. Hutton clashed with agricultural officials and pursued a hostile policy toward rival ginners in Uganda, trying to stifle competition through government regulation and monopoly privileges for the association.

After failed attempts at plantation agriculture in southern Nigeria, the BCGA fell back on smallholder production, but its efforts to integrate African producers into the world economy as cotton producers were fraught with contradiction. The association's mission was to deliver large quantities of cheap cotton to Lancashire, but as the merchant John Holt observed, paying low prices for cotton was not conducive to the expansion of cultivation. "Cheapening will not help that operation," he noted. "Dearness would be more likely to give the desired result."[232] Having grossly underestimated the prices at which cotton would appeal to African producers, the BCGA tried to get producers to grow more of it, searching for solutions in the intensification of labor and technical means like seeds, plows, insecticides, and expert supervision. BCGA experts ultimately had little to teach Africans about cotton, but the many rules they imposed added to the labor burden of farming families.

Political and agricultural officials in the African colonies built a substantial case against the BCGA at the end of its first decade of operation. Cooperation from the Colonial Office was not to be taken for granted, and despite the insistence of BCGA spokesmen that the private sector had to lead the way in cotton growing, Hutton and other BCGA figures believed that the association simply could not work without the CO's help. As Lancashire MP David Shackleton put it, "every object that [the BCGA] had hitherto sought had been ultimately secured through the assistance of the CO."[233]

Complaints against the BCGA came from two directions. First, colonial officials felt that the BCGA's special privileges and monopolies compromised state policy and made hypocrites of government leaders who had to defend a more or less laissez-faire approach to economic development in public while giving the BCGA grants, subsidies, and privileges. Second, and more importantly, officials believed that the BCGA worked incompetently, unscientifically, and against the best interests of the cotton industry and of colonial subjects.

Under Joseph Chamberlain's tenure, Colonial Office officials approved concessions like ginning monopolies and reduced rail freight, but Chamberlain's successors took a more skeptical view of the BCGA as its plans for Africa unfolded. Before the Liberal government came to power in 1906, Lyttleton tried to check Hutton's tendency to assume that the BCGA would be treated as if it were a branch of government. Lyttleton noticed that the BCGA failed to pay import duties on cotton seed and ginning equipment in the colonies, and he told the association to "make themselves acquainted with, and to adapt themselves to, the Customs requirements to which all other importers are expected to submit."[234] Later, Lyttleton's office informed Hutton that he could no longer communicate directly with Governor Lugard in Northern Nigeria. Lyttleton worried that the two were puffing up Nigeria's appeal as a cotton-producing country. Subsequent correspondence went through the CO, where officials in London could at least monitor, if not control, the two men's plans.[235]

The tenure of Lord Elgin and Winston Churchill in the Colonial Office was a high point for the BCGA, resulting in the Northern Nigerian railroad. The association showed its thanks by backing Churchill's reelection campaign in Manchester; Sir Alfred Jones even abandoned the Conservative Tariff Reform candidate, urging the city to "show its appreciation of Mr. Churchill's efforts to benefit the Cotton-Growing Association." The BCGA bought Churchill a silver dessert service as a parting gift when he took a post on the Board of Trade.[236] The next colonial secretary and undersecretary were deeply skeptical of the BCGA's work, however. J. E. B. Seely, who succeeded Churchill as colonial undersecretary, wrote a scathing memorandum in 1908 questioning the propriety of letting a for-profit business get so close to colonial policy makers. Hutton pleaded with Seely that "as the Association cannot at present be considered commercial, it seemed that it was rather premature to raise this question."[237] Officially, Seely backed down and praised the BCGA's experimental work. Hutton told the BCGA council later in 1908 that meetings at the CO "had been more satisfactory than for some time past," suggesting a fresh start after the exhausting fight for the Northern Nigerian railroad.[238]

Behind the scenes, however, the Liberal government was preparing to abandon the BCGA. Lord Crewe (who replaced Lord Elgin as colonial secretary) sent a memorandum to the prime minister in October 1908 informing him that "The Association is tending more and more to shed the not directly remunerative functions which are necessary for the encouragement and improvement of the industry, and to confine itself to the commercial and directly remunerative operations of buying and ginning the cotton. I do not consider that this development constitutes any ground of complaint against the Association, but its existence must be recognised."[239] The allegations in Lord Crewe's memorandum were true. The BCGA abandoned research work across Africa after about 1907, most notably in southern Nigeria, where the association's one-thousand-acre research station at Ibadan was turned over to the new government agricultural department in 1910 "in a very neglected condition."[240] Hutton slashed research spending, committing the association's limited resources to buying, ginning, and marketing the cotton that was already being grown in Africa. The failure to deliver large amounts of cotton to Lancashire and Lancashire's disinterest in funding the BCGA forced Hutton to retrench.

When Hutton approached Seely about altering the BCGA's charter to extend the seven-year abstention from dividend payments, Seely firmly told him that the BCGA's semiphilanthropic days were over. The association had to choose between agricultural research and commercial cotton buying. Hutton argued that he would have to "concentrate attention solely on those districts where there is a reasonable prospect of making profits," breaking promises made to farmers across the continent. Seely replied that "when the seven years have expired it would be better for the Association to become a purely business concern."[241] This was a return to sound Liberal policy, reflecting growing impatience with the BCGA's demands and disappointment with its lackluster achievements.

Colonial officials were also unhappy with the tendency of BCGA spokesmen to making extravagant promises that they were unable to deliver on, especially regarding Lugard's Northern Nigeria colony. During his tour of Nigeria, journalist E. D. Morel heard complaints about misleading BCGA propaganda and its deleterious effect on public opinion toward the colony. Morel insisted that CO officers were "without exception deeply interested in and anxious to assist in every way the effort to build up an export industry in cotton, and fully persuaded of the great importance and value of the work of the Association."[242] An influential officer in Northern Nigeria called cotton "promising," while another remarked that cotton was "going to be a big feature in the coming prosperity."[243] The problem was that the BCGA talked about Nigeria as "a cotton-growing country *par excellence.*" Such talk, Morel thought, "either now or potentially, is absurd. . . . To talk of Nigeria supplying the whole requirements of Great Britain (to say nothing of the promised surplus) is tantamount to saying that some day 'Pleasant Sunday Afternoon' excursions to the moon will be a regular feature of the national life." "These extravagances," Morel wrote, "have not helped the Association."[244] As late as 1916, the BCGA was still promising "that Nigeria will be able to produce the millions of bales that Lancashire requires."[245] The BCGA embarrassed colonial administrations by promising economic returns to Lancashire and Great Britain that the colonies could not possibly provide.

M. H. D. Beresford, acting governor of Northern Nigeria, opened the revolt against the BCGA in 1908 with a vicious report. Plantations and peasant production alike, he wrote,

> have not in my opinion proved to be a success. The history of this failure can be summed up as follows. The Association at the outset appeared to have been impressed with the idea that the cotton grown in Northern Nigeria could be vastly improved by importing Egyptian, Sea Island, or American Upland seeds. I think that this was a fundamental error, as it has proved to be in other countries. It would have been preferable to have instituted the earlier experiments with the native seed. . . . American experts were obtained, who, having little knowledge either of the country, its people, or their language, practically effected nothing.[246]

In the Southern Nigeria administration, Lieutenant Governor Thorburn said he "would be glad to see all connection between the B.C.G.A. (now that it is becoming a purely commercial concern) and the Government terminated."[247] C. A. B. Birstwistle, the commercial intelligence officer for Nigeria, agreed, and recommended that the government end all cooperation with the BCGA. "Far greater influence can be exercised by Government over natives in promising growing districts than by any private company or Association," he argued.[248] N. C. McLeod, the conservator of forests for Lagos, also thought the BCGA model had been an unmitigated failure. He wrote, "I am strongly of opinion that cotton cultivation in Southern Nigeria should be fostered by the Agricultural Department and that the B.C.G.A. should cease to have anything to do with this."[249]

P. H. Lamb was even more direct in his criticism. In a lengthy letter to Lugard, Lamb laid out his practical, political, and moral objections to BCGA policies. (Lugard mailed the report straight to Hutton. The BCGA copy is marked in Lugard's hand, "my only copy.") Drawing on his experience in Uganda and Nigeria, Lamb accused BCGA agents of "touring in agricultural districts . . . with the object of giving so called 'advice' not only to Political Officers but also direct to natives." These experts were "not for the most part highly qualified in agricultural matters." Lamb thought bad advice was worse than no advice at all, and maintained "that their giving official or semi-official advice on agricultural matters is a danger to the community." Lamb viewed "these semi-official peripatetic agents of the Association with as much apprehension as would be aroused in the Political staff were an association of lawyers to send their emissaries touring the country advising the Native Administration to reform their methods." "The natives come to ridicule the agricultural advice which he regards as emanating from the Government," Lamb warned, suggesting that the BCGA's failures undermined the legitimacy of colonial rule. Finally, Lamb found the BCGA's very premise narrow-minded. "Their employees must be prejudiced in favour of cotton and therefore inclined to encourage its growth in localities where other crops might prove far more profitable," he argued, alleging that "the commercial development of the country along sound lines is retarded." Lamb said he "cannot conscientiously recommend [cotton growing] on soils and in localities where other crops would obviously be more profitable to the grower."[250] From Lamb's perspective, the BCGA was not only incompetent, but worked against the values of trusteeship on which the colonial project was supposedly premised.

Conclusion

The BCGA worked as a for-profit development NGO, encouraging cotton growing without directly investing in land and labor. As Hutton observed in 1911, "It sounds like a paradox, but, though we are the Cotton-growing Association, our main policy has been to avoid growing cotton. I mean, of course, that we have thought it best to assist other people to grow it rather than to lock up our capital which is none too large."[251] This model did not work in Africa, but the failure of semiphilanthropic experiment sent the wrong messages to colonial planners. For the CO, the experience of failure justified the abandonment of commercial principles altogether, leading to projects that served neither the needs of African producers or British industry, culminating in embarrassing debacles like the post-1945 Gambia egg scheme and the Tanzania groundnut scheme.[252] Colonial agricultural officials turned to even more coercive, state-led models of development. The lesson learned was not that farmers had good reasons to ignore foreign demands for commodities, but that rural communities had to be managed, regulated, and educated by a powerful state to overcome the perceived social and cultural barriers that commercial enterprise had been unable to breach. The myth of the conservative peasant survived, to be tackled again in the 1950s and 1960s by a new generation of development planners with similar results.

"Peasant conservatism" was not a serious obstacle to development, though contemporaries and later development theorists believed it was the most important check on economic change. During his tours of West Africa, Himbury preached a gospel of wealth to would-be cotton farmers, and he found enthusiastic responses. At a village near Oyo, he "spoke strongly and told them men were sent into the world to improve themselves not just to live the life of the ordinary animal, and that if they planted cotton they would get a good price for it, and so be able to purchase more of life's comforts."[253] Himbury later remarked that his work "might be likened to a messenger from Mars advising British farmers to grow nothing but tulips. I wonder how many farmers would take this advice?"[254] He praised the "breadth of mind" exhibited by Africans who did take up export production of cotton, and he argued that an economic revolution had indeed been launched, despite its modest scale.

Across Africa, farmers adopted cotton growing where it was profitable and where it fit with the needs of local communities. Thomas Bassett showed that in Côte d'Ivoire, peasant communities in the second half of the twentieth century embraced a cost-effective development "package" of seeds, fertilizers, tools, techniques, and pesticides that offered high yields and good returns on cotton. The key was giving farmers a say in the formulation of agricultural policy, tailoring it to meet the needs of producers. There was nothing inimical to experimentation and progressive development in either the cotton plant or African peasantries. Farmers could and did transform centuries-old farming practices when "the opportunities and relative security offered by the cotton program" outweighed the usual "risks and uncertainties" of rural life.[255]

4

"King Cotton's Impoverished Retinue"

Making Cotton a "White Man's Crop" in the American South

American cotton-planters, proprietors of the greatest gold-producing staple in the world, are poor. They are practically in servitude. It is a tragedy of contemporary life that they who produce for the world the commodity without which modern civilization and industrial life could not proceed are themselves absolutely subservient and the poorest paid toilers in the United States.

—Daniel J. Sully

Daniel J. Sully presented this assessment of the Southern cotton industry in "King Cotton's Impoverished Retinue," the first of a three-part series for *Cosmopolitan* magazine in which the ruined cotton king called for revolutionary change in the growing and marketing of cotton. Sully added his voice to those of thousands of American farmers who were inspired by the cotton corners to push for higher cotton prices. Sully's own contribution to the South was ephemeral, but Southerners rallied around cotton as a symbol of economic oppression as well as economic opportunity. "Cotton populists" rekindled the agrarian political movement of the late nineteenth century, staging a revolt against their peripheral position in the global cotton textile industry. While they wanted to make more money from primary commodity production, they also sought to break the boom-and-bust cycle that the Sully corner exemplified.

Ellison D. Smith (better known as "Cotton Ed" Smith during his long career in the US Senate) argued in 1907 that the time had come for American farmers to earn a respectable income from cotton. The world had been transformed by technology, he observed:

Eighty years ago your grandfathers and mine never heard a steam whistle, they never heard a telephone bell, they never heard the click of a telegraph instrument; they never saw a machine that could print and fold and put on the markets of the world 10,000 copies hourly of a great daily that through the rural free delivery could be spread over an immense area in twenty-four hours. These are the forces that are spreading to the various districts of the earth and making the man in the backwoods as cosmopolitan as the man that walks the street, and keeps him in vital touch with the trend of the market.

Armed with information and access to markets, Smith claimed, "the toiler of the world is beginning to get an equal chance on the fighting line of life."[1] This narrative of progress would resonate with contemporary advocates of globalization, who argue that access to world markets and price information will empower entrepreneurs and stimulate economic development. But for Cotton Ed, development was not supposed to emancipate all of America's downtrodden farmers: he successfully campaigned for a seat in Congress by promising to "keep the negro down and cotton [prices] up." For Cotton Ed and the white farmers who organized in groups like the National Farmers' Union (NFU) and Southern Cotton Association (SCA) in the early twentieth century, cotton was destined to become a "white man's crop." There was no room in Cotton Ed's vision for African American farmers, and the idea that Africa itself would someday compete for America's share of the world cotton crop was laughable to most white Southerners.

Few outside of America recognized that white farmers and white labor were becoming increasingly important in the American cotton industry. According to Southern nationalists, the world had "overestimated the negro's importance as a factor in cotton-growing," due in part to the "picturesque" scene of "the black negro in the white cotton field" that dominated illustrations and photos of cotton in contemporary publications, postcards, and tourist photos.[2] As one American complained, the average European thought the South was "a land of swamps and alligators in which colored people do the only manual work."[3] By 1900, 60 percent of cotton farms and 66 percent of all cotton land were operated by white farmers, including "hundreds of thousands of small white farmers with their families who make cotton from planting to picking almost or entirely without negro labor."[4] Southern populists and their supporters, like Sully, insisted that American cotton was already in the hands of white farmers. They predicted that the role of white labor would necessarily grow as black workers moved to the cities and the North, and as the cotton frontier moved into the American Southwest. Most white cotton farmers viewed European efforts to grow cotton in Africa with amusement.

For African Americans in the South, the cotton-growing programs in Africa posed a challenge. They too tried to join the wave of "cotton populism," seeking higher earnings from cotton agriculture. Black farmers attended educational seminars and adopted new farming techniques intended to boost crop yields and end their dependency on cotton monoculture. Black farmers were systematically denied access to the cooperative tools white farmers were developing to increase the profitability of cotton agriculture, however. Unlike their white counterparts, some black Americans saw cotton growing in Africa as an inspiring movement rather than a threat to their livelihoods. For decades, Southern blacks had experimented with emigrationist and pan-African ideas, seeing Africa as a place of freedom for black peoples. The BCGA and other colonial cotton groups helped rekindle these ideas in the South. The *Textile Mercury*, which represented Lancashire's manufacturers, argued that a "new Exodus" was imminent: "Lancashire wants cotton; here are people [in America] who know how to grow it; the British colonies, dependencies and protectorates comprise ample lands for their location, and the reward is a grand one."[5] While little came of schemes like Leigh Hunt's plan to relocate black farmers to Sudan, the African American press followed colonial cotton projects and the exploits of scientists like John Wesley Hoffman with great interest. The message for African Americans was ambivalent, however. Reports from Africa proved that African peoples had a history and were not the "savages" of the colonial imagination, but many African Americans also accepted the idea of a colonial "civilizing mission." Black leaders like Hoffman and Booker T. Washington were eager to demonstrate the relative progress the African diaspora had achieved in America by bringing agricultural science to Africa itself.

Black scientists and educators worked to improve the lives of black cotton farmers in the South with new crops and cultivation methods, but white farmers won the real prize in the early twentieth century. Through their populist organizations and their representatives in Congress, white cotton farmers secured a range of subsidies and privileges that few black farmers were able to enjoy. White farmers used economic discrimination and outright terrorism to discourage the upward mobility of their black compatriots. The new partnership between wealthy and middle-income white farmers and the federal government later blossomed during the New Deal of the 1930s. The arrival of the first practical cotton harvesting machine in the 1940s sounded a death knell for the South's smallholders and sharecroppers, black or white. By the late twentieth century, cotton was a tightly regulated, heavily subsidized, and highly mechanized crop for the middle-class, white American farmer. The dream of cotton as a clear path toward economic success for workers in Africa and the African diaspora was abandoned.

Populism Reborn

American populism, especially in its Southern forms, has not fared well in recent historical thought. While mid-twentieth century historians like C. Vann Woodward argued that populism represented a vital strand of agrarian democracy, historians have since emphasized the movement's ugly stances on questions of race and class.[6] The blatant racism of Southern populism, along with the habit of using William Jennings Bryan's 1896 electoral defeat as the endpoint for studies of populism, have led many writers to dismiss or overlook the "cotton populists" of the early twentieth century. Populism was indeed broken as a national political force by 1900, but its socioeconomic critique, as political scientist Elizabeth Sanders has argued, survived and formed the core of Progressive-era agrarian reform in the United States.[7]

This chapter argues that white cotton farmers were central to those reforms, and that they framed their case for federal intervention in racial terms, as well as on a global scale. Southerners like "Cotton Ed" Smith argued that the average white farming family was "living upon a margin that is really not an enticing figure for the lowest negro laborer in the South." They pleaded with the world's manufacturers to not "drag the Southern cotton planter to the Indian level" by demanding cheap raw cotton.[8] Cotton populists were actively engaged with Lancashire and Europe, and they were well aware of the challenge the BCGA and other colonial cotton groups posed to the South. Their policies were formulated in an economic space defined by the world of cotton, rather than political borders.

Southern farmers began to organize around the issue of low cotton prices before Sully's corner. In 1900, a wealthy Georgia planter named Harvie Jordan formed the Southern (sometimes Georgia) Cotton Growers' Protective Association (SCGPA). Little more than a "letter-head organization," Jordan used the SCGPA to publish newsletters and pamphlets decrying low cotton prices; he urged farmers to organize but lacked any concrete plan of action or membership base.[9] Membership was not limited to farmers but included ginners, bankers, merchants, and "Every man who is willing to put his shoulder to the wheel and help in the work." This did not include black men; the bylaws limited membership to "white persons." Dues were fixed high enough at $50 to $100 per county chapter to discourage membership among the poorer class of white farmers and laborers as well.

Jordan's rhetoric followed the conventions of American populism, calling on farmers to "Help break the shackles which have bound the Southern farmer to Wall Street and Liverpool gamblers." He urged farmers to "Become freemen pricing your own money product at a fair and just value." For Jordan, the explanation of low cotton prices was not to be found in the laws of supply and demand, but rather in futures trading and the "false estimates gotten up by such men as Neil [one of many cotton brokers who issued crop estimates] for speculative purposes and to depress prices."[10] Jordan was one of the first to notice that spinning mills would rapidly exhaust the small 1900–1901 crop, leaving no surplus to hold cotton prices down in the next season. "There is no reason why the next crop, even if twelve million bales be harvested, should not sell for nine cents before it leaves the producers' hands," he predicted. Alluding to the victory of the populist Farmers' Alliance over the jute bagging trust a decade earlier, Jordan called for organized resistance against the "unjust oppression on the part of those with whom the cotton growers of the south have to deal."[11] Jordan's plan was to gather accurate crop information and to encourage farmers to store cotton instead of flooding the market at harvest time; he secured promises from Georgia bankers to help finance the withholding movement.[12]

No records of SCGPA membership are available, and it appears that Jordan's group was not very influential. In the Texas cotton belt, however, veterans of past populist movements seized on the rising prices of 1902 to launch their own organization—the National Farmers' Educational and Cooperative Union (today the National Farmers' Union, NFU). A poor cotton farmer and occasional journalist named Newton Gresham started the group. Raised in a tenant farming family in the aftermath of the Civil War, Gresham had been active in the Grange and other movements of the first Populist wave. According to the official NFU history, Gresham "was sitting on a log one day at a cross roads country store and observed the few woebegone and debt depressed farmers who came and went." Like "Mahomet," Gresham was inspired to preach a new populist crusade.[13] The NFU later became an important partner of New Deal agricultural programs in the 1930s, and in the second half of the century it voiced the domestic and international concerns of America's shrinking class of farm families.[14] The formation of the NFU was a direct response to the growing prominence of speculators in the cotton exchanges. Sully's corner raised awareness of the importance of cotton futures and speculation in the industry, but it also gave farmers hope that demand had truly outrun supply, giving farmers the upper hand at last.[15]

Like the SCA, the NFU was a white man's organization, although membership was open to "Indian[s] of industrious habits" as a concession to farmers in Oklahoma. Unlike Jordan's organization, an NFU member had to be "a farmer, farm laborer, rural mechanic, rural school teacher, physician or minister of the gospel." Merchants, bankers and all who belonged "to any trust or combine for the purpose of speculating in agricultural products of the necessities of life" were barred from membership.[16] As Sully and other brokers battled on the cotton exchanges, NFU membership skyrocketed from three thousand members to a hundred fifty thousand by 1904.[17] Sully fired Southern interest in the problems of cotton production and marketing by distributing leaflets and publishing notices in Southern papers urging farmers to hold their cotton back from the market. Southerners made the "great discovery" that "the price of cotton was not the remote, inevitable grinding of the law of Supply and Demand, as they had always supposed, but a mere man-made affair."[18] NFU members were attracted by the rhetoric of a war with Wall Street, but they were also drawn by more base interests: NFU branches were secret fraternities, with secret initiation rituals and oaths. The $1 membership fee "was worth the cost to find out what the secrets were for." The Ku Klux Klan used similar methods to recruit, but the KKK "charged more to see the show."[19]

As the New York *Chronicle* noted, the "Sully clique" succeed "partly because the total supply was actually very limited, but chiefly because producers of cotton were themselves participating in the campaign for higher prices, and therefore holding back their product."[20] Cotton farmers "walked around as though they were treading on air" after selling their crops in the 1903–4 season.[21] The price collapse after Sully's failure in March 1904 came as a shock to farmers. Cotton fell from a high of 17¢ in March to 7¢ in December. Hopes for a late recovery for the 1904–5 season were dashed by a Census Bureau report showing that almost twelve million bales had been ginned. Southern newspapers attacked the report as a fraud, but it soon became clear that the Bureau had actually underestimated the crop. Tempted by high prices during the Sully corner, farmers had ignored pleas to restrict plantings and had increased cotton acreage by nearly 12 percent. Meanwhile, the yield per acre was exceptionally high, thanks to good weather conditions. The final tally for the 1904–5 crop was a record-setting 13.5 million bales.

The ginning report was released one day before a coalition of farmers' groups met in Shreveport to discuss the growing boll weevil infestation. The Census report turned the Shreveport meeting into an anxious debate on the future of cotton in the South. The Georgia delegation, led by Harvie Jordan, proposed that cotton be banned from Texas to stop the spread of the boll weevil; this would also effect a dramatic reduction in the American cotton crop. Jordan called for the immediate organization of farmers across the South, repeating typical populist claims that a "farmers' trust" was needed to battle the phalanx of financial and industrial interests arrayed against them.[22] The conference adjourned with the creation of the short-lived National Cotton Association, having raised more issues than it resolved.[23]

In the cotton belt, unsatisfied farmers sought more radical remedies. Farmers in Alabama proposed to burn the "surplus" cotton (identified as one and then two million bales), and offered to sacrifice the first fifty bales if other towns agreed to participate.[24] The South Carolina Cotton Growers' Union quickly picked up the idea, promising to burn thousands of bales. Farmers in Georgia were the first to burn cotton, having "rolled 3,000 bales of cotton into the Court House square, marched around the huge pile singing hymns, and then set the cotton on fire" on December 28, 1904.[25] Newspapers across the country accused the Georgians of insanity. "IDIOTS TO BURN COTTON," cried the Fort Worth *Telegram*, summarizing North Carolina Sen. Benjamin Tillman's take on the matter. The New York *Tribune* called it "a scheme of folly and wickedness." An enterprising distillery placed an advertisement in the Atlanta *Constitution* telling farmers, "DO NOT BURN YOUR COTTON," while offering to buy one hundred thousand bales at 7.5¢ a pound, paid in whiskey.[26] Only a few papers praised the "burning frenzy," calling it "the cotton-raisers' only means of self defense."[27]

As the crisis developed, some skeptics claimed that only "a little old measly bale of 'dog tail' that was about to prove a drag on the market" had been destroyed.[28] As it became clear that nothing near three thousand bales had been burned, some papers reported that the affair was a hoax. On December 31, farmers in two Georgia towns responded by burning more cotton, while in Alabama, a cotton bonfire was "made a gala affair."[29] In Oklahoma, farmers "grew tired of being joked at and treated a village to a huge bonfire" of sixty bales. An NFU meeting in Ryan, Texas, agreed to burn cotton, while the farmers of Brason threatened to destroy a bale every week that passed without an improved price.[30] The fires were hastily extinguished in January when insurance companies raised warehouse rates and cancelled policies in counties affected by the demonstrations.[31]

Jordan used the crop-burning phenomenon to call for a new convention at New Orleans. More than thirty-five hundred representatives from across the South arrived to discuss cotton stockpiles, crop reductions, and financial issues. Backed by fiery orators like Georgia politician Tom Watson, Jordan forged a new group—the Southern Cotton Association—out of the regional organizations represented at the convention. Watson singled out New York broker Theodore Price for special abuse, calling him "the cold-blooded, cruel-hearted and utterly unscrupulous gambler, who is now exploiting the misery of the Southern people." (Price responded with a full-page ad in the local newspaper telling the farmers, "I am short cotton; I believe cotton will decline. . . . It makes no difference in price who holds the surplus, whether farmer, speculator, or spinner.") Watson called trusts "an invention of the devil," but citing the power of the coffee, coal, meat, and oil trusts, he urged farmers to "fight the devil with fire" by forming a cotton farmers' trust.[32]

Lancashire and the BCGA in the South

New York speculators were not the only people watching the activities of Southern cotton farmers. In Lancashire, cotton spinners openly expressed their fears that the American farmers were planting "the seeds of a gigantic cotton trust." "It is not realized in England to what an extent the American mind is attracted by the trust principle," they warned.[33] Americans had been following Lancashire's activities, too. While some, like J. W. Hoffman or Leigh Hunt, were enthusiastic about transferring American cotton—and African American farmers—to Africa, most Americans were skeptical of Lancashire's colonial cotton-growing project. Cotton expert Alfred Shepperson acknowledged that it was possible to grow cotton around the world, but he argued that no place could compete with the American South on the world market. According to Shepperson, the BCGA was "chasing rainbows" and showed "an amazing ignorance of the nature of the cotton plant and the proper methods of its cultivation."[34] Daniel J. Sully dismissed the BCGA as well, telling Southern farmers that their monopoly was unassailable.[35] The *Manufacturers' Record* alleged that "in every comparison made between a white county and a black one the black was the most fertile soil naturally, yet the white was nearly twice as productive" because white labor (allegedly) worked harder and with better tools and techniques. According to Southern nationalists, there was no reason to expect that Africans would do any better than African Americans.[36] One columnist used ugly stereotypes to mock the BCGA's mission:

> Our British friends consider the idea of making themselves independent of us by growing cotton in Africa at a dollar a pound. . . . There is something amusing in the suggestion of inducing the wild and wooly citizen of far Africa who wears no clothes, and whose article of diet consists of a fellow-citizen of the opposing faction served in various ways, to engage in cotton cultivation. Possibly the zebra of that country will be broken to draw the plow about the time the native biped is taught to guide it.[37]

An American who claimed to have briefly worked as a BCGA expert in Rhodesia offered an especially negative account, reporting that the African cotton industry was hampered by "a lack of transportation facilities and machinery, the unreliability of native labor and the unhealthiness of the climate for Europeans and Americans."[38]

For Southern farmers the very existence of the BCGA suggested that Lancashire was in a desperate position, proving the South's monopoly on cotton. The *Manufacturers' Record* argued that the cotton-growing association's money would be best spent in "the region unexcelled for that purpose—the South." The Southern states needed only "fair prices" and "the steady increase in white population" to continue expanding the cotton frontier westward.[39] Americans assured European manufactures that "they need have no anxiety about their future supplies, and that, if a fair and remunerative price is paid, America will grow all the cotton that the world needs."[40]

To the BCGA's dismay, Lancashire's cotton spinners took an interest in improving, rather than replacing, the American cotton supply. Sir Charles Macara and other Lancashire businessmen formed a "Lancashire Private Cotton Investigation Committee" in 1905 to negotiate with the SCA and NFU and to ascertain the true condition of America's cotton-growing industry. In 1906 the commission traveled over seven thousand miles across the United States, talking to farmers, ginners, brokers, and experts in a range of related areas.[41] Jordan and an NFU representative traveled to Vienna to address the International Cotton Federation in 1907, and Jordan invited Macara and other spinners to visit America later that year for what would be the Second International (or World) Cotton Congress in Atlanta. (A 1906 meeting between farmers and the Lancashire Private Commission was retroactively named the first congress.) Macara accepted the invitation, and planned a two-week, forty-six-hundred-mile tour of North America for his fellow cotton manufacturers, who paid an all-inclusive fee of £100 to join the expedition. The majority of the delegates were British cotton spinners, but German, Austrian, French, Belgian, Spanish, and Portuguese manufacturers also participated.

Strategies of Reform

Although some of the strategies pursued by the cotton populists were nationalist and protectionist, farmers and spinners found many points on which they agreed during the 1906 and 1907 conferences. Both sides initially claimed to be the injured party, each insisting that the other was making exceptional profits. At the 1906 meeting, the Americans offered to "show our hand down south open and broad and tell you within a farthing of what it costs to make cotton," but only when "we can ask [Lancashire] the cost of manufacturing and when we can ask you why it is, and have you explain it properly." When Harvie Jordan asserted that cotton had not been worthwhile to grow since the Civil War, English spinner H. W. MacAlister went on the attack. "No man will produce an article if it does not pay to produce it," he retorted.[42]

The SCA and NFU invited spinners to join a cartel, hoping to place cotton prices as high as the market would bear. E. D. Smith asked the spinners to share "a mutual profit and fix a stable price," but he warned, "If you disregard this plea we will use the financier and form ourselves into an organisation for simple self protection and then you will have to look out for your interests on the other side."[43] The Lancashire men insisted that textile-manufacturing profits were slender, and warned farmers that a fixed price would "be putting a bonus on mediocrity and slovenly methods."[44] (The BCGA should have taken note.)

Farmers and spinners both saw warehousing as a way of stabilizing cotton prices. Farmers hoped to hold back "surplus" cotton to keep prices high, while spinners wanted to regulate the supply to avoid sudden changes in prices. The SCA and NFU both believed that they could eliminate middlemen by selling direct to spinners from well-regulated and insured warehouses. During the 1880s and 1890s, the Farmer's Alliance had built warehouses and successfully marketed crops to Lancashire spinners; even smaller groups like the Mississippi Grange "had an agent in Liverpool, England, to handle consignments of cotton."[45] The NFU revived these plans in 1905 with launch of the Farmers' Union Cotton Company, which consisted of farmer-owned cooperative warehouses backed by local bankers. Members were supposed to hold their cotton at the warehouses for secret minimum prices, relying on fraternal ties for enforcement. After some financial troubles, the venture began taking cotton for a flat fee of 50¢ per bale, selling the cotton through sales offices in Liverpool and Manchester. Farmers received advances on cotton shipped to the central Memphis warehouse for sale in England, and the NFU issued receipts for cotton in outlying warehouses to help farmers secure credit from local banks.[46] The NFU and some individual farmers shipped cotton to the Manchester-based Cotton Buying Company, but no details of the arrangement survive.[47]

Harvie Jordan's alternative plan was to create a monopolistic warehouse company that would regulate prices by adjusting the flow of cotton out of its reserves. Opponents in Lancashire argued that low cotton prices were simply the result of economic laws that no warehouse could fix, but Jordan retorted, "Don't you think that the laws of supply and demand are violated when twelve months' supply of cotton is marketed in three or four months' time?"[48] Supporters of warehousing argued that "the laws of supply and demand would be truly operative" only when the seasonal cycle of cotton was broken.[49] Daniel Sully endorsed the warehouse proposal in 1905 and undertook a tour of the South to bolster the crop withholding and warehouse movement.[50] An alliance with New South spokesman Richard Edmonds made Sully's comeback possible; Edmonds's *Manufacturers' Record* had covered the Sully corner favorably and the paper reported widely on Sully's return from bankruptcy. Sully claimed, "I had won a skirmish or two . . . and on the 18th of March [1904] I lost a skirmish; but the cause is not lost." The speculator assured his supporters that he "had solemnly resolved to make the cause of the cotton growers of the South my cause, and to devote to it the energies of my life."[51] Together with Jordan,

Sully called for the abandonment of the saw gin along with improved baling, storage, and sampling methods. Sully claimed that $100 million a year
was lost through the careless treatment of cotton as it traveled from the
field to the factory.[52]

This message of agrarian reform resonated with farmers who were tired
of being told that low prices were merely the outcome of natural economic
forces. Referring to the five-cent price of 1898, Sully wrote:

> The explanation of the spinner regarding this five cent rate was that it was
> fixed by the laws of supply and demand. The Southern planter said that the
> cause of the ruinous rate was oppression. In my opinion it was neither. It was
> ignorance, ignorance on the part of the planter because he did not realize
> his impregnable position in having a monopoly of the most valuable fruit of
> the soil and because he did not assert his rights. And ignorance on the part
> of the spinners and manufacturers because they clung to the musty old idea
> that in buying their raw material at the lowest possible price and turning out
> finished products they were doing their full duty as business men.[53]

Sully called on the US government to adopt SCA proposals for "standard grades for cotton, standard dimensions for the bales, United States
bonded warehouses in which cotton may be stored, governmental bounties
to stimulate the yield for quality and quantity per acre, and bounties to
make possible a foreign trade in the products of American cotton-mills."[54]
Cotton receipts would give rural banks more liquid assets, thereby avert-
ing financial panics, Sully argued. Sully prophesied that export taxes on
cotton coupled with the reconstruction of the American merchant marine
would result in the transplantation of European mills to American soil and
American supremacy in textile exports.

Newspapers credited the propaganda work of Sully and the SCA for "the
skill displayed by planters in disposing of their product" in early 1905: the
farmers "learned that they can obtain a reasonable price for what they have
to sell if they will only study the conditions and apply the marketing of the
staple to the demand as it occurs."[55] According to one farmer interviewed
in June, "The cotton-buying districts in our towns and cities look like fall
with the wagons loaded with cotton, and the platforms of every railroad
station are lined with bales of cotton waiting to be shipped. Fully ten million dollars will be turned loose this summer for cotton carried over from
last year."[56] The victory was short-lived, however, and farmers continued to
sell most of their cotton in the autumn in subsequent years. The problem
was not a lack of warehouse facilities. While no accurate census of Southern cotton warehouses exists, a 1914 USDA survey produced an estimate
of 3,145 warehouses, capable of holding 9,344,520 flat (uncompressed) or
15,738,825 compressed bales—more than enough for the entire American
crop in most years.[57]

Cotton handling and packaging was another area where American farmers and Lancashire spinners saw a need for reform. Manufacturers received dirty and water-damaged bales, weighing anything from four hundred to six hundred pounds despite a nominal weight of five hundred pounds.[58] As British cotton expert J. A. Todd observed in 1919, "I am sorry to say that all of the work we have done in Africa, for nearly twenty years, has produced in no year one hundred thousand bales of cotton. You [Americans] are throwing away more than that every year—more than we have been able to do in twenty years."[59] Prevailing customs gave no incentives for quality in cotton handling. The ginner traditionally charged a flat fee for baling, and thus "as a matter of American business methods he will buy the cheapest, flimsiest bagging he can buy and make his profit as large as possible."[60] When farmers sold cotton outright to the ginner, they could pad their income by sending in wet, heavy cotton, which would be damaged by saw gins. "When we are skinned to death we are going to do some skinning, too," admitted E. D. Smith. "It is human nature." He said bluntly, "If a fellow is going to beat you out of $2.50 by speculation, by a drop in the market, we are going to fill the cotton with water. I might as well talk plain."[61] The BCGA avoided these problems by owning the ginneries and through agricultural legislation, but it seemed impossible to standardize quality regulations across thousands of independent American ginneries.

Entrepreneurs proposed new baling presses to better protect cotton and save weight on shipping, and Sir Charles Macara even brought BCGA bales from Africa to Atlanta in 1907 to show off the neat, tidy packages the association produced at its colonial ginneries (see fig. 4.1). American ginners opposed the new press technologies, however, and the geographical dispersion of the industry worked against modernization. Ginning had a low entry cost, with a saw gin plant costing as little as $4,000 in 1913.[62] In 1903 30,948 ginneries were active, with an average annual output of only 358 bales.[63] Consolidation in the industry was slow, and was due more to the retirement of old ginneries (some still using antebellum equipment) than to mergers and acquisitions. By 1918, only 19,259 gins were active, turning out an average of 618 bales per year.[64] New baling systems spread slowly, and the US National Cotton Association did not adopt a high density standard for bales until 1978.[65]

Despite their attempts at transatlantic cooperation, farmers and spinners could not agree on what constituted a fair price for cotton. Southerners wanted a price (10¢ or 15¢) that would ensure a comfortable income for a farming family, and many believed that they could dictate the price if farmers acted in unison. E. D. Smith declared, "It is not a questioning of cheapening the cost of the world's consumption. It is a question of getting a profit out of the world's necessity."[66] A Lancashire spinner replied that "The last user makes the price of cotton, and the last user is the man who

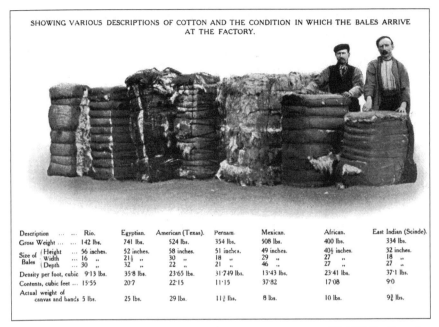

SHOWING VARIOUS DESCRIPTIONS OF COTTON AND THE CONDITION IN WHICH THE BALES ARRIVE
AT THE FACTORY.

Description	... ... Rio.	Egyptian.	American (Texas).	Pernam.	Mexican.	African.	East Indian (Scinde).
Gross Weight	142 lbs.	741 lbs.	524 lbs.	354 lbs.	508 lbs.	400 lbs.	334 lbs.
Size of Bales { Height ...	56 inches.	52 inches.	58 inches.	51 inches.	49 inches.	40½ inches.	32 inches.
Width ...	16 „	21½ „	30 „	18 „	29 „	27 „	18 „
Depth ...	30 „	32 „	22 „	21 „	46 „	27 „	27 „
Density per foot, cubic	9·13 lbs.	35·8 lbs.	23·65 lbs.	31·749 lbs.	13·43 lbs.	23·41 lbs.	37·1 lbs.
Contents, cubic feet ...	15·55	20·7	22·15	11·15	37·82	17·08	9·0
Actual weight of canvas and bands	5 lbs.	25 lbs.	29 lbs.	11⅞ lbs.	8 lbs.	10 lbs.	9¾ lbs.

Figure 4.1. Cotton bales displayed at 1907 Atlanta conference. IFMCSMA, *Second International Conference of Cotton Growers, Spinners, and Manufacturers, Held at Atlanta, Georgia, U.S.A., October 7th, 8th and 9th, 1907,* 59.

wears the shirt." "If planters hold cotton up to such a price that we can not pay for it and make a profit, we will close our mills," he said, to which one Southerner retorted, "And we will put them up in the South."[67]

One way to force Lancashire to pay more for cotton was to produce less of it, and the SCA and NFU both urged farmers to cut their cotton acreage and grow other crops. In 1905, farmers listened, cutting their plantings from more than thirty-one million acres to about twenty-seven million in the spring of 1905.[68] Walter Clark, a ginner and president of the SCA's Mississippi division, warned British and American manufacturers: "Whenever you have a surplus of goods, you curtail production, you shut down your mills. We did that last year. We had an overproduction of cotton. We curtailed production. You have taught us that."[69] Cotton farmers were effectively adopting the same short-time strategy Lancashire was using to combat high cotton prices. The effect of the 1905 campaign was short-lived, however, as the resultant high price encouraged farmers to plant five million more acres the following year. In 1908 the NFU tried again, observing that Lancashire was once again working on short time and did not have "the cotton to run on at even half time." "We have driven them to the last ditch," the NFU's president boasted, calling on farmers to plow up a tenth of the crop to drive prices higher.[70] This time crop reduction was a total failure; farmers actually cultivated a million more acres than the previous year and achieved yields 15 percent higher per acre.[71] Still, European cotton spinners took the crop-reduction movement very seriously. Swiss spinner Ernst Lang told his colleagues, "we do not consider whether [the Southern farmer] is able to live on his earnings or whether he finds it lucrative to continue cotton growing; our sole concern is to ask him to grow a sufficient supply of cotton. If he does not conform to this wish, we tell him that we shall grow cotton in new territories. . . . We need surely not be astonished if he gets tired of our attitude and answers by a counter move which might have serious consequences for us spinners."[72] Farmers continued to use the crop-reduction strategy for decades, having no other way of directly influencing commodity prices. The most dramatic demonstration was in 1932, when Gov. Huey Long of Louisiana called on the entire South to "drop a crop," taking a holiday from cotton production for an entire year.[73] Crop reduction was not an easy strategy to carry out and it rarely worked. Farmers knew that free-riding neighbors would benefit from the sacrifices of those who did participate.

Crop diversification appealed to more farmers, as it promised a de facto reduction in cotton acreage while adding new subsistence or cash crops. The NFU resolved that "in diversification lies our continued prosperity," while Harvie Jordan told farmers that "the strongest financial institution for every farmer is a well-filled corncrib and smokehouse."[74] Hoffman similarly urged black farmers to diversify and live frugally:

> He urged upon the farmers raising at home all produce needed for home consumption. . . . Reduce the acreage of cotton; if you have been planting forty acres, reduce the same to twenty, use the same amount of fertilizer, cultivate the land well, and it will yield as much cotton as forty acres poorly cultivated. Stop renting land; buy it if it is only five acres and produce your own home supply of food. Get away from the mortgage system; Live more economical; learn to save your money and not buy useless things.[75]

By 1904, farmers were celebrating the arrival of the boll weevil as "a blessing in disguise" because it forced farmers in stricken districts to diversify.[76] Seaman Knapp of the US Department of Agriculture cheerily told visiting Lancashire spinners that the boll weevil "clears out lazy farmers."[77]

For the poor farmer, growing less cotton and achieving self-sufficiency in foodstuffs promised freedom from the crop-lien merchant and higher prices for whatever cotton he could raise. "We have learned to plant potatoes and let cotton go," said one NFU farmer from Texas. "When you can get more money out of an eight million [bale] crop than a fifteen million crop, wouldn't it be wiser for us to take the eight million?" he asked.[78] As Georgia congressman L. F. Livingston put it, "We will grow our home supplies, and the rest that is planted in cotton is an absolute surplus and costs us nothing."[79] This was the inverse of what the BCGA wanted in Africa: American cotton growers wanted to become the very subsistence farmers that Europeans were trying so hard to wrench into the global commodity system in Africa.

The USDA promoted cash-crop rotations among farmers across the South.[80] Using the same "demonstration method" that inspired BCGA model farms in Africa, the USDA taught farmers how to use new tools, new methods, and new varieties of cotton and other crops. Agricultural extension work became "little short of a religion" in some parts of the South. "Proponents preached the doctrines of diversification, science, and efficiency with all the fervor of evangelists appealing to fallen sinners."[81] Agents of the USDA insisted that "A fair profit may be expected under average conditions where the crop is produced upon a cash basis and where a reasonable degree of knowledge is used in producing it."[82] Jordan was eventually won over by these arguments; as early as 1907 he promised European spinners that "the crop is bound to grow enormously, and we cannot deliver it in the old-fashioned way."[83]

The NFU was enthusiastic about agricultural education, and its original name—the Farmer's Educational and Cooperative Union—expressed the optimism of its founders that knowledge could bring wealth to farmers. "Ours is a schoolhouse organization," said a Texan member.[84] "Farmers' institutes" arranged by local farming groups and state and national agricultural agencies predated the NFU, but the group sponsored thousands more after its founding. Some eight hundred thousand farmers attended agricultural institutes in 1901–2, a number that grew to three million by 1913–14.[85] USDA lecturers taught farmers to boost crop yields dramatically in some districts and "proved that cotton could be grown in spite of the weevil." "Production in infested lands could outstrip and even double production on land free of the weevil but cultivated by old-fashioned methods." Yet, as C. Vann Woodward observed, "the clinching argument of the demonstration method was more pounds and bushels. More and more cotton. Always more cotton."[86]

Race and Cotton in the New South

While cotton futures and crop handling were important factors in cotton prices, European manufacturers agreed with Americans that the "chief problem of the American Cotton Crop today is the labour supply."[87] It was clear that black workers were leaving cotton farms and the South generally, and farmers and spinners alike wanted to find a solution to the labor problem. Some of the cotton populists envisioned a future where cotton, like wheat or corn, could be profitably produced by white yeoman farmers. This would take high prices as well as mechanization, but a satisfactory mechanical cotton harvester would not be developed until decades later.

In the interim, Southerners framed their demands for higher cotton prices around the needs of the white farmer and his family. As the quotes at the start of this chapter illustrate, white farmers believed that cotton at 5¢ or even 10¢ per pound (2.5d. to 5d.) was an immiserating crop. Samuel S. Dale, a sympathetic Yankee and editor of the *Textile World Record*, tried to paint a grim picture of Southern agriculture for visiting Lancashire spinners in 1906: "Ravaged by war and carpet bag governments, [the cotton farmer] has worked early and late, contended with frost, drought, blight, boll weevils and other pests, all the time facing year in and year out the most serious race issue that ever confronted the white man, only to find at the end of each season that he stood about nine hundred and ninety-nine chances out of a thousand of getting no more than 6 to 8 cents a pound for his cotton and being left in debt."[88] Until the cotton corners of the early twentieth century, American cotton farmers were growing more cotton and getting less for it. As historian C. Vann Woodward observed, "The cotton farmers produced a crop in 1894 that exceeded by two million bales any crop previously grown; yet they received $50,000,000 less for it than for the crop of 1882."[89]

Dale understood that, as English spinner H. W. MacAlister argued, "the man who wears the shirt" ultimately decided the price of cotton. Nonetheless, Dale appealed to Lancashire to understand the plight of the farmer—and specifically the white farmer—in terms of racial dignity:

> Whence comes this cry for cheap cotton? From Europe. Is it because the European consumer finds the American price "oppressive"? No. Eighty-five per cent. of Lancashire cotton products are exported, her best market being among the crowded millions of India, the poorest people on earth. A loin cloth is the wardrobe of many of them. . . . It is to supply this miserable population with cotton clothing that Europe seeks cheap cotton in America. . . . What I want to make clear is that from an American standpoint to concede it would be an outrage. It is to drag the Southern cotton planter to the Indian level.[90]

Sully drew farmers to his cotton corner in 1903–4 with similar rhetoric, and after his corner failed he declared, "The whole world is combined against the Southern farmers to keep down the price of their product." Echoing Dale's arguments, Sully told farmers that "The only difference between the ryot of India and the Southern farmer in the furrow behind his mule is that one breathes the air of liberty."[91]

White cotton farmers appealed to cotton spinners as fellow white men as well as business partners. As one South Carolina planter explained, they wanted cotton prices "at which our people in the South can educate their children and stop this waste; at a price that you can sell it to your Indian friends." A Tennessee farmer explained, "The only way to make a bale of cotton under present conditions is for the white man to make it, and have his children stay out of school."[92] "Cotton Ed" Smith argued that "Raising cotton was not a question of choice, it was a necessity. . . . We poured everything into the cotton crop—education, the future of our families, everything that we possessed." He credited Sully and other cotton speculators for forcing up the price of cotton: "We have paid off our debts, even though the cost was great, and it meant a sacrifice of education, comforts and almost life itself. Now we are independent, and we mean to be paid for this royal crop of ours such a price as will enable us to educate our children and enjoy of the comforts of life."[93]

While many white cotton farmers undoubtedly used child labor and suffered from low cotton prices, the claims these farmers made to Lancashire spinners must not be understood solely in economic terms. As historian Stephen DeCanio demonstrated, Southerners were not forced to grow cotton, and they did earn money from it. He observed that profit-seeking landlords and crop lien merchants would have demanded corn or other crops if they were in fact more valuable than cotton. Southerners grew cotton because they still had a comparative advantage in it.[94] White Southerners were not starving on cotton farms, but many were unable to buy the social and cultural trappings needed to distinguish themselves from their black neighbors. As two journalists put it, cotton prices before 1902–3 were "below the cost of production" when considering "any *reasonably high* standard of living" (emphasis added).[95]

Some observers tried to refute the argument that white and black labor were inherently different, and that black people were especially well suited to cotton cultivation. Alfred Holt Stone, a Mississippi plantation owner, lawyer, and committed white supremacist, argued that "white labor can accommodate itself to any work which can be performed by the Negro, whether it be the draining of Mississippi lowlands in 1860, or the digging of the Panama Canal a half century later."[96] Holt thought black peoples were pathologically lazy, and like some Southern elites, he saw immigration from Europe as the key to continued cotton production in the South: higher prices for cotton and lower wages for immigrants would allow planters to dispense with black labor. White yeomen farmers bitterly resented these efforts to equate white and black labor and to cheapen the cost of white labor through immigration. NFU members, who saw the problems of cotton agriculture as much in class terms as they did in racial terms, insisted that they did not want "Dagoes and people of that class [who] live on a handful of sour mush and a hunk of stale bread a day, and could raise cotton at four cents a pound, under contract to the spinners and then have money enough to send back to the old country for more of their kind."[97] Cotton populists like Harvie Jordan viewed the "the wholesale importation of foreign immigrants on southern farms for the supreme purpose of largely increasing the present supply of American cotton" as a nefarious plot hatched in "foreign spinning centres" to cheapen cotton.[98]

When British cotton experts visited the South, they were uncertain of the significance of black labor in the cotton industry. Members of the 1906 Lancashire Private Commission expressed frustration that they could not "ascertain the facts respecting the true value of the negro as a labourer." They found that some white Southerners "speak highly of his sterling working qualities, whilst others denounce him as devoid of energy and intelligence." "They exploit him unmercifully," commission members ruefully observed.[99] They found it "to be a fact" that

> the man who gets the most out of his negroes is the man who treats them as he would children. The average negro's mind appears to have no logical or reasonable basis; he is emotional and whimsical, controlled far more by fancies than common-sense. The nomadic instinct and an easy-going indolence are characteristic of his race. If treated as a white man and allowed to handle the money he earns, he spends it recklessly in vicious ways, and does no work until it is all gone. . . . On the whole, he is probably not so well off as in slavery days.[100]

They alleged that "improvements in the implements of cultivation have been very rare and exceedingly slowly introduced," and they blamed this on "the low order of intelligence which often characterises the negro agriculturalist."[101] It does not appear that the Lancashire men interviewed any black Americans.

When J. A. Todd toured the South on behalf of the International Cotton Federation in 1913, he concluded that black labor would continue to be an important factor in the cotton industry. Todd, who spent much of his career in Egypt, complained that African American labourers were coddled and overpaid compared to their peers in the global cotton peasantry: "The Egyptian *fellah* works patiently steadily and hard from sunrise to sunset. . . . Contrast this with the American negro, who not only must have his Sunday off, but also the whole day on Saturday; that day is usually spent in visiting the nearest town or village to buy rations, an excellent excuse for spending the whole day in idleness and a good deal of foolish extravagance."[102] Despite this "idleness," the African American worker still managed to produce more cotton per acre than the Egyptian *fellah* or Indian *ryot* and earned wages four to six times higher.[103]

Some white Southerners argued that black workers were overpaid and underworked after emancipation, describing what economists would later call a "backward-bending labor supply curve," in which higher wages led to fewer working hours. "Only a few years ago you could get a negro for forty cents a day and a little molasses and corn bread, and if he ran away, you could get a pair of hounds and catch him and put him back to work; and today we pay him $1.25 or $1.50," complained one farmer, who added, "the bigger price we pay the less he works." Many white Southerners insisted that high wages for cotton pickers meant less work, operating on the assumption that blacks would leave the labor market once their subsistence needs were met. One American claimed, "The high price of cotton has almost ruined the country. I mean as far as the negro is concerned."[104] Some Southerners disagreed about the economic rationality of African American workers, however, much as European colonial administrators debated the rationality of African peasants. Surprisingly, the inveterate racist E. D. Smith argued against the idea of a "backward-bending curve." He acknowledged that Southerners had lost social and political control over black labor, but he believed black workers would respond positively to wage incentives. Smith urged spinners to "Put the [cotton] price where we will bring the negro back from the saw-mill, from the streets of your different cities, and make it remunerative for him to go into the field."[105]

Lancashire spinners bought into the mythology of the "Old South," rejecting the idea that cotton was a crop for white men in America. Sir Charles Macara was perhaps the worst offender in perpetuating an "Old South" myth in Lancashire, though he was heartily encouraged in this by Southerners. The entertainment for the 1907 World Cotton Congress in Atlanta had an antebellum theme, and after the conference, Macara and other European spinners visited plantations in Alabama and Mississippi.[106] Macara's delegation of European spinners stopped in Heathman, Mississippi, to observe African American cotton pickers at work (see fig. 4.2), and then descended from their train to personally inspect the cotton fields (see fig. 4.3). He described his host near Heathman as "living in a solitary state, surrounded by his negro workers . . . a true type of the planter, and one who might easily have stepped from the pages of one of Mrs. Beecher Stowe's books." The next morning, Macara toured the estate with the planter's sons, "mounted and in planters' rig with pistols in their holsters," giving "the traditional picture of the Southern cotton planter as he goes about amongst his darkies."[107] Macara's companions called this "the most profitable day they had spent since their arrival in America, as it gave them just the opportunity they wanted for observation."[108] What they observed, however, was little more than a living museum.

Figure 4.2. African American cotton pickers at work near Heathman, Mississippi. IFMCSMA, *Second International Conference of Cotton Growers, Spinners, and Manufacturers, Held at Atlanta, Georgia, U.S.A., October 7th, 8th and 9th, 1907,* 29.

Figure 4.3. European cotton spinners inspecting a cotton field near Heathman, Mississippi. IFMCSMA, *Second International Conference of Cotton Growers, Spinners, and Manufacturers, Held at Atlanta, Georgia, U.S.A., October 7th, 8th and 9th, 1907,* 3.

The "Scientific Redemption of Africa" and the South

Black scientists and educators had their own ideas about the future of cotton agriculture. Their encounters with Africa and Africans produced two contradictory responses. On the one hand, black Southerners were eager to demonstrate their own advancement by aiding missionary and colonial efforts to transform Africa, implicitly supporting the claims of African backwardness on which colonial rule was premised. Yet black Americans also found a pan-African identity in Africa that connected the diasporic community to ancient civilizations, complex cultures, and skilled farmers and craftsmen. An individual like Hoffman could express both sentiments without acknowledging the inherent contradiction of the two ideas.

Booker T. Washington has been well studied as an African American apologist for colonialism. We have already seen how his educational philosophy encouraged the KWK and BCGA to seek out Tuskegee-trained men for their cotton-growing projects in Africa. In the South, Washington famously urged black Americans to "cast down your bucket where you are," to reach social and political freedom through hard work within a white-dominated system. For Washington, agriculture was the natural calling of the black man, and he believed that "Practical farming is . . . one of the most important things which Tuskegee Institute can teach." Washington discouraged urban migration and factory work, declaring, "As a general thing, the colored man is at his best in the country districts, where he is kept away from the demoralizing influences of city life."[109] Colonial officials would have sympathized; their reports on African labor throughout the twentieth century expressed similar sentiments. As Donald Spivey has argued, "The colonial powers in Europe could well appreciate an educational philosophy that stood for docility, heightened efficiency, and black subordination to white."[110]

Washington's students and colleagues carried this message to Africa as representatives of the "civilized world," often accepting European arguments about the racial or cultural inferiority of African societies. David Levering Lewis observed that "African American notables conceived of themselves as forming the vanguard of an African 'race' rising to greatness under Negro American tutelage," and that few black Americans questioned "the regnant European gospel of African moral and material backwardness."[111] Men employed in the cotton-growing campaigns were no exception to this. One of the Tuskegee men sent to Togo said, "I am glad that I can go back to my old home to carry there some part of the good which my race has learned in America."[112] A black-owned American newspaper described Hoffman's work in Nigeria in similar terms: "In more than one dusky breast he had stirred hopes of a future for the race, had awakened dreams hitherto foreign to these Africans, so lately emerged from a darkness as deep as their jungles. It is a rare good fortune that has permitted this earnest and gifted member of race to carry this message of better tiding to those of his blood."[113] This was not a new line of thinking; for much of the nineteenth century, various philanthropists and missionaries had been looking for schemes to "redeem" Africa. The idea that African Americans were the best agents of revitalization in Africa had a pedigree nearly as old.

African Americans were divided over several important issues relating to projects in Africa, however. Most important for the diasporic community in the United States was the end goal of any involvement in Africa. Earlier in the nineteenth century, many leaders rallied around the idea of permanent emigration. In their vision, American missionaries and colonists were paving the way for the full-scale repatriation of the African diaspora. Several colonization societies had put the idea to the test in Liberia beginning in the 1820s, and after the Civil War a wave of "exodus fever" gripped many African American communities. Africa seemed to be a land of political freedom and endless economic opportunity: "Potatoes were believed to grow large enough to feed an entire family. Sugar, syrup, and bacon could be obtained directly from trees, without the need to be processed, and cooking was done by the heat from the sun."[114] The skills African Americans had been compelled to hone in Southern cotton fields were recast as assets that would lead to the economic development of Africa. As a familiar cash crop, cotton was supposed to be the cornerstone of a new African economy. Leigh Hunt's far-fetched scheme of an African American emigration movement organized around cotton agriculture was only one of many cotton-based emigration projects, dating back to 1870s.[115] Religious leaders like Bishop Henry M. Turner were sure that "the uplift and resurgence of Africa would be led by African-Americans."[116] Charlatans like "Chief Sam" took advantage of the enthusiasm of many who hoped to escape poverty and political repression by moving to Africa.[117] White and black proponents of African missions also argued that the threat of losing the South's agricultural labor force would force white Americans to reassess their racist policies.[118]

Other leaders, like Booker T. Washington, opposed emigration schemes. From their perspective, the end goal of missionary work and colonization in Africa was the revitalization of the diasporic community in the Americas. By demonstrating the talents of black educators in Africa, proponents like Washington hoped to win points with whites back home. Black-owned newspapers championed this idea. In an article titled the "Scientific Redemption of Africa," the pan-Africanist writer Walter F. Walker praised Hoffman as an exemplar of the African diaspora's civilizing mission, a man who could stand as an equal with white scientists.[119]

The rhetoric of racial uplift through agriculture was as applicable in the South as it was in Africa. Hoffman saw little difference between his work in Africa and America. Before traveling to Nigeria his greatest success came in dairying and butter making, which he taught to young black men as "a practical way to better their condition." "He has chosen the South for his field of labor because of the magnificent opportunity to develop the agricultural resources of that section," one columnist wrote, praising "the efforts he has made and is still making for the elevation of his people."[120] A description of a "colored farmers' institute" offered by Hoffman in South Carolina in 1898 used similar language to Hoffman's own descriptions of his work in Nigeria. In both cases, black farmers were shown "new methods in farming which were far superior to those antiquated ones in which they had always been engaged, and that with their practical adoption and application upon their farms must come their success."[121] At another farmer's institute in South Carolina, Hoffman "told his audience to not be ashamed of hard work; work for the best salary or wages you can get, but work for anything, rather than to be idle."[122] Only a few years later he was in Nigeria telling farmers that "if they expected to live happy and contented lives they must develop the wonderful agricultural resources of their country." He explained to colonial officials that "The people can never be trained by one visiting their farms and showing them. They must first see for themselves how crops are produced under modern methods."[123]

After he left Nigeria, Hoffman continued to advocate a parallel path of development for Africans and the African diaspora. In America, he promoted his work in Africa, delivering public lectures about "Africa and her people" and exhibiting "specimens of native African handicrafts in Cloth, Leather, Iron, etc." (see fig. 4.4). Hoffman entertained audiences with tales of "the great wall city of Kano in Central Africa with a population of one hundred thousand, dating its civilization back to the 4th century."[124] He also brought several Nigerians to America to study at black colleges, including a Yoruba prince named Lattevi Ajayi, who maintained a long correspondence with Hoffman and who also introduced American folklorist John Lomax to Yoruba folktales.[125] Hoffman and Edward Blackshear, the principal of Prairie View Agricultural College, wrote a series of letters in 1909 urging Britain to adopt the Tuskegee model of agricultural education for Africans in the British Empire. Hoffman declared, "Back to the soil must be the cry of every African, and the Government ought to do everything to introduce the teaching of Agriculture in Africa." Blackshear warned that "the Anglo-Saxon race will just waste time and increase trouble by making the negroes a race of educated clerks." He argued, "If Africans can be made farmers, producers of cotton and other materials that can be utilized in English manufactures, then the African can become self-supporting. Self-support will lead to self-respect and to a true and natural

Figure 4.4. Advertisement for a lecture by J. W. Hoffman, ca. 1910. J. W. Hoffman Papers, Tuskegee University Archives. Reproduced by permission from the Tuskegee University Archives, Tuskegee University.

evolution to a higher state of civilization and culture."[126] Sir Alfred Jones paid to have the letters printed in a small pamphlet.

The other controversy over the diaspora's mission in Africa concerned the nature of Africans themselves. For antiemigrationists like Washington, Africa was a backward place in need of deliverance. From his perspective, slavery had been a "strangely providential" school that freed African Americans "from their ancestors' savagery and ignorance."[127] This line of thinking fit well with the racial rhetoric of European imperialism. It was also a potent weapon against the emigration movement; the idea that Africa was a homeland for African Americans did not fit well with an image of a primitive land populated with savages. One of Washington's pupils, who had been fired by the German government in Togo, toured the South spreading tall tales of cannibalism and barbarity. This undoubtedly hurt the idea of emigration, but it also caused Washington and Tuskegee a great deal of embarrassment.[128]

David Levering Lewis went too far in claiming that "None questioned the regnant European gospel of African moral and material backwardness," however.[129] If black Americans found a way to demonstrate their own racial progress by teaching in Africa, they also had to address the fact that Africans were not the primitive savages of the colonial imagination. The realization that African societies possessed long histories and sophisticated cultures had a powerful effect on visitors from the African diaspora. Black nationalist and pan-Africanist movements owed much to the reports of Americans in Africa, and of Africans in America.[130] For pan-African writers, Africa became a land with a history as travelers reported on their own journeys or appropriated knowledge produced by colonizers, such as the documentation of ancient ruins at Great Zimbabwe.[131] American travelers like the Bishop Henry M. Turner celebrated the "black men in positions of authority" they saw in places like Liberia and Sierra Leone, utterly disproving racist assertions that Africans were incapable of self-governance.[132] Turner in fact reversed Washington's arguments about slavery and the diaspora, viewing Africans as racially superior to "degenerated" African Americans.

Hoffman had his own diasporic experience of discovery in Nigeria, although his scanty writings suggest that he shared Washington's belief that educated black Americans were natural tutors to the "noble savages" of Africa, rather than a degenerated product of white-dominated society. Hoffman enthusiastically described Lagos as a thriving seaport of fifty thousand inhabitants, "less than 500 of whom are white men." It was "well laid out and built up with modern houses, [having] electric lights, telephones, street cars and an ice factory." He wrote about a railroad "that extends from Lagos 900 miles into the interior [and] is operated by natives, and a railroad, 200 miles long, is also operated by natives in every position except that of engineer." Hoffman praised the Yoruba peoples of southwestern Nigeria as "advanced in many of the fine arts," living in houses with "thatched roofs so perfectly constructed as to defy tropical rains."[133]

African American periodicals featured interviews with Hoffman on several occasions, although the stories misinterpreted some of Hoffman's descriptions of Africa and exaggerated his accomplishments. It is difficult to gauge the impact these articles had on readers, but Hoffman received at least two letters from black farmers in the South who had heard of his work in Africa through newspapers. One group of farmers in Pine Bluff, Arkansas, wrote to Hoffman in August 1904, asking him to teach them the same things he was teaching Nigerians. They embraced Hoffman's message of self-improvement through scientific commodity production, and they hoped Hoffman's work would "solve the mysterious & vexing problem concerning our race." Another group of farmers from Shelby County, Tennessee, wrote to Hoffman in Lagos asking him to pay them a visit. Unfortunately, their letter missed him by a year; Hoffman was back in the United States by the time the letter arrived. The Shelby County farmers wrote, "[we] think by what you say of Africa one could do some good." They were "much interested and anxious to know what we can about Africa," in addition to seeking agricultural advice from Hoffman.[134] Regrettably Hoffman did not have much to offer to these hopeful black farmers; he continued to hold farmers' institutes after his return to the United States, but preferred to work in the comfortable confines of academia.

Hoffman and the other Tuskegee scientists worked during a transitional period in the political consciousness of the African diaspora. African Americans participated in the first pan-African conference held in London in 1900, but it would take a later generation of writers and thinkers to articulate the experiences of the diaspora with those of Africans living under colonial rule. Pan-Africanism was not an explicitly anti-imperial stance in the first decade of the twentieth century. When travelers like Hoffman talked to the Lagos press or to Nigerian notables, they probably heard complaints about British abuses in a context of "seditious loyalty." For the African elites of Lagos, Accra, and other coastal cities, their aim was often to be recognized as "full Britishers" rather than to overthrow colonial rule entirely.[135] Hoffman can hardly be blamed for not joining an anti-imperialist movement that did not exist, yet in his later writings he ultimately rejected the fight for political equality his peers in West Africa and London were waging. As his pamphlet from Prairie View illustrates, Hoffman continued to preach Booker T. Washington's gospel of hard work and accommodation within an unjust system of political control.

Black Populists

Some black farmers realized that the tools white populists were developing could help them as much, or more, than the scientific training and self-help philosophy offered by men like Hoffman or Washington. The NFU and SCA barred black farmers from joining their organizations, but they needed black farmers to cooperate with warehousing and crop-reduction efforts. According to the 1900 census, white farmers operated 60 percent of the South's 1,418,000 cotton farms. Thus black Americans were responsible for up to 40 percent of the nation's cotton farms, without counting the black workers employed as seasonal laborers on white-operated farms. For a group like the SCA that hoped to corner cotton on the basis of a million-bale withholding movement, the role of African Americans in the cotton economy posed an enormous problem. How could white farmers hope to control the supply of cotton without abandoning their racist and segregationist beliefs?

For the most part, the leadership at the SCA and NFU simply ignored the problem. Partisans of Harvie Jordan at the Atlanta *Constitution* called on SCA members to pressure white landowners on crop reduction and crop withholding, recognizing that the majority of black farmers were tenants or sharecroppers. "The tenant, of his own volition, is not going to concern himself about the economic questions involved in a short crop this season and contribute to the end sought by short planting," warned the newspaper. The paper urged landowners to do their "duty to the South."[136] At the 1908 NFU convention, a speaker blamed black farmers for the failure of the crop-withholding schemes to stabilize the cotton price. "Rapid selling is caused by the tenant, the negro, who has to sell," he complained. The speaker offered no solutions, however.[137]

Black farmers did form their own movements. The Colored Farmers' Alliance of the 1880–90s left behind a network of county organizations after the collapse of the nationwide populist movement, but little is known about the group or its offshoots "since secrecy protected its members from landlord and merchant retaliation."[138] There is some evidence of cooperation between the white cotton populists and their black counterparts, however. In Texas, local NFU chapters allowed black farmers to use their warehouses on the same terms as white NFU members.[139] Arkansas's state union maintained cordial relations with the Colored Progressive Farmers' Union, loaning the group $1,000 to finance its operations. The Arkansas NFU even resolved to "invite them [black farmers] to bring all the cotton they can control to be weighed, handled and marketed, just as we do that of our own members."[140] Such cases were exceptions rather than the rule, however. In Mississippi, for example, the state NFU actively opposed efforts

to admit black farmers on grounds that they were overly burdened with crop liens and would overwhelm the cooperative credit and warehousing institutions created to help white farmers.[141]

The settlement at Mound Bayou in the Mississippi Delta region was perhaps the most ambitious attempt by black farmers to recast the social, political, and economic landscape for black cotton workers in the South.[142] Mound Bayou was founded in 1887 by settlers from Davis Bend, a post–Civil War experimental black community that collapsed in the 1870s under economic and legal pressure. Mound Bayou was built on land purchased from a railroad company on generous terms, with the intention of developing a prosperous community of landowning black cotton farmers along the railroad. Isaiah Montgomery, Mound Bayou's charismatic leader, was praised as a "Moses" who "carried his people from recent slavery to their new freedom in the wilderness." (Montgomery is best remembered for being the only black politician in Mississippi to vote *for* the disenfranchisement of black voters, in a misguided bid to ease racial tensions.) Under Montgomery's "masterful hand," settlers labored and made "the wilderness [blossom]."[143] As in so many other Southern communities, however, most of those blossoms appeared on the branches of *G. hirsutum*. Mound Bayou's charismatic leaders could see no further than cotton, and though they diversified into cottonseed oil, the town's fortunes rose and fell with cotton prices. The town survives today as a black enclave, but its model of black landownership and cotton commodity production proved disappointing as an emancipatory force for Southern blacks.

Black communities in the South also faced pressure from their erstwhile comrades in white farmers' organizations. The failure of crop reduction and withholding campaigns to boost cotton prices led white farmers to launch "extralegal attempts" to control the cotton crop in 1908.[144] Inspired by a night-riding campaign against a tobacco trust in Kentucky, white organizations in the cotton states launched a wave of terrorism against cotton gins and farmers who refused to reduce acreage or hold back cotton. In Arkansas a band of riders threatened to whip a man if he did not cut his plantings by half, while another man with a load of cotton in a wagon was forced to return home.[145] A Texas ginnery received a note stating: "Dear Friend: You are ordered to shut down your gin and keep it closed until further orders. Should you refuse to do so you may expect to find it in ashes. Do not be deceived. We mean business. Signed, NIGHT RIDERS."[146] In Mississippi, a group of black night riders allegedly imitated their white counterparts, threatening ginneries with arson if they continued processing cotton. A confession extracted from William Robinson identified him as an "agent of a negro lodge" intent on driving cotton prices higher.[147]

The night-riding campaign was poorly timed, coming on the heels of a Tennessee night-riding murder trial that garnered national attention.

Jordan and Barrett were quick to condemn night riding, and the NFU successfully reined in its members, who were the most likely culprits. But the 1908 SCA meeting in Memphis was brought to a standstill when one faction declared that the night riders "were an oppressed people fighting for what they believed to be right, working against overwhelming odds but always from the best motives."[148] Sporadic reports of cotton-related night riding continued for years. In 1911, for instance, "white-cappers" tried to drive black cotton pickers from fields in Texas, while other gangs attacked black and Mexican sharecroppers.[149]

These night-riding episodes illustrate how strongly Southern farmers believed in nostrums like crop reduction and warehousing, as well as the inherent weaknesses of their collective organizations. They faced a serious "free-rider" problem because any gains the organizations achieved would be shared by all cotton farmers in the form of higher cotton prices. Southern populists resorted to violence to force compliance with their schemes, drawing on half a century of experience in coercing their uncooperative neighbors. The fact that both white and black farmers were targeted by night riders was hardly a sign of softening racism among the vigilantes. White and black politicians and voters had faced terrorism since the end of the Civil War over political issues, and the extension of night riding to the economic sphere was a logical step for the vigilantes. Indeed, economic factors had a significant influence on political violence in the South. There was a strong correlation between lynching and low cotton prices across the late nineteenth and early twentieth centuries, suggesting that the cotton populists were perpetuating a decades-old problem.[150] While it is possible that black farmers' organizations may have engaged in extralegal violence of their own, as in the Mississippi case, it is far likelier that they were scapegoats for the actions of white night riders.

The Failure of Cotton Populism

The cotton populists proved to be their own worst enemies. White farmers spurned the black farmers and laborers who played a declining, but still significant role in producing the American cotton crop. Among the white organizations, leaders were able to cooperate on a few issues but they clashed over many minor political and personal disputes, ultimately derailing the cause of "cotton populism." Jordan criticized the NFU for supporting political candidates; as an SCA activist recalled, "The Grange and Farmers' Alliance went into politics and became opponents to merchants and business men generally, the result of which everybody knew."[151] NFU president Barrett argued that his political work was nonpartisan, aimed solely at reforming cotton marketing. Barrett argued, "People don't ask sheep stealers to be good. They go after them with shot guns. The ballot is the shot gun of the farmer."[152] Jordan's close cooperation with Sully and other speculators enraged the NFU, which had been founded on the premise that "Speculators and those engaged in distribution of farm products have organized and operate to the great detriment of the farming class."[153] The two groups fought openly in 1906 when the NFU called for 11¢ cotton in opposition to the SCA's "bread and meat line" of 10¢ per pound. Barrett caricatured Jordan as man who wore "patent leather shoes and led fashionable dances before he undertook seriously the work of farming operations," questioning his dedication to the cotton growers.[154]

When the SCA ran out of money in September 1906, the NFU began to destroy its rival.[155] Georgia politician Tom Watson, who had briefly served on the SCA Executive Council, backed the NFU in Georgia and tried to topple Jordan in the midst of a messy gubernatorial race, in which Watson and Jordan were both contenders.[156] Watson called the SCA "a mongrel association," little more than "the tool of Wall Street cotton gamblers and the special privilege manufacturers." He urged farmers to abandon it in favor of the NFU.[157] Barrett further humiliated Jordan by refusing to accompany him to the 1907 ICF conference in Vienna. Barrett maintained, "Ours is an organization of farmers," in contrast with Jordan's "nondescript organization of speculators, spinners, and apparently everybody else who wants to join." His ultimatum to Jordan and the SCA was clear: "Untie from Wall Street."[158] As the SCA started to collapse, NFU leaders rejected calls for a merger: "We have everything coming our way, and we do not propose to throw away our chance to benefit the real farmer," wrote one critic of Jordan.[159]

By late 1908, Jordan declared the SCA dead. "The farmers seem to have quit caring about these associations," he complained. "As long as there was interest in it we kept the price of cotton up. When the farmers' interest fell away the price of cotton went down." Critics pointed out more pressing problems, like the lack of support from farmers and financial interests. As the editors of the *Textile World Record* put it in a derisive article, Jordan's SCA declared itself "an amendment to the law of supply of demand" and expected the rest to fall into place.[160] After the SCA dissolved Jordan remained active in the Sea Island Cotton Growers' Association, a smaller organization he helped found in 1907. The group campaigned for import duties on Egyptian cotton.[161] He later testified before Congress on improved ginning and baling methods (he had launched a ginning company) and served on a federal commission investigating rural credit and agricultural cooperatives in Europe in 1913.[162]

SCA membership figures were never publicized, although a figure of a half-million was frequently quoted in the press. The NFU claimed to have five million members by 1908, although an internal NFU report showed only 935,837 active members spread across 17,938 local associations in

1907.[163] A later study of receipts for annual dues put the paying membership in the South in 1910 at only 87,227.[164] In the long run, the NFU gained most of its members in the west, moving outside the cotton belt.

The British and other European spinners who visited Atlanta in 1907 came away convinced that the South could vastly expand its cotton production, but that it desperately needed agricultural reform to increase yields, decrease waste, and hold down costs. At the 1908 ICF meeting in Paris, French spinner M. Méline picked up the Lancashire Private Commission's idea that Americans were in need of a colonial-style demonstration plantation. The French delegation hoped to use the American plantation as "a nursery of intelligent and energetic directors and planters taught by experience, and who could be called upon to render the greatest service in the colonial cotton growing of each Association." The Belgian delegation's report suggested that "the crop might even be doubled in eight years by judicious selection of the seed," while the Germans admitted, "it is quite certain that cotton in the States cannot nowadays be grown as cheaply as it was about a decade ago."[165] This was a sobering revelation for many cotton manufacturers. They had assumed that cotton was and must remain a cheap commodity, but their visits to the South showed them that prices were destined to rise. Macara sent cotton expert J. A. Todd on a secret tour of the South in 1913 to confirm the actual costs cotton farmers faced, and Todd affirmed that low prices, low yields, and the boll weevil brought farmers "to such a point as to come dangerously near the extinction of a reasonable profit."[166] Todd calculated a break-even point of about 7¢ per pound for an independent white farmer, noting that white and black sharecroppers would need to see 11¢ to turn a profit after handing over a quarter or more of their crop to their creditors. Todd ruefully concluded, "The profit on cotton growing is not nearly so high as had been imagined."[167]

The work of the BCGA, KWK, ACC, and other colonial cotton organizations had failed to provide a viable alternative to the American South. The ICF belatedly sponsored a campaign to revive Indian cotton production, but most spinners were resigned to the fact that America would continue to monopolize the cotton supply. Europeans manufacturers did not cross the Atlantic as a united group again until 1919. In the interim, American emissaries visited ICF conferences and gave combative speeches, telling the Europeans to accept the reality of rising cotton prices. James MacColl, head of the American cotton manufacturers' organization and normally an ally of the European spinners, warned other spinners: "The world cannot go on continually curtailing. You cannot run short time always!" "The markets are getting bare," he observed, adding that "The people are needing more shirts and clothes. They will be ready to pay 20 cents, if they have to pay it, but it is not a good thing for anybody to see the price of cotton as high as that."[168]

A few European spinners investigated the possibility of investing in American cotton agriculture, carrying vertical integration to its logical end by acquiring plantations to produce the raw materials their mills needed. The cotton populists encouraged foreign investment, although they argued that the best investment would be the relocation of Lancashire's mills to the South. Jordan boasted, "If our friends who are in the manufacture of American cotton in Manchester and Lancashire want to get nearer to the cotton fields of the south, let them move their mills to the cotton belt of the United States and settle down here as good American citizens."[169] South Carolina cotton magnate D. A. Tompkins received letters from England asking about plantation real estate, and his correspondents boasted that Lancashire was "ready to start 'buying up land, importing labour and growing their own cotton.'"[170] Jordan crowed that this "sounded the death knell for the BCGA," celebrating "the south's complete monopoly" on cotton.[171] Sir Charles Macara tried to buy a plantation after his 1907 visit, but his solicitors convinced him to cancel the project after finding that Southern state laws were hostile toward alien property owners.[172] Only one British group, the Fine Cotton Spinners' and Doublers' Association, actually bought Southern cotton land. The FCSDA was a massive combine of fine-spinning firms, and its directors (some of whom were on the 1906 and 1907 visits) wanted to guarantee a steady flow of high-quality long-stapled cotton to their mills. In 1911, the firm spent $2.5 million on thirty-eight thousand acres in Mississippi.[173] The FCSDA could have provided BCGA's entire working capital for what it paid for this land, illustrating the firm's skepticism about African cotton-growing schemes. The plantation proved unsuitable for the extra-long-staple cotton the firm preferred, but the FCSDA did grow cotton and make money on the Mississippi plantation for decades.[174]

Conclusion

On the surface, resurgent Southern populism looked very much like its failed predecessor of the 1890s. After the 1909–10 cotton corner, however, the American government increasingly sided with the cotton farmers in their war with the cotton exchanges. Southern politicians began to win victories on behalf of cotton farmers. Virginia-born Woodrow Wilson signed an array of agricultural reform bills during his first term as president, and the cotton populists were directly responsible for two of these legislative victories: the Cotton Futures Act and the Cotton Warehouse Act. Although urban Progressives claimed the laws as their own, the bills were the result of a decade of Southern agitation and they gave farmers many of the things they had hoped to accomplish on their own or in cooperation with Lancashire.

The American government had been gradually building a case for intervention in the cotton industry.[175] After a freak storm damaged large amounts of cotton in 1906, the New York Cotton Exchange attempted to dump the fiber on New England cotton mills at inflated prices. Northern manufacturers had the ear of influential politicians, and Congress quickly launched an investigation. The commissioner of corporations was charged with holding hearings and preparing a report on the NYCE's practices. The commissioner's report generally defended the cotton exchanges and cotton futures markets; the report demonstrated that futures trading had actually reduced annual fluctuations in cotton prices. The report did identify serious problems with the NYCE's grading and pricing policies, however, and it called for new federal descriptions of deliverable cotton grades.[176]

Rep. Charles Scott of Kansas used the momentum of the commissioner's hearings and the published report to propose a bill banning all cotton futures trading in 1910. Congress excoriated NYCE members during hearings on the bill, and agrarian leaders and sympathetic cotton manufacturers were given a soapbox in Washington, DC, to testify against the exchanges. The NFU enthusiastically supported the bill, despite charges that farmers "were on Easy Street with the best farm prices since the Civil War" and had no grounds for complaint against the exchanges.[177] The hearings were given teeth by federal indictments against Brown, Hayne, Patten, and others cotton brokers charged with cornering cotton in 1910. The Scott Bill cleared the House of Representatives with a vote of 160–41, but it died in committee in the Senate. Sen. James Clarke of Arkansas revived the hearings and proposed a cotton futures tax as a rider on the Underwood-Simmons Tariff Bill in 1913. The bill taxed futures transactions a tenth of a cent per pound, or $50 per one-hundred bale contract. The tax would have been refunded if cotton bales were physically delivered to a buyer. The bill amounted to an attack on hedging, as manufacturers rarely wanted to accept cotton from futures contracts, which could be of a wide range of grades.[178]

The financial press reacted with horror, protesting that "such radical and uncalled-for legislation would not only put out of business the various cotton exchanges of the country but work incalculable harm to all those handling the staple in any way, including the planters, whom it is the apparent intention to benefit."[179] Like the Scott Bill, the Clarke amendment failed in the Senate. But the cumulative effect of four years of hearings and investigations wore down the NYCE. The exchange's president admitted in 1913 that his organization had developed policies and tendencies that "served to render of little value the use of exchanges as a hedge" and agreed to initiate reforms in cooperation with the European cotton exchanges and European cotton spinners.[180]

Real victory for farmers came in 1914, when "Cotton Ed" Smith, by then a Democratic senator for South Carolina, joined forces with Rep. Frank Lever to pass the Cotton Futures Act. (The bill is sometimes mistakenly called the Smith-Lever Act; that 1914 law funded agricultural colleges and USDA extension services, another victory for the populists.) Southern politicians pushed the bill through the Senate, and the vote in the House was carried by Southern Democrats and Progressive allies in the North.[181] The law was ruled unconstitutional in 1915, but only the grounds that it was a revenue act, and therefore had to originate in the House rather than the Senate. Congress passed a corrected version in 1916. The Cotton Futures Act responded to the immediate complaints of manufacturers, who said that the NYCE contract "permitted delivery of cotton that the buyer could not use."[182] It also reflected the demands of farmers, however, who wanted to restrict futures trading. The law stated that "the delivery of cotton under the contract shall not be effected by means of 'setoff' or 'ring' settlement, but only by the actual transfer of the specified cotton mentioned in the contract."[183] When contracts matured, cotton actually had to change hands, and while this provision did not eliminate short selling, which farmers also wanted to ban, it did discourage industry outsiders from speculating in cotton. Brokers could still "offset" contracts by selling or buying them before maturity, but any speculator hoping to corner the market would need to consider the logistics of handling and storing cotton bales if they were forced to hold contracts until the delivery date.

Most importantly, the law empowered the USDA to intervene in cotton marketing by requiring brokers to use new standardized USDA grades. Every bale had to be marked and numbered for identification. By creating "a uniform system by which farmers could classify and price their crops," the law freed manufacturers from the chore of sorting through and reselling or repurposing low-quality bales that were frequently mixed in with large orders, and the provision allowed farmers to benefit from premiums on top-quality cotton.[184] The law also gave a federal agency the power to shape markets, and the USDA used this power to promote the interests of American farmers over domestic and foreign consumers of cotton.[185]

The full effect of the First World War will be examined in the last chapter, but the outbreak of war in 1914 led to another set of legislative victories for the cotton populists. When the shooting started in August, international commodity markets suspended trading and cotton prices plummeted. Southern politicians desperately lobbied for a federal warehouse bill and proposed dozens of schemes to help farmers deal with the largest cotton crop in history. Critics fought hard against these proposals. Why, they asked, should the farmer be given "extraordinary measures . . . devised to enable him to realize on the cotton before it is actually sold, and thus get him deeper into debt?" Farmers "always have extravagant ideas as to what they ought to get for their output," they complained.[186] Victory finally came in 1916, when Congress passed the Warehouse Act. In conjunction with the Federal Farm Loan Act and the 1913 passage of the Federal Reserve Act, the bill gave farmers access to cheap credit on warehoused cotton. By depositing their cotton in federally licensed warehouses, farmers got receipts that could be used to obtain federally backed credit.[187]

Farmers had other victories as well. The Clayton Anti-Trust Act of 1914 exempted farmers' cooperatives from its provision, implicitly acknowledging that they exhibited trust-like characteristics but accepting that they played a positive role in the economy.[188] The congressional attack on the NYCE gave the USDA the power to define cotton grades, and USDA authority gradually crept into other areas of cotton handling, storage, and marketing. Yet the legislative victories of the cotton farmers undermined the farmers' movement. The federal government assumed responsibility for tasks that the NFU and other farmers' organizations had sought to provide through cooperative methods. With federal licensing available to all warehouses, cotton farmers had little incentive to store cotton in a cooperative if a commercial rival was cheaper or more accessible.

African Americans gained little from federal agricultural legislation. Intellectual leaders like Washington and Hoffman hoped that efficient, scientific cotton agriculture would transform Southern black farmers into a prosperous group of yeoman, with economic gains gradually leading to social and political progress. As the night-riding incidents and experimental failures like Mound Bayou showed, however, cotton was not a universal engine for progress. Laws like the Warehouse Act and Cotton Futures Act did little to help the small farmer or sharecropper, white or black. Only those with access to credit and capital could weather the year-to-year fluctuations in the cotton market and improve efficiency with new machines, pesticides, and fertilizers. Abandoning cotton and moving northward ultimately proved to be the most effective means of self-improvement for African Americans.

5

Cotton, Development, and the "Imperial Burden"

"The commercial interdependence of nations was illustrated in a manner never to be forgot when the Great War of 1914 broke out," American historian James Scherer observed in 1916.[1] Scherer had been working on the first comprehensive history of cotton from antiquity to the present when the war began, and the conflict provided a dramatic conclusion for his story. Cotton had been the emblematic industry of what many scholars regard as the first era of "globalization," and the war shattered the international division of labor and free trading conditions that had made global economic integration possible. As Europe mobilized for war, the machinery of international trade ground to a halt. Stock exchanges and commodity markets around the world closed their doors.[2] In Africa, expatriate employees of the BCGA and the Colonial Office, as well as many local farmers, abandoned cotton and joined the war effort. Africans waited apprehensively to see whether the war would ruin their trade, or perhaps even topple their colonial rulers. In Lancashire, merchants stopped buying textiles and mills stopped making them. Mill operatives and their employers enlisted and prepared to join the fight in France. Meanwhile, across the Atlantic, American farmers were preparing to harvest the biggest cotton crop in history, over sixteen million bales.

The war produced calamitous changes in the cotton industry, and marked the end of the Atlantic-centered world of cotton. The nineteenth century began with the emergence of a bipolar system, concentrating textile manufacturing in Britain and cotton agriculture in the United States. Africa, the vital source of labor for this system, was marginalized. The colonial cotton projects of the early twentieth century marked another transition, this time toward a multipolar system in which cotton agriculture and cotton manufacturing diffused across the globe. After the First World War, the world of cotton fractured into several competing systems, representing the efforts of imperial powers to achieve self-sufficiency and shut out competitors. Lancashire and the American South remained important centers in this environment, but their influence waned. Instead of replacing the American South, Britain's African colonies joined a growing cast of peripheral commodity producers scattered across Africa, Asia, and Latin America.

This chapter explores the immediate impact of the First World War on the BCGA and farmers in Africa and America, and traces the divergent paths of development that emerged after the war. On both sides of the Atlantic, the state assumed a larger role in cotton agriculture, but the outcomes for farmers were very different. Helped by an interventionist federal government, American cotton farmers—or at least a privileged group of white farmers—weathered the economic crisis brought on by the war and its aftermath. Though their fortunes fluctuated across the 1920s and 1930s, American cotton farmers continued to expand on a state-supported, capital-intensive path of development. By the 1950s, cotton was firmly entrenched as a crop for white, middle-class farmers in the South and Southwest. Protected by federal subsidies and federal manipulation of domestic and global markets for cotton, these farmers finally realized a long-sought goal: the total mechanization of cotton agriculture.

Meanwhile, Lancashire's cotton textile industry entered a terminal pattern of decline. Worried by the collapsing free-trade system on which Lancashire had grown rich, cotton capitalists and mill workers alike demanded quick results from colonial cotton projects. BCGA proponents like E. D. Morel had strongly advocated for the association's demand-side model for cotton growing, arguing that it represented a partnership between Britain's capital and Africa's labor, but after 1918 the rhetoric of imperial development in Britain shifted toward a more racist and unapologetically exploitative form. The BCGA ended its semiphilanthropic mission of development. It continued working in African colonies but ceded its scientific responsibilities to the Empire Cotton Growing Corporation, which worked closely with colonial agricultural departments to improve African agriculture. Ralph Austen observed that the adoption of cotton and other cash crops by African farmers before 1914 represented the "low-cost expansion of market opportunities for small farmers to produce goods for attractive external markets." Farmers used free BCGA seeds and newly constructed railroads and ginneries to access new markets, and some profited. By the 1920s and 1930s, however, colonial policies shifted: "export markets and rural production were managed in ways which frustrated or contradicted the self-perceived interests of peasants."[3] Unlike their peers in Francophone Africa, farmers in British colonies were not forced to grow cotton to meet specific demands from Lancashire. Farmers were, however, forced to grow cotton—despite its low commercial appeal—to pay taxes, and in some cases cotton became a convenient experimental tool for colonial planners hoping to reshape African societies and landscapes. African farmers endured labor-intensive regulations and lower prices for their cotton; when farmers across Africa finally gained freedom from colonial rule in the 1950s and 1960s, many abandoned cotton in favor of more lucrative crops.

Wartime Disruptions

While "cotton populists" in America agitated for higher prices and began to draw the federal government into the cotton industry, American farmers continued to plant more and more cotton (see table 5.1). In the 1913–14 season, more than 65 percent of the cotton crop was sold to foreign buyers. There were few overseas buyers as the bumper crop of 1914–15 came to market, however. Cotton exchanges in Liverpool, Bremen, Havre, and New York were shuttered in July and August as the war began, and little business could be done without them. Prices for cotton in American ports collapsed as bales accumulated on wharves and in warehouses.

Table 5.1. American cotton production, 1914–26

	American bales (500-pound bale equivalents)	Acreage	Average price (New Orleans, Upland cotton)
1914	16,134,930 bales	36,045,000 acres	7.3 cents/pound
1915	11,191,820	31,412,000	11.2
1916	11,449,930	34,985,000	17.28
1917	11,302,375	33,841,000	27.12
1918	12,040,532	36,008,000	28.76
1919	11,420,763	33,566,000	35.36
1920	13,439,603	35,878,000	15.89
1921	8,360,153	30,509,000	16.9
1922	10,319,843	33,036,000	22.9
1923	10,810,234	37,122,000	28.7
1924	14,497,361	41,360,000	22.9
1925	17,167,011	46,448,000	19.6
1926	18,796,934	47,087,000	12.5

Source: Bureau of the Census, *Cotton Production and Distribution* (1920), 12, 31; (1926), 24.

The US government acted quickly to save Wall Street from disaster as financial markets fell apart, but appeals from Southern politicians and farm leaders for intervention in the cotton market initially fell on deaf ears. As prices plummeted, desperate cotton farmers circulated schemes for a federal buy-up of the entire crop or for the "valorization" of cotton through bank notes issued against warehoused cotton. The National Farmers' Union launched a crash campaign of warehouse building, and state legislatures in Texas and South Carolina passed warehouse bills and began constructing new facilities.[4] President Woodrow Wilson tried to find relief for his fellow Southern Democrats, but Congress blocked special measures for the cotton belt. Wilson inaugurated the "buy-a-bale" movement, urging private citizens to buy and hold cotton in lieu of a federal stockpiling program. Gimbel's department store in New York bought a stock of ten thousand bales to sell to patriotic customers, while the American Tobacco Co. offered to trade tobacco for cotton, pound for pound. Companies around the nation switched from jute bagging to cotton, in a patriotic gesture.[5]

Wilson convinced private bankers to form a pool to stabilize cotton prices at 6¢, but the bankers issued only $28,000 out of a fund that was supposed to put $150 million at the disposal of Southern planters.[6] As the economic situation in the South worsened, Wilson worried that "Southerners in Congress might join with German-American and Irish-American elements to force a retaliatory arms embargo against the British for suppression of the cotton trade with Central Europe."[7] The NFU and the Georgia state legislature in fact demanded tariff retaliation against Britain for its expanding blockade, which prevented cotton sales to Germany and Austria.[8] Southern congressmen frantically pushed for the passage of a federal warehouse law before the fall session adjourned, and South Carolina Rep. Frank Lever extracted a promise from the House leadership to vote on his warehouse bill in the next session. In early 1915 Congress passed a preliminary warehouse bill, later reinforced by the 1916 Federal Warehouse Act, which allowed the Federal Reserve to issue banknotes to farmers against cotton stored in federal facilities.[9]

In Britain, Sir Charles Macara privately, and then publically, asked the British and American governments to buy five million bales of cotton. He thought this would be enough to stabilize prices while also establishing a strategic reserve of the fiber. The "two governments vitally concerned could protect millions of people engaged in the growing, handling and manufacturing of cotton from appalling disaster," Macara said, adding there was "the possibility of no ultimate loss" to taxpayers.[10] Neither government moved. Macara was also rebuffed by his colleagues in Lancashire when he proposed a private-sector stockpile, and he bitterly remarked that his colleagues in Lancashire were "indifferent as to the steps that could be taken to minimise the effects of war on their industry."[11]

Macara nonetheless made himself useful to the war effort. As president of the International Cotton Federation, he enjoyed access to confidential data on cotton mill equipment, stockpiles, and consumption in Europe, which he promptly surrendered to the Allies. Macara also helped the British government manage industrial production and recruit military volunteers.[12] In Lancashire, the FMCSA was so horrified by Macara's proposals for price-fixing and collective management that they forced him to resign as FMCSA president. Macara grumbled that too many in Lancashire "took the view that it was to their advantage to get cotton at the lowest price, even at the expense of the ruin of the growers."[13]

Macara also joined a campaign to declare cotton a wartime material, making it contraband for neutral countries trading with Germany and its allies. Germany had been a major consumer of American cotton before the war (see table 5.2). For all of the belligerents, cotton was "the pivot and crux of the whole situation" because of its vital role in modern warfare. The most important military use of cotton was in guncotton (cellulose nitrate), used in ammunition propellant and explosives. Cotton is a very pure source of cellulose and two cotton manufacturing byproducts, mill waste and linters (fibers that were scraped from seeds before crushing), provided a cheap supply. Scherer estimated that the German army alone required at least four hundred thousand bales every year to keep its guns firing. A single battleship might consume twelve bales of cotton for every minute of combat.[14] Aside from delivering death, cotton also went into tents, tarpaulins, uniforms, tires, and bandages. While British observers noted that Germans were experimenting with wood cellulose for explosives and textile manufacturing, cotton trade leaders were convinced that Germany would have run out of ammunition in 1915 had all cotton imports been cut off in August 1914.[15] "Why not buy up the whole of the coming American cotton crop," Lord Beresford asked, and "resell it afterwards even at a loss? What is this latter compared with the sacrifices we are sustaining daily with our Armies in the field?"[16]

Table 5.2. British and German imports of American cotton

	United Kingdom	Germany	Total US exports
1912	4,343,108 bales	3,156,171 bales	11,070,251 bales
1913	3,716,898	2,443,886	9,124,591
1914	3,581,501	2,884,324	9,521,881
1915	3,919,749	294,191	8,807,157
1916	2,760,890	0	6,168,140
1917	2,895,415	0	6,176,134

Source: Bureau of the Census, *Cotton Production and Distribution* (1918), 69.

Succumbing to public pressure, the British government declared cotton contraband on August 20, 1915. To ease tensions with America, "A secret agreement . . . was negotiated by Ambassador Cecil Spring Rice and Sir Richard Crawford of the British Embassy with W. P. G. Harding of the Federal Reserve Board and Theodore Price [the cotton speculator and financial journalist]." Britain agreed to "buy enough cotton to stabilize the price at ten cents a pound." After 1915, cotton prices climbed steadily in response to strong demand and a greatly decreased supply. Southern politicians hastily dropped their principled isolationism to back Wilson's program for intervention as the economic picture in the South improved.[17]

In Lancashire, business owners tried to carry on with their regular trade as far as possible, to the extent of hoarding labor and resources needed for war work. At the peak of war production in early 1918, only a quarter of Lancashire's cotton operatives were working on military contracts.[18] Lancashire faced a new cotton crisis in 1917, however, as the escalation of submarine warfare and a shrinking supply of American cotton drove prices in Britain and continental Europe to record levels. Fierce competition for raw materials led to short time and factory shutdowns. The situation grew so dire in the summer of 1917 that manufacturers voluntarily formed the Cotton Control Board (CCB) to regulate the trade. Government heartily approved and gave the CCB's decrees the force of law. A. H. Dixon (head of the Fine Cotton Spinners and Doublers Association) became chairman, hoping to ensure "the maximum of self-government by employers and employed in the trade" and a minimum of government intervention.[19] The object of the CCB was not to support industrial output for the war effort, but rather to organize short time and manage employment to "maintain the tranquility and the morale of Lancashire."[20] While the CCB did not survive into the postwar era, its existence illustrated the end of Lancashire's fervent commitment to laissez-faire economic policy, an attitude that extended to Lancashire's colonial cotton project.

The BCGA and the Wartime Crisis

Chairman J. Arthur Hutton saw the war as an opportunity to prove the value of the semiphilanthropic British Cotton Growing Association. The war caused immediate shipping shortages, which depressed cash-crop prices in Africa and sent prices for imported goods soaring. Colonial officers feared that farmers would abandon cash crops altogether as export markets evaporated, reversing a decade of work aimed at connecting African producers to world markets.[21] Invoking the BCGA's philanthropic mission, Hutton promised to support African cotton industries even if it meant buying cotton for more than it was worth in Liverpool. The BCGA succeeded in protecting colonial cotton growers from great disruptions during the war, but this victory ironically came at the expense of support from government leaders and important cotton firms in Lancashire. By the end of the war, Britain's government and Lancashire's leading business figures were convinced that the semiphilanthropic model of the BCGA was outmoded and unnecessary.

The BCGA's fate was probably sealed before the war began. Reports critical of the association's methods and the competence of its staff accumulated in the Colonial Office, putting the BCGA's privileged relationship with government in jeopardy. BCGA president Lord Derby urged Hutton to abandon the semiphilanthropic position and take the association forward as a strictly commercial operation in late 1913. Derby had no illusions about the success of this venture, telling the BCGA council that "the public would not be likely to subscribe £250,000 additional capital unless it could be shown that the Association were in a position to make profits." Hutton pleaded "for two or three years longer without committing [the association] to any definite policy," arguing that "it would be for the benefit of cotton growing generally, because if it was decided to work on a purely commercial basis it was probably the Association would lose the cooperation of the Government."[22] Hutton knew about the charges leveled at the association by colonial officials, but he also knew that government support was necessary for the regulations and monopolies that the BCGA increasingly relied upon.

In early 1914, Treasury officials wrote to Lord Emmott, the colonial undersecretary and former MP for Oldham. The Treasury warned Emmott that any further government aid for the BCGA was "a hopeless dream." Like Derby, Emmott had supported "winding up the present Association and starting a new body on purely business lines," and he was surprised to hear that Hutton "attache[d] great importance to maintaining, what I may call, the trustee character of the Association as regards the production of cotton. . . . they wish to keep their semi-philanthropic attitude in giving the largest possible price to the native and not in making a profit out of screwing down the price that they pay to the seller."[23] Hutton was trapped by the contradictory premise of the BCGA's semiphilanthropic mission. While convinced "that we must try and preserve for ever if possible the public character of the Association," he nonetheless insisted that "we must work on more or less commercial lines in order to enable us to raise the large sums of capital that will ultimately be required." Hutton continued to entertain ideas of raising more capital in the private sector, but W. H. Himbury was convinced that private investment would never materialize. Government was the BCGA's only hope, Himbury argued.[24]

When the war broke out, Hutton tried to demonstrate the importance of the BCGA's semiphilanthropic model. In terms of bales produced for export, the cotton industries of Uganda and the Caribbean were the most successful British cotton-growing regions by 1914, and thus were the most threatened by the war. Hutton pushed for ambitious partnerships between the BCGA, colonial governments, and private businesses to protect cotton exports from these areas. In Uganda, financing the crop was the main problem. Buyers wanted Ugandan cotton, but there was not enough money available to buy it and ship it under wartime freight and insurance rates. Worried colonial officials reported, "The natives have been encouraged by the Government to extend their cotton cultivation as far as possible, and its cessation would mean not only a material reduction in the receipts from poll-tax, but also a serious risk of disaffection among the natives and possibly of famine."[25] After lengthy negotiations, the BCGA and colonial government agreed to put up the capital together, sharing the risk. The BCGA demanded that local cotton-buying firms be forced to cooperate in purchasing the entire Ugandan crop at prices set by the BCGA.[26]

Back in London, the Treasury was unenthused by the idea of the CO taking financial responsibility for Uganda's cotton. Treasury officials had not directly dealt with the BCGA before and were not impressed by the association's philanthropic credentials. One skeptical official commented, "The Treasury need shed no official tear over the failure of this scheme."[27] The BCGA insisted that the goal of the financing plan was to protect farmers from exploitation by firms that might try to buy up the crop at bargain prices, but the Treasury concluded that the real goal was to "help keep down maximum [prices]." Despite opposition from rival merchants in Uganda, who argued that the BCGA was merely shutting out competitors, the plan was approved. Uganda's wartime cotton crop was purchased by the BCGA and cooperating merchant firms at a fixed price. The BCGA framed its cotton buy-up in Uganda as a philanthropic rescue mission, risking Lancashire's capital to honor a promise made to African farmers. As it turned out, the BCGA made a good deal of money on the crop when it finally reached foreign markets.

The problem in the Caribbean was more complicated, as the Sea Island cotton crop grown there had one principal buyer, the Fine Cotton Spinners' and Doublers' Association (FCSDA). Hutton had previously clashed with the FCSDA over cotton prices, suggesting that the firm "ought to look upon West Indian cotton-growing from a statesmanlike point of view," rather than "from a *purely business* point of view."[28] When the war started, Hutton urged planters to continue growing cotton, and he appealed to the FCSDA to buy up the entire crop at a fixed price. The FCSDA's directors took this to mean that they "should get the offer of all the Cotton at the minimum prices," while Hutton thought "the arrangement was to guarantee a minimum price, and that if it was possible to obtain higher prices from other Spinners the [BCGA] should be entitled to do so."[29]

The FCSDA responded by undercutting the BCGA in the islands, sending out a buying agent who "impressed on the community that cotton should bring high prices, and that he is prepared to give higher prices than the Association do, as the Association are purchasing the cotton for themselves." The agent alleged that "the Fine Spinners seem to regard it that the B.C.G.A. are not doing their best, and as there is a demand they wish to encourage more planting."[30] Hutton sent an urgent telegram to Francis Watts, commissioner of agriculture for the West Indies, stating, "We are informed certain individual arranging [to] buy cotton in West Indies undervalue. Strongly recommend planters continue to ship [to the] Association." Hutton claimed Sea Island cotton was fetching from 31d. to 36d. per pound in Liverpool, compared to the 22d. the FCSDA buyer was promising.

After an exchange of angry letters with FCSDA director H. W. Dixon, the two sides met. Dixon "asked if it was inimical to the interests of the B.C.G.A. that an increase in cotton production should be made, if such increase did not come through the B.C.G.A," suggesting that Hutton was jealous of competition. Dixon further charged that the BCGA was out to fleece the FCSDA, arguing that guaranteeing remunerative prices for planters did not require a public auction of scarce cotton.[31] Hutton complained to a CO official, "they are certain to put their private interests in front of everything else. . . . The whole thing has been a great blow to me for it has rather upset my confidence in human nature. I certainly thought that the people who were at the head of the Fine Spinners were more broadminded and philanthropic."[32] Hutton unsuccessfully conspired to have the government "commandeer the whole of the crop and for it to be dealt with by the Association who would sell it to the Spinners to fulfill Government contract," illustrating his willingness to seek state intervention whenever he deemed it necessary to protect BCGA projects.[33]

The BCGA had to turn to government and the FCSDA for financing in both cases because its own capital was inadequate to handle the quantities of cotton being produced in the colonies. Furthermore, the BCGA's capital was shrinking, as operational losses from its seed distribution, research, ginning, and buying activities eroded Lancashire's investment. The BCGA had received a series of small grants from the British government to offset some of these losses, but the last of these was due to expire in 1917. Hutton believed it was imperative to secure its renewal as a symbol of continuing government support for colonial cotton growing. He also hoped to capitalize on changing attitudes about the empire in Lancashire and the rest of Britain. Shortages of raw materials forced many in government and the private sector to reevaluate the wisdom of depending on free trade and the world market. By 1916, Lord Derby could confidently state that "the whole trend of National movement at the present moment is towards making Great Britain and Ireland, with its Colonies and Dependencies, a self supporting Empire."[34] At a mass meeting of manufacturers and workers, Hutton lectured Lancashire on the necessity of further government support for imperial development, blaming Lancashire itself for past failures:

> It was essential in the interests of Lancashire and for the whole of the country, that some substantial and material help should be given by the Government. . . . The Chairman [Hutton] suggested that the apathy of the Lancashire cotton trade had something to do with the matter, as Lancashire had not given the enthusiastic support to the Association which it deserved, and if the cotton trade wanted anything done now, it was for Lancashire to bring the necessary pressure. If the trade is really in earnest about this question, it is probably that great things could be done, as the favourable moment appears to have arrived; the Association have laid the foundations of a magnificent business proposition and it now remains for the Government to say what is the best thing to be done.[35]

The BCGA managed to get the workers and capitalists of Lancashire to once again lobby government on the association's behalf. Hutton continued to tout the BCGA's semiphilanthropic approach to cotton. He told colonial officials, "most of his colleagues had been brought up in a business school and there were frequent conflicts on policy, and the Imperial Grant was always a very useful lever," suggesting that all nonpaying BCGA work would immediately cease if the grant was not renewed.[36]

BCGA balance sheets showed that grants defrayed about 60 percent of the association's operating losses, and Hutton threatened to end services like the distribution of free seed across the empire if he did not receive another grant. "The Association have spent £177,886 of their capital in developing the industry," Hutton reported, candidly saying that "so far as Lancashire is concerned the direct return obtained is almost infinitesimal. The Government have however derived immediate benefits [in tax revenue] as a direct result of the Association's work."[37] Hutton's appeal, backed up by Lancashire notables and trade unions, attracted the government's attention. Chancellor of the Exchequer Andrew Bonar-Law personally went to bat for the association. He told Treasury officials, "a total cessation of the grant would be taken to mean that the Government had lost confidence in their work." According to Bonar-Law, Britain owed "much to Lord Derby and to Lancashire (where the operatives have put up part of the Association's funds)." He asked the British government "to agree to this small concession to them."[38] This intercession won a one-year grant of £1,000, but the Treasury inserted an explicit statement that it was the last grant the association would ever receive from the imperial government. It did not help matters that the BCGA paid its first dividend (2.5 percent on subscribed capital) as it was begging for the renewed grant, making it look like something of a war profiteer.[39]

The Empire Cotton Growing Committee and Corporation

In the end, no colonial cotton was left to rot for lack of buyers, but the BCGA's wartime experience made powerful enemies. J. W. McConnel, an FCSDA boss who also served on the BCGA council, led an independent campaign to create the Empire Cotton Growing Committee (ECG Committee). The ECG Committee was a spin-off of the Empire Resources Development Committee (ERDC), which was itself a parliamentary group formed to stimulate colonial production of badly needed wartime supplies. The ERDC marked a major turn in government attitudes toward the colonies; its members rejected the old Liberal idea that colonies were best developed by private industry alone. Instead, the ERDC assumed the Chamberlainite position that the empire was "a collection of undeveloped estates which the metropolis had definite rights to treat as imperial possessions."[40]

ERDC members challenged prewar policies that had protected African land and labor from "capitalistic exploitation." The committee concluded that colonial officials and private capitalists had both failed to adequately utilize the resources of the colonies. "[At] great sacrifice of life and treasure we have given millions of natives in Africa security of life and property," the committee argued. "We can fairly claim that the native shall in return bear their share of the Imperial burden."[41] British policy makers dropped the guise of "philanthropic" colonial development and ordered colonial administrations to produce raw materials for British industry. Fortunately for African farmers, the wartime shortage of resources and the subsequent postwar economic crash prevented the committee from fully implementing a harsh policy of economic exploitation.[42]

Hutton at first refused to sit on the Empire Cotton Growing Committee with McConnel. He even threatened to resign from the BCGA, saying McConnel had "gone out of his way on several occasions to injure the Association." Government officials told Hutton that McConnel "was the widest-read man in the World on this particular subject," and Hutton grudgingly agreed to participate.[43] McConnel's position on cotton growing was clear: experimental and "missionary" work should be in government hands, while buying and ginning should be done by private firms on a self-supporting but highly regulated basis. The merchants on the BCGA council feared that the new committee "were endeavouring to obtain control of all African produce," using the war as an excuse to force merchants into a noncompetitive role as government buying agents.[44]

By the time the ECG Committee began to take testimony on the future of Britain's cotton industry in 1917, Hutton was despondent. His only hope was that the BCGA might be "reconstituted on a stronger basis, and with a stronger official status" in recognition of its wartime work.[45] Using evidence from the Sudan Plantations Syndicate, Hutton made a case for the preservation of the semiphilanthropic model through a new, semiofficial BCGA. Private capitalists and government could work in partnership, developing cotton growing in Africa together. When asked, "You really mean to make the whole thing a minor Department of State?" Hutton answered, "Absolutely."[46]

Weeks of further testimony changed Hutton's mind about the advisability of private-public partnerships. McConnel and other witnesses criticized the BCGA's scientific and "missionary" efforts, arguing that only a scientifically oriented government agency could overcome the problems of agrarian development in the empire. Hostile witnesses attacked Hutton and other BCGA officials for their management of cotton buying and ginning, alleging that their expertise as merchants was no substitute for real experience in agriculture. McConnel wrote that it was "premature and presumptuous" for the BCGA to ask for new powers as a government department, and argued that this could happen only if the BCGA "would no longer be nominally an Association for profit."[47]

As the war dragged on and ECG Committee hearings continued, Hutton warned his colleagues in the BCGA Executive Council that "it would be a great mistake if the business was run by a Government Department."[48] A cotton department without the businessmen of the BCGA was doomed, he thought. Under personal attack, Hutton resigned as BCGA chairman in January 1918. He cited his failing health and high stress level, but also lashed out at a government he thought was stingy and unappreciative of his work. Political leaders like Lord Derby and Lord Emmott accepted Hutton's resignation with relief, and the BCGA council appointed the more diplomatic W. H. Himbury to the chairmanship. Hutton was made an honorary vice-president and continued to attend occasional BCGA meetings, but his dominance of the association was over.[49] Emmott and Derby hoped to have Hutton knighted to ensure that his departure would not jeopardize the reputation of the BCGA, but the government refused on grounds that Hutton had previously declined such an honor, and that his wartime work did not merit special honors.[50]

From the outside, Hutton complained that a business conspiracy was out to disband the philanthropic BCGA, "who were not out for profits." The FCSDA and McConnel were the villains in this drama, supposedly undermining two decades of work for the benefit of a few Lancashire spinners. Hutton admitted that "the Association had not made the progress hoped for, and there was no chance of making cotton cultivation a success unless it had the whole weight and backing of the Government." Still, he "did not see how the ECGC were going to work any better than the Association had done, and the Committee had not the organisation or the experience which the Association possessed. The Association had suffered because commercial bodies had looked upon them with jealousy, and on the other hand some Government officials had treated them as a commercial body who were not entitled to preferential treatment."[51] The only remedy was that government "appoint the Association the Government agents in all matters of cotton growing."[52] But the BCGA's lackluster record in Africa and the enemies it had made among the ranks of CO officials, as well as in Lancashire, sealed its fate.

McConnel had his own plans for the BCGA and the Empire Cotton Growing Committee. Although his personal clash with Hutton led to some unwarranted attacks on the BCGA leadership, McConnel's broad critique of the association was sound. Competing with and even hoping to replace the American supply of long-staple cotton was fruitless, he argued. Hutton's early claims "that the production of cotton in America has reached, or nearly reached its limits" were nonsense. Britain should have invested in specialty long-staple cottons from the beginning, McConnel argued, and these were the varieties that were thriving in the Caribbean, Egypt, Uganda, and Sudan. As a fine-spinner, McConnel had a clear interest in creating a larger supply of these fibers, which were in high demand for automobile tires and other new uses. He made a nationalist argument as well, pointing out that the survival of Lancashire as an economic power depended on the growth of fine-spinning, the only field where Britain retained a strong competitive advantage in the world marketplace. "No invidious comparison is intended between different districts in Lancashire," he said, nonetheless noting "the fact that on the whole British spindles and looms are employed on much finer work than those of most other countries."[53]

McConnel's opinion was that colonial agricultural departments, rather than the BCGA, had done the most important work in encouraging cotton growing, and he made a case for restructuring the BCGA as a nonprofit utility company. The BCGA would "act as agent for the Empire Cotton Growing Committee for marketing crops where this is desired by the local Government." McConnel wanted the BCGA to "forego the appropriation of any profits made in the business carried on under the agreement, provided that the Association is guaranteed against permanent loss arising therefrom."[54] Effectively the BCGA would become a state-subsidized, nonprofit ginning utility.

When the war ended, Lancashire demanded a strong government role in cotton growing. In Parliament, Lancashire's MPs thought "the BCGA had done good work, but there was a feeling . . . that the work which had been done should now materialise into something realistic."[55] While BCGA policies were all too real for African farmers, it was clear in Lancashire that they had done little to supply Britain with cotton. Labor organizations reminded government that operatives had subscribed to the BCGA "without any prospect of any return on their money." They had "during the war, made great sacrifices, for example by agreeing to short time, and they considered that the Government had a duty to help them now."[56] In the final settlement, the ECG Committee was given control over all cotton research and propaganda in the Empire. The BCGA—shorn of Hutton's leadership—was allowed to retain its profit-making work, operating ginneries as a utility company. By 1916, the BCGA was already beginning to replace the phrase "semiphilanthropic" with "semicommercial," reflecting the shift away from research and propaganda.[57]

The ECG Committee evolved into the Empire Cotton Growing Corporation (ECGC), a quasi-private entity that supported scientific research on a grand scale. It was funded by a small levy on cotton imported into Britain and by a £1 million gift from the government. The gift was in fact an involuntary contribution from colonial subjects in Egypt, who were forced in 1918–19 to sell cotton through a government program that siphoned off excess profits.[58] By taking responsibility for financing research, the ECGC was able to direct scientific experiments into the subjects and places its leadership found most promising. As a CO official warned in 1920, "If [private industry in] Lancashire has to bear the cost of stimulating cotton production, it will be entitled to choose the site and there is no reason why it should give Uganda, Nigeria, Nyasaland, or the Sudan any preference over, say, Brazil."[59]

Essentially an independent department of agriculture for the British Empire, the ECGC was charged with encouraging the growth of cotton, researching soils and climates, experimenting with new varieties and farming techniques, and battling cotton pests. The ECGC sponsored cotton research in universities and published the *Empire Cotton Growing Review*, a journal reporting on scientific and policy achievements in the empire. The ECGC did not neatly replace or augment the BCGA, as some historians have suggested.[60] The BCGA was in fact reconstructed to serve the objectives of the imperial government and the new ECGC cotton-growing regime. Committed to commercial tasks like buying and ginning cotton, the BCGA became a profitable company, returning regular dividends to the thousands of investors who had supported it since 1902. Still, its operations were haunted by the association's semiphilanthropic past. The BCGA continued to receive special benefits like reduced freight from colonial governments, on grounds that the colonial cotton sector could not stand on its own in the world economy.[61] Government agricultural departments continued to police cotton cultivation and especially cotton markets throughout the colonial period and beyond, perpetuating and expanding regulatory policies the BCGA had initiated. BCGA operations continued until 1972, when the association was wound up. Faced with nationalization threats in Nigeria and Malawi, the BCGA sold its remaining ginneries to Ralli Brothers.[62]

The End of an Atlantic World of Cotton

During the First World War, Macara presciently warned manufacturers and farmers of the dangers of volatile cotton prices. "It is just as important to prevent too rapid a depreciation in the price of the raw material as it is to prevent a further undue inflation of it," he said. "It will be found that skilful management is as essential in emerging from the war, as it was in entering upon the war."[63] Unfortunately for everyone involved, skillful management gave way to reckless enthusiasm on both sides of the Atlantic. The result was the collapse of a century-old division of labor and the spread of cotton agriculture and cotton manufacturing far beyond the Atlantic region.

In the American South, the war repeated the cycle of the prewar cotton crisis. Despair at low cotton prices in 1915 caused farmers to cut acreage, leading to a series of short crops. Pessimism gave way to exuberance as cotton prices reached new records in 1917. The South enjoyed great returns from cotton between 1917 and 1920. There were "marveling reports of debt settlements, forty-five-dollar suits, six-dollar shirts, eight-dollar shoes, and most spectacular of all, the automobile invasion of the rural South."[64] In 1919, a South Carolina planter launched the American Cotton Association (ACA) to revive the cotton populist movement, which had faded after the collapse of the Southern Cotton Association and the subsequent expansion of the National Farmers' Union outside the cotton belt.[65] The ACA hoped to keep cotton prices high through warehousing and crop diversification strategies, but its efforts were overshadowed by new USDA-sponsored programs.[66] Government had taken the reins of the cotton economy in the South.

Farmers and spinners also met that year in New Orleans for the Second (actually third) World Cotton Congress. The Washington (1906) and Atlanta (1907) conferences both ended with farmers and manufacturers at an impasse. In 1919, high prices for textiles and raw cotton gave all sides of the industry confidence that a new era of prosperity was beginning. American spinner J. R. MacColl told the audience, "It is a good time to brush aside old and inefficient methods. The economic world is being reconstructed. The cotton industry cannot stand still, but must join in the forward march."[67] Cotton speculator Theodore Price urged the industry to use "voluntary cooperation or financial compulsion" to regulate itself, using the cotton exchanges to control speculation and limit market fluctuations. Price asked, "is it not true that a great many people would be benefited by the more deliberate and gradual operation of the law of supply and demand which would probably thus be insured?"[68] Few Europeans attended the conference, however, and no representatives of the colonial cotton-growing programs bothered to attend. British cotton expert J. A. Todd delivered what amounted to a surrender speech on behalf of colonial cotton to the audience at New Orleans. He admitted "that all of the work we have done in Africa, for nearly twenty years, has produced in no year one hundred thousand bales of cotton. You [Americans] are throwing away more than that every year—more than we have been able to do in twenty years."[69] Todd assured the audience, "We have never yet reached the limit of the world's demand for cotton good," and he encouraged Americans to continue expanding cotton production.[70] American farmers took this message to heart. As they saw it, the war had brought about a new order. The ACA's president declared, "The old day of low-price labor and low-cost cotton has gone forever. The old economic claims of the all-cotton system have been broken and gone to the scrap heap, never again to be forged . . . these things have made the South poor, not rich."[71]

At the end of the war, farmers "bought new lands at inflated prices, and mortgaged themselves to the limit" to take advantage of record cotton prices.[72] By 1920, cotton supplies caught up with world demand and prices tumbled. Between July and December, cotton fell from 40¢ per pound to 13¢. The worst elements of cotton populism returned as night riders threatened cotton pickers and burned gins and warehouses across the cotton belt. The boll weevil was also on the march, and in 1921 it destroyed the entire US Sea Island crop, in addition to ravaging 30 percent of the Upland cotton crop. The next two decades saw wild fluctuations in cotton prices as farmers alternately increased and reduced acreage. USDA programs encouraged farmers to gradually adopt new machines, fertilizers, pesticides, and crop varieties, helping farmers with good land and access to credit to earn a living in the tumultuous 1920s and 1930s. Franklin Roosevelt's New Deal brought even more aid to cotton farmers, but wealthy landowners benefited disproportionately. Sharecroppers and smallholders could not weather the large annual fluctuations in cotton prices, nor did they have the capital required to access key federal programs. Groups like the Southern Tenant Farmers' Union fought unsuccessfully to bring government assistance to the classes that needed it most in the South.

Government assistance brought scientific techniques, credit, and state regulation of cotton handling and marketing to the industry, but the biggest transformation came with the arrival of an effective mechanical harvester. "A successful cotton picker has been just right around the corner of the late eighty-seven years," quipped one observer in 1937, but by the 1940s several companies had developed workable machines.[73] Like Whitney's cotton gin, the mechanical cotton harvester's success depended on changing market conditions as much as it did on technology. The saw gin rapidly removed fiber from the seeds of *G. hirsutum,* but early nineteenth-century manufacturers spurned the short and uneven cotton that resulted. Ultimately the low price of saw-ginned cotton forced manufacturers to adapt their spindles to the stuff. Machine-harvested cotton was (and remains) dirtier than hand-picked cotton, contaminated with leaf and boll fragments and other debris. The viability of American machine-harvested cotton depended on a host of interrelated components. First, the rising cost of labor in South and the low price of cotton produced elsewhere in the world meant that American farmers had to mechanize, or go out of business. In America, only the highest grades of cotton were worth hand-picking at the prices prevailing after 1945. Second, the mechanical harvester relied on a collection of other technologies that helped farmers grow large amounts of cotton as cheaply as possible. As historian Clyde Woods noted, the American cotton belt experienced a mechanical revolution as well as "biological, chemical, hydraulic, geological, and organizational revolutions."[74] Without fertilizers, pesticides, groundwater irrigation, and capital, the large-scale plantations on which harvesters efficiently worked would have been impossible. Chemical "harvest-aid materials" were especially important. Early harvesting machines had failed because they collected too much debris from the cotton plant, and the success of the new harvesters owed much to new chemicals, which "defoliate plant leaves, accelerate boll opening, enhance seed cotton drying in the field, and, in some cases, desiccate green plant material."[75] Where human hands had once deftly plucked clean cotton and skipped over unripe bolls, machines and chemicals could now sweep entire fields of cotton. The widespread use of chemicals in cotton cultivation, especially pesticides, had a devastating impact on human and environmental health in the South and beyond.[76]

From the 1930s and 1940s, American cotton farming became an agrotechnical system, backed by state power. African American farmers and laborers were rarely the beneficiaries of this new system. The Rust brothers, who invented one of the more successful cotton harvesters, were well aware that their machine meant that "75% of the labor population would be thrown out of employment."[77] The Southern Tenant Farmers' Union warned that black and white laborers were all doomed to be "displaced by the mechanical cotton picker, flame cultivator, mechanical cotton chopper, four-row cultivator and other labor-saving devices."[78]

Economic historian Donald Holley argued that the mechanical harvester and other innovations "emancipated" Southern farm workers, and especially African Americans, from the most arduous elements of cotton production. Recognizing that the substitution of machines for human labor meant unemployment for many, Holley claimed that African Americans were further "emancipated" from social oppression by being driven out of the South through unemployment. African Americans were certainly emancipated from cotton, a crop that under the social and political conditions of the South would never favor the economic advancement of black people. Holley's evidence from the Arkansas delta illustrates the racialized dynamics of the new cotton economy in the South: the number of white farmers there fell from 57,298 in 1935 to 40,446 by 1954, and to 15,229 in 1974. For black farmers, the decrease was far greater: from 48,640 in 1935, their ranks fell to 22,522 in 1954. By 1974, only 1,230 remained. While figures vary from region to region, the trend across the South is unmistakable: black farmers were nearly eliminated from commercial cotton agriculture, while a sizable core of white farmers managed to endure.[79] Fewer than twenty-thousand cotton farmers remain in the United States today, and a tiny fraction of them identify as African Americans. This transition toward capital-intensive cotton cultivation was built on technology and government support, but it also occurred in a period of intensifying violence and political oppression aimed at black Americans in the 1950s and 1960s. As Clyde Woods concluded, viewing the transition merely as a "mechanical revolution" masks the "astoundingly brutal attack upon rural African American communities and labor [which] the transformation involved."[80] The result today is a cotton industry that is emphatically a "white man's industry," to borrow an early-twentieth-century phrase. Despite the benefits of mechanization and state regulation, the American cotton industry still requires subsidies to compete with machine- and hand-picked cotton from other parts of the world.

These interventions were unable to halt America's fall from monopoly producer to second-rate power over the second half of the twentieth century. On the other end of the old bipolar cotton system, Lancashire manufacturers fared much worse. They enjoyed few benefits from the state over the course of the twentieth century, despite intensifying efforts to extract cotton from Britain's colonies. Lancashire's initial response to the end of the First World War was exuberant. Shipping shortages and cotton rationing had starved cloth markets around the world, and the German, Belgian, Austrian, French, and Russian cotton textile industries were more or less out of commission. Demand for cloth was incredible, and prices for finished textiles soared (table 5.3). Oldham mills paid out a staggering 40 percent dividend to shareholders in 1920. Exports of cotton piece goods had grown by only 20 percent between 1918 and 1920, but their value rose by nearly 125 percent. Instead of rebuilding cash reserves, restoring wages to labor, or investing in colonial cotton, mill owners spent this windfall on a recapitalization spree. Few new spindles were added; rather, firms were refloated at much higher prices. New investors scrambled to join the cotton export boom, and about 40 percent of Lancashire's cotton spindles changed hands between 1918 and 1920.[81] Most of the fine-spinners in Bolton "kept out of the evil boom reflotations," seeing it as irrational.[82] Trade unions were also skeptical; the workers feared that "mills will be required to earn more to pay interest on increased capital, and this will send up the price of goods, prevent orders from being secured, and keep down the wages of the workers."[83]

Table 5.3. Trade statistics for Lancashire, 1913–31

	Average margin*	Average mill dividend	Average mill profit	Cotton piece goods exports (million pounds)	Value of cotton exports (million £)
1913	3.43d.	7.25%	£5,366	1291.4	126.5
1914	2.82	6.88	531	1046.9	102.6
1915	3.25	5	–150	866.7	85.2
1916	2.19	6	4,004	959	117.2
1917	6.18	7.5	5,739	908.6	144.8
1918	24.62	16.25	14,403	675.2	178.7
1920	29.88	40.21	n/a	809.5	401.4
1922	7	4.01	n/a	813.8	186.9
1931	2.98	1.46	n/a	334.6	56.6

Source: Robson, *Cotton Industry*, 334–38.
Note: Figures shown for American Upland middling cotton and 32s yarn. "Margin" is the trade term for the difference in the prices of raw cotton and finished yarn.

When cotton prices crashed, Lancashire's cloth producers could not slash costs quickly enough. Recapitalized firms with heavy loan charges and commitments to new shareholders found they could not compete with firms that had remained aloof. Old firms with paid-off machines preferred selling yarn at cost to letting their machinery sit idle.[84] After 1920, Lancashire firms, especially those in the American cotton-consuming sector, colluded in a number of price-fixing and work-sharing schemes to ease competitive pressures.[85] Sir Charles Macara and other spinners appealed for government aid, observing that "Recourse to legislation has been resorted to already in the matter of raising funds for the development of the cotton fields of the Empire." Macara failed to see "why we should hesitate again to obtain powers from the Government if those powers will assist us in putting the cotton trade into a prosperous state."[86] But there was no hope for Lancashire. Colonial schemes like the SPS at Gezira and a new BCGA venture in the Punjab did not produce enough cheap cotton to save Oldham's mills. Fine-spinning firms fared better, but by the late 1930s Lancashire was a shadow of its former self. By the 1970s, cotton spinning had nearly died out in Britain. New producers like Japan and India seized many of Lancashire's prized markets, including those the BCGA had helped make in Africa. Cotton was no longer centered on a neat division of labor between America and Europe, and the labor of Africans and the

African diaspora was no longer viewed as the crucial factor in the production of cheap cotton.

The possibility of cooperation across racial divides waned alongside Lancashire's fortunes. E. D. Morel continued to advocate for partnership between white workers in Britain and black workers in Africa, but his tone became more paternalistic. (Morel also published ugly statements about African troops stationed in occupied Germany, jeopardizing his antiracist credentials.)[87] In *The Black Man's Burden*, published in 1920, Morel condemned colonial capitalism as racist, immoral, and economically unproductive. Yet he continued to celebrate the BCGA as an alternative model, and he expressed hope that British workers would see "the human associations connected with the raw material they handle." Morel had joined the socialist movement during the First World War, and he came to see the industrial working class as the vanguard of "a great democratic drive for the honest, just, and humane treatment of the coloured races."[88] Unfortunately, Lancashire's working class was in no mood for racial solidarity. White men refused to labor next to black men from Britain's African and West Indian colonies. Rioters attacked black men and women in Liverpool and other British cities in 1919, blaming them for unemployment and housing shortages.[89] Other riots broke out across Britain, with white crowds attacking black people, many of whom had been in Britain for decades. The mill towns of Lancashire did not experience acute racial violence, but the mood across Britain shifted. No longer confident in their status as citizens of the wealthiest and most powerful empire on earth, Britons became increasingly defensive about securing their own privileges within Britain, and keeping imperial subjects in the colonies. While only a few hundred black seamen were in Liverpool during the 1919 riots, they symbolized the erosion of imperial order for many in Lancashire. They were men out of place, competing with white men for jobs in Britain instead of laboring in faraway colonies on Britain's behalf.[90] Hardening racial attitudes in Britain contributed to harsher policies within the empire, dooming Morel's dream of cross-racial cooperation through organizations like the semiphilanthropic BCGA.

The geographic shift of the cotton industry away from Lancashire and the American South reflected change on a global scale, as empires collapsed and new nation-states sought to take control of their own economic destinies. Nationalist governments "believed that they needed to make the transition to industrial capitalism more swiftly, including the mobilization of labor, territory, markets, and raw materials." As in earlier colonial regimes, state power substituted for market incentives in many of these new industrializers. Sven Beckert observed that "State-directed economic planning, which had claimed its first great victories in Europe's scattered imperial possessions, was by the 1950s the globe's efficient and seemingly inevitable norm."[91] Beckert argues, however, the global reorganization of the cotton industry also reflected an unmooring of capitalism from state institutions that had used war, slavery, and empire to fuel economic growth during the eighteenth and nineteenth centuries. Capitalists were eager to pursue lower costs across national borders. Sometimes this meant chasing subsidies and tariff protections offered by industrializing states. By the late 1940s, even Lancashire manufacturers concluded that it was "better to employ our capital abroad . . . than to sit at home mourning the loss of so much of our . . . export business."[92] By the time protectionist policies began to yield to free trade in the 1980s and 1990s, the cotton industry had shifted from a bipolar system (American agriculture and British manufacturing) to a multipolar world with many competing agricultural and manufacturing regions. Low wages in agriculture and manufacturing helped China emerge as a cotton superpower in this era, but the growth of global trade and the mobility of capital ensure that there is no dominant core today in either cotton agriculture or textile manufacturing. Depending on one's point of view, cotton has either given poor workers across the planet a chance to earn an income from farming or manufacturing, or it has driven them into a merciless "race to the bottom" as buyers of raw cotton and textiles seek ever-lower prices.

Cotton and Development in Colonial and Postcolonial Africa

The Empire Cotton Growing Corporation represented a new, scientifically oriented phase in the economic development of Britain's African colonies. Some scholars, like James C. Scott, date the onset of the "development era" to a later period, arguing that post-1945 developments were entirely new and that "The point of departure for colonial policy was a complete faith in what officials took for 'scientific agriculture' on the one hand and nearly total skepticism about the agricultural practices of Africans on the other."[93] Colonial administrators of the 1920s and 1930s (many of them new to the job and scientifically trained) tended to believe that they were the first people to seriously investigate the challenges of economic development in Africa. Helen Tilley shifted this date back to 1918 for Britain's empire, but still concluded that before this point "neither the agricultural departments nor the Colonial Office adopted a consistent or coherent approach. Agricultural activities proceeded in an ad hoc fashion, and only a few scientific studies were supported through botanical stations and field surveys."[94]

These conclusions were based on the writings of colonial officials, who experienced a severe case of institutional amnesia. Just as post-1945 administrators paid little attention to past experience, the ECGC and other colonial economic branches forgot that twenty years of lackluster experiments had preceded the new development mission of the 1920s. G. Howard Jones claimed in his influential 1934 study of West African agriculture that "until the last few years it was nobody's special business to help the native peasant, and especially the African small grower, to farm better." The BCGA's experts and their partners in the colonial government had made a substantial effort to transform the way cotton was grown by African farmers, but the failures of the cotton-growing campaign obscured any lessons that might have been learned. Indeed, the new colonial science was marked by an "unlearning" of the agricultural and economic lessons of the BCGA's experiences as much as it was by new scientific knowledge of plants and soils. By the 1930s Jones could confidently claim that African agriculture was characterized by a "general unskilfulness and lack of precision" caused by the cultural backwardness of African peoples.[95] Jones disregarded evidence accumulated by BCGA experts attesting to the many advantages of indigenous African farming techniques, like mixed cropping.

O. T. Faulkner, who became Nigeria's director of agriculture in 1921, exemplified this new wave of scientific administration in colonial Africa. Faulkner "insisted that useful agricultural advice could not be given unless it was based on research carried out in local conditions, and tested and verified by experiment." Officials like Faulkner dedicated their resources to research, believing that basic science was the first step toward any plan of development. As a result, extension work was "rather soft-pedalled," hurting farmers who in previous years had been told to look to BCGA or CO officials for expert advice, new seeds and tools, and marketing assistance.[96] Scientists like Faulkner rejected the BCGA's attempts to blend commercial agriculture with research, seeing sound science as the true foundation of economic change and growth.

Gradually, colonial scientists realized that "the luxurious foliage [of tropical Africa] rested on fragile foundations."[97] They paid greater attention to local conditions and local agricultural techniques. The ECGC's goal shifted from finding an American cotton that would grow in Africa, toward broader studies of plant breeding, pests, and environmental conditions. The Allen variety was successful enough as an interim crop, and in Nigeria the ECGC focused on evolving "a strain of cotton thoroughly suited to Nigerian environment, and exhibiting at the same time the particular qualities as to length, strength, colour, texture, and so forth, which Lancashire requires, coupled with the highest acreage-yield and lint-percentage attainable under Nigerian conditions."[98] The ECGC recognized that farmers had choices, and would grow only cotton if it brought good prices.

African cotton growers got a mixed lot from the postwar shift toward scientific development. The end of the BCGA's "philanthropic" cotton buying after 1918 coincided with a postwar frenzy for cotton and cotton goods, and farmers initially benefited from high prices. There was no protection, however, when the crash came. Until the 1930s, when state-controlled marketing boards reinstated fixed prices in many colonies, African farmers suffered from violent fluctuations in cotton prices. The end of the BCGA's scientific mission freed African farmers from J. A. Hutton's schemes for the transplantation of American cotton to African soil, but the new scientific colonial regime brought its own problems to Africa. The failure of peasant agriculture to produce large amounts of cotton inspired megalomaniacal projects aimed at bending land and labor to the needs of cotton cultivation. In Sudan, the irrigation works at Gezira were completed and significantly extended, and French Soudan and Portuguese Mozambique saw similar projects in the interwar period.[99] According to Western visitors, the Gezira scheme was a model of colonial benevolence: the farmer was "installed upon good land with a full supply of water, with English overseers to guide him in sowing, and an assured income." "I never met a more content, happy-looking body of people," wrote a visiting missionary in 1930. "They were no longer serfs and slaves. . . . They were free, independent, and contented agriculturalists."[100] Sudanese farmers were also locked into an agro-technical complex they could not control, forced to grow cotton in exchange for access to land and water for food production. Farmers were utterly at the mercy of the Sudan Plantations Syndicate for water, seeds, and chemicals, and were forced to sell their cotton to the syndicate.

The success of the Gezira model in producing cotton for export encouraged "the belief that agricultural problems could be easily solved by 'crash programmes' involving heavy investment in irrigation and mechanisation."[101] The farmers, the syndicate, and the state prospered for a time, but the enormous technical and financial structure proved inflexible when hard times struck. When cotton prices slumped after 1929, the SPS continued to pay dividends to investors while the Sudanese government continued servicing loans for the irrigation works, but these payments were possible only because of lower prices the SPS offered to Sudanese farmers for their produce, and by cutting services.[102]

The BCGA supported a similar irrigated cotton project in Punjab, where the Indian government had been creating "canal colonies" from the late nineteenth century onward. The Punjab project had many similarities to the Gezira scheme, reflecting a desire on the part of British administrators to create "an entirely new society on barren wasteland, under the aegis of state authority but with the active involvement of the native population." Much of the agricultural land was dedicated to wheat and fodder crops for transport animals, but the BCGA introduced American long-staple cotton around 1916 with the stated purpose of growing "improved cottons for export to the textile mills of Lancashire."[103] A key difference between the Punjab canal colonies and Gezira, however, was the level of corporate control over farm routines. While the Sudan Plantations Syndicate closely monitored and effectively managed almost all of the agricultural process from planting to harvest to marketing, the day-to-day work in Punjab was largely left to subtenants, working as renters or sharecroppers. The colonial government evidently could not imagine imposing the kind of social control exercised in Africa in India, and hoped that a capitalist class would quickly emerge among the Punjabi tenants to lead the region's economic development.

The BCGA established a major seed farm at the Lower Bari Doab colony and at its peak the BCGA-Punjab Ltd. subsidiary of the BCGA was the largest renter in all of Punjab, with seventy thousand acres. The core seed farm appears to have been operated as a wage-labor plantation, but to cultivate the rest of its vast holdings the association was "entirely dependent on the subtenancy system." As in Africa, the BCGA worked to eradicate local cotton varieties, which, "apart from providing generally lower yields, were less competitive as marketable commodities [in Liverpool]." In cooperation with the Indian agriculture department, the BCGA tasked farmers with sowing only "pure seed," planted in orderly rows. Farmers were expected to abandon traditional farming techniques and adopt new plows and other tools to prepare and maintain fields according to "scientific" guidelines. Without the domineering influence of a colonial or corporate overlord, however, the BCGA found that it could not force Punjabi farmers to grow the kinds of cotton the association wanted in the way they wanted it grown. Many tenant farmers grew a mix of crops and focused on wheat, which they could eat in the event of a crisis. Subtenants focused on achieving high returns in the shortest time. They had no vested interest in the land, and cotton appealed to them as a cash crop with a ready market, thanks to the BCGA's buying stations. The colonial government became concerned about the enthusiasm of subtenants for cotton: "Good land is being overtaxed by continued croppings of cotton, and inferior land, which is capable of bearing good fodder crops, is being made weaker still by attempts to grow cotton on it." Farmers effectively mined the soil, extracting cotton as quickly as possible while leaving behind a barren waste. The BCGA also found that Punjabi farmers were mixing American seeds with hardy indigenous varieties. Following its African precedent, the BCGA pushed for a 1925 law regulating ginneries and restricting access to seed, but this bill was ineffective. Historian Imran Ali found that "By the 1930s, seed quality had begun to suffer, and it became increasingly difficult, and expensive, to obtain pure American seed."[104] The "adulterated" cotton fetched lower prices on the world market, forcing farmers to expand cultivation even further to maintain their incomes. Without the carrot of high prices or the stick of coercive micromanagement, the BCGA found itself in the same predicament the CSA encountered a century earlier, when a cycle of adverse selection led to the simultaneous deterioration of Indian cotton quality and Indian cotton prices. The end result in Punjab was extensive growth in the irrigated colonies but not real development. Like American sharecroppers in the late nineteenth century and Gezira tenants of the mid twentieth century, Punjabi farmers fell into debt and found themselves chained to an unpredictable world commodity market.

Where gigantic irrigation works and social engineering projects were impractical, colonial planners developed a more nuanced approach to peasant agriculture, giving up on "the introduction of 'sound' European agricultural practices such as planting in pure stands, deep plowing, crop rotation, and clean weeding." Agricultural officials did learn a few lessons from the BCGA's failures in Africa: they focused less on high cotton yields and exotic varieties, developing a new appreciation for "the variability of local climatic and soil conditions and the dynamics of local farming systems."[105] But prescriptive rules for cotton planting and rigid policies aimed at checking soil erosion and eradicating pests and disease forced farmers to intensify their labor inputs, often without incentives like higher prices or bonuses to encourage superior cotton.[106] In Nyasaland, for example, the government dropped all pretenses of a competitive market for cotton in 1923 and gave the BCGA a monopoly in the colony. "Government officials no longer insisted that minimum rates should reflect upward trends in the cotton market, as they had periodically done in the past."[107]

Richard Roberts argued that across Africa, colonial planners used cotton agriculture to "impose order on African societies and to render intelligible Africans' economic and social behavior."[108] In too many cases, cotton production became a convenient tool by which colonial officials forced Africans into economic activities associated with an abstract idea of "progress," paying little attention to economic utility. An especially egregious case occurred in southern Sudan during the 1930s, when British administrators forced cotton on Africans "for purely ideological reasons." The British knew that the cotton produced would be economically insignificant to the colony, but as one administrator put it, cotton growing was part of "a long-term process of education" in commodity production, taxpaying, and participation in the colonial and global economic system.[109]

Things did not improve much after the Second World War, when the "second colonial occupation" further reined in the independence of farmers across Africa. The historian Cyril Ehrlich was optimistic that the failure of post-1945 projects like the Tanzania groundnut scheme might change the direction of colonial development toward a market-based approach: "Beset by economic crises, groundnut fiascos, and a [Colonial Development Corporation] deficit of more than £8 million, we are thinking again. We are discovering that things have to be produced before they can be distributed; that the problem of production is never finally solved; that 'enterprise' can be something more than a term of abuse."[110] Ehrlich's hopes were misplaced. Instead of learning from past mistakes, colonial officials looked for new models, turning to scholarly fads like "modernization theory." Raymond Dumett noted several decades ago that "descriptions of spectacular achievements have always been more fashionable than the analysis of projects that ended in stagnation or failure," and colonial officials readily borrowed models from America or Europe instead of reexamining indigenous practices or the long history of failed colonial agricultural experiments.[111] The BCGA's history in Africa illustrated that market conditions were much more important than scientific knowledge in determining the success or failure of cotton, but the lessons were forgotten.

Across Africa, "the agricultural extension agent replaced the district officer as the embodiment of colonial authoritarianism" as colonial powers intensified their efforts to extract wealth from the colonies.[112] Proponents of cotton growing abandoned positive inducements in favor of more regulation and discipline. A telling example was a 1946 law in Nyasaland that threatened peasant farmers with heavy fines and imprisonment for flouting agricultural regulations.[113] Colonial officials dropped the market incentives that lay at the heart of the original BCGA project, but retained the idea that extraeconomic control wielded by the state was necessary to propel Africa toward economic growth.

Two films sponsored by the ECGC illustrate the divergent paths of development that resulted from the BCGA's work.[114] *Black Cotton* (1927) focused on Nigeria, where the cotton industry continued to be subject to a moderate level of colonial regulation. In some parts of Nigeria, farmers willingly chose cotton as the best cash crop available. In a matter-of-fact style, the film shows Nigerians harvesting, transporting, selling, and ginning cotton. The film's text celebrates cotton as a "purely native" industry and the narration avoids racist language. It makes no mention of the ECGC or the BCGA, whose gins were likely depicted in the film. *Black Cotton* concludes with a sympathetic portrayal of Nigerian cloth-making techniques, emphasizing the skill of Nigerian craft workers. The film was shown in other African colonies by Julian Huxley as part of a research project for the Colonial Advisory Committee on Native Education. According to Huxley, students in Kenya and Uganda responded favorably to the film's depiction of Nigerian cotton and Nigerian cotton farmers: "I saw the women picking cotton from the pods and put in the sacks, and how they gin it by machines called gins. Also how they tie in bales, and how they make clothing. All these were shown to us. And we were pleased with them." "We found that the people of Nigeria are now civilized," one student reported.[115] Some of the BCGA's supporters, like, E. D. Morel, would have been proud of this film. (Many in Lancashire would have grimaced at seeing Nigerian handicraft weavers busily at work as late as 1927, however.) The film illustrated how the BCGA's "philanthropic" business investment had provided mechanical gins as well as an export market to serve a thriving local industry. African farmers were subject to regulation and compelled to use certain seeds and chemical inputs, but were otherwise left to work out their own futures as cotton farmers.

A 1967 children's textbook for African students titled *The Story of Nigerian Cotton* attests to the durability of the agricultural compromise reached by farmers, the BCGA, and the colonial and postcolonial state in Nigeria. The book examines the life of Adamu, a prosperous farmer living near Gombe, who grew cotton in rotation with groundnuts and food crops. Adamu was exactly the kind of farmer the BCGA had in mind when it began its work in Nigeria in 1902: he used ox-drawn plows, hired wage labor during harvest time, and used cottonseed "carefully chosen by Government Officers." His community ensured that all farmers "cut down and burn[ed] all their cotton bushes" to limit insect problems, and he sold his cotton only in a government-regulated market. (Despite Adamu being a model farmer, the government cotton inspector forced him to "pick out a lot of the unripe cotton" and separate stained cotton.) With the benefit of good land and a little capital, Adamu cooperated with the government and the local BCGA ginnery to grow cash crops while also meeting his family's subsistence needs. Balancing food crops, groundnuts, and cattle helped insulate him from the vagaries of the cotton market. The book highlighted the durability of the government-centered model of cotton agriculture the BCGA pioneered, and like *Black Cotton*, also emphasized the persistence of hand-spinning and weaving in the face of industrial competition.[116]

If Nigeria offered a model of compromise—the BCGA accepting the autonomy and economic priorities of African farmers, and African farmers accepting a certain level of surveillance and regulation—other parts of the British Empire offered very different examples of evolution in colonial agricultural policies. *Cotton Growing in the Sudan* (ca. 1925) painted a drastically different picture, highlighting a statist and racist project of economic, environmental, and social engineering. The film was not intended to be shown as an educational piece, at least not in the format available in the archive. *Cotton Growing in the Sudan* was a souvenir of mill owner Arthur Birtwistle's tour of southern Sudan with other shareholders in the Sudan Plantations Syndicate. The film is rife with colonial tropes and unflattering "ethnographic" scenes of Sudanese men and women. In several scenes, Africans move large bags and baskets of cotton by hand and wait in regimented lines for white colonial officials to inspect the fiber. Film historian Tom Rice concluded, "The locals are objectified as further 'discoveries,' while the British are shown as supervisors, organising and modernising this still undeveloped land. Even when the British are pictured with the locals away from work, the staged shots still emphasise cultural differences."[117] The Sudan film presents a stark contrast to the film on the Nigerian cotton industry. Instead of Africans serving as the agents of their own economic progress, the film depicts Africans as hopelessly backward, in need of European expertise to develop the resources of their own country. This is the view of Africans and African agriculture embodied in the Gezira scheme and later in the Zande scheme in southwestern Sudan, which sought a wholesale transformation of the region and its peoples through export commodity production. Colonial managers hoped to conjure a cotton export industry, complete with a textile factory, out of the Sudanese countryside. An American anthropologist studying the Zande project reported that "compulsion was considered necessary for a few years," and he observed that the "punishment of individuals became more frequent" when farmers were unable to perform their prescribed roles as cotton farmers.[118]

Two models of cotton development emerged from the colonial experience: one requiring gigantic infusions of capital to construct irrigation works, and one that depended on smallholder initiative. Both involved the technocratic control of cottonseeds, cotton harvesting, and cotton marketing, to protect the quality of cotton and (at least ostensibly) to ensure that farmers received the best possible prices for their cotton. These models continued after the end of formal colonial rule in part because they were embedded in the new national political and economic systems. As Joseph Hodge has shown, they also continued because the same colonial personnel continued to operate them, "enabling the perpetuation of their ideals and practices in the postcolonial world."[119] Colonial experts had a lingering influence on the independent states of Africa, but their work also provided models for other parts of the world. The countries that supposedly offered alternative models for development for postcolonial Africa—the USSR and China—in fact copied British and French irrigated cotton projects on a grand scale in their own countries, leading to huge increases in cotton output in Central Asia but also disastrous environmental consequences.[120]

While scholars of development have digested many of the lessons of failed state-led development schemes, the seemingly intractable problems of economic growth and effective governance in Africa continue to tempt experts to recommend "large, capital-intensive projects that substantially raise the productivity of a labor force effectively controlled by the state apparatus." As Keith Hart argued, "Nothing can beat a big irrigation scheme from this point of view. The requirements for capital planning, water control, and managerial supervision make government central to such schemes."[121] Mozambique's government, for example, has perpetuated some elements of Portuguese colonial policy by focusing on dams, irrigation, and cotton exports at the expense of local farmers and the environment.[122]

Conclusion

The BCGA and Lancashire turned to Africa for new cotton supplies because they believed cotton was "the black man's crop," and they believed that black labor and raw cotton were both inherently cheap commodities. As a private venture, the BCGA was not successful. Lancashire's half-million pound investment would have better been used building nothing but cotton gins in places like southern Nigeria and Uganda, rather than fixing cotton prices in pioneer areas, subsidizing white planters, and paying for agricultural research. While colonial officials in British, French, and Portuguese colonies resorted to racist explanations to justify their coercive interventions in the lives of African farmers, the BCGA's experience in fact vindicated the antiracist sentiments of key supporters like E. D. Morel. Morel concluded in 1914, "The tropical African native is neither the half child nor half devil of popular imagination. He is at bottom a keen man of business, a trader, and an agriculturist." If Africans chose not to grow cotton, it was because it was not economically attractive. Morel warned, "In the measure in which this is recognized the modern intervention of the white race in tropical Africa will be a success or a disaster to both white and black."[123] Unfortunately, most colonial officials did not heed Morel's advice, and continued to force specific types of cotton and work regimes on farmers whose labor would have been more profitably applied elsewhere. As international NGOs gradually displaced colonial administrations in the work of African development, myths of the "backwardness" of African farmers remained. As Frederick Cooper has argued, the image of the "conservative peasant" or "backward African" merely "concealed the fact that that the leading colonial powers had neither transformed nor exploited Africa as their earlier promises had implied."[124]

The lasting impact of Lancashire's engagement with African and American farmers lay in the idea of development. While the BCGA's work ushered in a new era of state-led, scientifically oriented development policies that tended to discourage private entrepreneurship and market incentives, the efforts of the American cotton populists generated positive results, at least for white American farmers. Beginning with the Cotton Futures Act of 1914, federal legislation and the work of the USDA accomplished nearly all that the cotton populists demanded. The South was transformed, though not necessarily for the better. State-led agricultural extension work targeted those who needed help the least, the "better class" of white farmers who could afford to take the risks, invest in education, and get credit to buy new machines, seeds, and chemical inputs. "Chained to the old cultural methods and the credit system," poor Southern farmers—white and black—were finished off by the New Deal of the 1930s. Its money went to landlords and bigger commercial farmers, and the changes it brought to tenancy arrangements among poor farmers "broke their tie to the land."[125] Today American cotton remains a "white man's crop." Across the southern and southwestern United States, about 18,600 farms grow cotton in highly mechanized operations. They produce seventeen million bales annually, about half the amount produced by China, the world's leader in cotton agriculture.[126] Only 408 of these cotton farmers identify as African Americans.[127] White or black, these American farmers produce cotton that "is so uncompetitive on the world market that they receive enormous federal subsidies to continue to farm it, subsidies that in some years equal the GDP of the country of Benin." As Beckert explains, in 2001 these subsidies "amounted to triple that year's USAID payments to all of Africa, a part of the world where production costs for cotton were only about a third of what they were in the United States."[128]

Cotton agriculture brought misery to millions of farmers in Africa during the colonial period, but the crop did not fail for immutable economic or ecological reasons. Cotton did succeed in several regions of the continent where farmers found ways to fit cotton production into sustainable agricultural patterns. To take one example, many Ugandan farmers prospered by growing cotton. Blessed with an acclimated variety of Egyptian cotton, Ugandans found a ready market for their high-quality produce. Lancashire's lack of influence on colonial policy making and the declining influence of cotton in the British economy meant that Ugandan farmers were free to move into new commodities like coffee when better opportunities emerged after 1945. During the late twentieth century, many former colonies experienced a "peasant cotton revolution" as national governments supplied new seeds, training, chemicals, and— perhaps most importantly—credit to farmers as part of a campaign of economic development through export agriculture. In places like Côte d'Ivoire, where farmers saw real economic gains from cotton agriculture, the industry has thrived. In other places, where governments insist on cotton above other crops, farmers continue to manipulate agricultural services to their best advantage, such as in Mali, where farmers grow cotton to gain access to subsidized fertilizers for use on maize. Malian farmers reported, "Cotton is now an old man! We used to get money from it, but no longer. . . . Maize and beans are better for cash now-a-days. All we need is fertilizer."[129] Frederick Cooper reminds us that "The best success stories of colonial economies, such as cocoa production in the Gold Coast or Nigeria, reflected above all the initiatives of African farmers, and colonial authorities happily benefited from their efforts without asking too many questions about the producers' subject positions or how they adapted 'traditional' kinship systems to agricultural innovation."[130] Colonial ideas of race were often invoked to explain the failure of cash-crop industries, but never to explain their success.

Notes

Introduction

1. Passenger list for steamer *Akobo*, box 2, folder 1, John Wesley Hoffman Papers, The Tuskegee University Archives, Tuskegee University (Hoffman Papers hereafter); Pipkin, *Negro in Revelation*, 413. Throughout the book, the lower-case terms "northern" and "southern" are used to describe geographical regions. When referring to the British colonial administrations of Northern Nigeria and Southern Nigeria, which were amalgamated in 1914, they are capitalized.

2. Atwater and Woods, *Dietary Studies*.

3. "John Wesley Hoffman," *Indianapolis Freeman*, July 21, 1906, 1–2.

4. The royal metaphor was first popularized in David Christy's apologia for slavery, *Cotton Is King*.

5. Farnie, "Merchants as Prime Movers," 20.

6. Sandberg, *Lancashire in Decline*, 3.

7. Riello, *Cotton*, 266–67, 6–7.

8. Beckert, *Empire of Cotton*, 103–6.

9. North, *Economic Growth*, 67–74.

10. O'Rourke and Williamson, *Globalization and History*, ch. 3. Distance still mattered, but it was distance from railroads and seaports—a function of a region's integration or disintegration with the world market—that most influenced prices.

11. Copeland, *Cotton Manufacturing Industry*, 284–85.

12. Kriger, *Cloth in West African History*, ch. 2; Beckert, *Empire of Cotton*, 9–10; Inikori, "Commercial Agriculture," 16–17.

13. Inikori, *Africans and the Industrial Revolution*.

14. Johnson, *River of Dark Dreams*, 420.

15. The term "cotton crisis" has also been used to describe periods in the 1860s, 1920s, and 1930s, and it has been used as recently as the 2000s. See Farnie, "Cotton Famine"; McCorkle Jr., "Louisiana and the Cotton Crisis"; Snyder, *Cotton Crisis*; Yartey, "Tackling Burkina Faso's Cotton Crisis."

16. For definitions of development, see the short essay in Williams, *Keywords*, 102–4; and extended discussions in Leys, *Rise and Fall*; Cowen and Shenton, *Doctrines of Development*; Hodge, *Triumph of the Expert*; Tilley, *Africa as a Living Laboratory*.

17. Throughout the book I use "white" and "black" as actors' categories and dispense with quotation marks around them. The people examined in this book believed these racial categories were real, and these concepts profoundly shaped the way they viewed economics, agriculture, and imperialism. My thinking on the creation and historical evolution of race as a category has been heavily influenced by the work of Painter, *Creating Black Americans*; Painter, *History of White People*.

18. Hunt, *Farmer Movements*, 56.
19. Watts and Little, "Introduction," 13.
20. Beckert, "Cotton: A Global History," 52.
21. Hopkins, "History of Globalization," 19.
22. Cooper, *Colonialism in Question*, 96; see also Bennison, "Muslim Universalism."
23. Hopkins, "Introduction."
24. Appadurai, *Modernity at Large*; see also essays in Appadurai, *Globalization*.
25. Goody, *Ghana Observed, Africa Reconsidered*, 2.
26. Austen, *African Economic History*, 5.
27. Isaacman, *Mother of Poverty*, 1.
28. Marx, *Eighteenth Brumaire*, ch. 1.
29. Quote from Angus Burgin in "Interchange," 521.
30. Julia Ott in ibid., 506.
31. Austin, *Labour, Land, and Capital*, 4.
32. Cooper, *Colonialism in Question*, 105.
33. Manning, "African Empires," 602.
34. Cooper, *Colonialism in Question*, 239.
35. For two critiques of the reliance in African historiography on the "container" provided by the colonial state and colonial economy, see Roberts, *Two Worlds of Cotton*, 22; Mitchell, *Rule of Experts*, ch. 3 and 9.
36. Sittert, "Imperialism in Africa," 118.
37. Tosh, "Cash-Crop Revolution," 80–81; for a more recent summary of this historiographical shift see Nyambara, "Colonial Policy," 82–83.
38. Lonsdale and Berman, "Coping with the Contradictions"; my reading of Lonsdale and Berman is strongly influenced by Cooper, *Colonialism in Question*, 50–51.
39. Watts, *Silent Violence*, 363; for the latter expression, see Hopkins, *Economic History*, 189.
40. Manning, "African Empires," 600; see also Manning, *Dahomey*, 263–64.
41. For a representative sample of the different takes on British cotton in Africa, see Johnson, "Cotton Imperialism"; Ratcliffe, "Cotton Imperialism"; Watts, *Silent Violence*; Nonnenmacher and Onyeiwu, "Cotton Paradise."
42. Pitcher, *Politics in the Portuguese Empire*, 3.
43. Isaacman, *Mother of Poverty*.
44. Roberts, *Two Worlds of Cotton*, 13.
45. Ibid., 6.
46. Sunseri, "Baumwollfrage."
47. Beckert, *Empire of Cotton*, 342.
48. Ibid., 344.
49. Ibid., 358.
50. Moseley and Gray, "Introduction," 7.
51. Beckert, *Empire of Cotton*, 341.
52. Isaacman, *Mother of Poverty*, 26; see also Pitcher, "Sowing the Seeds of Failure."
53. Pitcher, "Sowing the Seeds of Failure," 64.
54. Watts, *Silent Violence*, 156.
55. Nworah, "West African Operations."
56. Egboh, "BCGA in the Lagos Colony," 98.

57. Hogendorn, *Nigerian Groundnut Exports*; Hogendorn, "Cotton Campaign."

58. Hart, *Political Economy*, 112.

59. See the essays in Guha and Spivak, *Selected Subaltern Studies* and other publications in the Subaltern Studies series.

60. Chakrabarty, "Conditions for Knowledge," 179.

61. Cooper, "Conflict and Connection."

62. See, for example, the essays in Lawrance, Osborn, and Roberts, *Intermediaries, Interpreters, and Clerks.*

63. Some grades of American long-staple cotton are called "medium-staple." That description went out of use some time after the Civil War, and returned in the twentieth century. The sources used in this study classify cotton exclusively as "short" or "long." See Watt, *Cotton Plants.*

64. Bureau of Manufacturers, "Monthly Consular and Trade Report," 67.

65. Shepperson, *Cotton Facts*, 3.

66. Scherer, *World Power*, 424.

67. Rose, *Firms, Networks, and Business Values*, 162.

68. Ibid., 216–17.

69. Oldham MCSA Annual Report, 1904, D-AAN/1/1/2/1, Oldham Local Studies and Archives. Germany and France combined had only 14,584,601 spindles in that year.

70. McIvor, *Organised Capital*, 28.

71. McIvor, "Employers Associations"; McIvor, *Organised Capital.*

72. McIvor, *Organised Capital*, 53.

73. Nworah, "West African Operations"; Egboh, "Adventures of the BCGA"; Johnson, "Cotton Imperialism." Later works, such as Watts's *Silent Violence*, mischaracterize the BCGA's level of support within the British government, in addition to mislabeling the association as the "cotton growers' association." In Stephen Constantine's *British Colonial Development Policy* the author takes the BCGA's propaganda at face value and incorrectly assumes that Britain's imperial government gave strong support to the cotton-growing movement.

74. Wardle, "History of the BCGA," i.

75. Cain and Hopkins, *British Imperialism*, 400, 52.

76. For a survey of the literature, see Burton, *Imperial Turn*; Bernard Porter offers trenchant criticism of the new imperial studies in *Absent-Minded Imperialists*; see also Darwin, *Empire Project*, 14–15.

77. Chase-Dunn, "Core Capitalism"; Carlton, "How American Is the American South?"

78. See recent contributions by Carlton and Coclanis, "Southern Textiles"; Engerman, "Southern Industrialization"; see also Wright, *Old South, New South*; Sanders, *Roots of Reform*, ch. 1.

79. Levi and Havinden, *African Agriculture*, 145.

Chapter 1

1. Davis, *Late Victorian Holocausts.*

2. Sandberg, *Lancashire in Decline*, 262.

3. Robson, *Cotton Industry*, 332.

4. Ibid., 336.

5. Baker and Hahn, *Cotton Kings*, ch. 2–4.

6. *Manchester Cotton Factory Times*, October 31, 1902.

7. Boyle, *New Orleans Cotton Exchange*, 1–18.

8. Woodman, *King Cotton*, 269–94.

9. Smith, *Cotton Exchanges*, 2–3:258.

10. Copeland, *Cotton Manufacturing Industry*, 38.

11. Lipartito, "Cotton Futures Market," 53.

12. Ibid., 58; for a broad discussion of futures markets, see Telser and Higinbotham, "Organized Futures Markets."

13. Pietruska, "Cotton Guessers."

14. Smith, *Cotton Exchanges*, 2–3:290.

15. Quoted in Moore, *Forecasting*, 5.

16. To measure crop condition, the USDA asked agents to compare a cotton field to a "normal" crop on a scale of 1 to 100. But according to the USDA, "normal" was "*not* an *average* condition but a condition *above* the average, giving promise of *more than an average crop*. Furthermore a normal condition does *not* indicate a *perfect* crop, or a crop that is or promises to be the very largest in quantity and the very best in quality that the region reported upon may be considered capable of producing . . . [and] it does not represent a crop of extraordinary character, such as may be produced here and there by the special effort of some highly skilled farmer with abundant means, or such as may be grown on a bit of land of extraordinary fertility, or even such as may be grown quite extensively once in a dozen years in a season that is extraordinarily favorable to the crop to be raised." Quoted in ibid., 59.

17. Shepperson, *Cotton Facts*, iv.

18. Barrett, *Farmers' Union*, 66.

19. Cowing, *Populists, Plungers, and Progressives*, 14. Cowing notes that in Chicago's wheat exchange, brokers were ostracized for demanding delivery instead of settling with cash.

20. Fite, *Cotton Fields No More*, 48.

21. Smith, *Cotton Exchanges*, 2–3:52.

22. Hunt, *Farmer Movements*.

23. Smith, *Cotton Exchanges*, 2–3:xviii.

24. Sanders, *Roots of Reform*, 299.

25. Smith, *Cotton Exchanges*, 2–3:258.

26. Annual Report for 1903, Oldham Master Cotton Spinners' Association, D-AAN 1/1/2/1, Oldham Local Studies and Archives (OLSA hereafter).

27. Copeland, *Cotton Manufacturing Industry*, 354–60. According to Copeland, American mills were increasingly relying on futures to eliminate the costs of warehousing (182).

28. "Cotton Consumption of Europe and the World," *New York Commercial & Financial Chronicle*, November 1, 1902, 949.

29. *New York Commercial & Financial Chronicle*, September 6, 1902, 508.

30. Baker and Hahn, *Cotton Kings*, ch. 3–4.

31. Sully, "King Cotton's Impoverished Retinue," 259.

32. Sully, "High Price of Cotton," 199.

33. *New York Commercial & Financial Chronicle*, May 16, 1903, 1052–53.

34. Boyle, *New Orleans Cotton Exchange*, 115.

35. Ibid., 115–16.

36. "Cotton Nets Daniel Sully Many Millions," *Atlanta Constitution*, May 10, 1903.

37. "Two Views of the Cotton Situation," *Baltimore Manufacturers' Record*, July 2, 1903, 479.

38. *New York Commercial & Financial Chronicle*, September 5, 1903, 480–81.

39. *New York Commercial & Financial Chronicle*, November 21, 1903, 2000.

40. Thomas P. Grasty, "Are We to Have Cotton Famines?" *Baltimore Manufacturers' Record*, December 3, 1903, 381.

41. Robson, *Cotton Industry*, 340.

42. Sully, "High Price of Cotton," 197.

43. Sully, "King Cotton's Impoverished Retinue," 417.

44. Harvie Jordan, "Georgia Cotton Growers! Do You Want Good Prices for Your Cotton Next Fall?" SCGPA, n.d. but ca. 1900, Pamphlet 620, Hargrett Broadside collection, University of Georgia Special Collections (Hargrett Broadsides hereafter).

45. "Sully, Cotton King, Forced to the Wall," *Boston Journal*, March 19, 1904, 5.

46. "Suggestions to Spinners," *Baltimore Manufacturers' Record*, November 26, 1903, 363.

47. *Baltimore Manufacturers' Record*, August 25, 1904, 119.

48. See, for example, the copy in *Omaha World Herald*, January 8, 1904, 9.

49. "Pointed Paragraphs," *Wall Street Daily News*, March 10, 1904, 2.

50. "Bulls Rush Cotton Up," *New York Times*, January 29, 1904.

51. Memberships usually sold for $10,000 (Smith, *Cotton Exchanges*, pt. 2–3, 258).

52. "Cotton Breaks and Rallies," *New York Sun*, January 8, 1904.

53. "The Cotton Situation," *Bennettsville (SC) Marlboro Democrat*, January 15, 1904, 4. Japanese mills consumed 20 percent more cotton between July 1904 and July 1905, a significant increase but nowhere near Sully's predictions.

54. Sully, "High Price of Cotton," 202.

55. "Plan to Raise Prices of Raw Cotton Higher," *Washington Times*, January 5, 1904.

56. *Olympia Daily Recorder*, January 25, 1904, 2; see also *New York Commercial & Financial Chronicle*, January 2, 1904, 5.

57. Thomas P. Grasty, "The Readjustment of Cotton-Goods Prices," *Baltimore Manufacturers' Record*, September 1, 1904, 150.

58. See, for example, "The Future of Cotton," *Washington Times*, February 7, 1904.

59. *New York Commercial & Financial Chronicle*, April 15, 1905, 1391.

60. *New York Commercial & Financial Chronicle*, January 2, 1904, 5.

61. *New York Commercial & Financial Chronicle*, May 23, 1903, 1108.

62. "Panic in Cotton Pit," *New York Times*, February 3, 1904.

63. "Sully to the Rescue," *Dallas Morning News*, February 5, 1904.

64. "Generalship of Cotton King," *Charlotte Observer*, February 5, 1904.

65. "Spot Cotton Dealers to Fight the Bears," *New York Times*, February 7, 1904.

66. "Cotton Slumps Again," *New York Times*, February 4, 1904.

236   *Notes to pp. 42–46*

67. "Cotton King Will Serve Meals to His Clerks Till the Rush Is Over," *Fort Worth Star-Telegram*, February 9, 1904.
68. "Cotton," *Times* (London), March 16, 1904.
69. "Failure of Mr. Sully," *Times* (London), March 19, 1904.
70. "Speculators vs. Merchants," *New York Times*, April 10, 1904; see also "Sully Is Thrown into Bankruptcy," March 23, 1904, and "Sully to Fight Hawley and Ray," March 27, 1904.
71. "War upon the Cotton Growers," *Baltimore Manufacturers' Record*, April 21, 1904, 299.
72. "The Sully Failure," *Baltimore Manufacturers' Record*, March 24, 1904, 200.
73. "The Sully Failure," *New York Commercial & Financial Chronicle*, March 26, 1904, 1196.
74. Editorial, *Times* (London), March 21, 1904, 9.
75. Webster, "Slave of Cotton," 302.
76. "The Sully Failure," *New York Commercial & Financial Chronicle*, March 26, 1904, 1196.
77. Editorial, *Baltimore Manufacturers' Record*, February 18, 1904, 87, and February 25, 1904, 107; Burkett and Poe, *Cotton*, 56.
78. "Cotton Acreage and Condition," *New York Commercial & Financial Chronicle*, June 4, 1904, 2307.
79. *New York Commercial & Financial Chronicle*, May 16, 1903, 1052–53.
80. Boyle, *New Orleans Cotton Exchange*, 117.
81. *New York Commercial & Financial Chronicle*, April 23, 1910, 1079; June 25, 1910, 1650; March 25, 1911, 772.
82. Baker and Hahn, *Cotton Kings*, ch. 7–8.
83. Boyle, *New Orleans Cotton Exchange*, 121.
84. *New York Commercial & Financial Chronicle*, June 27, 1903, 1376.
85. Sandberg, *Lancashire in Decline*, 110.
86. Annual Report for 1903, D-AAN 1/1/2/1, OLSA; Keir Hardie, speech to the House of Commons, February 19, 1904, vol. 156, col. 452. For trade union views, see Employers' Parliamentary Association minutes, June 19, 1903, B14/17/1, Greater Manchester County Record Office (GMRCO hereafter).
87. William Field, speech to the House of Commons, May 11, 1904, vol. 134, col. 1028. See also Field's speeches on July 1, 1903, vol. 124, col. 1026; July 8, 1903, vol. 125, col. 16; February 16, 1904, vol. 129, col. 1475; February 19, 1904, vol. 130, col. 496–97; April 12, 1904, vol. 133, col. 7. Field unsuccessfully attempted to revise the 1892 Gambling Act to include cotton futures transactions. He also tried to give the Royal Commission on Food Supplies (a body charged with protecting and rationing commodity supplies during war) the power to seize cotton exchanges in the interests of national welfare.
88. Editorial, *Times* (London), March 21, 1904, 9.
89. Huberman, "Early Evidence of Worksharing"; Fowler, *Lancashire Cotton Operatives*, 242.
90. Chapman, *Unemployment*, 34–35.
91. *Manchester Cotton Factory Times*, March 7, 1902.
92. There is no modern biography of Macara, but see Mills, *Sir Charles Macara*; Macara, *Recollections*. A gentleman's agreement allowed Macara, representing

Manchester, to hold the presidency. This reassured other districts, who feared that Oldham's enormous weight in the federation would dictate Lancashire's policy. McIvor, "Sir Charles Wright Macara," 9; On the Brooklands Agreement, see McIvor, *Organised Capital,* ch. 5.

93. Clarke, *Lancashire and the New Liberalism,* 99.

94. Copeland, *Cotton Manufacturing Industry,* 361–62; Rose, *Firms, Networks, and Business Values,* 73–74.

95. Huberman, "Early Evidence of Worksharing," 16.

96. Oldham MCSA Annual Report, 1902, 1, D-AAN/1/1/2/1, OLSA.

97. Employers' Parliamentary Association, minutes, July 11, 1902, B14/17/1, GMCRO.

98. Editorial, *Times* (London), January 5, 1904, 7.

99. Participation in local and national associations among spinning firms increased from 42 to 60 percent between 1903 and 1905. Participation increased to only 64 percent in 1913 during a brutal lockout struggle with organized labor. McIvor, *Organised Capital,* 63.

100. *Manchester Cotton Factory Times,* 1901–14.

101. FMCSA Annual Report, 1904, 11, B14/4/9/1, GMCRO.

102. Oldham Operative Spinners, Monthly Report for July 1904, 229, D-TU 2/1/109, OLSA.

103. IFMCSMA, *Sixth International Congress,* 82.

104. Bolton & District Operative Cotton Spinners Provincial Association, 31st Annual Report, 12–3, FT 21/7, Bolton Archives History Centre, Bolton Library and Museum Services (Bolton Archives hereafter).

105. White, *Limits of Trade Union Militancy,* 27.

106. This sum is for Burnley, a weaving town, in 1910. McGhee, "Englishman's Bigger Dollar," 13152–58. The figures are comparable to those given by Young (*American Cotton Industry,* 132–33).

107. Hutton, *Cotton Crisis,* 10; Lazonick, *Competitive Advantage,* 170.

108. *Manchester Cotton Factory Times,* May 30, 1902; January 30, 1903.

109. *Manchester Cotton Factory Times,* February 19, 1910; Fowler and Wyke, *Barefoot Aristocrats,* 111, 251–52; Great Britain Board of Trade, *Trade Unions,* xxxvi.

110. Oldham Operative Spinners, Monthly Report, August 1902, 275, D-TU 2/1/107, OLSA.

111. *Times* (London), June 15, 1904, 12.

112. Dangerfield, *Strange Death,* ch. 4.

113. Bolton & District Operative Cotton Spinners Provincial Association, 24th Annual Report, 1903, 5, FT 21/7, Bolton Archives.

114. McIvor, "Employers Associations," 121–38.

115. White, *Limits of Trade Union Militancy,* 83.

116. Oldham Operative Spinners, Monthly Report for January 1910, D-TU 2/1/115, OLSA.

117. Lazonick, *Competitive Advantage;* Mass and Lazonick, "The Performance of the British Cotton Industry, 1870–1913," 17–20.

118. Watts, *Cotton Supply Association;* Redford, *Manchester Merchants and Foreign Trade,* 1:12; Harnetty, *Imperialism and Free Trade,* 36; Ratcliffe, "Cotton Imperialism," 90. For the standard revisionist account, which downplays the idea of an actual

shortage of cotton in Lancashire, see Farnie, "Cotton Famine"; see also David Surdam's effective rebuttal in "Monarch or Pretender?"

119. Harnetty, *Imperialism and Free Trade*, 36, 45–46, 100.

120. Hose, "West African Cotton," 82; see also Vincent, "Cotton Growing in Southern Nigeria."

121. BCGA minutes, February 18, 1902, BCGA 1/1/1, Records of the British Cotton Growing Association, University of Birmingham Special Collections (BCGA hereafter).

122. Oldham MCSA Annual Report for 1902, 1, D-AAN/1/1/2/1, OLSA.

123. Minutes, April 9, 1902, BCGA 1/1/1.

124. "Interviews with West African Governors," 17, in BCGA/2/1/1.

125. Raven-Hill, "Touched on the Raw Material," 201. The editors of *Punch* rather unusually included an explanation of the cartoon, suggesting that the sufferings of the Sully corner were quickly forgotten outside Lancashire.

126. Beckert, *Empire of Cotton*, 356.

127. Roberts, *Two Worlds of Cotton*, 81.

128. Carland, *Colonial Office and Nigeria*, 3; Havinden and Meredith, *Colonialism and Development*, 4.

129. Hodge, *Triumph of the Expert*, 45.

130. Reginald Antrobus to Hutton, April 24, 1902, BCGA 6/3; West Indies Committee minutes, September 13, 1911, BCGA 1/4/5. For CO officials' backgrounds, see Constantine, *British Colonial Development Policy*, 21.

131. Hutton and Hutton, *Hutton Families*, 85. The family history is reticent about the broader context of the invoice and makes no reference to the slave trade.

132. Voyage 83947 in Eltis et al., "Voyages, the Trans-Atlantic Slave Trade Database."

133. Brooks, *Yankee Traders*, 68, 70.

134. Hutton, *Voyage to Africa*.

135. Lynn, "Change and Continuity," 344–45.

136. Hutton and Hutton, *Hutton Families*, 88.

137. Ratcliffe, "Cotton Imperialism," 93, 105n59.

138. Nworah, "West African Operations."

139. Atkins to Hutton, April 12, 1902, BCGA 6/3. Jones's takeover left a lasting impression, as several scholars have mistakenly attributed the founding of the BCGA to Jones. See references in Dumett, "Obstacles to Government-Assisted Agricultural Development."

140. Jones to Hutton, April 12, 1902, BCGA 6/3.

141. Davies, *Trade Makers*, 97–107.

142. Jones to Morel, March 17, 1903, F3/4 9, Edmund Dene Morel Papers, London School of Economics Archive (Morel Papers hereafter).

143. Annual reports, 1902, 1910, BCGA 2/1.

144. Transcript of speech, 1902 dinner meeting, 7, BCGA 10/4/7; Jones to Morel, September 28, 1902, F8/95/94, Morel Papers.

145. J. A. Hutton, "The Work of the B.C.G.A.," 1904, 39, BCGA 2/2/1.

146. BCGA Annual report for 1903, BCGA 2/1.

147. Transcript of Hutton's speech, 1903 dinner meeting, 3, BCGA 10/4/7.

148. Ibid., 9.

149. G. B. Zochonis, a Manchester merchant and friend of Hutton's, may have also given Morel the idea, though Zochonis warned that Newton had not been consulted. Zochonis to Morel, December 20, 1902, F3/3, Morel Papers.

150. See Morel to Hutton, March 25, 1903, F10/5/160, Morel Papers.

151. Wardle, "History of the BCGA," 35–36; see also Nworah, "Liverpool 'Sect'"; Nworah, "West African Operations."

152. Holt to Morel, June 20, 1902, F8/84 219; Holt to Morel, November 5, 1902, F8/84 263, Morel Papers. Holt did take a business interest in cotton later, opening a ginnery in Lagos. The BCGA may have used some dirty tricks to punish Holt; their ginneries claimed to be full and refused to process his cotton while they ginned cotton from other merchants, and in June 1904, a mysterious fire burned a gin and a bale of Holt's cotton. Holt's firm sold the equipment to the BCGA in 1908 for £265 (Himbury tour diary, BCGA 7/3/1; Executive Committee minutes, January 16, 1908, BCGA 1/3/1).

153. BCGA annual reports, BCGA 2/2/1–18.

154. Hutton, "The Work of the B.C.G.A.," February 1904, BCGA 2/1/1.

155. Hutton, *Cotton Crisis,* 9–10.

156. "The Empire's Cotton Supply," *Liverpool West African Mail,* March 18, 1904, 1283.

157. BCGA Organisation Committee minutes, February 24, 1905, BCGA 1/4/3; Manchester Subcommittee minutes, July 27, 1906, BCGA 1/4/2.

158. Shelford, "Ten Years' Progress," 347.

159. Duke of Marlborough, speech to the House of Lords, May 10, 1906, vol. 156, col. 1425.

160. Hazzledine, *White Man in Nigeria,* 190.

161. Ibid., 4.

162. Morel, *Affairs of West Africa,* 188–200; Morel, *Nigeria,* 222–49. For a more moderate example of pro-BCGA propaganda, see Orr, *Making of Northern Nigeria,* 209–18.

163. Grant, *Civilised Savagery,* ch. 3 and 4.

164. Morel explicitly contrasted the BCGA's free-market model with the horrors seen elsewhere in colonial Africa in his 1920 book *Black Man's Burden.* Morel tried to convince Liverpool merchant John Holt to support the BCGA as an alternative to the "Leopoldian" model, but Holt retorted, "I have not associated myself with that movement and don't intend to as I regard it as another affairs of Jones promoted for his own advertisement chiefly and accompanied by the usual hypocritical humbug of imperialism, patriotism and such-like catchwords, the purpose of which is personal and material ends." Quoted in Nworah, "West African Operations," 232.

165. Editorial, *Lagos Weekly Record,* June 16, 1904, 5.

166. Editorial, *Liverpool West African Mail,* August 10, 1906, 464.

167. David Shackleton, speech to the House of Commons, April 5, 1905, vol. 144, col. 544, 553.

168. Imperial Institute and the BCGA, *Handbook of an Exhibition,* vi; Tewson, *BCGA Golden Jubilee,* 17.

169. Hutton, *Cotton Crisis,* 14.

170. Oldham Chamber of Commerce minutes, March 19, 1906, D-ABJ 1/3, OLSA.

171. "Cotton-Growing Exhibition at the Imperial Institute." *Times* (London), June 2, 1905.

172. Hutton daybook 2, May 4, 1905, BCGA 7/2/2; minutes, May 2, 1905, BCGA 1/2/1; Manchester Subcommittee, October 11 and 25, 1905, BCGA 1/4/2.

173. BCGA Organisation Committee minutes, June 23, 1905, BCGA 1/4/3.

174. David Shackleton, speech to the House of Commons, April 5, 1905, vol. 144, col. 553.

175. BCGA Organisation Committee minutes, April 27, 1906, BCGA 1/4/3.

176. Manchester Subcommittee minutes, August 23, 1904, BCGA 1/4/2; see also Oldham MCSA minutes, July 28, 1905, D-AAN 1/1/5/9, OLSA.

177. BCGA Organisation committee, December 13, 1904, February 16, 1905, BCGA 1/4/3.

178. Clarke, *Lancashire and the New Liberalism*, 95–96; McIvor, *Organised Capital*, 72; Nworah, "West African Operations"; Redford, *Manchester Merchants and Foreign Trade*, 1:7.

179. FMCSA report, June 1905, FET 4/1/1, Bolton Archives.

180. Poster, September 1905, BCGA 10/4/1.

181. Bolton Employers' minutes, October 18, 1905, FET 1/1/4; March 11, 1910, FET 1/1/15, Bolton Archives.

182. Kershaw & Bamford to Oldham MCSA, October 24, 1905, OLD 2/5/1, Records of the Oldham Master Cotton Spinners' Association, John Rylands University Library Special Collections (JRUL hereafter).

183. John Dunkerley & Sons to Oldham MCSA, November 8, 1905, OLD 2/5/1, JRUL.

184. The figures include ring and doubling spindles and some looms, converted by the Oldham MCSA into "spindle equivalents." FMCSA Levy Return book, 1904–19, D-AAN 1/2/2/1, OLSA.

185. Harold Cliff (Oldham MCSA) to BCGA, n.d. but 1905–6, OLD 2/5/5, JRUL.

186. Smallbrook Mill directors to Oldham MCSA, October 26, 1905, OLD 2/5/1, JRUL.

187. Manchester Subcommittee minutes, July 27, 1906, BCGA 1/4/2.

188. Oldham MCSA General Committee minutes, July 28, 1905, D-AAN 1/1/5/9, OLSA.

189. Notes of a deputation to Townley Mills, November 2, 1905, OLD 2/5/1, JRUL.

190. BCGA Annual reports; BCGA West Africa indents, vols. 1–2, M257/1–2, Manchester Libraries, Information and Archive, Manchester City Council (MLIA hereafter).

191. Letter in BCGA-FMCSA correspondence, March 4, 1910, OLD 2/5/2, JRUL.

192. FMCSA minutes, February 7, 1910, OLD 2/5/3/1, JRUL. The Executive Council's minutes were not released to the general BCGA council, and until 1910 the manufacturers heard only censored reports of what was actually happening in the field.

193. Minutes, January 7, 1908, BCGA 1/2/1.

194. Executive Committee minutes, October 14, 1909, December 3, 1909, BCGA 1/3/1.

195. Executive Committee minutes, October 14, 1909; November 4, 1909, BCGA 1/3/1.

196. *Manchester Cotton Factory Times,* June 13, 1902.

197. Minutes, June 20, 1902, BCGA 1/1/1.

198. *Manchester Cotton Factory Times,* September 18, 1903.

199. Annual Report, 1904, 56–66, BCGA 2/2/1. The total subscribed capital then stood at about £32,000.

200. Minutes, 1906, BCGA 1/4/2.

201. *Manchester Cotton Factory Times,* August 19, 1904; Organisation Subcommittee minutes, February 24, 1905; BCGA 1/4/3.

202. Bolton & District Cardroom, Quarterly Report, September 1905, 5, G12/36, GMCRO. When the BCGA was wound up in 1972, the Amalgamated Association of Spinners' and Twiners' Associations still held several hundred share certificates (see ACS/3/3/19, JRUL).

203. Manchester Subcommittee minutes, September 27, 1905, BCGA 1/4/2.

204. *Manchester Cotton Factory Times,* February 9, 1906.

205. Oldham Cardroom minutes, May 2, 1906, D-TU 2/1/20, OLSA. The chairman was eventually convinced to contribute, in order to "have done with the thing for good, and in the event of again being asked to subscribe the Association could say that their members had done their share already." Ibid., May 23, 1906.

206. Bolton Spinners, 25th Annual Report, 6, 1904, FT 21/7, Bolton Archives.

207. *Manchester Cotton Factory Times,* July 20, 1906.

208. Manchester Subcommittee minutes, October 31, 1906, BCGA 1/4/2. McNiel was surprised to find that in Colne, a weaving town, "some of the Socialists are actively helping us towards a Day's Wage collection."

209. William Lazonick argues that relations between mule spinners and "piecers," their assistants, deteriorated throughout the late nineteenth and early twentieth century. Piecers faced increased workloads and diminished hopes of promotion to mule spinning, and turned to the cardroom unions for organization against the mule minders as much as against mill owners. Lazonick, *Competitive Advantage,* ch. 3.

210. White, *Limits of Trade Union Militancy,* 75.

211. Oldham Cardroom minutes, May 11, 1910; June 8, 1910, D-TU 2/1/24, OLSA.

212. Oldham Cardroom, Private Quarterly Report, June 5, 1910, D-TU 2/1/24, OLSA.

213. Miscellaneous minutes, July 10, 1914, BCGA 1/4/6.

214. Amalgamated Association of Operative Cotton Spinners, Annual Report, December 1905, BCGA 2/2/5.

215. Cardoom minutes, March 31, 1905, D-TU 2/1/19, OLSA.

216. "Minutes of meeting with employers and labour," June 10, 1910, BCGA 1/4/6.

217. *Textile World Record (Boston)* 39, no. 5 (August 1910): 549–50. The *Cotton Factory Times* responded to these charges indignantly, getting an apology of sorts out of the American paper (*Cotton Factory Times,* September 2, 1910).

218. ICF 1911, "Colonial Cotton Growing and Germany," 100, BCGA 2/1/9.

219. "Statement of Capital subscribed to by the different Organisations," enclosed in Oldfield (BCGA) to Marsland (Operative Spinners), July 4, 1913, ACS 6/6/1, JRUL.

220. Davis and Huttenback, *Pursuit of Empire*, 314.

221. Lancashire gentry were targeted in a 1906 "County Movement" that brought in a few major subscribers. Manchester Subcommittee minutes, February 28, 1906, BCGA 1/4/2.

222. Nelson, "Welfare Capitalism."

223. Marrison, *British Business and Protection*, 26, 42–43; Trentmann, *Free Trade Nation.*

224. Hyam, *Elgin and Churchill*; Clarke, "End of Laissez Faire."

225. Jones to Morel, February 13, 1902, F8/95/56; Jones to Morel, March 31, 1902, F8/95/58, Morel Papers. Jones also served on Chamberlain's Tariff Commission and paid for the distribution of ten thousand copies of the commission's report on cotton textiles in Lancashire. Marrison, *British Business and Protection*, 131.

226. J. A. Hutton, "The Work of the B.C.G.A.," BCGA 2/2/2.

227. Howard Reed, "Cotton Growing within the British Empire," pamphlet reprinted from *Cooperative Wholesale Society Annual*, 1911, in BCGA 2/2/11.

228. George Harwood, speech to the House of Commons, April 27, 1904, vol. 133, col. 1390.

229. CO minutes, March 21, 1907, BCGA 1/5/2.

230. See J. A. Hutton to Chamberlain, May 6, 1898, JC 9/5/3/13 and clipping from *Guardian*, August 4, 1898, JC 9/5/2/6, Joseph Chamberlain Papers, University of Birmingham Special Collections (Chamberlain Papers hereafter).

231. Matthew Ridley, speech to the House of Commons, February 10, 1904, vol. 129 (1904), col. 923.

232. House of Commons debate, August 22, 1907, as reported in BCGA annual report, 1907, BCGA 2/2/7.

233. Clarke, *Lancashire and the New Liberalism*, 96.

234. Hyam, *Elgin and Churchill*, 45, 435.

235. Dumett, "Joseph Chamberlain"; Cain and Hopkins, *British Imperialism*, 330–35.

236. Churchill, speech to the House of Commons, May 1, 1906, vol. 156, col. 400.

237. Hyam, *Elgin and Churchill*, 452.

238. Connections between free trade ideology and humanitarianism in Africa ran deep; see Nworah, "Liverpool 'Sect.'"

239. Hogendorn, "Cotton Campaign"; Wardle, "History of the BCGA," ch. 2.

240. Lord Elgin, speech to the House of Lords, May 10, 1906, vol. 156, col. 1422–43.

241. BCGA-CO minutes, March 21, 1907, BCGA 1/5/1.

242. Hogendorn, "Cotton Campaign," 54.

243. Carland, *Colonial Office and Nigeria*, 169.

244. Sir Gilbert Parker, speech to the House of Commons, May 28, 1908, vol. 189, col. 1314.

245. "The Nigerian Railway," *Times* (London), August 23, 1907.

246. "Mr. Churchill in Liverpool," *Times* (London), December 6, 1909.

247. "The Northwest Manchester Bye-Election," *Annual Register*, 83.
248. Wardle, "History of the BCGA," 72.
249. Holt to Morel, December 17, 1908, F8/87 553, Morel Papers.
250. BCGA Executive minutes, November 17, 1908, November 4, 1909, December–January 1909–10, BCGA 1/3/1.
251. Speech by Lord Derby at the Nottingham Chamber of Commerce Banquet, January 17, 1911, BCGA 2/2/11, reprinted from *The Trader* (n.d.).
252. BCGA-CO minutes, May 6, 1913, BCGA 1/5/2.
253. BCGA CO letters, July 16, 1913, BCGA 6/1/3.
254. BCGA executive minutes, September 18, 1913, BCGA 1/3/2.
255. Wardle, "History of the BCGA," 551–52.
256. Johnson, "Cotton Imperialism."
257. "The South the Resort for the Cotton Industry," *Baltimore Manufacturers' Record*, October 5, 1905, 284.
258. Davis and Huttenback, *Pursuit of Empire*, ch. 3.

Chapter 2

1. Howarth, "Cotton Cultivation in West Africa," 115. For a closer analysis of BCGA fund-raising, see Robins, "Lancashire and the Undeveloped Estates."
2. Hutton was not alone in thinking this; Sir Alfred Jones suggested in a 1903 speech that Americans would soon consume their entire domestic crop (*West Africa*, March 14, 1903, p. 256). Americans did little to discourage such speculation. A 1902 US Census Bureau report marked in Hutton's handwriting predicted: "At the present rate of progress it will not be long before the *entire cotton supply* of the States on the Atlantic sea-board *will be taken at home*" (emphasis in the original, in BCGA 2/2/1).
3. Isaacman, *Mother of Poverty*, 9.
4. Bassett, *Peasant Cotton Revolution*, 15.
5. Schanz, "Colonial Cotton Growing," 1910.
6. For a survey of railroad debacles, see the essays in Davis and Wilburn, *Railway Imperialism*; on African cotton soils, see Dunn, *Cotton in Africa*, 8–9; Prentice, *Cotton*, 136–51.
7. Barth, *Travels and Discoveries*, 2:332–33.
8. Livingstone, *Missionary Travels*, 399.
9. Letter from Thomas Clegg, quoted in Coates, *Cotton Cultivation in Africa*, 25.
10. Masefield, *Handbook of Tropical Agriculture*, 3; Isaacman and Roberts, "Introduction," 13–14; Tilley, *Africa as a Living Laboratory*, 28.
11. Porter, "Cotton and Climate," 47; Beckert, *Empire of Cotton*, 4.
12. Isaacman, *Mother of Poverty*, 3.
13. Evidence of J. Arthur Hutton, June 8, 1916, BCGA 2/6/1. See also Hutton, "Notes on the development of cotton growing in new districts," Records of the Empire Cotton Growing Committee, BT 55/25 no. 22, The National Archives (TNA hereafter); quote from Hutton to J. Bottomley, Queensland Dept. of Agriculture, December 10, 1906, BCGA 2/6/13.

14. Schanz, "Colonial Cotton Growing . . . 1911."

15. Scott, *Seeing Like a State*, 189.

16. See Zimmerman, "German Alabama," 1371.

17. "Conference of Growers and Manufacturers," 27.

18. Douglass, *Life and Times*, 300.

19. Clipping, *Liverpool West African Mail*, April 17, 1903, in BCGA 2/1/1.

20. "Cotton Growing Movement," *Lagos Weekly Record*, January 30, 1904.

21. Quoted in "Corner on Cotton," 387.

22. Burkett and Poe, *Cotton*, 36–37.

23. Minutes of a meeting with Sir Percy Girouard, January 12, 1911, BCGA 1/4/6. See also "Italians in the Cotton Fields," *Baltimore Manufacturers' Record*, April 7, 1904, 250; and Clune, "Black Workers, White Immigrants."

24. For British capital in Latin America, see Platt, *Finance, Trade, and Politics*.

25. Argentina Ministerio de Agricultura, *Cotton Cultivation*.

26. Untitled pamphlet, n.d., in BCGA 2/2/2.

27. Pearse, *Brazilian Cotton*, 53.

28. Baron G. V. Rosen, quoted in Beckert, *Empire of Cotton*, 345.

29. IFMCSMA, *Fifth International Congress*, 71; for a preliminary account of the Dutch effort, see van der Eng, "'De-Industrialisation'and Colonial Rule."

30. Cotton Supply Association, *Cotton Culture*, 5.

31. Smith, *Cotton Trade of India*, 28; see also Dejung, "Boundaries of Western Power."

32. Quoted in Beckert, *Empire of Cotton*, 254.

33. See, for example, *Textile World Record (Boston)* 39, no. 6 (September 1910): 656. In the original formulation, related by John Bright, a worker interjected, "O Lord! But not Surat" after a public prayer for more cotton. Bright, *Speech of Mr. Bright*, 5.

34. Hazareesingh, "Cotton, Climate, and Colonialism"; Hazareesingh, "Territories of Conquest."

35. BCGA minutes, November 7, 1911, BCGA 1/2/1.

36. IFMCSMA, *Seventh International Congress*, 111.

37. "West African Correspondence no. 4," 1906, Africa Confidential Print no. 835, Records of the Colonial Office, CO 879/92/835, TNA.

38. BCGA India Subcommittee minutes, September–December 1904, September–November 1911, BCGA 1/4/1.

39. Beckert, "Tuskegee to Togo," 28; Sunseri, "Baumwollfrage," 31.

40. Bassett, *Peasant Cotton Revolution*, 55; see also Roberts, *Two Worlds of Cotton*, 40.

41. Zimmerman, "German Alabama," 1395; Zimmerman, *Alabama in Africa*, ch. 1.

42. Rönnbäck, "Idle and the Industrious."

43. Speech by Alfred Emmott, IFMCSMA, *Second Conference of Growers and Spinners*, 113–14.

44. Col. Alfred B. Shepperson, "The Foreign Textile Situation," *Baltimore Manufacturers' Record*, September 17, 1903, 155.

45. Roberts, *Two Worlds of Cotton*, 30.

46. Ibid., 35, 82; Bassett, *Peasant Cotton Revolution*, ch. 2–3.

47. Sunseri, "Baumwollfrage," 33.

48. Havinden and Meredith, *Colonialism and Development*, 89.

49. Nworah, "Liverpool 'Sect'"; Nworah, "West African Operations."

50. Kidd, *Control of the Tropics*, 53.

51. Morel, *Affairs of West Africa*, 198.

52. Hopkins, *Economic History*, 231–36.

53. Untitled, anonymous illustration in BCGA pamphlet, 1907, BCGA 2/2/7.

54. Hutton to Morel, May 16, 1905, F9/2 189, Morel Papers.

55. Antrobus to Hutton, April 24, 1902, BCGA 6/3; minutes, June 20, 1902, BCGA 1/1/1.

56. Morel to Lugard, November 9, 1904, F10/10 582, Morel Papers.

57. Interview with Captain Orr, July 20–21, 1904, BCGA 1/5/3; minutes, April 4, 1903, BCGA 1/1/1.

58. "New British Cabinet," *New York Times*, October 6, 1903; Carland, *Colonial Office and Nigeria*, 157. Carland's account shows how Lyttelton was manipulated by Lugard into endorsing a scheme that would have let Lugard run Nigeria from Britain, breaking the traditional policy of leaving decision-making to the "man on the spot."

59. Dunstan, "British Cotton Cultivation."

60. BCGA-CO minutes, especially October 13, 1904, BCGA 1/5/1.

61. Egboh, "BCGA in the Lagos Colony," 81.

62. BCGA-CO minutes, April 5, 1906, BCGA 1/5/1.

63. CO minutes, March 8, 1906, BCGA 1/5/1.

64. BCGA-CO minutes, January 25, 1906, BCGA 1/5/1.

65. Simpson, "Report on Cotton Growing," Africa Confidential Print, CO 879/89/792, TNA.

66. Hopkins, *Economic History*, 232.

67. See especially Austin, *Labour, Land, and Capital.*

68. For an introduction to Meillassoux's approach, see Meillassoux, "Reproduction to Production"; for applications of this approach, see Watts, *Silent Violence*, 2012; Mandala, *Work and Control.*

69. Tosh, "Cash-Crop Revolution."

70. Austin, *Labour, Land, and Capital*, 79.

71. Tosh, "Cash-Crop Revolution," 89.

72. IFMCSMA, *Second International Congress*, 96.

73. Roberts, *Two Worlds of Cotton*, ch. 4.

74. Enclosure in no. 157, "Correspondence on Cotton," Correspondence with colonies, no. 953, CO 869/105; W. S. Sharpe to Lugard, April 27, 1904, West African correspondence, CO 879/84/745, TNA.

75. BCGA minutes, January 30, 1913, BCGA 1/2/1.

76. Enclosure with dispatch no. 306, Hoffman to colonial secretary, Lagos, December 31, 1903, box 1, folder 2, J. W. Hoffman Papers.

77. Interview with Sir William Manning, January 30, 1913, BCGA 1/2/7.

78. BCGA Executive Committee minutes, July 10, 1903, BCGA 1/1/1; Paton to Hoffman, September 1, 1903, box 1, folder 4, Hoffman Papers; BCGA-CO minutes, May 12, 1904, BCGA 1/5/1.

79. "West Africa Correspondence no. 4," Africa confidential print, CO 879/92/835, TNA.

80. BCGA Executive Committee minutes, October 28, 1915, BCGA 1/3/2.

81. Report by Hesketh Bell, September 28, 1910, enclosed in CO to BCGA, November 5, 1910, BCGA 6/1/1.

82. Thorburn to Harcourt, enclosed in June 14, 1912, BCGA 6/1/2; Lambert to Hutton, September 3, 1915, BCGA 6/1/4.

83. BCGA Executive Committee minutes, November 19, 1913, BCGA 1/3/2.

84. Wallis to CO, April 22, 1914, enclosed in CO to BCGA, June 2, 1914, BCGA 6/1/3.

85. Himbury, West Africa tour diary, 34, 1904–5, BCGA 7/3/1.

86. Lugard, *Lugard and the Amalgamation of Nigeria*, 112.

87. Dumett, "Obstacles to Government-Assisted Agricultural Development," 167; Zimmerman, "German Alabama," 1387; Mandala, *Work and Control*, 265; Wardle, "History of the BCGA," 551.

88. Himbury, West Africa tour diary, 141, 1905, BCGA 7/3/1.

89. Engdahl, "Exchange of Cotton," 153.

90. Egerton to CO, January 17, 1907, "West Africa Correspondence no. 4," Africa confidential print, CO 879/92/835, TNA.

91. Report by Hesketh Bell, September 28, 1910, enclosed in CO to BCGA, November 5, 1910, BCGA 6/1/1. Compare to Roberts, *Two Worlds of Cotton*, ch. 9, for French reactions to the same predicament.

92. CO correspondence, November 10, 1910, BCGA 6/1/1.

93. Enclosure in no. 157, "Correspondence on Cotton," Correspondence with colonies, no. 953, CO 869/105, TNA.

94. Morel, *Nigeria*, 243.

95. Hose, "West African Cotton," 250.

96. Hogendorn, "Cotton Campaign," 64–65.

97. CO correspondence, July 1910, BCGA 6/1/1.

98. Lugard, *Lugard and the Amalgamation of Nigeria*, 112.

99. Morel, *Nigeria*, 58.

100. 1905 figures include the Lagos Colony, which was absorbed into the Southern Nigeria administration in 1906. 1908 Annual Report, BCGA 2/2/9.

101. *Cotton: Its Preparation, Transportation and Marketing*, 43.

102. *Lagos Weekly Standard*, January 23, 1907, 1.

103. CO minutes, December 13, 1906, BCGA 1/5/1.

104. BCGA-CO minutes, quoted in Wardle, "History of the BCGA," 74.

105. Antrobus to Hutton, June 15, 1907, West African Correspondence no. 49, CO 879/92/835, TNA.

106. Wardle, "History of the BCGA," 73–83.

107. Beckert, *Empire of Cotton*, 370.

108. Bassett, *Peasant Cotton Revolution*, 52; Beckert, "Tuskegee to Togo," 30; Watts, *Silent Violence*, 173; Olukoju, *"Liverpool" of West Africa*, 59.

109. Roberts, *Two Worlds of Cotton*, 94–95.

110. Ibid., 86.

111. Minutes, October 16, 1907, BCGA 1/2/1.

112. Hopkins, *Economic History*, 220; Hogendorn, *Nigerian Groundnut Exports*.

113. Hutton daybook no. 3, November 19, 1907, BCGA 7/2/3.

114. Olukoju, *"Liverpool" of West Africa*, 39.

115. Lamb to CO, August 2, 1914, enclosed in August 8, 1914, BCGA 6/1/4.

116. Lamb, Report on Northern Nigerian Cotton, July 1914, enclosed in October 19, 1914, BCGA 6/1/4.

117. Lamb, untitled report, March 4, 1915, BCGA 6/1/4.

118. Watts, *Silent Violence*, 173.

119. John Anderson to Lord Derby, December 28, 1915, BCGA 6/1/4.

120. Copy of a memo from Milner to Hugh Clifford, August 7, 1920, Empire Cotton Growing Committee records, no. 239, BT 55/25, TNA.

121. Minutes, July 28, 1916, BCGA 1/2/2.

122. Watts, *Silent Violence*, 173.

123. See, for instance, Duff, *Nyasaland*, xxiv; Watts, *Silent Violence*, 1983; Egboh, "Adventures of the BCGA."

124. Isaacman, *Mother of Poverty*, 26.

125. Maier, "Slave Labor and Wage Labor," 84; Knoll, "Decision-Making for the German Colonies," 137–38.

126. Phillips, *Enigma of Colonialism*.

127. BCGA minutes, March 24, 1903, BCGA 1/1/1.

128. Himbury, West Africa tour diary, June 27, 1904, 64, BCGA 7/3/1.

129. E. D. Morel, "Free Labour in Tropical Africa," 639–40; Cadbury 256/1, Cadbury Papers, University of Birmingham Special Collections.

130. IFMCSMA, *Second International Congress*, 97.

131. Hutton, *Cotton Crisis*, 17.

132. Tewson, *BCGA Golden Jubilee*.

133. IFMCSMA, *Second International Congress*, 97.

134. Quoted in Nworah, "West African Operations," 326.

135. BCGA London Reports, March 9–11, 1904, BCGA 1/5/3.

136. Elgee to CO, March 4, 1904, quoted in Egboh, "BCGA in the Lagos Colony," 95.

137. BCGA-CO meeting reports, November 23–24, 1904, BCGA 1/5/2.

138. CO to BCGA, March 8, 1904; Atkins to CO, March 30, 1904; West African correspondence no. 25, CO 879/84/745, TNA.

139. Personnel files, BCGA 4/1. At least six Americans were hired, but none lasted more than two years in Africa. Shelby Neely (sometimes rendered Shelly in documents) died of blackwater fever at Onitsha in 1905.

140. Lovejoy and Hogendorn, *Slow Death for Slavery*, 60.

141. Enclosure from Shelby Neely in Lugard to CO, July 28, 1904, West African Correspondence, no. 25, CO 879/84/745, TNA.

142. Quoted in E. D. Morel, "Empire-Grown Cotton," 45, 1904, BCGA 2/1/1.

143. Ibid. Morel told Himbury, the BCGA's manager in West Africa, "I always said it was a mistake on the part of the B.C.G.A. to spend any money on plantations, and in Southern Nigeria of all places in the world." He warned, "I hear a good many opinions about the B.C.G.A., and the most frequent one perhaps is that Jones and [Sir Ralph] Moor will ruin the show. This is for your private guidance." Morel to Himbury, January 16, 1905, F10/10 954, Morel Papers.

144. Egboh, "Adventures of the BCGA," 75.

145. Hutton daybook 1, October 20, 1904, BCGA 7/2/1.
146. BCGA minutes, December 6, 1904, BCGA 1/2/1.
147. Hutton daybook 1, October 20, 1904, BCGA 7/2/1.
148. 1st Annual Report, August 1905, BCGA 2/1/1.
149. Moyamba had been leased at 1s. per acre by a government agent; the BCGA found this price outrageous and protested that they "could not in any case afford to give more than –/3 an acre with any prospect of making the plantation pay." BCGA-CO minutes, May 12, 1904; February 9, 1905, BCGA 1/5/1.
150. Hutton daybook 1, October 20, 1904, BCGA 7/2/1.
151. BCGA London Reports, March 9–11, 1904, BCGA 1/5/3.
152. Tamuno, *Nigerian State*, 263.
153. Nworah, "West African Operations," 319.
154. BCGA West Africa indents, 2:21–27, M257/2, MLIA.
155. Nworah, "West African Operations," 319. Nworah's citation for the protest in the House of Commons is incorrect; the correct date is March 2, 1905, vol. 142, col. 181.
156. Himbury, West Africa tour diary, 127, 130, 1904–5, BCGA 7/3/1.
157. Ibid., 131.
158. Ibid.
159. The location is still in use as an agricultural research station and school. Morel, *Nigeria*, 225; Idachaba, *Agricultural Research Policy*, 15.
160. Himbury, *New Cotton Fields*, 5.
161. BCGA minutes, January 12, 1911, BCGA 1/2/1.
162. "Interview with Mr. Walker," April 5, 1904, BCGA 1/5/3.
163. Samuel Simpson, "Report on the Cotton Growing Industry, British Central Africa Protectorate," August 12, 1905, Africa confidential print, CO 879/89/792, TNA.
164. This figure is based on a search of the Board of Trade records of registered companies at the National Archives, Kew.
165. West African Cotton Growing Company Ltd., BT 31/10051/75184, Companies Registration Office, files of dissolved companies, TNA.
166. New Cotton Fields Ltd., BT 31/10009/74794, Companies Registration Office, files of dissolved companies, TNA.
167. New Cotton Fields Ltd., prospectus, September, 1902, BCGA 6/3; Harlan and Smock, *Washington Papers*, 6:506–7; "Downing, Henry Francis."
168. Jamaica Cotton Co. Ltd., BT 31/10819/82059; Demerara Cotton Syndicate Ltd., BT 31/10964/83285, TNA.
169. San Tomas Cotton Estates Ltd., BT 31/12213/95965, TNA.
170. East African Cotton Syndicate to Hutton, enclosed letter, n.d. but ca. May 1905, Hutton daybook 2, BCGA 7/2/2.
171. Rhodesia Cotton Syndicate Ltd., BT 31/10535/79583, TNA.
172. Nyasa Cotton Estates Ltd., BT 31/13515/114072, TNA.
173. East African (Jubaland) Cotton Growers' Association, BT 31/13751/118615, TNA.
174. Green, *Peasant Production*, 66–69, 150–55; Nieboer, *Slavery as an Industrial System*.

175. Gareth Austin's exhaustive study of Asante supports the key assertions of the theory; see *Labour, Land, and Capital*, 155–70; see also Green, "Economics of Slavery."

176. Falconer, *Horseback through Nigeria*, 302.

177. Mandala, *Work and Control*, ch. 3.

178. Himbury, West Africa tour diary, 72, 1904–5, BCGA 7/3/1.

179. Typescript document, "Notes by Mr. Himbury on AFRICAN LABOUR," n.d. but ca. 1920, in BCGA 1/4/6.

180. Lever to Morel, April 11, 1911, F8/100 114, Morel Papers.

181. BCGA-CO minutes, April 5, 1906, BCGA 1/5/1.

182. Minutes of a meeting with Sir Percy Girouard, January 12, 1911, BCGA 1/4/6.

183. Minutes, April 9, 1902, BCGA 1/1/1. By 1913, the BCGA had answered 62,113 letters. Milne, *Sir Alfred Jones*, 68.

184. Davies, *Sir Alfred Jones*, 106–9. BCGA West Indies Committee minutes, BCGA 1/4/5. Jones transformed the Canary Islands into a vibrant vacation spot and an exporter of fruit to Europe, and used bananas to rebuild the Jamaican economy. He hoped cotton would do the same for the smaller West Indian islands.

185. BCGA minutes, December 2, 1902, BCGA 1/1/1.

186. BCGA West Indies Committee minutes, July 14, 1905, BCGA 1/4/5.

187. BCGA reports, 1903–4, BCGA 2/1/1–2; 1st Annual Report of Chartered Association, August 1905, BCGA 2/1/3.

188. BCGA minutes, April 7, 1908, BCGA 1/2/1.

189. BCGA minutes, November 3, 1908, BCGA 1/2/1.

190. Nevis Ltd. to Hutton, September 17, 1908, enclosure in Hutton daybook 3, BCGA 7/2/3; Algernon E. Aspinall to Hutton, October 2, 1908, BCGA 6/3.

191. BCGA West Indies Committee minutes, September 13, 1911, BCGA 1/4/5.

192. Jaquay, "Caribbean Cotton."

193. See Schnurr, "Calamatous Commodity."

194. Annual Report, December, 1912, BCGA 2/1/11.

195. Wardle, "History of the BCGA," 575.

196. H. H. Lardner, "The Cotton Growing Problem," February 1904, in BCGA 2/2/3.

197. Hutton, *Work of the BCGA*, 35.

198. Quoted in Phillips, *Enigma of Colonialism*, 71.

199. BCGA-CO Reports, March 8, 1906, BCGA 1/5/2. On the Jamaican banks, see Turner, "Co-Operative Bank."

200. van Beusekom, *Negotiating Development*, xxiv.

201. Mandala, *Work and Control*, 128.

202. BCGA-CO Report, May 9, 1912, BCGA 1/5/2.

203. Wardle, "History of the BCGA," 566–67.

204. BCGA Executive Committee minutes, August 25, 1910, BCGA 1/3/1.

205. Ehrlich, *Uganda Company*, 18.

206. BCGA-CO Reports, January 30, 1908, BCGA 1/5/2.

207. BCGA-CO minutes, January 26, 1910, BCGA 1/5/1.

208. Grant, *Civilised Savagery*, ch. 3–4.

209. Interview with Sir William Manning, January 30, 1913, BCGA 1/2/7. This account contains several passages regarding the government position on labor migration and plantations that were censored in the copy of the report the general BCGA council saw (BCGA minutes, January 30, 1913, BCGA 1/2/1.
210. BCGA Executive Council minutes, March 19, 1912, BCGA 1/3/1.
211. BCGA Executive Council minutes, August 25, 1910, BCGA 1/3/1.
212. BCGA minutes, November 2, 1911, BCGA 1/2/1.
213. BCGA Executive Council minutes, November 2, 1911, BCGA 1/3/1.
214. Evidence of J. Arthur Hutton, June 8, 1916, 36, BCGA 2/6/1.
215. Wardle, "History of the BCGA"; Nworah, "West African Operations."
216. Hodge, *Triumph of the Expert*, 68.
217. A. E. Evans to CO, January 18, 1910, "Correspondence on cotton," no. 953, CO 879/105, TNA.

Chapter 3

1. Phillips, *Enigma of Colonialism*, 14.
2. Schanz, "Colonial Cotton Growing," 152.
3. Beckert, "Tuskegee to Togo"; Zimmerman, "German Alabama."
4. Isaacman and Roberts, "Introduction," 26.
5. Wardle, "History of the BCGA," ii.
6. Gibbons, *New Map of Africa*, 308.
7. "Notes by Mr. Himbury on AFRICAN LABOUR," typescript, n.d. but ca. 1920, in BCGA 1/4/6.
8. See letter from Hutton to Joseph Chamberlain, May 6, 1898, Chamberlain Papers, JC 9/5/3/13, University of Birmingham Special Collections. See Abraham, "Hut Tax War"; on violence and the creation of colonial order in British colonies, see Robins, "Colonial Cuisine."
9. Lugard to Hutton, December 20, 1904, West African correspondence, CO 879/84/745, TNA.
10. Mandala, *Work and Control*, 112. The rebates were not abolished until 1921.
11. Hanson, *Landed Obligation*, 169.
12. Swindell, "Struggle for Transport Labor," 153.
13. Gardner, *Taxing Colonial Africa*, 58, 112–13.
14. Engdahl, "Exchange of Cotton," 116.
15. Wrigley, *Crops and Wealth*, 16.
16. John Holt to Morel, July 13, 1906, F8/3, Morel Papers, quoted in Nworah, "West African Operations," 324.
17. BCGA Executive Committee minutes, May 17, 1912, BCGA 1/3/1.
18. Hogendorn, "Cotton Campaign," 59.
19. Lamb to CO, August 2, 1914, enclosed in CO to BCGA, August 8, 1914, BCGA 6/1/4. Lamb's point was not that peasants should *not* be pressured to grow crops, but rather that they should grow whatever would pay the best and earn the colony the most revenue.
20. Robinson, "Non-European Foundations," 119–20.

21. Lawrance, Osborn, and Roberts, "Introduction," 6.

22. Mandala, *Work and Control*, 111.

23. Newbury, *Patrons, Clients, and Empire*, 5.

24. Lawrance, Osborn, and Roberts, "Introduction," 6.

25. Foster-Carter, "Modes of Production"; Berman, "Articulation."

26. Watts, *Silent Violence*, 75; Austen, *African Economic History*, 4, 137–38.

27. Cooper, "Analagous to Slavery," 116–29.

28. Baillaud, "Cultivation of Cotton," 146.

29. Untitled memorandum, Hazzledine to Residents, n.d., in West African Correspondence, Africa confidential print, CO 879/84/745, TNA.

30. Hesketh Bell, report on Northern Nigeria, n.d. but July 1910, BCGA 6/1/1.

31. Bashir Salau, *West African Slave Plantation*, 111–28.

32. Lovejoy and Hogendorn, *Slow Death for Slavery*, 8, 86.

33. African Lakes Co. to BCGA, March 10, 1909, BCGA 6/3. Britons used the Portuguese term "capitão" in Nyasaland to denote an "overseer under Government surveillance," rather than an established hereditary leader (Duff, *Nyasaland*, 97).

34. *Lagos Weekly Record*, February 23, 1903, 1.

35. MacGregor, "Lagos, Abeokuta and the Alake," 478–79.

36. "Cotton Growing Movement at Abeokuta," *Lagos Weekly Record*, January 30, 1904, 8.

37. Himbury, West Africa tour diary, 144, 1905, BCGA 7/3/1.

38. BCGA annual reports, 1904–7, BCGA 2/1.

39. Walker, "Scientific Redemption of Africa," 5.

40. *Lagos Weekly Record*, July 1, 1905, 3.

41. Editorial, *Lagos Weekly Record*, June 16, 1904, 5.

42. For a brief account of the Alake's visit and accounts of other African visitors to the UK in the same period, see Green, *Black Edwardians*, 25–26.

43. "The Alake's Impressions," *Lagos Weekly Record*, July 30, 1904, 5.

44. Quoted in "The Alake in England," *Lagos Weekly Record*, July 9, 1904, 5; see also "Alake at Manchester," July 16.

45. See coverage and article reprints in *Lagos Weekly Record*, June 18, 1904, 6–7.

46. *Otago Witness*, October 19, 1904, 18. At least one student was fined £12 for insulting the Alake.

47. Rigby and Booth, *Modernism and Empire*, 189–91.

48. "John Bull and the Prince," *Chicago Record*, reproduced in the *Dawson Daily*, September 5, 1904.

49. The exposition organizers replied that they were willing to consider "the visit of King Gladebo [*sic*], the Monarch who rules over Yomboland [*sic*] in the Nigeria Territory of West Africa," but nothing ever came of it. Wallis B. Stevens to Hoffman, March 19, 1904, box 1, folder 1, Hoffman Papers.

50. Byfield, *Bluest Hands*, 50–51.

51. *Lagos Standard*, January 22, 1908, 6.

52. "Agriculture and Trade at Abeokuta," *Lagos Weekly Record*, February 28, 1903, 7.

53. Egba Government Gazette, quoted in Egboh, "BCGA in the Lagos Colony," 88.

54. "The Cotton Growing Movement," *Lagos Weekly Record*, January 30, 1904, 8.

55. Ibid., 4.

56. *Lagos Standard,* January 23, 1907, 1.

57. Tamuno, *Nigerian State,* 263; Nworah, "West African Operations."

58. For an overview of the rise and demise of tolls, see Falola, "Yoruba Toll System," passim.

59. Hutton, *Work of the BCGA,* 31.

60. *Lagos Weekly Record,* August 1, 1903, 5.

61. MacGregor, "Lagos, Abeokuta and the Alake," 481; Falola, "Yoruba Toll System," 78–79. MacGregor genuinely liked Gbadebo; other British administrators complained that MacGregor and Gbadebo "walked arm-in-arm" and that MacGregor "once held the regal umbrella over the Alake's head!" Tamuno, *Nigerian State,* 80–81.

62. *West African Mail,* July 15, 1904, quoted in *Lagos Weekly Record,* August 6, 1904, 5.

63. "West Africa Correspondence no. 4" Africa confidential print, CO 879/92/835, TNA.

64. Taylor, "Colonial Economy in Uganda," 18–19; Sathyamurthy, *Political Development of Uganda,* 212.

65. Wrigley, *Kingship and State,* 123; Newbury, *Patrons, Clients, and Empire,* 128.

66. Engdahl, "Exchange of Cotton," 60–61.

67. Reproduced in Low, *Mind of Buganda,* 60.

68. "Report on the Introduction and Establishment of the Cotton Industry in the Uganda Protectorate," November 1909, reproduced in Ehrlich, *Uganda Company,* 21; see also Low, *Buganda in Modern History,* 88.

69. BCGA minutes, August 12, 1913, BCGA 1/2/1. See also *Visit of the Kabaka of Uganda to Manchester,* BCGA pamphlet, July 28–31, 1913, in BCGA 1/4/6.

70. *Nairobi East African Standard,* September 6, 1913, 9.

71. *Kampala Uganda Herald,* September 12, 1913, 3–4, and September 26, 1913, 13.

72. Wrigley, *Crops and Wealth,* 16.

73. For two classic works in this genre, see Amin, *Accumulation on a World Scale;* Frank, *Dependent Accumulation and Underdevelopment.*

74. Mandala, *Work and Control,* 107.

75. Eric Hobsbawm, "Peasants and Politics," quoted in Scott, *Weapons of the Weak,* xv.

76. Ibid., 291.

77. Quoted in Lovejoy and Hogendorn, *Slow Death for Slavery,* 47.

78. Quoted in Schnurr, "Boom and Bust," 129.

79. Engdahl, "Exchange of Cotton," 69.

80. West Africa Correspondence no. 4, Hutton to Elgin, January 6, 1906, CO 879/92/835, TNA.

81. Dumett, "Obstacles to Government-Assisted Agricultural Development," 167; Zimmerman, "German Alabama," para. 34; Mandala, *Work and Control,* 265; Wardle, "History of the BCGA," 551.

82. Egerton to CO, January 17, 1907, "West Africa Correspondence no. 4," Africa confidential print, CO 879/92/835, TNA.

83. Hastings, *Nigerian Days,* 74.

84. Taylor, "Colonial Economy in Uganda," 37.
85. Engdahl, "Exchange of Cotton," 58.
86. MacKenzie, "Experts and Amateurs," 188.
87. Hodge, *Triumph of the Expert.*
88. This expression is borrowed from Mitchell, *Rule of Experts.*
89. Beckert, "Tuskegee to Togo," 22; Zimmerman, *Alabama in Africa.*
90. J. A Hutton, manuscript notes for a 1902 speech in Liverpool, BCGA 10/4/7.
91. Pamphlet of letters on African education by Hoffman, Blackshear, and Sir Alfred Jones, privately published, 1909, box 1, folder 3, Hoffman Papers.
92. Quoted in Egboh, "Adventures of the BCGA," 72. See also Personnel records, BCGA 4/2/1.
93. Beckert, "Tuskegee to Togo," 507.
94. Personnel records, BCGA 4/1; Dunstan, "British Cotton Cultivation," 18.
95. Northrup, *Bend in the River*, 140n; Emmott, "Cotton-Growing," 446.
96. BCGA minutes, September 20, 1902, BCGA 1/1/1. I have not been able to locate any biographical information about J. R. Prince.
97. BCGA Finance & Correspondence Committee minutes, May 8, 1903, BCGA 1/1/1. Hoffman commanded more than his black peers at £350 a year, the same paid to the Neely brothers. The highest-paid BCGA expert was Edward Fisher [or Fischer], who earned £500 his first year in Gold Coast, rising to £600 for two subsequent years. BCGA 4/1.
98. Pine Bluff residents to Hoffman, August 14, 1904, box 1, folder 1, Hoffman Papers. For Hoffman's promotion in the press, see Moses, *Black Nationalism*, 206.
99. Pamphlet of letters on African education by Hoffman, Blackshear, and Sir Alfred Jones, privately published, 1909, box 1, folder 3, Hoffman Papers.
100. According to BCGA records, Shelby Neely and a British agricultural assistant died in Nigeria, and four others, including Hoffman, were invalided. Personnel file, BCGA 4/2/1. Himbury, West Africa tour diary, 30, 47, 52, 131–44, BCGA 7/3/1.
101. See correspondence and contracts, box 1, folders 1 and 2 and box 3, folder 1, Hoffman Papers.
102. Hutton to CO, August 2, 1907, in BCGA 2/6/13.
103. A. R. Slater, acting governor of Gold Coast to A. Bonar Law, August 20, 1915, BCGA 6/1/4.
104. Hersey, *Conservation*, 155.
105. Woodward, *Origins of the New South*, 409.
106. See BGCA reports collection, J. A. Hutton set, BCGA 2/2.
107. Typescript report to CO, Lagos, December 1903, box 1, folder 2, Hoffman Papers.
108. Hodge, *Triumph of the Expert*, ch. 2.
109. Rönnbäck, "Idle and the Industrious," 124–25, 138.
110. Guggisberg and Guggisberg, *We Two*, 102. It is not clear who is speaking in this passage: F. G. Guggisberg notes in the preface to the book, "Throughout the book my wife talks—I write."
111. BCGA Executive Committee minutes, July 3, 1903, BCGA 1/1/1.
112. Engdahl, "Exchange of Cotton," 54–55.
113. Egboh, "Adventures of the BCGA," 73.

114. Typescript report to CO, Lagos, April 1904, box 1, folder 2, Hoffman Papers.

115. Quoted in Roberts, *Two Worlds of Cotton*, 82.

116. Watts, *Silent Violence*, 195; Bassett, *Peasant Cotton Revolution*, 33.

117. Bassett, *Peasant Cotton Revolution*, 58.

118. Austen, *African Economic History*, 139; see also Mandala, *End of Chidyerano*, especially 174–77.

119. Mulwafu, *Conservation Song*, 27.

120. Hart, *Political Economy*, 56.

121. Faulkner and Mackie, *West African Agriculture*, 120.

122. Mandala, *Work and Control*, 206, 231.

123. Showers, *Imperial Gullies*, 257.

124. See discussion and references in Tosh, "Cash-Crop Revolution," 87.

125. Beinart and Coates, *Environment and History*, 55.

126. Quoted in Beckert, *Empire of Cotton*, 364.

127. BCGA-CO minutes, October 13, 1904, BCGA 1/5/1.

128. BCGA minutes, June 2, 1908, BCGA 1/2/1.

129. "Appeal to Employers and Operatives," December 12, 1906, OLD 2/5/5, JRUL.

130. Egboh, "BCGA in the Lagos Colony," 84.

131. Quoted in Ehrlich, *Uganda Company*, 18.

132. Ibid., 18; Engdahl, "Exchange of Cotton," 86; Doyle, *Crisis & Decline in Bunyoro*, 131–32.

133. Mandala, *Work and Control*, 147.

134. Hill, *Migrant Cocoa-Farmers*; for an updated assessment, see Austin, *Labour, Land, and Capital*.

135. Himbury to Hoffman, February 10, 1905, box 1, folder 4, Hoffman Papers.

136. Egboh, "BCGA in the Lagos Colony," 81.

137. Hutton to CO, February 5, 1908, in BCGA 2/6/13. On African cotton varieties, see BCGA Executive Committee minutes, July 28, 1903, BCGA 1/1/1; J. C. Atkins, "The Supply of Cotton," 1904, 6, in BCGA 2/1/1.

138. T. Dawe, "A Simple Guide for Peasant Growers on the Cultivation of Cotton in Uganda," Leaflet no. 18, Agricultural Department, July 1908, BCGA 2/2/9.

139. Hutton daybook 1, January 5, 1905, BCGA 7/2/1. Quote from Tyler, *American Upland Cotton*, 35.

140. Bassett, *Peasant Cotton Revolution*, 57.

141. Roche, *International Cotton Trade*, 56; Kriger, *Cloth in West African History*, 27.

142. Faulkner and Mackie, *West African Agriculture*, 118.

143. Bassett, *Peasant Cotton Revolution*, 33; Morel, *Nigeria*, 236.

144. Boyle to CO, October 22, 1912, enclosed in Southern Nigerian government report, October 28, 1912, BCGA 6/1/2.

145. See miscellaneous correspondence in BCGA 6/3 and Beckert, *Empire of Cotton*, 304–5.

146. BCGA-CO minutes, November 16, 1905, BCGA 1/5/1.

147. Hutton, Sudan tour diary, 193, 1911–12, BCGA 7/3/2.

148. Simpson to CO, November 28, 1913, BCGA 6/1/3.

149. Quoted in McCracken, "Experts and Expertise," 103.

150. "Nyasaland Cotton Ordinance," 1910, enclosed in August 19, 1911, BCGA 6/1/2.

151. Olukoju, "Economic Relations," 99.

152. Hutton to CO, July 20, 1911, Correspondence on Cotton no. 953, CO 879/105, TNA.

153. Lamb to CO, September 9, 1911, Correspondence on Cotton, attachment no. 152, CO 879/105, TNA.

154. Lamb, "Account of Tour."

155. Wrigley, *Crops and Wealth*, 31. Wrigley notes that Simpson was "publically rebuked" in 1920 by the Development Commission for his hostility to white planters, and Wrigley suggests that Simpson's attitudes were deeply shaped by his experience in Nyasaland, where "there had been land-grabbing on a large scale, and where, moreover, European agriculture had enjoyed only a very moderate measure of success."

156. Simpson to CO, February 6, 1914, BCGA 6/1/3.

157. For a fascinating account of how Eli Whitney and other American inventors worked to convince manufacturers to use the inferior lint produced by saw gins, see Lakwete, *Inventing the Cotton Gin*.

158. BCGA West Africa indents, vol. 2:52, M257/2, MLIA.

159. Simpson to CO, November 28, 1913, BCGA 6/1/3.

160. Oldham Local Studies, Oldham Master Cotton Spinners' Association letter to members, September 1913, OLD 2/5/3/2, JRUL.

161. Engdahl, "Exchange of Cotton," 88.

162. "West Indian Cotton Growing Conference," August 1908, 29, BCGA pamphlet no. 29, BCGA 2/2/8.

163. BCGA Executive Committee minutes, March 4, 1909, BCGA 1/3/1.

164. Jaquay, "Caribbean Cotton"; Frankel, *Capital Investment in Africa*, 274.

165. Hutton, Sudan tour diary, 22–23, 1911–12, BCGA 7/3/2.

166. Hutton, *Cotton-Growing Resources*, 15–16.

167. Engdahl, "Exchange of Cotton," 161.

168. Hodge, *Triumph of the Expert*, 67.

169. Egerton to BCGA, January 17, 1907, West African Correspondence, Africa confidential print, CO 879/92/835, TNA.

170. MacGregor to Hoffman, October 20, 1914, box 1, folder 5, Hoffman Papers. See Hodge, *Triumph of the Expert*, 67; Bassett, *Peasant Cotton Revolution*, 32–33.

171. *Lagos Weekly Record*, December 12, 1903, 6. See also Walker, "Scientific Redemption of Africa," 4.

172. Typescript report to CO, Lagos, December 1903, box 1, folder 2, Hoffman Papers.

173. Unknown to the BCGA, Dudgeon was charged by the CO with investigating the association's operations and conducting his own scientific inquiries, revealing early doubts about the BCGA's competence. "West African Correspondence," no. 51, August 1905, Africa confidential print, CO 879/84/745, TNA.

174. Dunstan, "British Cotton Cultivation," 16; Hodge, *Triumph of the Expert*, 66.

175. Samuel Simpson, "Report on the Cotton Growing Industry, British Central Africa Protectorate," August 12, 1905, Africa confidential print, CO 879/89/792, TNA.

176. Hutton, Sudan tour diary, 12, 1911–2, BCGA 7/3/2.

177. Mulwafu, *Conservation Song*, 31.

178. Quoted in Mandala, *Work and Control*, 133.

179. Oldham Chamber of Commerce, "Growth of Cotton in the Empire: West Coast of Africa," 7, 1902, in BCGA 2/1/1.

180. Lucas, *Historical Geography*, 3:252. Lucas is specifically referring to Northern Nigeria in this passage.

181. BCGA West Africa indents, vol. 1:2, 21–27, M257/1, MLIA.

182. BCGA West Africa indents vols. 1–2, M257/1–2, MLIA.

183. Hutton daybook 1, September 20, 1904, BCGA 7/2/1.

184. West Africa indents, vol. 2:161–63, M257/2, MLIA.

185. BCGA meeting with McCall, December 15, 1911, BCGA 6/1/2; Undersecretary of State H. J. Read to Hutton, April 11, 1912, BCGA 6/1/2.

186. Hutton, Sudan tour diary, 26, 34, 1911–12, BCGA 7/3/2; see West African Committee minutes, September 16 and 20 and November 9, 1904, Hutton daybook 1, BCGA 7/2/1.

187. Hart, *Political Economy*, 56.

188. I am indebted to Maurits Ertsen for his critique of this section, and for allowing me to see portions of his draft manuscript, "Improvising Planned Development on the Gezira Plain."

189. Oslund, "Getting Our Hands Dirty," 5; Scott, *Seeing Like a State*.

190. Hunt craved adventure. His first commercial success came in Seattle, where launched a newspaper and got rich speculating in land along the frontier. He dabbled in railroads and gold mines in China and Korea (where he personally shot at and killed illegal placer miners) before turning to Sudan. The only biography is a hagiographic work written by one of Hunt's descendants; Rand, *High Stakes*.

191. Quoted in ibid., 184.

192. Ibid., 187; Hunt's tales of big game hunting and adventure on the upper Nile impressed Roosevelt, and Hunt personally coordinated and financed part of Roosevelt's 1909 African safari. Bederman and Stimpson, *Manliness & Civilization*, 281n149.

193. Rand, *High Stakes*, 201.

194. Ibid., 188–89.

195. Harlan and Smock, *Washington Papers*, 8:153–54, 288.

196. Mollan, "Productive for the State," 2.

197. Rand, *High Stakes*, 190.

198. Werhner and Beit were to hold a majority stake of 201,000 shares to Hunt's 199,000.

199. Rand, *High Stakes*, 196.

200. "Field for Educated Negroes," *Indianapolis Freedman*, May 20, 1905.

201. John Jerry Powell to Washington, March 23, 1907, in Harlan and Smock, *Washington Papers*, 8:232.

202. Rand, *High Stakes*, 244–45.

203. Mather, *Egypt and the Anglo-Egyptian Sudan*, 30, 39.

204. Ibid., 46–47; minutes, March 4, 1913, BCGA 1/2/1.

205. Communications with government officials in 1911–13 reveal increasing frustration with the BCGA, especially with Hutton. When Hutton tried to schedule

a meeting with Lord Grey at the Foreign Office, he was told that Grey had already heard from "cotton men" about Sudan and "had nothing further to add." Grey was referring to an International Cotton Federation delegation that had bypassed the BCGA to lobby for the development of the Gezira Scheme. BCGA India Committee, November 10, 1911, BCGA 1/4/1.

206. Hutton, Sudan tour diary, 171–72, 1911–12, BCGA 7/3/2.

207. Hutton to Derby, February 1, 1913, BCGA 6/3.

208. Hutton Sudan tour diary, 161, BCGA 7/3/2.

209. N. Barton to Hutton, January 28, 1913, BCGA 6/3.

210. Maurits Ertsen, personal communication, December 17, 2013; Hutton, Sudan tour diary, 252, BCGA 7/3/2.

211. Sanderson, "Ghost of Adam Smith," 115.

212. Drummond, *British Economic Policy*, 48.

213. BCGA Executive Committee minutes, July 25, 1912, BCGA 1/3/2; see also several letters between Hutton, Kitchner, and Lord Derby in BCGA 6/3.

214. Warburg, *Sudan under Wingate*, 24–25; Daly, *Empire on the Nile*, 53.

215. Hutton, Sudan tour diary, 183, 1911–12, BCGA 7/3/2.

216. N. Barton to Hutton, January 28, 1913, BCGA 6/3.

217. Bernal, "Cotton and Colonial Order," 97.

218. Beer, "Social Development in the Gezira Scheme," 43; Warburg, *Sudan under Wingate*, 160.

219. Allen, "Irrigation in the Sudan," 258.

220. Tignor, "Sudanese Private Sector," 190.

221. BCGA Executive Committee minutes, July 24, 1913, BCGA 1/3/2.

222. Sikainga, *Slaves into Workers*, 43 and ch. 3–4.

223. Anonymous, "Sudan Cotton Fields," 118ff.; Hodgkinson, "Development of Cotton," 339.

224. Keun, *British Sudan*, 8, 13, 20–21.

225. Barnard Linnott, "Sudan Cotton Field," Empire Marketing Board poster series, ca. 1933, CO 956/351 and CO 956/484, TNA.

226. Dickson, *Old Reliable in Africa*, 321–22.

227. "Notes on the development of cotton growing in new districts," no. 22, Empire Cotton Growing Committee, BT 55/25, TNA.

228. Barnett, *Gezira Scheme*.

229. Jobin, *Dams and Disease*, 321–55.

230. Wardle, "History of the BCGA," 544–49.

231. Drummond, *British Economic Policy*, 48.

232. John Holt to Morel, June 20, 1902, F8/84 219, Morel Papers.

233. Manchester Chamber of Commerce, Joint West Africa Committee Minutes, December 10, 1908, M 8/4/21, MLIA.

234. CO to BCGA, January 11, 1905, no. 51, "West African correspondence," Africa confidential print, CO 879/84/745, TNA.

235. Antrobus to Hutton, March 31, 1905, in ibid.

236. Minutes, October 6, 1908, BCGA 1/2/1.

237. BCGA-CO minutes, July 30, 1908, BCGA 1/5/1.

238. BCGA minutes, August 4, 1908, BCGA 1/2/1.

239. CO draft memorandum, October 23, 1908, BCGA 11/1/19.

240. The location is still in use as an agricultural research station and school. Morel, *Nigeria*, 225; Idachaba, *Agricultural Research Policy*, 15.

241. BCGA-CO minutes, January 12, 1909, BCGA 1/5/2.

242. Morel, *Nigeria*, 244.

243. Orr, *Making of Northern Nigeria*, 209; Hastings, *Nigerian Days*, 227.

244. Morel, *Nigeria*, 223.

245. Report on BCGA meeting with employers' and operatives' associations, December 13, 1916, enclosed in Minutes, BCGA 1/2/2.

246. M. H. D. Beresford, January 18, 1909, in CO draft memorandum, October 23, 1908, BCGA 11/1/19.

247. Memorandum, Lieutenant Governor Thorburn to CO, November 19, 1908, BCGA 11/1/19.

248. C. A. B. Birstwistle, "Minute of the Commercial Intelligence Officer," November 16, 1908, in CO draft memorandum, October 23, 1908, BCGA 11/1/19.

249. N. C. McLeod, November 19, 1908, in CO draft memorandum, October 23, 1908, BCGA 11/1/19.

250. Lamb, Confidential report, n.d., enclosed in Lugard to Hutton, August 27, 1913, BCGA 6/1/3.

251. Minutes, January 12, 1911, BCGA 1/4/6.

252. Hodge, *Triumph of the Expert*, ch. 7.

253. Himbury, West Africa tour diary, 39, 1904–5, BCGA 7/3/1.

254. Himbury, "Empire Cotton," 269.

255. Bassett, *Peasant Cotton Revolution*, 183.

Chapter 4

1. Sully, "King Cotton's Impoverished Retinue," 253; Sully, "Cotton Century"; Sully, "The Remedy"; IFMCSMA, *Second Conference of Growers and Spinners*, 44–45.

2. Burkett and Poe, *Cotton*, 36.

3. "Englishmen for Southern Mills," *Baltimore Manufacturers' Record*, September 20, 1906, 226.

4. Burkett and Poe, *Cotton*, 37; see also Hahn, *Roots of Southern Populism*; Beckert, *Empire of Cotton*, 289.

5. *Textile Mercury* quoted in "Grasping at Straws," *Baltimore Manufacturers' Record*, March 12, 1903, 151.

6. Woodward, *Tom Watson*; Woodward, *Origins of the New South*. The literature on populism is vast and still growing, but for critical studies of populism and racial politics, see Goodwyn, *Democratic Promise*; Hahn, *Roots of Southern Populism*; Sanders, *Roots of Reform*; Gaither, *Populist Revolt*; Clemens, *People's Lobby*, 67. Charles Postel has tried to rehabilitate populism in *Populist Vision*, arguing that the movement was a modern and progressive force in American politics, rather than a reactionary movement.

7. Sanders, *Roots of Reform*.

8. "Conference of Growers and Manufacturers," 29, 212.

9. Saloutos, *Farmer Movements*, 153.

10. "Georgia Cotton Growers! Do You Want Good Prices for your Cotton next Fall?" 1900, Hargrett Broadside 620.

11. Woodward, *Origins of the New South*, 198.

12. "County sub-Organizations," n.d. but 1900, Hargrett Broadside C64; "Georgia Bankers will aid Georgia Cotton Growers," n.d. but 1900, Hargrett Broadside 619.

13. Barrett, *Farmers' Union*, 104–5.

14. Crampton, *National Farmers' Union*; Field, *Harvest of Dissent*.

15. Fite, *Cotton Fields No More*, 63.

16. Barrett, *Farmers' Union*, 108.

17. Fite, *Cotton Fields No More*, 22; Saloutos, *Farmer Movements*, 187.

18. Webster, "Slave of Cotton," 302.

19. Hunt, *Farmer Movements*, 56; Saloutos, *Farmer Movements*, 187–88.

20. "The Sully Failure," *New York Commercial & Financial Chronicle*, March 26, 1904, 1196.

21. "Conference of Growers and Manufacturers," 176.

22. Burkett and Poe, *Cotton*, 58–59.

23. "Growers Combine," *Bamberg (SC) Herald*, December 29, 1904.

24. "Want to Burn Cotton," *Montgomery Advertiser*, December 9, 1904.

25. Fite, *Cotton Fields No More*, 65.

26. Advertisement, *Atlanta Constitution*, January 4, 1905, 2.

27. "The Cotton-Raisers' Only Means of Self-Defence," *Dallas Morning News*, January 8, 1905.

28. "Cotton Burning," *Fort Worth Telegraph*, January 9, 1905; "That Georgia Cotton Burning," *Earlington (KY) Bee*, January 5, 1905.

29. *Biloxi Daily Herald*, January 2, 1905, 1.

30. *Charlotte Daily Observer*, January 3, 1905, 1.

31. "Insurance Men to Stop Cotton Burning," *Fort Worth Telegram*, January 11, 1905.

32. Watson, *Life and Speeches*, 310, 315; Boyle, *New Orleans Cotton Exchange*, 148–49.

33. "The Lancashire Private Cotton Investigation Commission," 86; "Last spring," 6.

34. Alfred Shepperson, "The Foreign Textile Situation," *Baltimore Manufacturers' Record*, September 17, 1903, 155. See also *New York Commercial & Financial Chronicle*, June 18, 1904, 2408.

35. Thomas P. Grasty, "Sully's Message to the South," *Baltimore Manufacturers' Record*, December 10, 1903, 404.

36. "Views of Economists about the South," *Baltimore Manufacturers' Record*, February 4, 1904, 42.

37. Albert Phenis, "Spinners Invited by Southern Financiers," *Baltimore Manufacturers' Record*, September 22, 1904, 223.

38. "Rhodesian Yarns," *Baltimore Manufacturers' Record*, November 16, 1905, 447. Most Americans remained skeptical of African cotton, but Harvie Jordan eventually accepted that Africa might challenge the South in cotton production. In 1907 he stated, "we are in error as regards the idea that foreign countries do not possess land and climatic conditions favorable to the production of the best grades

of cotton in large quantities." "American Cotton Abroad," *Baltimore Manufacturers' Record*, June 27, 1907, 753.

39. "Views of Economists about the South," *Baltimore Manufacturers' Record*, February 4, 1904, 42, and October 27, 1904, 349.

40. IFMCSMA, *Second Conference of Growers and Spinners*, 3–4.

41. Sir Charles Macara, Tootal Broadhurst, and the firms of Armitage & Sons, Hoyle & Sons, Ashton Bros, Barlow & Jones, J. Orr & Sons, Horrockses, Calico Printers Ltd., William Calvert & Sons, Hollins Mill, Renyers, and Rylands all paid for the expedition. See "Lancashire Private Cotton Investigation Commission," 85; Lancashire Private Investigation Commission, *Cotton Growing Area*.

42. "Conference of Growers and Manufacturers," 21, 55.

43. IFMCSMA, *Third International Congress*, 87.

44. "Conference of Growers and Manufacturers," 52, 56, 65, 69.

45. Fite, *Cotton Fields No More*, 52; Postel, *Populist Vision*, 119.

46. Barrett, *Farmers' Union*, 137.

47. Charles Gay, "Selling Cotton Direct to Spinners," *Textile World Record (Boston)* (September 1909): 691.

48. IFMCSMA, *First International Congress*. "Cotton Conference at Washington," *Boston Manufacturers' Record*, May 3, 1906, 437.

49. *New York Commercial & Financial Chronicle*, November 21, 1908, 1325.

50. "Cotton Bears Fighting Sully," *Atlanta Constitution*, March 18, 1905; "Daniel Sully Indorses [*sic*] S.C.A.," *Atlanta Constitution*, March 26, 1905.

51. "Sully Hearing Postponed," *Atlanta Constitution*, April 7, 1904, 6.

52. "D. J. Sully's New Scheme," *New York Times*, April 26, 1904; Alfred Phenis, "Sully's Cotton Improvement Plan," *Baltimore Manufacturers' Record*, April 28, 1904, 322–23; Sully, "King Cotton's Impoverished Retinue," 260.

53. Sully, "King Cotton's Impoverished Retinue," 258–59.

54. Sully, "The Remedy," 548.

55. *New York Commercial & Financial Chronicle*, April 15, 1905, 1391.

56. Hermann and Gardner, *Cooperative Cotton Marketing*, 10.

57. Nixon, *Cotton Warehouses*, 14.

58. "Conference of Growers and Manufacturers," 83–84, 88, 104–5, 128.

59. *Official Report, World Cotton Conference*, 107.

60. *Cotton: Its Preparation, Transportation and Marketing*, vol. 2, p. 78; Conant, "Cotton Tare," 7.

61. "Conference of Growers and Manufacturers," 113, 134b.

62. "Birmingham," *Iron Age*, 167. Saw ginnery prices in that year ranged from $4,000 to $10,000, with $50,000 buying a modern ginnery with a high-pressure gin compression system and attached seed-crushing plant.

63. Bureau of the Census, *Cotton Ginning*, 8.

64. Bureau of the Census, *Cotton Production and Distribution, 1919–20*, 39; Britton, *Bale O' Cotton*.

65. The "Universal Density" or UD standard calls for bales pressed to twenty-eight pounds and three feet; Mangialardi and Anthony, "Cotton Bale Presses," 16.

66. "Conference of Growers and Manufacturers," 65.

67. Ibid., 178.

68. Smith, *Cotton Exchanges*, 2–3:29.

69. "Conference of Growers and Manufacturers," 203.

70. Smith, *Cotton Exchanges*, 2–3:337.

71. Barrett, *Farmers' Union*, 128; Smith, *Cotton Exchanges*, 2–3:337.

72. IFMCSMA, *Fifth International Congress*, 286.

73. Snyder, *Cotton Crisis*, 33–55; Daniel, *Breaking the Land*, 18–22.

74. Smith, *Cotton Exchanges*, 2–3:329, 335.

75. "Colored Farmers' Institute," *Charleston Weekly News & Courier*, October 26, 1898, 7. The original text was misprinted; this text is my interpretation of the author's meaning.

76. Fite, *Cotton Fields No More*, 81.

77. "Lancashire Private Cotton Investigation Commission," 85.

78. "Conference of Growers and Manufacturers," 171.

79. Ibid., 196.

80. Woodward, *Origins of the New South*, 409.

81. Fite, *Cotton Fields No More*, 68.

82. Mercier and Savely, *Knapp Method*, 142.

83. IFMCSMA, *Fourth International Congress*, 35, 50–51.

84. "Conference of Growers and Manufacturers," 169.

85. Postel, *Populist Vision*, 277.

86. Woodward, *Origins of the New South*, 411–12.

87. "Report by Prof. John A. Todd on His Visit to the American Cotton Belt, July–September 1913," IFMCSMA report, September 25, 1913, BCGA 11/5/9.

88. "Conference of Growers and Manufacturers," 211.

89. Woodward, *Origins of the New South*, 269.

90. "Conference of Growers and Manufacturers," 54, 212.

91. Sully, "King Cotton's Impoverished Retinue," 261.

92. "Conference of Growers and Manufacturers," 145, 34.

93. "Cotton Conference at Washington," *Baltimore Manufacturers' Record*, May 3, 1906, 437.

94. DeCanio, *Agriculture in the Postbellum South*, 112–13, 261.

95. Burkett and Poe, *Cotton*, 39.

96. Stone, "Negro and Agricultural Development," 10; for Stone's biography see Hollandsworth, *Portrait of a Scientific Racist*.

97. Quoted in Saloutos, *Farmer Movements*, 208.

98. "Speeches in Birmingham," 22. See also Clune, "Black Workers, White Immigrants."

99. IFMCSMA, *Fourth International Congress*, 342.

100. Ibid.

101. Ibid., 339.

102. Ibid., 13.

103. Todd, *World's Cotton Crops*, 107.

104. Quoted in Clune, "Black Workers, White Immigrants," 208.

105. "Conference of Growers and Manufacturers," 22, 27–28, 32–34.

106. "Brilliant Social Side to Cotton Convention," *Atlanta Constitution*, October 8, 1907, 10.

107. Macara, *Recollections*, 129.

108. "European Cotton Spinners Welcome," *New Orleans Picayune*, October 13, 1907.

109. Washington, "Tuskegee Does Its Work," 433.

110. Spivey, *Schooling for the New Slavery*, 109.

111. Preface to Campbell, *Middle Passages*, xiii.

112. Washington, "Tuskegee Does Its Work," 440.

113. "John Wesley Hoffman," *Indianapolis Freeman*, July 21, 1906.

114. Fierce, *Pan-African Idea*, 14. The author was presumably referring to the many products of the oil palm tree.

115. Walker, "Scientific Redemption of Africa"; Moses, *Black Nationalism*, 206–7; Zimmerman, *Alabama in Africa*, 13.

116. Fierce, *Pan-African Idea*, 16.

117. Negassa, "Chief Alfred Charles Sam."

118. See discussion of Leigh Hunt in ch. 3, for example. Fierce, *Pan-African Idea*, 14.

119. Walker, "Scientific Redemption of Africa."

120. "A Noted Negro Scientist," *Indianapolis Freeman*, January 17, 1903.

121. Untitled clipping, Charleston, SC, August 8, 1898, box 2, folder 2, Hoffman Papers.

122. "Colored Farmers' Institute," *Charleston Weekly News & Courier*, October 26, 1898.

123. Enclosure to despatch no. 306, Hoffman to CO, Lagos, December 31, 1903, box 1, folder 2, Hoffman Papers.

124. Poster, "Lecture on Africa," n.d. but ca. 1910, Hoffman Papers. The poster claims that Hoffman visited India, Egypt, and the Soudan, but I have not been able to corroborate any travel outside southern Nigeria. BCGA records do not indicate that Hoffman ever visited Kano, much less crossed the Sahara.

125. Miscellaneous letters, Hoffman Papers; Lomax, "African Prince."

126. Pamphlet of letters on African education by Hoffman, Blackshear, and Sir Alfred Jones, privately published, 1909, box 1, folder 3, Hoffman Papers.

127. David Levering Lewis's preface in Campbell, *Middle Passages*, xiii.

128. Fierce, *Pan-African Idea*, 181–82.

129. Lewis, in Campbell, *Middle Passages*, xiii.

130. There is an expansive literature on pan-Africanism and African diasporic identity, which I cannot hope to do justice to in this book. For an introduction, see Campbell, *Middle Passages*; Adeleke, *UnAfrican Americans*; Painter, *Creating Black Americans*, ch. 8 and 9.

131. Bressey, "Geographies of Solidarity," 249.

132. Campbell, *Middle Passages*, 120.

133. Walker, "Scientific Redemption of Africa," 4–5.

134. Pine Bluff farmers to Hoffman, August 14, 1904, box 1, folder 1; Shelby County farmers to Hoffman, September 27, 1906, box 1, folder 3, Hoffman Papers.

135. Bressey, "Geographies of Solidarity," 247, 250.

136. Editorial, *Atlanta Constitution*, February 23, 1905, 6.

137. Smith, *Cotton Exchanges*, 2–3:352.

138. Sanders, *Roots of Reform*, 121.

139. Saloutos, *Farmer Movements*, 192–93.

140. Barrett, *Farmers' Union*, 208–9.

141. Saloutos, *Farmer Movements*, 192–93.

142. This paragraph is based on Rosen, *New Lanark to Mound Bayou*, 119–46; Hermann, *Pursuit of a Dream*; Dattel, *Cotton and Race*, 332–34.

143. Quoted in Dattel, *Cotton and Race*, 340.

144. Fite, *Cotton Fields No More*, 66.

145. "Night Riders Place Warning at Gin," *Dallas Morning News*, September 16, 1908.

146. "Nightriderism and the Cotton Farmer," *Dallas Morning News*, October 1, 1908.

147. "Five Years in the Pen," *Palestine (TX) Daily Herald*, October 9, 1908.

148. "Night Riders Roasted," *Bryan (TX) Morning Eagle*, November 13, 1908, 1.

149. "Night Riders in Texas," *Daily Ardmoreite* (Ardmore, OK), September 12, 1911, 5.

150. Beck and Tolnay, "Killing Fields."

151. *Macon Telegraph*, March 3, 1905. See also "Jordan Outlines Work ahead of Association," *Atlanta Constitution*, March 27, 1905, 7.

152. Barrett, *Farmers' Union*, 77.

153. Fite, *Cotton Fields No More*, 63.

154. "10 Cts. Price Demanded by Association," *Atlanta Constitution*, September 8, 1906, 1; Saloutos, *Farmer Movements*, 191.

155. "Not One Cent in Treasury, Says Jordan," *Atlanta Constitution*, September 7, 1906, 1.

156. C. S. Barret, "How Harvie Jordan Got Rid of Watson," *Atlanta Constitution*, November 9, 1906, 1.

157. "Union Will Never Merge with S.C.A.," *Atlanta Constitution*, May 1, 1907, 6.

158. "Barret Not to Co. with Jordan," *Atlanta Constitution*, April 25, 1907, 9, and "Union Will Never Merge with S.C.A.," May 7, 1907, 6.

159. "Harvie Jordan Roasted," *Atlanta Constitution*, May 1, 1907, 6.

160. "Southern Cotton Association," 71.

161. US Congress, House of Representatives, Ways and Means Committee, *Tariff Hearings*, 60th Cong. (1908–9), 2nd session, 1909, 4733–34.

162. "Agricultural Credit."

163. Woodward, *New South*, 413.

164. Fisher, *Farmers' Union*, 12, 16.

165. IFMCSMA, *Fifth International Congress*, 113, 90, 117.

166. Todd, *World's Cotton Crops*, 114–15.

167. J. A. Todd, "Report by Professor John A. Todd on his Visit to the American Cotton Belt, July–September 1913," 12, September 25, 1913, in BCGA/11/5/9.

168. IFMCSMA, *Seventh International Congress*, 20, 62–63.

169. Quoted in "Speeches in Birmingham," 22.

170. Clune, "Black Workers, White Immigrants," 215.

171. "Spinners to Join in a Conference," *Atlanta Constitution*, April 7, 1906, 8.

172. Macara, *Recollections*, 129–30.

173. Nelson, "Welfare Capitalism"; Rose, *Firms, Networks, and Business Values*, 174–75.

174. Brandon, *Cotton Kingdom*, 128–31.

175. See Baker and Hahn, *Cotton Kings*, ch. 8–9.

176. Smith, *Report of the Commissioner.*

177. Cowing, *Populists, Plungers, and Progressives*, 44.

178. Hoffman, "Cotton Futures Act," 477.

179. *New York Commercial & Financial Chronicle*, July 5, 1913, 5.

180. Ibid., April 12, 1913, 1049. See Hoffman, "Cotton Futures Act," 480; Robins, "A Common Brotherhood."

181. Sanders, *Roots of Reform*, 309–10.

182. Hoffman, "Cotton Futures Act," 469.

183. 7 *US Code*, §15b, para. h.1.D.

184. Markham, *Financial History*, 2:96.

185. Quark, *Global Rivalries.*

186. *New York Commercial & Financial Chronicle*, August 29, 1914, 565.

187. Tindall, *New South*, 13; Sanders, *Roots of Reform*, 299.

188. Postel, *Populist Vision*, 277; Sanders, *Roots of Reform*, 287.

Chapter 5

1. Scherer, *World Power*, 360.

2. Ferguson, *The Pity of War*, ch. 7.

3. Austen, *African Economic History*, 232.

4. Tindall, *New South*, 33–48.

5. *New York Commercial & Financial Chronicle*, September 26, 1914, 868–69, and October 3, 1914, 945. The future of jute supplies from India were in question, so the move had pragmatic aspects.

6. Link, *Wilson and the Progressive Era*, 149–50.

7. DeConde, "South and Isolationism," 338; Link, *Wilson and the Progressive Era*, 169–70.

8. Gaughan, "Militant Interventionism," 775.

9. Abrams, "Wilson and the Southern Congressmen," 432–33.

10. *New York Commercial & Financial Chronicle*, October 10, 1914, 1008.

11. Macara, *Social and Industrial Reform*, 104–5.

12. Macara, *Recollections*, 233.

13. Macara, *Social and Industrial Reform*, 234; see also Robins, "A Common Brotherhood."

14. Scherer, *World Power*, 365–66.

15. In fact, German experiments with wood cellulose were successful, and cheap wood pulp gradually replaced cotton around the world in explosives manufacture. Ironically, the cotton blockade of Germany encouraged the growth of the wood-based rayon industry, cotton's first synthetic competitor.

16. "The Case of Cotton," *Times* (London), August 12, 1915.

17. Link, *Wilson and the Progressive Era*, 171; Gaughan, "Militant Interventionism."

18. Singleton, "British War Effort," 606.

19. Macara, *Social and Industrial Reform*, 250.

20. Henderson, *Cotton Control Board*, 5.

21. Olukoju, "Elder Dempster," 261–63; Olukoju, *"Liverpool" of West Africa*, ch. 2.

22. BCGA minutes, November 4, 1913, BCGA 1/2/1.

23. Minutes from Lord Emmott re: the BCGA and associated correspondence, February 1914, Correspondence with colonies, CO 323/641, TNA.

24. Ibid.

25. H. J. Read to Treasury, October 27, 1914, "Scheme of the British Cotton Growing Association for financing the Ugandan cotton crop," Treasury Papers, T 1/11740, TNA.

26. Wardle, "History of the BCGA," ch. 3.

27. Minutes, February 5, 1915, "Scheme of the British Cotton Growing Association for financing the Ugandan cotton crop," Treasury Papers, T 1/11740, TNA.

28. Executive Committee minutes, July 11, 1912, BCGA 1/3/1.

29. Executive Committee minutes, April 22, 1915, BCGA 1/3/2.

30. Executive Committee minutes, December 22, 1916, BCGA 1/3/2.

31. Executive Committee minutes, January 10, 1917, BCGA 1/3/2.

32. Hutton to W. C. Bottomley, January 29, 1917, BCGA 6/3.

33. Minutes of a meeting with Bolton mill directors, August 21, 1917, BCGA 1/4/6.

34. BCGA minutes, July 28, 1916, BCGA 1/2/2.

35. BCGA minutes, November 7, 1916, BCGA 1/2/2.

36. BCGA-CO minutes, July 1, 1915, BCGA 1/5/1.

37. BCGA report, BCGA grant renewal appeal file, 1916, Treasury Papers, T 1/11903, TNA.

38. Memorandum to Treasury, January 27, 1916, BCGA grant renewal appeal file, Treasury Papers, T 1/11903, TNA.

39. Hutton personally received £272.3.8 for his shares. Executive Committee minutes, July 28, 1916, BCGA 1/3/2.

40. Constantine, *British Colonial Development Policy*, 38.

41. H. Wilson-Fox, quoted in ibid.

42. Ibid., 51–56.

43. Executive Committee minutes, February 15, 1917, BCGA 1/3/2.

44. Executive Committee minutes, October 10, 1917, BCGA 1/3/2.

45. Ibid.

46. Evidence of J. Arthur Hutton, October 31, 1917, ECGC testimony, BT 55/28, TNA.

47. McConnel, "Imperial Cotton Growing," February 28, 1917, BCGA 2/6/5.

48. Executive Committee minutes, November 15, 1917, BCGA 1/3/2.

49. Executive Committee minutes, February 5, 1918, BCGA 1/3/2.

50. Memorandum and attached correspondence, February 11, 1918, Secretary for the Colonies correspondence, CO 323/786, TNA.

51. Executive Committee minutes, November 5, 1918, BCGA 1/3/2.

52. BCGA minutes, November 5, 1918, BCGA 1/2/2.

53. McConnel, "Report on the Cotton Supplies of the British Empire after the War," n.d. but 1917–18, BCGA 2/6/3.

54. "Report to the Board of Trade of the ECGC," 1920, BCGA 2/6/15.

55. Minutes, March 16, 1920, BCGA 1/4/6.

56. ECGC report to the CO, May 13, 1920, Secretary for the Colonies correspondence, CO 323/844, TNA.

57. Wardle, "History of the BCGA," 107.

58. Baldwin, speech to the House of Commons, June 13, 1921, vol. 143, cols. 24–25.

59. Minutes on ECGC, June 10, 1920, Secretary for the Colonies correspondence, CO 323/844, TNA.

60. Onyeiwu, "Deceived by African Cotton," 89.

61. Olukoju, *"Liverpool" of West Africa*, 178.

62. Shareholders were offered 10d. stakes in Ralli or a 100d. buyout (33 percent over market value) for their 12.5d. BCGA shares. Ralli buyout documents, BCGA 5/4.

63. Macara, *Social and Industrial Reform*, 170.

64. Tindall, *New South*, 60.

65. Ibid., 114–18, ch. 4.

66. Hermann and Gardner, *Cooperative Cotton Marketing*, 23.

67. *World Cotton Conference*, 104.

68. Ibid., 114.

69. Ibid., 107.

70. Ibid.

71. Ibid., 119.

72. Tindall, *New South*, 111–12.

73. Quoted in Dattel, *Cotton and Race*, 354.

74. Woods, *Development Arrested*, 160.

75. Supak and Snipes, *Cotton Harvest Management*, 1.

76. Daniel, *Toxic Drift*.

77. Quoted in Aiken, *Cotton Plantation South*, 105.

78. Quoted in Whayne, *New Plantation South*, 224.

79. Figures from Holley, *Second Great Emancipation*, 189.

80. Woods, *Development Arrested*, 160.

81. Fowler and Wyke, *Barefoot Aristocrats*, 156.

82. Bowker, *Lancashire under the Hammer*, 58.

83. Macara, *Getting the World to Work*, 322.

84. Levi and Havinden, *African Agriculture*, 130; Olukoju, "Faulkner Blueprint."

85. Bowden and Higgins, "Short-Time Working and Price Maintenance"; Rose, *Firms, Networks, and Business Values*, 221–23.

86. Macara, *New Industrial Era*, 53.

87. Reinders, "Racialism on the Left."

88. Morel, *Black Man's Burden*, 153.

89. Jenkinson, *Black 1919*; Evans, "Across the Universe."

90. Rich, *Race and Empire*, ch. 6.

91. Beckert, *Empire of Cotton*, 426, 437.

92. Calico Printers' Association, quoted in Singleton, *Lancashire on the Scrapheap*, 120.

93. Scott, *Seeing Like a State*, 226.

94. Tilley, *Africa as a Living Laboratory*, 128.

95. Jones, *Earth Goddess*, 167, 135.

96. Levi and Havinden, *African Agriculture*, 130; Olukoju, "Faulkner Blueprint."
97. Tilley, *Africa as a Living Laboratory*, 154.
98. Duff, *Cotton Growing in Nigeria*, 25.
99. Roberts, *Two Worlds of Cotton*, ch. 10; Newitt, *Mozambique*, 466.
100. Cash, *Changing Sudan*, 21.
101. Levi and Havinden, *African Agriculture*, 145.
102. Cross, "British Attitudes," 229–30.
103. This paragraph and the next are based on Ali, *Punjab under Imperialism*, quotes at 6, 226.
104. Ibid., 234–35.
105. Hodge, *Triumph of the Expert*, 149.
106. Mandala, *Work and Control*, ch. 6.
107. Ibid., 163.
108. Roberts, *Two Worlds of Cotton*, 287.
109. Sanderson, "Ghost of Adam Smith," 108–9; Daly, *Imperial Sudan*, 91.
110. Ehrlich, *Uganda Company*, 2.
111. Dumett, "Obstacles to Government-Assisted Agricultural Development," 156.
112. Cooper, "Africa and the World Economy," 127.
113. Green, "Lasting Story," 263.
114. Both films can be viewed at http://www.colonialfilm.org.uk.
115. Quoted in Rice, "Black Cotton."
116. Tiffen, *Nigerian Cotton*, 8, 12, 16.
117. Rice, *Cotton Growing in the Sudan*.
118. Reining, *Zande Scheme*, 31.
119. Hodge, "Colonial Experts"; quote from Oslund, "Getting Our Hands Dirty," 9.
120. Beckert, *Empire of Cotton*, 435–36.
121. Hart, *Political Economy*, 88.
122. Isaacman and Isaacman, *Delusion of Development*.
123. Morel, "Free Labour," 643.
124. Cooper, "Analagous to Slavery," 126.
125. Daniel, *Breaking the Land*, 16, 19.
126. National Cotton Council, "Frequently Asked Questions."
127. Pennick and Gray, "U.S. Cotton Program."
128. Beckert, *Empire of Cotton*, 429, 438.
129. Laris and Foltz, "Cotton as Catalyst?"; Bassett, *Peasant Cotton Revolution*, 180.
130. Cooper, *Colonialism in Question*, 144.

Bibliography

Archival Sources

Bolton Archives History Centre, Bolton Library and Museum Services (Bolton Archives)

Amalgamated Association of Operative Cotton Spinners, Minders and Twisters (FT). Annual reports 1895–1925.
Bolton and District Card and Ring Room Operatives' Association (FT). Minutes, financial records, reports 1895–1925.
Bolton and District Cotton Manufacturers' Association (FET). Minutes, accounts, letter books, levy books 1895–1925.
Bolton and District Managers' Carders' and Overlookers' Association (FT). Correspondence, financial records 1895–1925.
Bolton Master Cotton Spinners' Association (FET). Minutes, financial records, correspondence, levy books, annual reports, mule spinning surveys and calculations, trade dispute files, cuttings 1895–1925.
Bolton Operative Bleachers' Dyers' and Finishers' Association (FT). Minutes, reports, correspondence, accounts 1895–1925.
Bolton Operative Cotton Spinners' Provincial Association (FT). Annual reports, agreements, wage returns, rule books 1895–1925.
Cotton Spinners' and Manufacturers' Association (FET). Minutes, annual reports, correspondence, price lists, yearbooks 1901–25.
Darwen Cotton Manufacturers' Association (FET). Minutes, accounts, levy books, membership lists, letter books 1897–1925.
Federation of Master Cotton Spinners' Associations (FET). Annual reports, yearbooks, price lists, agreements 1905–25.

Greater Manchester County Record Office (GMCRO)

Bolton & District Card & Blowing Room Operatives Association (G12). Annual reports and balance sheets 1895–1921.
Cotton Employers' Parliamentary Association (B14). Minute books 1899–1911.
Federation of Master Cotton Spinners' Associations (B14). Annual reports 1904–25.
N. & N. East Lancashire Cotton Spinners' and Manufacturers' Association (B14). Minute books 1895–1925.
Rochdale Card and Blowing Room and Ring Spinners Association (G1). Minutes, correspondence 1895–1925.

The John Rylands University Library, University of Manchester (JRUL)

Amalgamated Association of Operative Cotton Spinners and Twiners (ACS). Minute books, BCGA correspondence, ca. 1900–1925.
Cotton Factory Times, 1898–1920.
Oldham Master Cotton Spinners' Association (OLD). Official reports, published material, BCGA correspondence 1904–20.

London School of Economics Archives

Edmund Dene Morel Papers (Morel Papers). Correspondence, published material 1900–1916.

Manchester Libraries, Information and Archives (MLIA)

Manchester Chamber of Commerce Joint West Africa Committee (M8). Minutes 1902–14.
Records of the British Cotton Growing Association (M257). West Africa indents, foreign order books, share register 1902–14.

The National Archives of the United Kingdom (TNA)

Companies Registration Office records (BT 31). Records of dissolved companies, 1902–14.
Colonial Office records (CO). Africa confidential print, correspondence with colonies, BCGA correspondence 1902–25.
Empire Cotton Growing Committee records (BT 55/25-27). Mimeographed papers and correspondence, report of committee 1913–21.
Treasury Papers (T 1/11740, 1/11903). Uganda financing scheme papers; BCGA grant renewal application 1914–16.

Oldham Local Studies and Archives (OLSA)

Oldham & Rochdale Cardoom Operatives Association (D-TU). Minutes, quarterly reports 1900–1920.
Oldham and Rochdale Textile Employers' Association (D-AAN). Minutes, annual reports, levy books 1902–19.
Oldham Chamber of Commerce (D-AJB). Minutes 1901–10.
Oldham Operative Cotton Spinners Association (D-TU). Minutes and reports 1902–10.

Tuskegee University, Archives and Special Collections

John Wesley Hoffman Papers (Hoffman Papers), 1880s–1920s.

University of Birmingham Special Collections

British Cotton Growing Association Papers (BCGA). Minutes, publications, reports, tour diaries, daybooks, clippings, correspondence 1902–25.
Cadbury Papers (Cadbury). Correspondence, clippings, 1902–14.
Joseph Chamberlain Papers (Chamberlain Papers). West Africa communications, Colonial Office correspondence, West Africa & Malta diary, Tariff Reform correspondence 1898–1904.

University of Georgia Special Collections

Hargrett Broadside Collection (Hargrett Broadside). Cotton pamphlets, ca. 1890–1920.

Published Sources

Abraham, A. "Nyagua, the British, and the Hut Tax War." *International Journal of African Historical Studies* 5, no. 1 (1972): 94–98.
Abrams, Richard M. "Woodrow Wilson and the Southern Congressmen, 1913–1916." *Journal of Southern History* 22, no. 4 (November 1956): 417–37.
Adeleke, Tunde. *UnAfrican Americans: Nineteenth-Century Black Nationalists and the Civilizing Mission.* Lexington: University Press of Kentucky, 1998.
"Agricultural Credit." Senate Document 214. Washington, DC: GPO, October 1913.
Aiken, Charles S. *The Cotton Plantation South Since the Civil War.* Baltimore: Johns Hopkins University Press, 2003.
Ali, Imran. *The Punjab under Imperialism, 1885–1947.* Princeton, NJ: Princeton University Press, 1988.
Allen, R. W. "Irrigation in the Sudan." *African Affairs* 23, no. 92 (1924): 257–64.
Amin, Samir. *Accumulation on a World Scale: A Critique of the Theory of Underdevelopment.* New York: Monthly Review Press, 1974.
Anonymous. "A New-Comer to the Sudan Cotton Fields." *Empire Cotton Growing Review* 1, no. 2 (April 1924): 116–20.
Appadurai, Arjun. *Globalization.* Durham, NC: Duke University Press, 2001.
———. *Modernity at Large: Cultural Dimensions of Globalization.* Minneapolis: University of Minnesota Press, 1996.
Argentina Ministerio de Agricultura. *Cotton Cultivation.* Buenos Aires: Anderson & Co., 1904.
Atwater, Wilbur Olin, and Charles D. Woods. *Dietary Studies with Reference to the Food of the Negro in Alabama in 1895 and 1896.* Washington, DC: GPO, 1897.

Austen, Ralph A. *African Economic History: Internal Development and External Dependency.* London and Portsmouth, NH: James Currey and Heinemann, 1987.

Austin, Gareth. *Labour, Land, and Capital in Ghana: From Slavery to Free Labour in Asante, 1807–1956.* Rochester, NY: University of Rochester Press, 2005.

Baillaud, E. "Cultivation of Cotton in Western Africa." *African Affairs* 2, no. 6 (1903): 132–48.

Baker, Bruce, and Barbara Hahn. *The Cotton Kings: Capitalism and Corruption in Turn-of-the-Century New York and New Orleans.* New York: Oxford University Press, 2015.

Banerjee, Debdas. *Colonialism in Action: Trade, Development, and Dependence in Late Colonial India.* Hyderabad: Orient Blackswan, 1999.

Barnett, T. *The Gezira Scheme: An Illusion of Development.* London: F. Cass, 1977.

Barrett, Charles Simon. *The Mission, History and Times of the Farmers' Union.* Nashville: Marshall & Bruce Co., 1909.

Barth, Heinrich. *Travels and Discoveries in North and Central Africa, Being a Journal of an Expedition Undertaken under the Auspices of H.B.M.'s Government, in the Years 1849–1855.* 3 vols. New York: Harper & Brothers, 1857.

Bashir Salau, Mohammed. *The West African Slave Plantation: A Case Study.* New York: Palgrave Macmillan, 2011.

Bassett, Thomas J. *The Peasant Cotton Revolution in West Africa.* Cambridge: Cambridge University Press, 2001.

Beck, E. M., and Stewart E. Tolnay. "The Killing Fields of the Deep South: The Market for Cotton and the Lynching of Blacks, 1882–1930." *American Sociological Review* 55, no. 4 (August 1990): 526–39.

Beckert, Sven. "Cotton: A Global History." In *Interactions: Transregional Perspectives on World History,* edited by Jerry H. Bentley, Renate Bridenthal, and Anand A. Yang, 48–63. Honolulu: University of Hawai'i Press, 2005.

———. *Empire of Cotton: A Global History.* New York: Knopf, 2014.

———. "From Tuskegee to Togo: The Problem of Freedom in the Empire of Cotton." *Journal of American History* 92, no. 2 (September 2005): 498–526.

Bederman, Gail, and Catharine R. Stimpson. *Manliness & Civilization.* Chicago: University of Chicago Press, 1996.

Beer, C. W. "Social Development in the Gezira Scheme." *African Affairs* 54, no. 214 (1955): 42–51.

Beinart, William, and Peter Coates. *Environment and History: The Taming of Nature in the USA and South Africa.* London: Routledge, 1995.

Bennison, Amira. "Muslim Universalism and Western Globalization." In *Globalization in World History,* edited by A. G. Hopkins, 74–97. New York: Norton, 2002.

Berman, Bruce J. "The Concept of 'Articulation' and the Political Economy of Colonialism." *Canadian Journal of African Studies* 18, no. 2 (1984): 407.

Bernal, Victoria. "Cotton and Colonial Order in Sudan: A Social History with Emphasis on the Gezira Scheme." In *Cotton, Colonialism, and Social History in Sub-Saharan Africa,* edited by Allen F. Isaacman and Richard L. Roberts, 96–118. Portsmouth, NH: Heinemann, 1995.

"Birmingham." *The Iron Age* 92, no. 3 (July 1913): 166–67.

Bowden, S., and D. M. Higgins. "Short-Time Working and Price Maintenance: Collusive Tendencies in the Cotton-Spinning Industry, 1919–1939." *The Economic History Review* 51, no. 2 (1998): 319–43.

Bowker, B. *Lancashire under the Hammer.* London: L. & Virginia Woolf, 1928.

Boyle, James E. *Cotton and the New Orleans Cotton Exchange; a Century of Commercial Evolution.* Garden City, NY: Country Life Press, 1934.

Brandon, Robert L. *Cotton Kingdom of the New South: A History of the Yazoo Mississippi Delta from Reconstruction to the Twentieth Century.* Cambridge, MA: Harvard University Press, 1967.

Bressey, Caroline. "Geographies of Solidarity and the Black Political Diaspora in London before 1914." In *Indigenous Networks: Mobility, Connections and Exchange,* edited by Jane Carey and Jane Lydon, 241–61. New York: Routledge, 2014.

Bright, John. *Speech of Mr. Bright, M.P., in the Town Hall, Birmingham, December 18, 1862.* London: Joseph Allen and Son, 1862.

"British Cotton Cultivation." Report to the Board of Trade on Cotton Cultivation in the British Empire and in Egypt, Cd. 2020. United Kingdom, Parliament, 1904.

Britton, Karen Gerhardt. *Bale O' Cotton: The Mechanical Art of Cotton Ginning.* College Station: Texas A & M University Press, 1992.

Brooks, George E. *Yankee Traders, Old Coasters & African Middlemen; a History of American Legitimate Trade with West Africa in the Nineteenth Century.* Brookline: Boston University Press, 1970.

Bureau of Manufacturers. "Monthly Consular and Trade Report." Washington, DC: Department of Commerce and Labor, January 1908.

Bureau of the Census. *Cotton Ginning.* Bulletin no. 2. Washington, DC: GPO, 1903.

———. *Cotton Production and Distribution, Season of 1916–1917.* Bulletin 135. Washington, DC: GPO, 1918.

———. *Cotton Production and Distribution, Season of 1919–1920.* Bulletin 145. Washington, DC: GPO, 1920.

———. *Cotton Production and Distribution, Season of 1925–1926.* Bulletin 160. Washington, DC: GPO, 1926.

Burkett, Charles William, and Clarence Hamilton Poe. *Cotton, Its Cultivation, Marketing, Manufacture, and the Problems of the Cotton World.* New York: Doubleday, Page & Company, 1906.

Burton, Antoinette M., ed. *After the Imperial Turn: Thinking with and through the Nation.* Durham: Duke University Press, 2003.

Byfield, Judith A. *The Bluest Hands: A Social and Economic History of Women Dyers in Abeokuta (Nigeria), 1890–1940.* Portsmouth, NH: Heinemann, 2002.

Cain, P. J., and A. G. Hopkins. *British Imperialism, 1688–2000.* 2nd ed. London: Longman, 2001.

Campbell, James T. *Middle Passages: African American Journeys to Africa, 1787–2005.* New York: Penguin, 2006.

Carland, John M. *The Colonial Office and Nigeria, 1898–1914.* Stanford, CA: Hoover Institution Press, 1985.

Carlton, David L. "How American Is the American South?" In *The South as an American Problem,* edited by Larry J. Griffin and Don H. Doyle, 33–56. Athens: University of Georgia Press, 1995.

Carlton, David L., and Peter Coclanis. "Southern Textiles in a Global Context." In *Global Perspectives on Industrial Transformation in the American South,* edited by

Susanna Delfino and Michele Gillespie, 151–74. Columbia: University of Missouri Press, 2005.

Cash, W. Wilson. *The Changing Sudan.* London: Church Missionary Society, 1930.

Chakrabarty, Dipesh. "Conditions for Knowledge of Working-Class Conditions: Employers, Government and the Jute Workers of Calcutta." In *Selected Subaltern Studies,* edited by Ranajit Guha and Gayatri Chakravorty Spivak, 179–232. Oxford: Oxford University Press, 1988.

Chapman, Sydney J. *Unemployment; the Results of an Investigation Made in Lancashire and an Examination of the Report of the Poor Law Commission.* Economic Series 12. Manchester: University of Manchester Press, 1909.

Chase-Dunn, C. "The Development of Core Capitalism in the Antebellum United States: Tariff Politics and Class Struggle in an Upwardly Mobile Semiperiphery." In *Studies of the Modern World-System,* edited by Albert J. Bergesen, 189–230. New York: Academic Press, 1980.

Christy, David. *Cotton Is King: The Culture of Cotton, and Its Relation to Agriculture, Manufacturers, Commerce; to the Free Colored People; and to Those Who Hold That Slavery Is in Itself Sinful.* Cincinnati: Moore, Wilstach, Keys & Co., 1855.

Clarke, P. F. "The End of Laissez Faire and the Politics of Cotton." *The Historical Journal* 15, no. 3 (September 1972): 493–512.

———. *Lancashire and the New Liberalism.* Cambridge: Cambridge University Press, 1971.

Clemens, Elisabeth Stephanie. *The People's Lobby: Organizational Innovation and the Rise of Interest Group Politics in the United States, 1890–1925.* Chicago: University of Chicago Press, 1997.

Clune, Erin Elizabeth. "Black Workers, White Immigrants, and the Postemancipation Problem of Labor." In *Global Perspectives on Industrial Transformation in the American South,* edited by Susanna Delfino and Michele Gillespie, 199–221. Columbia: University of Missouri Press, 2005.

Coates, Benjamin. *Cotton Cultivation in Africa.* London: C. Sherman & Son, 1858.

Conant, Luther. "Cotton Tare." Washington, DC: Bureau of Corporations, Department of Commerce and Labor, 1912.

Constantine, Stephen. *The Making of British Colonial Development Policy: 1914–1940.* London: F. Cass, 1984.

Cooper, Frederick. "Africa and the World Economy." In *Confronting Historical Paradigms: Peasants, Labor, and the Capitalist World System in Africa and Latin America,* edited by Frederick Cooper et al., 84–201. Madison: University of Wisconsin Press, 1993.

———. *Colonialism in Question: Theory, Knowledge, History.* Berkeley: University of California Press, 2005.

———. "Conditions Analagous to Slavery: Imperialism and Free Labor Ideology in Africa." In *Beyond Slavery,* edited by Frederick Cooper, Thomas C. Holt, and Rebecca J. Scott, 107–49. Chapel Hill: University of North Carolina Press, 2000.

———. "Conflict and Connection: Rethinking Colonial African History." *American Historical Review* 99, no. 5 (December 1994): 1516–45.

Copeland, Melvin Thomas. *The Cotton Manufacturing Industry of the United States.* Cambridge, MA: Harvard University Press, 1912.

"The Corner on Cotton." *Bulletin of the National Association of Wool Manufacturers* 33, no. 4 (December 1903): 384–90.

Cotton: Its Preparation, Transportation and Marketing. 2 vols. Washington, DC: GPO, 1913.

Cotton Supply Association. *Cotton Culture in New or Partially Developed Sources of Supply.* Manchester: John J. Sales, 1862.

Cowen, Michael, and Robert W. Shenton. *Doctrines of Development.* London: Routledge, 1996.

Cowing, Cedric B. *Populists, Plungers, and Progressives; a Social History of Stock and Commodity Speculation, 1890–1936.* Princeton: Princeton University Press, 1965.

Crampton, John A. *The National Farmers Union: Ideology of a Pressure Group.* Lincoln: University of Nebraska Press, 1965.

Cross, P. "British Attitudes to Sudanese Labour: The Foreign Office Records as Sources for Social History." *British Journal of Middle Eastern Studies* 24, no. 2 (1997): 217–60.

Daly, M. W. *Empire on the Nile: The Anglo-Egyptian Sudan, 1898–1934.* Cambridge: Cambridge University Press, 1986.

———. *Imperial Sudan: The Anglo-Egyptian Condominium, 1934–1956.* Cambridge: Cambridge University Press, 1991.

Dangerfield, George. *The Strange Death of Liberal England.* New York: Capricorn Books, 1961.

Daniel, Pete. *Breaking the Land: The Transformation of Cotton, Tobacco, and Rice Cultures Since 1880.* Urbana: University of Illinois Press, 1985.

———. *Toxic Drift: Pesticides and Health in the Post-World War II South.* Baton Rouge: Louisiana State University Press, 2007.

Darwin, John. *The Empire Project: The Rise and Fall of the British World-System, 1830–1970.* Cambridge: Cambridge University Press, 2009.

Dattel, Eugene R. *Cotton and Race in the Making of America: The Human Costs of Economic Power.* Chicago: Ivan R. Dee, 2009.

Davies, Peter N. *Sir Alfred Jones: Shipping Entrepreneur Par Excellence.* London: Europa Publications, 1978.

———. *The Trade Makers; Elder Dempster in West Africa, 1852–1972.* London: Allen & Unwin, 1973.

Davis, Clarence B., and Kenneth E. Wilburn, eds. *Railway Imperialism.* New York: Greenwood Press, 1991.

Davis, Lance Edwin, and Robert A. Huttenback. *Mammon and the Pursuit of Empire: The Political Economy of British Imperialism, 1860–1912.* Cambridge: Cambridge University Press, 1986.

Davis, Mike. *Late Victorian Holocausts: El Niño Famines and the Making of the Third World.* London: Verso, 2001.

DeCanio, Stephen J. *Agriculture in the Postbellum South: The Economics of Production and Supply.* Cambridge: MIT Press, 1974.

DeConde, Alexander. "The South and Isolationism." *Journal of Southern History* 24, no. 3 (August 1958): 332–46.

Dejung, Christof. "The Boundaries of Western Power: The Colonial Cotton Economy in India and the Problem of Quality." In *The Foundations of Worldwide*

Economic Integration: Power, Institutions, and Global Markets, 1850–1930, edited by Christof Dejung and Niels P. Petersson, 133–57. Cambridge: Cambridge University Press, 2013.

Dickson, Harris. *Old Reliable in Africa.* New York: Frederick A. Stokes, 1920.

Douglass, Frederick. *The Life and Times of Frederick Douglass: From 1817–1882.* London: Christian Age Office, 1882.

"Downing, Henry Francis (1846–1928)." *The Black Past: Remembered and Reclaimed.* http://www.blackpast.org/?q=aah/downing-henry-francis-1846-1928.

Doyle, Shane. *Crisis & Decline in Bunyoro: Population & Environment in Western Uganda 1860–1955.* London: James Currey, 2006.

Drummond, Ian M. *British Economic Policy and the Empire 1919–1939.* London: Allen and Unwin Ltd., 1972.

Duff, Sir Hector Livingston. *Cotton Growing in Nigeria.* London: Billing and Sons, Ltd., 1921.

———. *Nyasaland under the Foreign Office.* London: George Bell and Sons, 1906.

Dumett, Raymond E. "Joseph Chamberlain, Imperial Finance and Railway Policy in British West Africa in the Late Nineteenth Century." *The English Historical Review* 90, no. 355 (1975): 287–321.

———. "Obstacles to Government-Assisted Agricultural Development in West Africa: Cotton-Growing Experimentation in Ghana in the Early Twentieth Century." *Agricultural History Review* 23, no. 2 (1975): 156–72.

Dunn, Read P. *Cotton in Africa.* Memphis: National Cotton Council, 1950.

Dunstan, Wyndham. *British Cotton Cultivation.* Report to the Board of Trade on Cotton Cultivation in the British Empire and in Egypt, 1904, Cd. 2020.

Egboh, Edmund O. "The Adventures of the British Cotton Growers' Association in Southern Nigeria, 1902–1913." *Quarterly Review of Historical Studies* 18, no. 2 (1978): 71–93.

———. "British Cotton Growing Association Enterprise in the Lagos Colony and Protectorate, 1902–1905." *Bulletin de l'I.F.A.N. T.* 41. sér. B, no. 1 (1979): 72–99.

Ehrlich, Cyril. *The Uganda Company Limited: The First Fifty Years.* Kampala: Uganda Company Ltd., 1953.

Eltis, David, et al. "Voyages, the Trans-Atlantic Slave Trade Database." http://www.slavevoyages.com.

Emmott, Alfred. "Cotton-Growing in the British Empire." *Journal of the Society of Arts* 52, no. 2681 (April 1904): 439–57.

Engdahl, Torbjörn. "The Exchange of Cotton: Ugandan Peasants, Colonial Market Regulations, and the Organisation of International Cotton Trade, 1904–1918." PhD diss., University of Uppsala, 1999.

Engerman, Stanley L. "Southern Industrialization: Myths and Realities." In *Global Perspectives on Industrial Transformation in the American South,* edited by Susanna Delfino and Michele Gillespie, 14–25. Columbia: University of Missouri Press, 2005.

Evans, Neil. "Across the Universe: Racial Violence and the Post-War Crisis in Imperial Britain, 1919–25." In *Ethnic Labour and British Imperial Trade: A History of Ethnic Seafarers in the UK,* edited by Diane Frost, 59–88. London: Frank Cass, 1995.

Falconer, John Downie. *On Horseback through Nigeria; Or, Life and Travel in the Central Sudan.* London: T. F. Unwin, 1911.

Falola, Toyin. "The Yoruba Toll System: Its Operation and Abolition." *Journal of African History* 30, no. 1 (January 1989): 69–88.

Farnie, Douglas A. "The Cotton Famine in Great Britain." In *Great Britain and Her World, 1750–1914,* edited by Barrie M. Ratcliffe, 153–78. Manchester: Manchester University Press, 1975.

———. "The Role of Merchants as Prime Movers in the Expansion of the Cotton Industry, 1760–1990." In *The Fibre That Changed the World,* edited by Douglas A. Farnie and David J. Jeremy, 15–56. Oxford: Oxford University Press, 2004.

Farnie, Douglas A., and David J. Jeremy. "The Role of Cotton as a World Power, 1780–1990." In *The Fibre That Changed the World,* edited by Douglas A. Farnie and David J. Jeremy, 3–14. Oxford: Oxford University Press, 2004.

Faulkner, O. T., and J. R. Mackie. *West African Agriculture.* Cambridge: Cambridge University Press, 1933.

Ferguson, Niall. *The Pity of War.* New York: Basic Books, 1999.

Field, Bruce E. *Harvest of Dissent: The National Farmers Union and the Early Cold War.* Lawrence: University Press of Kansas, 1998.

Fierce, Milfred C. *The Pan-African Idea in the United States, 1900–1919.* New York: Garland Publishing, 1993.

Fisher, Commodore B. *The Farmers' Union.* Lexington: University of Kentucky Press, 1920.

Fite, Gilbert Courtland. *Cotton Fields No More: Southern Agriculture, 1865–1980.* Lexington: University Press of Kentucky, 1984.

Foster-Carter, Aidan. "The Modes of Production Controversy." *New Left Review,* I, no. 107 (1978): 47–77.

Fowler, Alan. *Lancashire Cotton Operatives and Work, 1900–1950: A Social History of Lancashire Cotton Operatives in the Twentieth Century.* Burlington: Ashgate, 2003.

Fowler, Alan, and Terry Wyke, eds. *The Barefoot Aristocrats: A History of the Amalgamated Association of Operative Cotton Spinners.* Littleborough: George Kelsall, 1987.

Frank, Andre Gunder. *Dependent Accumulation and Underdevelopment.* New York: Monthly Review Press, 1979.

Frankel, Sally Herbert. *Capital Investment in Africa.* London: Howard Fertig, 1938.

Gaither, Gerald H. *Blacks and the Populist Revolt: Ballots and Bigotry in the "New South."* Tuscaloosa: University of Alabama Press, 1977.

Gardner, Leigh A. *Taxing Colonial Africa: The Political Economy of British Imperialism.* Oxford: Oxford University Press, 2012.

Gaughan, Anthony. "Woodrow Wilson and the Rise of Militant Interventionism in the South." *Journal of Southern History* 65, no. 4 (November 1999): 771–808.

Gibbons, Herbert Adams. *The New Map of Africa (1900–1916); a History of European Colonial Expansion and Colonial Diplomacy.* New York: The Century Co., 1916.

Goodwyn, Lawrence. *Democratic Promise: The Populist Moment in America.* New York: Oxford University Press, 1976.

Goody, Jack. *Ghana Observed, Africa Reconsidered.* Legon: Institute of African Studies, 2007.

Grant, Kevin. *A Civilised Savagery: Britain and the New Slaveries in Africa, 1884–1926.* New York: Routledge, 2005.

Great Britain Board of Trade. *Report by the Chief Labour Correspondent of the Board of Trade on Trade Unions in 1902–04.* London: Darling & Son, Ltd., 1906.

Green, Erik. "The Economics of Slavery in the Eighteenth-Century Cape Colony: Revising the Nieboer-Domar Hypothesis." *International Review of Social History* 59, no. 01 (April 2014): 39–70.

————. "A Lasting Story: Conservation and Agricultural Extension Services in Colonial Malawi." *Journal of African History* 50, no. 2 (2009): 247–67.

————. *Peasant Production and Limits to Labour: Thyolo and Mzimba Districts in Malawi, Mid-1930s to Late-1970s.* Lund Series in Economic History 35. Stockholm: Almqvist & Wiksell International, 2005.

Green, Jeffrey P. *Black Edwardians: Black People in Britain, 1901–1914.* London: Frank Cass, 1998.

Guggisberg, Decima Moore, and Sir Frederick Gordon Guggisberg. *We Two in West Africa.* London: William Heinemann, 1909.

Guha, Ranajit, and Gayatri Chakravorty Spivak, eds. *Selected Subaltern Studies.* Oxford: Oxford University Press, 1988.

Hahn, Steven. *The Roots of Southern Populism: Yeoman Farmers and the Transformation of the Georgia Upcountry, 1850–1890.* 2nd ed. Oxford: Oxford University Press, 2006.

Hanson, Holly Elisabeth. *Landed Obligation: The Practice of Power in Buganda.* Portsmouth, NH: Heinemann, 2003.

Harlan, Louis R., and Raymond W Smock, eds. *The Booker T. Washington Papers.* 14 vols. Urbana: University of Illinois Press, 1977.

Harnetty, Peter. *Imperialism and Free Trade: Lancashire and India in the Mid-Nineteenth Century.* Vancouver: University of British Columbia Press, 1972.

Hart, Keith. *The Political Economy of West African Agriculture.* Cambridge Studies in Social Anthropology 43. Cambridge: Cambridge University Press, 1982.

Hastings, Archibald Charles Gardiner. *Nigerian Days.* London: J. Cape, 1930.

Havinden, Michael Ashley, and David Meredith. *Colonialism and Development: Britain and Its Tropical Colonies, 1850–1960.* London: Routledge, 1993.

Hazareesingh, Sandip. "Cotton, Climate and Colonialism in Dharwar, Western India, 1840–1880." *Journal of Historical Geography* 38, no. 1 (2012): 1–17.

————. "Territories of Conquest, Landscapes of Resistance: The Political Ecology of Peasant Cultivation in Dharwar, Western India, 1818–1840." *Journal of Historical Geography* 42 (2013): 88–99.

Hazzledine, George Douglas. *The White Man in Nigeria.* 1904. Reprint, New York: Negro Universities Press, 1969.

Henderson, Sir Hubert Douglas. *The Cotton Control Board.* Oxford: Clarendon Press, 1922.

Hermann, Janet Sharp. *The Pursuit of a Dream.* Jackson: University of Mississippi Press, 1981.

Hermann, O. W., and Chastina Gardner. *Early Developments in Cooperative Cotton Marketing.* Washington, DC: Farm Credit Administration, 1936.

Hersey, Mark D. *My Work Is That of Conservation: An Environmental Biography of George Washington Carver.* Athens: University of Georgia Press, 2011.

Hill, Polly. *The Migrant Cocoa-Farmers of Southern Ghana: A Study in Rural Capitalism.* Cambridge: Cambridge University Press, 1963.

Himbury, W. H. "Empire Cotton." *Journal of the Royal African Society* 17, no. 68 (July 1918): 262–75.

———. *The Exploration and Development of New Cotton Fields within the British Empire.* Manchester: BCGA, 1921.

Hodge, Joseph Morgan. "Colonial Experts, Developmental and Environmental Doctrine, and the Legacies of Late British Colonialism." In *Cultivating the Colonies,* edited by Christina Folke Ax, Niels Brimnes, Niklas Thode Jensen, and Karen Oslund, 300–326. Athens: Ohio University Press, 2011.

———. *Triumph of the Expert: Agrarian Doctrines of Development and the Legacies of British Colonialism.* Athens: Ohio University Press, 2007.

Hodgkinson, C. M. "Development of Cotton Land on the Gezira Plain." *Empire Cotton Growing Review* 2, no. 4 (October 1925): 337–40.

Hoffman, I. Newton. "The Cotton Futures Act." *Journal of Political Economy* 23, no. 5 (May 1915): 465–89.

Hogendorn, Jan S. "The Cotton Campaign in Northern Nigeria, 1902–1914: An Early Example of a Public/Private Planning Failure in Agriculture." In *Cotton, Colonialism, and Social History in Sub-Saharan Africa,* edited by Allen F. Isaacman and Richard L. Roberts, 50–70. Portsmouth, NH: Heinemann, 1995.

———. "Economic Initiative and African Cash Farming: Pre-Colonial Origins and Early Colonial Developments." In *Colonialism in Africa, 1870–1960: The Economics of Colonialism,* edited by Lewis H Gann and Peter Duignan, 283–328. Hoover Institution 127. Cambridge: Cambridge University Press, 1975.

———. *Nigerian Groundnut Exports: Origins and Early Development.* Ahmadu Bello University History Series. Zaria: Ahmadu Bello University Press, 1978.

Hollandsworth, James G. *Portrait of a Scientific Racist: Alfred Holt Stone of Mississippi.* Baton Rouge: Louisiana State University Press, 2008.

Holley, Donald. *Second Great Emancipation: The Mechanical Cotton Picker, Black Migration and How They Shaped the Modern South.* Little Rock: University of Arkansas Press, 2000.

Hopkins, A. G. *An Economic History of West Africa.* New York: Columbia University Press, 1973.

———. "The History of Globalization—and the Globalization of History?" In *Globalization in World History,* edited by A. G. Hopkins, 11–46. New York: Norton, 2002.

———. "Introduction." In *Global History: Interactions between the Universal and the Local,* 1–38. New York: Palgrave Macmillan, 2006.

Hose, John. "Britain and the Development of West African Cotton, 1845–1960." PhD diss., Columbia University, 1970.

Howarth, William. "Cotton Cultivation in West Africa." *Textile World Record* 35, no. 2 (May 1908): 114–16.

Huberman, M. "Some Early Evidence of Worksharing: Lancashire before 1850." *Business History* 37, no. 4 (1995): 1–24.

Hunt, Robert Lee. *A History of Farmer Movements in the Southwest, 1873–1925.* College Station: Texas A & M University Press, 1935.

Hutton, J. Arthur. *The Cotton Crisis: Paper Read before the Economic Section of the British Association, Cambridge, August 22, 1904.* Manchester: BCGA, 1904.

———. *The Development of the Cotton-Growing Resources of the Empire.* Manchester: BCGA, 1917.

———. *The Work of the British Cotton Growing Association.* Manchester: BCGA, 1904.

Hutton, J. Arthur, and Peter Coates Hutton. *Hutton Families.* Manchester: Privately printed, 1939.

Hutton, William. *A Voyage to Africa Including a Narrative of an Embassy to One of the Interior Kingdoms in the Year 1820; with Remarks on the Course and Termination of the Niger, and Other Principal Rivers in That Country.* London: Longman, Hurst, Rees, Orme, and Brown, 1821.

Hyam, Ronald. *Elgin and Churchill at the Colonial Office 1905–1908: The Watershed of the Empire-Commonwealth.* London: Macmillan, 1968.

Idachaba, Francis Sulemanu. *Agricultural Research Policy in Nigeria.* Research report 17. International Food Policy Research Institute, 1980.

IFMCSMA. *Report of the First International Congress,* Zürich, May 23–27, 1904. Manchester: Marsden and Co., Ltd., 1904.

———. *Report of the Second International Congress,* Manchester, June 5–7 and 9, and Liverpool, June 8, 1905. Manchester: Thiel & Tangye, 1905.

———. *Report of the Third International Congress,* Bremen, June 25–27, 1906. Manchester: Taylor, Garnett, Evans & Co., 1906.

———. *Report of the Fourth International Congress,* Vienna, May 27–29, 1907. Manchester: Taylor, Garnett, Evans & Co., 1907.

———. *Report of the Fifth International Congress,* Paris, June 1–3, 1908. Manchester: Taylor, Garnett, Evans & Co., 1908.

———. *Report of the Sixth International Congress,* Milan, 1909. Manchester: Taylor, Garnett, Evans & Co., 1909.

———. *Report of the Seventh International Cotton Congress,* Brussels, 1910. Manchester: Taylor, Garnett, Evans & Co., 1910.

———. *Second International Conference of Cotton Growers, Spinners, and Manufacturers, Held at Atlanta, Georgia, U.S.A., October 7th, 8th and 9th, 1907.* Manchester: Taylor, Garnett, Evans & Co., 1908.

Imperial Institute, and the BCGA. *Handbook of an Exhibition Illustrating British Cotton Cultivation & the Commercial Uses of Cotton.* London: Imperial Institute, 1905.

Inikori, Joseph. E. *Africans and the Industrial Revolution in England: A Study in International Trade and Development.* Cambridge: Cambridge University Press, 2002.

———. "The Development of Commercial Agriculture in Pre-Colonial West Africa." *African Economic History Working Paper Series* No. 9, 2013.

"Interchange: The History of Capitalism." *Journal of American History* 101, no. 2 (2014): 503–36.

Isaacman, Allen F. *Cotton Is the Mother of Poverty: Peasants, Work, and Rural Struggle in Colonial Mozambique, 1938–1961.* Portsmouth, NH: Heinemann, 1996.

Isaacman, Allen F., and Barbara S. Isaacman. *Dams, Displacement and the Delusion of Development: Cahora Bassa and Its Legacies in Mozambique, 1965–2007.* Athens: Ohio University Press, 2013.

Isaacman, Allen F., and Richard L. Roberts. "Introduction." In *Cotton, Colonialism, and Social History in Sub-Saharan Africa*, 1–26. Portsmouth, NH: Heinemann, 1995.

Jaquay, Barbara Gaye. "The Caribbean Cotton Production: An Historical Geography of the Region's Mystery Crop." PhD diss., Texas A & M University, 1997.

Jenkinson, Jacqueline. *Black 1919: Riots, Racism and Resistance in Imperial Britain*. Liverpool University Press, 2009.

Jeremy, David. "Organization and Management in the Global Cotton Industry, 1800–1990s." In *The Fibre That Changed the World*, edited by Douglas A. Farnie and David J. Jeremy, 191–248. Oxford: Oxford University Press, 2004.

Jobin, William R. *Dams and Disease: Ecological Design and Health Impacts of Large Dams, Canals, and Irrigation Systems*. New York: Routledge, 1999.

Johnson, Marion. "Cotton Imperialism in West Africa." *African Affairs* 73, no. 291 (1974): 178–87.

Johnson, Walter. *River of Dark Dreams: Slavery and Empire in the Cotton Kingdom*. Cambridge, MA: Harvard University Press, 2013.

Jones, G. Howard. *The Earth Goddess: A Study of Native Farming on the West African Coast*. London: Longmans, Green and Co., 1936.

Keun, Odette. *A Foreigner Looks at the British Sudan*. London: Faber & Faber, 1930.

Kidd, Benjamin. *The Control of the Tropics*. New York: MacMillan, 1898.

Knoll, Arthur J. "Decision-Making for the German Colonies." In *Germans in the Tropics*, edited by Arthur J. Knoll and Lewis H. Gann, 131–49. New York: Greenwood Press, 1987.

Kriger, Colleen E. *Cloth in West African History*. Lanham: AltaMira Press, 2006.

Lakwete, Angela. *Inventing the Cotton Gin: Machine and Myth in Antebellum America*. Baltimore: The Johns Hopkins University Press, 2003.

Lamb, P. H. "Account of Tour in Cotton Belt of United States." *The Agricultural Journal of British East Africa* 3, no. 1 (April 1910): 1–10.

"The Lancashire Private Cotton Investigation Commission." *Textile World Record* 32, no. 2 (November 1906): 84–88.

Lancashire Private Investigation Commission. *Report of the Members of the Commission on Their Visit to the Cotton Growing Area of the United States of America*. Manchester: Privately printed, 1906.

Laris, Paul, and Jeremy D. Foltz. "Cotton as Catalyst? The Role of Shifting Fertilizer in Mali's Silent Maize Revolution." *Human Ecology* 42, no. 6 (2014): 857–72.

"Last spring . . ." *Fibre & Fabric* 44, no. 1130 (October 27, 1906): 6–7.

Lawrance, Benjamin N., Emily Lynn Osborn, and Richard L. Roberts, eds. *Intermediaries, Interpreters, and Clerks: African Employees in the Making of Colonial Africa*. Madison: University of Wisconsin Press, 2006.

Lawrance, Benjamin N., Emily Lynn Osborn, and Richard L. Roberts. "Introduction: African Intermediaries and the 'Bargain' of Collaboration." In *Intermediaries, Interpreters, and Clerks: African Employees in the Making of Colonial Africa*, 3–34. Madison: University of Wisconsin Press, 2006.

Lazonick, William. *Competitive Advantage on the Shop Floor*. Cambridge, MA: Harvard University Press, 1990.

Levi, John, and Michael Ashley Havinden. *Economics of African Agriculture*. Harlow: Longman, 1982.

Leys, Colin. *The Rise & Fall of Development Theory*. Bloomington: Indiana University Press, 1996.

Link, Arthur Stanley. *Woodrow Wilson and the Progressive Era, 1910–1917*. New York: Harper, 1954.

Lipartito, K. J. "The New York Cotton Exchange and the Development of the Cotton Futures Market." *Business History Review* 57, no. 1 (1983): 50–72.

Livingstone, David. *Missionary Travels and Researches in South Africa: Including a Sketch of Sixteen Years' Residence in the Interior of Africa*. London: Harper & Bros., 1857.

Lomax, John A. "Stories of an African Prince." *Journal of American Folklore* 26 (January 1913): 1–12.

Lonsdale, John, and Bruce Berman. "Coping with the Contradictions: The Development of the Colonial State in Kenya, 1895–1914." *Journal of African History* 20, no. 4 (January 1979): 487–505.

Lovejoy, Paul E., and Jan S. Hogendorn. *Slow Death for Slavery: The Course of Abolition in Northern Nigeria, 1897–1936*. Cambridge: Cambridge University Press, 1993.

Low, D. A. *Buganda in Modern History*. Berkeley: University of California Press, 1971.

———. *The Mind of Buganda: Documents of the Modern History of an African Kingdom*. Berkeley: University of California Press, 1971.

Lucas, Sir Charles Prestwood. *A Historical Geography of the British Colonies*. Oxford: The Clarendon Press, 1913.

Lugard, Frederick J. D. *Lugard and the Amalgamation of Nigeria*. Edited by Anthony Hamilton Millard Kirk-Greene. London: F. Cass, 1968.

Lynn, Martin. "Change and Continuity in the British Palm Oil Trade with West Africa, 1830–55." *Journal of African History* 22, no. 3 (1981): 331–48.

Macara, Charles W. *Getting the World to Work*. Manchester: Sherratt and Hughes, 1922.

———. *The New Industrial Era*. Manchester: Sherratt and Hughes, 1923.

———. *Recollections*. London: Cassell, 1921.

———. *Social and Industrial Reform: Some International Aspects*. Manchester: Sherratt & Hughes, 1919.

MacGregor, William. "Lagos, Abeokuta and the Alake." *Journal of the Royal African Society* 3, no. 12 (July 1904): 464–81.

MacKenzie, John M. "Experts and Amateurs: Tsetse, Nagana and Sleeping Sickness in East and Central Africa." In *Imperialism in the Natural World*, edited by John M MacKenzie, 187–212. Manchester: Manchester University Press, 1990.

Maier, Donna J. E. "Slave Labor and Wage Labor in German Togo, 1885–1914." In *Germans in the Tropics*, edited by Arthur J. Knoll and Lewis H. Gann, 73–92. New York: Greenwood Press, 1987.

Mandala, Elias Coutinho. *The End of Chidyerano: A History of Food and Everyday Life in Malawi, 1860–2004*. Portsmouth, NH: Heinemann, 2005.

———. *Work and Control in a Peasant Economy: A History of the Lower Tchiri Valley in Malawi, 1859–1960*. Madison: University of Wisconsin Press, 1990.

Mangialardi, Gino J., and W. Stanley Anthony. "Cotton Bale Presses at Gins, 1960–2004." The National Cotton Ginners Association, 2005. http://www.cotton.org/ncga/techpubs/upload/1823-Cotton_Bale_Presses_at_Gins.pdf.

Manning, Patrick. "African Empires in the Twentieth Century: Designing Assessments at Global, Imperial, and National Levels." In *Africa, Empire, and Globalization*, edited by Toyin Falola and Emily Brownell, 591–609. Durham, NC: Carolina Academic Press, 2011.

———. *Slavery, Colonialism and Economic Growth in Dahomey, 1640–1960*. Cambridge: Cambridge University Press, 2004.

Markham, Jerry W. *A Financial History of the United States*. 3 vols. New York: M. E. Sharpe, 2002.

Marrison, Andrew J. *British Business and Protection, 1903–1932*. Oxford: Clarendon Press, 1996.

Marx, Karl. *The Eighteenth Brumaire of Louis Bonaparte*. Translated by Saul K. Padover. Marxist Internet Archive, 2006. https://www.marxists.org/archive/marx/works/1852/18th-brumaire/.

Masefield, G. B. *A Handbook of Tropical Agriculture*. Oxford: Clarendon Press, 1949.

Mass, William, and William Lazonick. "The Performance of the British Cotton Industry, 1870–1913." *Research in Economic History* 9 (1984): 1–44.

Mather, Sir William. *Egypt and the Anglo-Egyptian Sudan: Resources and Development, Especially in Relation to Cotton-Growing*. Southhampton: Hampshire Advertiser, 1910.

McCorkle, J. L., Jr. "Louisiana and the Cotton Crisis, 1914." *Louisiana History* 18, no. 3 (1977): 303–21.

McCracken, John. "Experts and Expertise in Colonial Malawi." *African Affairs* 81, no. 322 (January 1982): 101–16.

McGhee, Zach. "The Englishman's Bigger Dollar." *The World's Work*, July 1910, 13152–58.

McIvor, Arthur. "Employers Associations and Industrial Relations in Lancashire, 1890–1939: A Comparative Study of the Development, Organisation and Labour Relations Strategies of Employers' Combinations in the Cotton, Building and Engineering Industries." PhD diss., University of Manchester, 1983.

———. *Organised Capital: Employers' Associations and Industrial Relations in Northern England, 1880–1939*. Cambridge: Cambridge University Press, 1996.

———. "Sir Charles Wright Macara." In *Dictionary of Business Biography*, 4:7–14. London: Butterworths, 1985.

Meillassoux, Claude. "From Reproduction to Production." *Economy and Society* 1, no. 1 (February 1972): 93–105.

Mercier, William Benjamin, and Harvey E. Savely. *The Knapp Method of Growing Cotton*. Garden City and New York: Doubleday, Page & Company, 1913.

Mills, William Haslam. *Sir Charles W. Macara, Bart.; a Study of Modern Lancashire*. Manchester: Sherratt & Hughes, 1917.

Milne, A. H. *Sir Alfred Lewis Jones, K.C.M.G., a Story of Energy and Success*. Liverpool: H. Young & Sons, 1914.

Mitchell, Timothy. *Rule of Experts: Egypt, Techno-Politics, Modernity*. Berkeley: University of California Press, 2002.

Mollan, Simon. "'Productive for the State and to Commerce'—Financing Business in the Anglo-Egyptian Sudan: The Case of the Sudan Plantations Syndicate,

1904–1913." Paper presented at the Economic History Society Annual Conference, University of Durham, April 2003.

Moore, Henry Ludwell. *Forecasting the Yield and the Price of Cotton.* New York: Macmillan, 1917.

Morel, E. D. *Affairs of West Africa.* London: W. Heinemann, 1902.

———. *The Black Man's Burden.* Manchester: National Labour Press, 1920.

———. "Free Labour in Tropical Africa." *The Nineteenth Century and After* 75, no. 445 (March 1914): 629–43.

———. *Nigeria, Its Peoples and Its Problems.* 2nd ed. London: Murray, 1912.

Moseley, William G., and Leslie C. Gray. "Introduction." In *Hanging by a Thread: Cotton, Globalization, and Poverty in Africa,* edited by William G. Moseley and Leslie C. Gray, 1–34. Athens: Ohio University Press, 2008.

Mosely Industrial Commission to the United States of America. *Reports of the Delegates.* Manchester: Co-operative Printing Society, 1903.

Moses, Wilson Jeremiah. *The Golden Age of Black Nationalism, 1850–1925.* New York: Oxford University Press, 1988.

Mulwafu, Wapulumuka Oliver. *Conservation Song: A History of Peasant-State Relations and the Environment in Malawi, 1860–2000.* Cambridge: White Horse Press, 2011.

National Cotton Council. "Frequently Asked Questions." http://www.cotton.org/edu/faq/.

Negassa, Semhar. "Chief Alfred Charles Sam (c. 1880–c. 1930s?)." *The Black Past: Remembered and Reclaimed.* http://www.blackpast.org/aaw/chief-alfred-charles-sam-c-1880-c-1930s.

Nelson, Lawrence J. "Welfare Capitalism on a Mississippi Plantation in the Great Depression." *Journal of Southern History* 50, no. 2 (May 1984): 225–50.

Newbury, Colin. *Patrons, Clients, and Empire: Chieftancy and Over-Rule in Asia, Africa, and the Pacific.* Oxford: Oxford University Press, 2003.

Newitt, M. D. D. *A History of Mozambique.* Bloomington: Indiana University Press, 1995.

Nieboer, H. J. *Slavery as an Industrial System: Ethnological Research.* New York: B. Franklin, 1971.

Nixon, Robert L. *Cotton Warehouses: Storage Facilities Now Available in the South.* USDA Bulletin 216. Washington, DC: GPO, 1916.

Nonnenmacher, Tomas, and Steve Onyeiwu. "Illusion of a Cotton Paradise: Explaining the Failure of the British Cotton Growing Association in Colonial Nigeria." *Journal of European Economic History* 34, no. 1 (Spring 2005): 121–48.

North, Douglass C. *The Economic Growth of the United States, 1790–1860.* Englewood Cliffs, NJ: Prentice-Hall, 1961.

Northrup, David. *Beyond the Bend in the River: African Labor in Eastern Zaire, 1865–1940.* Athens: Ohio University Center for International Studies, 1988.

"The Northwest Manchester Bye-Election," In *The Annual Register 1908,* 82–83. London: Longmans, Green & Co., 1909.

Nworah, K. D. "The Liverpool 'Sect' and British West African Policy, 1895–1915." *African Affairs* 70, no. 281 (1971): 349–64.

———. "The West African Operations of the British Cotton Growing Association, 1904–1914." *African Historical Studies* 4 (1971): 315–30.

Nyambara, P. S. "Colonial Policy and Peasant Cotton Agriculture in Southern Rhodesia, 1904–1953." *International Journal of African Historical Studies* 33, no. 1 (2000): 81–111.

Official Report World Cotton Conference, New Orleans, Louisiana, October 13–16, 1919. Boston: Executive Committee, 1919.

Olukoju, Ayodeji. "Economic Relations between Nigeria and the United States in the Era of British Colonial Rule, Ca. 1900–1950." In *The United States and West Africa: Interactions and Relations,* edited by Alusine Jalloh and Toyin Falola, 90–111. Rochester, NY: University of Rochester Press, 2008.

———. "Elder Dempster and the Shipping Trade of Nigeria during the First World War." *Journal of African History* 33, no. 2 (1992): 255–71.

———. "The Faulkner 'Blueprint' and the Evolution of Agricultural Policy in Inter-War Colonial Nigeria." In *The Foundations of Nigeria: Essays in Honor of Toyin Falola,* edited by Adebayo Oyebade, 403–22. Trenton: Africa World Press, Inc., 2003.

———. *The "Liverpool" of West Africa: The Dynamics and Impact of Maritime Trade in Lagos, 1900–1950.* Trenton: Africa World Press, Inc., 2004.

Onyeiwu, Steve. "Deceived by African Cotton: The British Cotton Growing Association and the Demise of the Lancashire Textile Industry." *African Economic History,* no. 28 (2000): 89–121.

O'Rourke, Kevin H., and Jeffrey G. Williamson. *Globalization and History: The Evolution of a Nineteenth-Century Atlantic Economy.* Cambridge, MA: MIT Press, 1999.

Orr, Charles William James. *The Making of Northern Nigeria.* London: MacMillan & Co., 1911.

Oslund, Karen. "Getting Our Hands Dirty." In *Cultivating the Colonies,* edited by Christina Folke Ax, Niels Brimnes, Niklas Thode Jensen, and Karen Oslund, 1–16. Athens: Ohio University Press, 2011.

Painter, Nell Irvin. *Creating Black Americans: African-American History and Its Meanings, 1619 to the Present.* Oxford and New York: Oxford University Press, 2006.

———. *The History of White People.* New York: W. W. Norton & Company, 2010.

Pearse, Arno S. *Brazilian Cotton; Being the Report of the Journey of the International Cotton Mission through the Cotton States of São Paulo, Minas Geraes, Bahia, Alagôas, Sergipe, Pernambuco, Parahyba, Rio Grande Do Norte.* Manchester: Taylor, Garnett, Evans & Co., 1921.

Pennick, Jerry, and Heather Gray. "U.S. Cotton Program & Black Farmers in the United States." Federation of Southern Cooperatives, 2006. http://www.federationsoutherncoop.com/cottonstudy/cotton2.htm.

Phillips, Anne. *The Enigma of Colonialism: British Policy in West Africa.* London: James Currey, 1989.

Pietruska, Jamie L. "'Cotton Guessers.'" In *The Rise of Marketing and Market Research,* edited by Hartmut Berghoff, Uwe Spiekermann, and Philip Scranton, 49–72. London: Palgrave Macmillan, 2012.

Pipkin, James Jefferson. *The Negro in Revelation, in History, and in Citizenship.* St. Louis: N. D. Thompson Publishing Co., 1902.

Pitcher, M. Anne. *Politics in the Portuguese Empire: The State, Industry, and Cotton, 1926–1974.* Oxford: Clarendon Press, 1993.

————. "Sowing the Seeds of Failure: Early Portuguese Cotton Cultivation in Angola and Mozambique, 1820–1926." *Journal of Southern African Studies*, 1991, 43–70.

Platt, D. C. M. *Finance, Trade and Politics in British Foreign Policy, 1815–1914*. Oxford: Oxford University Press, 1968.

Porter, Bernard. *The Absent-Minded Imperialists: Empire, Society, and Culture in Britain*. Oxford: Oxford University Press, 2004.

Porter, Philip W. "A Note on Cotton and Climate: A Colonial Conundrum." In *Cotton, Colonialism, and Social History in Sub-Saharan Africa*, edited by Allen Isaacman and Richard Roberts, 43–49. Portsmouth, NH: Heinemann, 1995.

Postel, Charles. *The Populist Vision*. Oxford: Oxford University Press, 2007.

Prentice, A. N. *Cotton; with Special Reference to Africa*. London: Longman, 1972.

Quark, Amy A. *Global Rivalries: Standards Wars and the Transnational Cotton Trade*. Chicago: University of Chicago Press, 2013.

Rand, Laurance B. *High Stakes: The Life and Times of Leigh S. J. Hunt*. New York: P. Lang, 1989.

Ratcliffe, B. M. "Cotton Imperialism: Manchester Merchants and Cotton Cultivation in West Africa in the Mid-Nineteenth Century." *Historical Papers* 16, no. 1 (1981): 101–23.

Raven-Hill, Leonard. "Touched on the Raw Material." *Punch* 127 (September 21, 1904), 201.

Redford, Arthur. *Manchester Merchants and Foreign Trade*. 2 vols. Manchester: Manchester University Press, 1934.

Reinders, Robert C. "Racialism on the Left: E. D. Morel and the 'Black Horror on the Rhine.'" *International Review of Social History* 13, no. 1 (1968): 1–28.

Reining, Conrad C. *The Zande Scheme: An Anthropological Case Study of Economic Development in Africa*. Evanston: Northwestern University Press, 1966.

"Report of the Conference of Growers and Manufacturers of Cotton." Typescript, 1906. Http://www.cs.arizona.edu/patterns/weaving/other/conf_ctn1_1. pdf. University of Arizona On-Line Digital Archive of Documents on Weaving and Related Topics.

Rice, Tom. "Black Cotton." *Colonial Film: Moving Images of the British Empire*, 2009. http://www.colonialfilm.org.uk/node/1322.

————. "Cotton Growing in the Sudan." *Colonial Film: Moving Images of the British Empire*, 2009. http://www.colonialfilm.org.uk/node/837.

Rich, Paul B. *Race and Empire in British Politics*. Cambridge: Cambridge University Press, 1986.

Riello, Giorgio. *Cotton: The Fabric That Made the Modern World*. Cambridge: Cambridge University Press, 2013.

Rigby, Nigel, and Howard J. Booth. *Modernism and Empire: Writing and British Coloniality 1890–1940*. Manchester: Manchester University Press, 2000.

Roberts, Richard L. *Two Worlds of Cotton: Colonialism and the Regional Economy in the French Soudan, 1800–1946*. Stanford: Stanford University Press, 1996.

Robins, Jonathan E. "Colonial Cuisine: Food in British Nigeria, 1900–1914." *Cultural Studies—Critical Methodologies* 10 (December 2010): 457–66.

————. "Coercion and Resistance in the Colonial Market: Cotton in Britain's African Empire." In *Global Histories, Imperial Commodities, Local Interactions*, edited by Jonathan Curry-Machado, 100–20. New York: Palgrave Macmillan, 2013.

————. "A Common Brotherhood for Their Mutual Benefit: Sir Charles Macara and Internationalism in the Cotton Industry, 1904–1914." *Enterprise and Society* 16, no. 4 (2015): 847–88.

————. "Lancashire and the 'Undeveloped Estates': The British Cotton Growing Association Fundraising Campaign, 1902–1914." *Journal of British Studies* 52, no. 4 (2015): 869–97.

Robinson, Ronald. "Non-European Foundations of European Imperialism: Sketch for a Theory of Collaboration." In *Studies in the Theory of Imperialism*, edited by Roger Owen and Bob Sutcliffe, 117–40. London: Longman, 1972.

Robson, R. *The Cotton Industry in Britain*. London: Macmillan, 1957.

Roche, Julian. *The International Cotton Trade*. Abingdon: Woodhead Publishing, 1994.

Rönnbäck, Klas. "The Idle and the Industrious: European Ideas about the African Work Ethic in Precolonial West Africa." *History in Africa* 41 (June 2014): 117–45.

Rose, Mary B. *Firms, Networks, and Business Values: The British and American Cotton Industries Since 1750*. Cambridge: Cambridge University Press, 2000.

Rosen, Joel Nathan. *From New Lanark to Mound Bayou: Owenism in the Mississippi Delta*. Durham, NC: Carolina Academic Press, 2011.

Saloutos, Theodore. *Farmer Movements in the South, 1865–1933*. Berkeley: University of California Press, 1960.

Sandberg, Lars G. *Lancashire in Decline: A Study in Entrepreneurship, Technology, and International Trade*. Columbus: Ohio State University Press, 1974.

Sanders, Elizabeth. *Roots of Reform: Farmers, Workers, and the American State, 1877–1917*. Chicago: University of Chicago Press, 1999.

Sanderson, G. N. "The Ghost of Adam Smith: Ideology, Bureaucracy, and the Frustration of Economic Development in the Sudan, 1934–1940." In *Modernization in the Sudan: Essays in Honor of Richard Hill*, 101–20. New York: Lilian Barber Press, 1985.

Sathyamurthy, T. V. *The Political Development of Uganda: 1900–1986*. Aldershot: Gower, 1986.

Schanz, Moritz. "Colonial Cotton Growing and Germany, 1910." In *7th IFMCSMA Conference Report*, 173–200. Manchester: Taylor, Garnett, Evans & Co., 1910.

————. "Colonial Cotton Growing and Germany, 1911." In *8th IFMCSMA Conference Report*. Manchester: Taylor, Garnett, Evans & Co., 1911.

Scherer, James A. B. *Cotton as a World Power; a Study in the Economic Interpretation of History*. New York: F. A. Stokes, 1916.

Schmidt, Arno. *Cotton Growing in the Anglo-Egyptian Sudan*. Manchester: Taylor, Garnett, and Evans, 1913.

Schnurr, Matthew. "The Boom and Bust of Zululand Cotton, 1910–1933." *Journal of Southern African Studies* 37, no. 1 (2011): 119–34.

————. "Cotton as a Calamitous Commodity: The Politics of Agricultural Failure in Natal and Zululand, 1844–1933." *Canadian Journal of African Studies* 47, no. 1 (April 2013): 115–32.

Scott, James C. *Seeing Like a State: How Certain Schemes to Improve the Human Condition Have Failed.* New Haven: Yale University Press, 1998.

———. *Weapons of the Weak: Everyday Forms of Peasant Resistance.* New Haven: Yale University Press, 1985.

Shelford, Frederic. "Ten Years' Progress in West Africa." *Journal of the Royal African Society* 6, no. 24 (1907): 341–49.

Shepperson, Alfred. *Cotton Facts.* New York: Shepperson Publishing, 1901.

Shepperson Publishing. *Cotton Facts.* New York: Shepperson Publishing, 1912.

Showers, Kate Barger. *Imperial Gullies: Soil Erosion and Conservation in Lesotho.* Columbus: Ohio University Press, 2005.

Sikainga, Ahmad Alawad. *Slaves into Workers: Emancipation and Labor in Colonial Sudan.* Austin: University of Texas Press, 1996.

Singleton, John. "The Cotton Industry and the British War Effort, 1914–1918." *The Economic History Review,* New Series, 47, no. 3 (August 1994): 601–18.

———. *Lancashire on the Scrapheap: The Cotton Industry, 1945–1970.* Oxford: Published for the Pasold Research Fund by Oxford University Press, 1991.

Sittert, Lance van. "Imperialism in Africa." In *The Great Divergence,* edited by K. S. Jomo, 116–36. Oxford: Oxford University Press, 2006.

Smith, Herbert Knox. *Report of the Commissioner of Corporations on Cotton Exchanges.* 3 vols. Washington, DC: GPO, 1908.

Smith, Samuel. *The Cotton Trade of India: Being a Series of Letters Written from Bombay in the Spring of 1863.* London: Effingham Wilson, 1863.

Snyder, Robert E. *Cotton Crisis.* Chapel Hill: University of North Carolina Press, 1984.

"Speeches in Birmingham." *Fibre & Fabric* 44, no. 1142 (January 1907): 21–24.

Spivey, Donald. *Schooling for the New Slavery: Black Industrial Education, 1868–1915.* Westport, CT: Greenwood Press, 1978.

Stone, Alfred Holt. "The Negro and Agricultural Development." *Annals of the American Academy of Political and Social Science* 35, no. 1 (January 1910): 8–15.

Sully, Daniel J. "The Dawn of the Cotton Century." *Cosmopolitan,* March 1909, 408–17.

———. "Is the High Price of Cotton the Result of Manipulation?" *North American Review,* February 1904, 194–204.

———. "King Cotton's Impoverished Retinue." *Cosmopolitan,* February 1909, 253–63.

———. "The Remedy." *Cosmopolitan,* April 1909, 546–53.

Sunseri, Thaddeus. "The Baumwollfrage: Cotton Colonialism in German East Africa." *Central European History* 34, no. 1 (2001): 31–51.

Supak, James R., and Charles E. Snipes, eds. *Cotton Harvest Management: Use and Influence of Harvest Aids.* The Cotton Foundation Reference Book Series, No. 5. Memphis: The Cotton Foundation, 2001.

Surdam, D. G. "King Cotton: Monarch or Pretender? The State of the Market for Raw Cotton on the Eve of the American Civil War." *Economic History Review* 51, no. 1 (1998): 113–32.

Swindell, K. "The Struggle for Transport Labor in Northern Nigeria, 1900–1912: A Conflict of Interests." *African Economic History* 20 (1992): 137–59.

Tamuno, Tekena N. *The Evolution of the Nigerian State: The Southern Phase, 1898–1914*. London: Longman, 1972.

Taylor, Thomas Frank. "The Role of the British Cotton Industry in the Establishment of a Colonial Economy in Uganda, 1902–1939." PhD diss., Syracuse University, 1981.

Telser, Lester G., and Harlow N. Higinbotham. "Organized Futures Markets: Costs and Benefits." *Journal of Political Economy* 85, no. 5 (1977): 969–1000.

Tewson, William Francis. *The British Cotton Growing Association: Golden Jubilee, 1904–1954*. Stockport: Cloister Press, 1954.

Tiffen, Mary. *The Story of Nigerian Cotton*. Ibadan: Evans Brothers Ltd, 1967.

Tignor, R. L. "The Sudanese Private Sector: An Historical Overview." *Journal of Modern African Studies* 25, no. 2 (1987): 179–212.

Tilley, Helen. *Africa as a Living Laboratory: Empire, Development, and the Problem of Scientific Knowledge, 1870–1950*. Chicago: University of Chicago Press, 2011.

Tindall, George Brown. *The Emergence of the New South, 1913–1945*. Baton Rouge: Louisiana State University Press, 1967.

Todd, John Aiton. *The World's Cotton Crops*. London: A. & C. Black, 1915.

Tosh, John. "The Cash-Crop Revolution in Tropical Africa: An Agricultural Reappraisal." *African Affairs* 79, no. 314 (1980): 79–94.

Trentmann, Frank. *Free Trade Nation: Commerce, Consumption, and Civil Society in Modern Britain*. Oxford: Oxford University Press, 2008.

Turner, W. M. "The Christiana People's Co-Operative Bank, Ltd." *West Indian Bulletin* 6 (1906): 250–53.

"Two Years of the Southern Cotton Association." *Textile World Record* (February 1907): 70–73.

Tyler, Frederick Jared. *Varieties of American Upland Cotton*. Bureau of Plant Industry, no. 163. Washington, DC: GPO, 1910.

US Congress, House of Representatives, Ways and Means Committee. *Tariff Hearings*, 60th Cong. (1908–9), 2nd session, Washington, DC: GPO, 1909.

van Beusekom, Monica M. *Negotiating Development: African Farmers and Colonial Experts at the Office Du Niger, 1920–1960*. Portsmouth, NH: Heinemann, 2002.

van der Eng, Pierre. "'De-Industrialisation'and Colonial Rule: The Cotton Textile Industry in Indonesia, 1820–1942." Paper presented at the International Economic History Conference, Helsinki, 2006.

Vincent, Brian. "Cotton Growing in Southern Nigeria: Missionary, Mercantile, Imperial and Colonial Government Involvement versus African Realities c. 1845 to 1939." PhD diss., Simon Fraser University, 1977.

Walker, Walter F. "Scientific Redemption of Africa." *Alexander's Magazine* 1, no. 4 (August 1905): 3–5.

Warburg, Gabriel. *The Sudan under Wingate: Administration in the Anglo-Egyptian Sudan, 1899–1916*. London: Cass, 1971.

Wardle, William A. "A History of the British Cotton Growing Association, 1902–39, with Special Reference to Its Operations in Northern Nigeria." PhD diss., University of Birmingham, 1980.

Washington, Booker T. "How Tuskegee Does Its Work." *Frank Leslie's Popular Monthly*, 1901, 429–41.

Watson, Thomas. *The Life and Speeches of Thomas E. Watson.* Nashville: Privately printed, 1908.

Watt, Sir George. *The Wild and Cultivated Cotton Plants of the World.* London: Longmans, Green, and Co., 1907.

Watts, Isaac. *The Cotton Supply Association.* Manchester: Tubbs & Brook, 1871.

Watts, Michael J. *Silent Violence: Food, Famine, & Peasantry in Northern Nigeria.* 2nd ed. Athens: University of Georgia Press, 2012.

Watts, Michael J., and Peter D. Little. "Introduction." In *Living under Contract: Contract Farming and Agrarian Transformation in Sub-Saharan Africa,* 3–18. Madison: University of Wisconsin Press, 1994.

Webster, Henry Kitchell. "Slave of Cotton." *The American Magazine,* July 1906, 302–10.

Whayne, Jeannie M. *A New Plantation South: Land, Labor, and Federal Favor in Twentieth-Century Arkansas.* Charlottesville: University of Virginia Press, 1996.

White, Joseph L. *The Limits of Trade Union Militancy: The Lancashire Textile Workers, 1910–1914.* Westport, CT: Greenwood Press, 1978.

Williams, Raymond. *Keywords: A Vocabulary of Culture and Society.* Rev. ed. New York: Oxford University Press, 1985.

Woodman, Harold D. *King Cotton & His Retainers; Financing & Marketing the Cotton Crop of the South, 1800–1925.* Lexington: University of Kentucky Press, 1968.

Woods, Clyde Adrian. *Development Arrested: The Blues and Plantation Power in the Mississippi Delta.* London: Verso, 1998.

Woodward, C. Vann. *Origins of the New South, 1877–1913.* Baton Rouge: Louisiana State University Press, 1951.

———. *Tom Watson, Agrarian Rebel.* New York: The Macmillan Company, 1938.

Wright, Gavin. *Old South, New South: Revolutions in the Southern Economy Since the Civil War.* 2nd ed. Baton Rouge: Louisiana State University Press, 1996.

Wrigley, Christopher. *Crops and Wealth in Uganda: A Short Agrarian History.* Kampala: East African Institute of Social Research, 1959.

———. *Kingship and State: The Buganda Dynasty.* Cambridge: Cambridge University Press, 1996.

Yartey, Charles Amo. "Tackling Burkina Faso's Cotton Crisis." *IMF Survey Magazine,* February 25, 2008. http://www.imf.org/external/pubs/ft/survey/so/2008/CAR022508B.htm.

Young, Thomas M. *The American Cotton Industry; a Study of Work and Workers.* London: Methuen & Co, 1902.

Zimmerman, Andrew. "A German Alabama in Africa: The Tuskegee Expedition to German Togo and the Transnational Origins of West African Cotton Growers." *The American Historical Review* 110, no. 5 (2005): 1362–98.

———. *Alabama in Africa: Booker T. Washington, the German Empire, and the Globalization of the New South.* Princeton: Princeton University Press, 2010.

Index

Fine Cotton Spinners' and Doublers'
Association (FCSDA), 22, 66, 207,
212; Mississippi plantation, 66, 196.
See also spinning: fine
First World War: American neutrality,
203, 205; cotton prices, 202–3;
cotton supplies, 202–8; impact in
Lancashire, 205, 210, 217–18
fixed prices: abandonment of, 125–26;
in America, 174; BCGA policy,
90–94; and cotton quality, 93, 129,
174; marketing boards, 221
food. *See* agriculture, subsistence;
intercropping
free riding, 62, 65, 178, 193
free trade, 25, 31, 67–70. *See also* Tariff
Reform

Gambia, 91, 102, 120, 135
Gbadebo I (Alake of Abeokuta), 27;
American tour, 251n49; in Britain,
124; as cotton promoter, 123–26
gender, 97, 137
"gentlemanly capitalists," 66
Gezira, 26, 118, 149–58; as a model,
210–11, 222, 227. *See also* Sudan
Plantations Syndicate
Ghana. *See* Gold Coast
ginning: American, 176; BCGA
ginneries, 55, 83–84, 88–89, 94;
profitability, 95–97; roller gin, 139,
145; as technological breakthrough,
97–98, 125, 226. *See also* British
Cotton Ginning Company;
monopoly
globalization, 7–10, 14, 200; of cotton
industry, 21–22, 217–20; and
integration, 90, 93, 97, 166, 205
Gold Coast, 29, 53; and BCGA, 92–93,
114; cocoa, 102, 120
Gresham, Newton, 169

Hardie, Keir, 44
Hazzledine, George D., 58
Himbury, William H., 18, 211; in
Africa, 92, 102, 105, 123; and
Africans, 108, 118, 164

historiography: African, 7–8; of
capitalism, 9–11; colonial, 11–13
121; economic, 8–11; global, 7–8,
200; Marxian, 9, 17, 24, 87–88,
121–22, 127; of populism, 6, 27,
168, 258n6
Hoffman, John Wesley, 1, 6, 131, 134;
and African Americans, 178, 185–
89, 190; 262n124, and Africans, 90,
124, 133; pan-Africanism, 189–90;
scientific work, 105, 123, 133–35,
146
Holt, John, 56, 69
Hopkins, Anthony G., 7–8, 17, 24, 66,
87
humanitarianism, 59, 82–84. *See also*
Morel, E. D.
Hunt, Leigh, 150–52, 186
Hutton, J. Arthur: African cotton, 140,
147; and Africans, 83–84, 88, 102;
BCGA management, 18, 55–56, 148,
206; ideology, 67, 119, 155–56, 208;
Indian cotton, 77–79; and Jones,
54–55; and Morel, 55; resignation,
61, 210–11; and SPS, 149, 152–53;
trade unions, 65; West African trade,
52–54, 86

J. P. Coates, 22
Jones, Alfred: and Africa, 54, 77; and
BCGA, 54, 66, 69; and Caribbean,
109; and Churchill, 160; death, 70;
and Hoffman, 189; and Morel, 54;
Tariff Reform, 67
Jordan, Harvie: European spinners,
173, 179; immigration, 182;
industrialization, 196; and NFU,
193–95; organizing work, 168–71,
174
Joyce, James, 124

Kabaka. *See* Cwa, Daudi
Kano, 98, 122, 187
Keun, Odette, 157
Kingsley, Mary, 82–83
Kitchener, Herbert, 154–55
Knapp, Seaman A., 134, 178